Fodor's 98

Bermuda

The complete guide, thoroughly up-to-date

Packed with details that will make your trip

The must-see sights, off and on the beaten path

What to see, what to skip

Mix-and-match vacation itineraries

City strolls, countryside adventures

Smart lodging and dining options

Essential local do's and taboos

Transportation tips, distances and directions

Key contacts, savvy travel tips

When to go, what to pack

Clear, accurate, easy-to-use maps

Books to read, videos to watch, background essays

Fodor's Travel Publications, Inc.
New York • Toronto • London • Sydney • Auckland
www.fodors.com/

Fodor's Bermuda

EDITOR: Stephen Wolf

Editorial Contributors: Robert Andrews, David Brown, Rachel Christmas Derrick, Honey Naylor, Heidi Sarna, Helayne Schiff, M.T. Schwartzman (Gold Guide Editor), Dinah A. Spritzer

Editorial Production: Tracy Patruno

Maps: David Lindroth Inc., *cartographer*; Steven K. Amsterdam, *map editor*

Design: Fabrizio La Rocca, *creative director*; Guido Caroti, *associate art director*; Jolie Novak, *photo editor*

Production/Manufacturing: Robert B. Shields

Cover Photograph: Jonathan Wallen

Copyright

Special Sales

Fodor's Travel Publications are available at special discounts for bulk purchases for sales promotions or premiums. Special editions, including personalized covers, excerpts of existing guides, and corporate imprints, can be created in large quantities for special needs. For more information, contact your local bookseller or write to Special Markets, Fodor's Travel Publications, 201 East 50th Street, New York, NY 10022. Inquiries from Canada should be directed to your local Canadian bookseller or sent to Random House of Canada, Ltd., Marketing Department, 1265 Aerowood Drive, Mississauga, Ontario L4W 1B9. Inquiries from the United Kingdom should be sent to Fodor's Travel Publications, 20 Vauxhall Bridge Road, London SW1V 2SA, England.

PRINTED IN THE UNITED STATES OF AMERICA

10 9 8 7 6 5 4 3 2 1

CONTENTS

ON THE ROAD WITH FODOR'S

WE'RE ALWAYS THRILLED to get letters from readers, especially one like this:

It took us an hour to decide what book to buy and we now know we picked the best one. Your book was wonderful, easy to follow, very accurate, and good on pointing out eating places, informal as well as formal. When we saw other people using your book, we would look at each other and smile.

Our editors and writers are deeply committed to making every Fodor's guide "the best one"—not only accurate but always charming, brimming with sound recommendations and solid ideas, right on the mark in describing restaurants and hotels, and full of fascinating facts that make you view what you've traveled to see in a rich new light.

About Our Writers

Our success in achieving our goals—and in helping to make your trip the best of all possible vacations—is a credit to the hard work of our extraordinary writers.

Ben Davidson wrote one of Chapter 9's Portraits, based on his exploration of the Bermuda Railway Trail. Formerly an editor of *Sunset* magazine, he now specializes in travel writing and photography.

New York–based freelance writer **Rachel Christmas Derrick** has been revisiting the Bahamas for more than 15 years. Her articles about these Atlantic islands and other locales around the world have appeared in numerous newspapers and magazines, including the *New York Times, Washington Post, Boston Globe, Los Angeles Times, Travel & Leisure, Newsweek, Essence,* and *Ms.*

Honey Naylor's featured articles have appeared in *Travel & Leisure, Travel Holiday, USA Today, The Times-Picayune,* and *New Orleans Magazine.* She has traveled extensively throughout the Caribbean, but there's no place she prefers to Bermuda, which she calls the most civilized of the islands.

New This Year

This year, Fodor's joins Rand McNally, the world's largest commercial mapmaker, to bring you a **detailed color map** of Bermuda. Just detach it along the perforation and drop it in your tote bag.

We're also proud to announce that the American Society of Travel Agents has endorsed Fodor's as its guidebook of choice. ASTA is the world's largest and most influential travel trade association, operating in more than 170 countries, with 27,000 members pledged to adhere to a strict code of ethics reflecting the Society's motto, "Integrity in Travel." ASTA shares Fodor's devotion to providing smart, honest travel information and advice to travelers, and we've long recommended that our readers consult ASTA member agents for the experience and professionalism they bring to the table.

On the Web, check out **Fodor's site (www.fodors.com/)** for information on major destinations around the world and travel-savvy interactive features. The Web site also lists the 85-plus stations nationwide that carry the **Fodor's Travel Show,** a live radio call-in program that airs every weekend. Tune in to hear guests discuss their wonderful adventures—or call in to get answers for your most pressing travel questions.

How to Use This Book

Organization

Up front is the **Gold Guide,** an easy-to-use section divided alphabetically by topic. Under each listing you'll find tips and information that will help you accomplish what you need to in Bermuda. You'll also find addresses and telephone numbers of organizations and companies that offer destination-related services and detailed information and publications.

The first chapter in the guide, **Destination: Bermuda,** helps get you in the mood for your trip. New and Noteworthy cues you in on trends and happenings, What's Where gets you oriented, Pleasures and Pastimes describes the activities and sights that really make Bermuda unique, Fodor's Choice showcases our top picks, and Festivals and Seasonal Events alerts you to special events you'll want to seek out.

Cruising to Bermuda, Chapter 2, addresses everything from the eccentricities of the six ships that ply the island's waters to ways to get the most for what you pay for a cruise. It also has helpful charts that list rates, the facilities and activities offered, and the ever-important passenger-to-crew ratios.

The **Exploring** chapter is subdivided into Hamilton, the town of St. George, the West End, and the Parishes sections; each subsection recommends a walking or driving tour and lists local sights alphabetically, including sights that are off the beaten path. The remaining chapters cover dining; lodging; nightlife and the arts; outdoor activities, beaches, and sports; and shopping.

At the end of the book you'll find **Portraits,** wonderful essays about Bermuda's history, landscapes, and its Railway Trail, followed by suggestions for any pretrip research you want to do, from recommended reading to a handful of videos about the island.

Icons and Symbols

★   Our special recommendations
✕   Restaurant
   Lodging establishment
   Good for kids (rubber duckie)
☞   Sends you to another section of the guide for more information
✉   Address
☎   Telephone number
☺   Opening and closing times
   Admission prices (those we give apply to adults; substantially reduced fees are almost always available for children, students, and senior citizens)

Numbers in white and black circles that appear on the maps, in the margins, and within the tours correspond to one another.

Credit Cards

The following abbreviations are used: **AE,** American Express; **DC,** Diners Club; **MC,** MasterCard; and **V,** Visa.

Don't Forget to Write

You can use this book in the confidence that all prices and opening times are based on information supplied to us at press time; Fodor's cannot accept responsibility for any errors. Time inevitably brings changes, so always confirm information when it matters—especially if you're making a detour to visit a specific place. In addition, when making reservations be sure to mention if you have a disability or are traveling with children, if you prefer a private bath or a certain type of bed, or if you have specific dietary needs or other concerns.

Were the restaurants we recommended as described? Did our hotel picks exceed your expectations? Did you find a museum we recommended a waste of time? If you have complaints, we'll look into them and revise our entries when the facts warrant it. If you've discovered a special place that we haven't included, we'll pass the information along to our correspondents and have them check it out. So send us your feedback, positive *and* negative: email us at editors@fodors.com (specifying the name of the book on the subject line) or write the Bermuda editor at Fodor's, 201 East 50th Street, New York, New York 10022. Have a wonderful trip!

Karen Cure
Editorial Director

North America

Bermuda

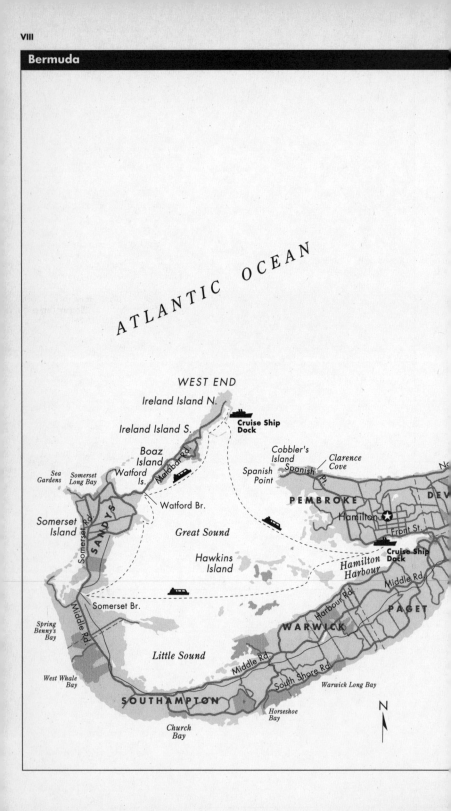

ATLANTIC OCEAN

WEST END

Ireland Island N.

Ireland Island S.

Cruise Ship Dock

Boaz Island

Cobbler's Island

Clarence Cove

Spanish Point

Spanish Pt.

Watford Is.

Maldbar Rd.

Sea Gardens

Somerset Long Bay

PEMBROKE

DE

Watford Br.

Somerset Island

Somerset Rd.

SANDYS

Great Sound

Hamilton ★

Front St.

Cruise Ship Dock

Hawkins Island

Hamilton Harbour

Middle Rd.

PAGET

Somerset Br.

Spring Benny's Bay

Little Sound

WARWICK

Middle Rd.

West Whale Bay

Middle Rd.

Harbour Rd.

South Shore Rd.

Warwick Long Bay

SOUTHAMPTON

Horseshoe Bay

Church Bay

N

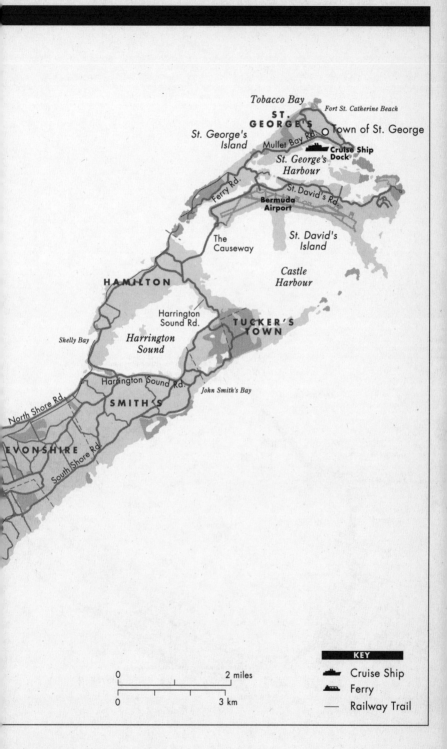

Tobacco Bay

Fort St. Catherine Beach

**ST.
GEORGE'S**

St. George's
Island

Mullet Bay Rd.

○ Town of St. George

**Cruise Ship
Dock**

St. George's
Harbour

Ferry Rd.

St. David's Rd.

**Bermuda
Airport**

St. David's
Island

The
Causeway

Castle
Harbour

HAMILTON

Harrington
Sound Rd.

**TUCKER'S
TOWN**

Shelly Bay

Harrington
Sound

Harrington Sound Rd.

SMITH'S

John Smith's Bay

North Shore Rd.

EVONSHIRE

South Shore Rd.

0			2 miles
0			3 km

KEY

Cruise Ship

Ferry

Railway Trail

x

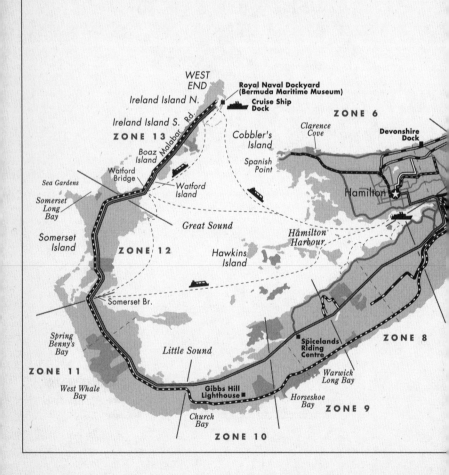

ATLANTIC OCEAN

WEST
END
Ireland Island N.
Royal Naval Dockyard
(Bermuda Maritime Museum)
Cruise Ship
Dock
ZONE 6
Clarence
Cove
Devonshire
Dock
Ireland Island S.
ZONE 13
Cobbler's
Island
Malabar Rd.
Boaz
Island
Spanish
Point
Watford
Bridge
Watford
Island
Sea Gardens
Hamilton
Somerset
Long
Bay
Great Sound
Somerset
Island
ZONE 12
Hawkins
Island
Hamilton
Harbour
Somerset Br.
Spring
Benny's
Bay
Little Sound
Spicelands
Riding
Centre
ZONE 8
ZONE 11
Warwick
Long Bay
West Whale
Bay
Gibbs Hill
Lighthouse
Horseshoe
Bay
ZONE 9
Church
Bay
ZONE 10

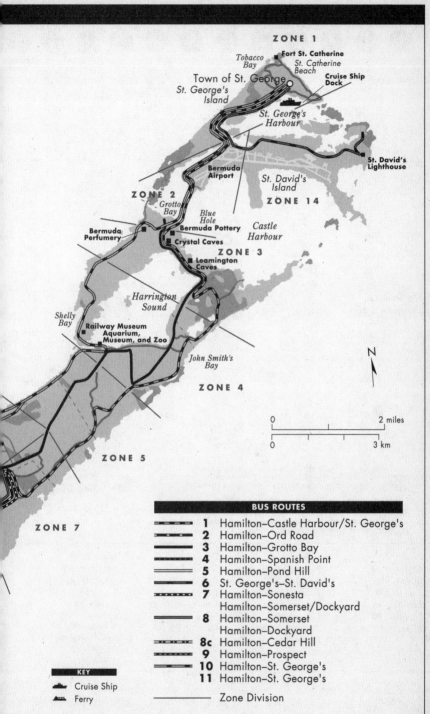

ZONE 1

Tobacco Bay ■ **Fort St. Catherine**
St. Catherine Beach

Town of St. George
St. George's Island ○ **Cruise Ship Dock**

St. George's Harbour

St. David's Lighthouse

Bermuda Airport

St. David's Island

ZONE 2

Grotto Bay

ZONE 14

Blue Hole
Bermuda Pottery

Castle Harbour

Bermuda Perfumery

Crystal Caves

ZONE 3

■ **Leamington Caves**

Harrington Sound

Shelly Bay

■ **Railway Museum Aquarium, Museum, and Zoo**

John Smith's Bay

ZONE 4

N

ZONE 5

0 ———— 2 miles
0 ———— 3 km

ZONE 7

BUS ROUTES

1	Hamilton–Castle Harbour/St. George's
2	Hamilton–Ord Road
3	Hamilton–Grotto Bay
4	Hamilton–Spanish Point
5	Hamilton–Pond Hill
6	St. George's–St. David's
7	Hamilton–Sonesta
	Hamilton–Somerset/Dockyard
8	Hamilton–Somerset
	Hamilton–Dockyard
8c	Hamilton–Cedar Hill
9	Hamilton–Prospect
10	Hamilton–St. George's
11	Hamilton–St. George's
	Zone Division

KEY

⛴ Cruise Ship
⛴ Ferry

World Time Zones

Numbers below vertical bands relate each zone to Greenwich Mean Time (0 hrs.).
Local times frequently differ from these general indications,
as indicated by light-face numbers on map.

Algiers, **29**
Anchorage, **3**
Athens, **41**
Auckland, **1**
Baghdad, **46**
Bangkok, **50**
Beijing, **54**

Berlin, **34**
Bogotá, **19**
Budapest, **37**
Buenos Aires, **24**
Caracas, **22**
Chicago, **9**
Copenhagen, **33**
Dallas, **10**

Delhi, **48**
Denver, **8**
Djakarta, **53**
Dublin, **26**
Edmonton, **7**
Hong Kong, **56**
Honolulu, **2**

Istanbul, **40**
Jerusalem, **42**
Johannesburg, **44**
Lima, **20**
Lisbon, **28**
London
(Greenwich), **27**
Los Angeles, **6**
Madrid, **38**
Manila, **57**

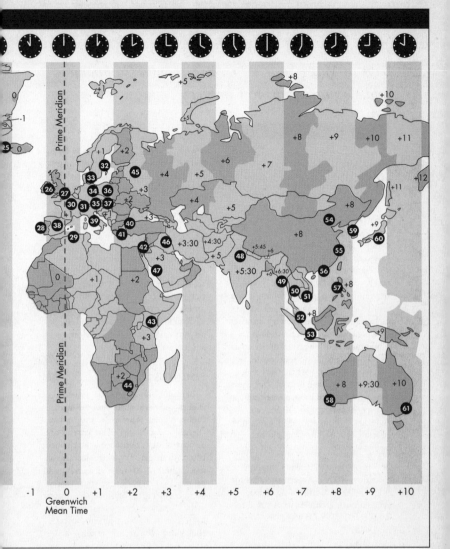

SMART TRAVEL TIPS A TO Z

Basic Information on Traveling in Bermuda, Savvy Tips to Make Your Trip a Breeze, and Companies and Organizations to Contact

A
AIR TRAVEL

MAJOR AIRLINE OR LOW-COST CARRIER?

Most people choose a flight based on price. Yet there are other issues to consider. Major airlines offer the greatest number of departures; smaller airlines—including regional, low-cost, and no-frill airlines—usually have a more limited number of flights daily. Major airlines have frequent-flyer partners, which allow you to credit mileage earned on one airline to your account with another. Low-cost airlines offer a definite price advantage and fewer restrictions, such as advance-purchase requirements. Safety-wise, low-cost carriers as a group have a good history, but **check the safety record before booking** any low-cost carrier; call the Federal Aviation Administration's Consumer Hotline (☞ Airline Complaints, *below*).

➤ MAJOR AIRLINES: **Air Canada** (☎ 800/776–3000). **American** (☎ 800/433–7300). **Continental** (☎ 800/231–0856). **Delta Airlines** (☎ 800/241–4141). **US Airways** (☎ 800/428–4322).

➤ FROM THE U.K.: **British Airways** (☎ 0181/897–4000; 0345/222–111 outside London) has three flights a week from Gatwick.

GET THE LOWEST FARE

The least-expensive airfares to Bermuda are priced for round-trip travel. Major airlines usually require that you **book far in advance and stay at least seven days** and no more than 30 to get the lowest fares. Ask about "ultrasaver" fares, which are the cheapest; they must be booked 90 days in advance and are nonrefundable. A little more expensive are "supersaver" fares, which require only a 30-day advance purchase. Remember that penalties for refunds or scheduling changes are stiffer for international tickets, usually about $150. International flights are also sensitive to the season: **plan to fly in the off season** for the cheapest fares. If your destination or home city has more than one gateway, **compare prices to and from different airports.** Also price flights scheduled for off-peak hours, which may be significantly less expensive.

To save money on flights from the United Kingdom and back, **look into an APEX or Super-PEX ticket.** APEX tickets must be booked in advance and have certain restrictions. Super-PEX tickets can be purchased at the airport on the day of departure—subject to availability.

DON'T STOP UNLESS YOU MUST

When you book, **look for nonstop flights** and **remember that "direct" flights stop at least once.** International flights on a country's flag carrier are almost always nonstop; U.S. airlines often fly direct. Try to **avoid connecting flights,** which require a change of plane. Two airlines may jointly operate a connecting flight, so ask if your airline operates every segment—you may find that your preferred carrier flies you only part of the way.

USE AN AGENT

Travel agents, especially those who specialize in finding the lowest fares (☞ Discounts & Deals, *below*), can be especially helpful when booking a plane ticket. When you're quoted a price, **ask your agent if the price is likely to get any lower.** Good agents know the seasonal fluctuations of airfares and can usually anticipate a sale or fare war. However, waiting can be risky: The fare could go *up* as seats become scarce, and you may wait so long that your preferred flight sells out. A wait-and-see strategy works best if your plans are flexible, but if you must arrive and depart on certain dates, don't delay.

CHECK WITH CONSOLIDATORS

Consolidators buy tickets for scheduled flights at reduced rates from the airlines, then sell them at prices that beat the best fare available directly from the airlines, usually without advance restrictions. Sometimes you can even get your money back if you need to return the ticket. Carefully read the fine print detailing penalties for changes and cancellations, and **confirm your consolidator reservation with the airline.**

➤ CONSOLIDATORS: **United States Air Consolidators Association** (✉ 925 L St., Suite 220, Sacramento, CA 95814, ☎ 916/441–4166, ℻ 916/441–3520).

AVOID GETTING BUMPED

Airlines routinely overbook planes, knowing that not everyone with a ticket will show up, but sometimes everyone does. When that happens, airlines ask for volunteers to give up their seats. In return these volunteers usually get a certificate for a free flight and are rebooked on the next flight out. If there are not enough volunteers the airline must choose who will be denied boarding. The first to get bumped are passengers who checked in late and those flying on discounted tickets, **so get to the gate and check in as early as possible,** especially during peak periods.

Always **bring a photo ID to the airport.** You may be asked to show it before you are allowed to check in.

ENJOY THE FLIGHT

For more legroom, **request an emergency-aisle seat**; don't, however, sit in the row in front of the emergency aisle or in front of a bulkhead, where seats may not recline.

If you don't like airline food, **ask for special meals when booking.** These can be vegetarian, low-cholesterol, or kosher, for example.

Some carriers have prohibited smoking throughout their systems; others allow smoking only on certain routes or even certain departures from that route, so **contact your carrier regarding its smoking policy.**

COMPLAIN IF NECESSARY

If your baggage goes astray or your flight goes awry, complain right away. Most carriers require that you file a claim immediately.

➤ AIRLINE COMPLAINTS: U.S. Department of Transportation **Aviation Consumer Protection Division** (✉ C-75, Room 4107, Washington, DC 20590, ☎ 202/366–2220). **Federal Aviation Administration (FAA) Consumer Hotline** (☎ 800/322–7873).

The major gateway to Bermuda is Bermuda International Airport, on the east end of the island, approximately 9 mi from Hamilton and 17 mi from Somerset.

Flying time from New York, Boston, Raleigh/Durham, and Baltimore is about 2 hours; from Atlanta, 2¾ hours; from Toronto, 3 hours; and from London, 7 hours.

TRANSFERS

Taxis are readily available at the airport. The approximate fare (not including tip) to Hamilton is $20; to St. George's, $10; to south shore hotels, $25; and to the West End (Dockyard), $38. A surcharge of 25¢ is added for each piece of luggage stored in the trunk or on the roof. Fares are 25% higher between midnight and 6 AM and all day on Sunday and public holidays. Depending on traffic, the driving time to Hamilton is about 30 minutes; it's about one hour to the West End.

Bermuda Hosts Ltd. has round-trip transportation to hotels and guest houses aboard air-conditioned 6- to 25-seat vans and buses. Reservations are recommended. One-way fares, based on zones, are as follows: Zone 1 (to Grotto Bay Beach Hotel), $5; Zone 2 (to the Flatts Village area), $7; Zone 3 (to Cobb's Hill Road), $9; Zone 4 (to Church Rd.), $11; and Zone 5 (westward to Dockyard), $13.

➤ AIRPORT INFORMATION: **Bermuda International Airport** (✉ 2 Kindley Field Rd., St. George's, ☎ 441/293–1640).

➤ BUS TRANSFERS: **Bermuda Hosts Ltd.** (☎ 441/293–1334, ℻ 441/293–1335).

B

BUS TRAVEL

Bermuda's pink-and-blue buses travel the island from east to west. You can buy tickets at most post offices. To find a bus stop outside Hamilton, look for either an easily identifiable stone shelter or a striped pole by the road. These poles can be short or tall, pink and blue, green and white, or black and white. Remember to **wait on the proper side of the road**—driving in Bermuda is on the left. Bus drivers will not make change, so **carry plenty of coins**; the fare depends on your destination.

Bermuda is divided into 14 bus zones, each about 2 mi long. Within the first three zones, the rate is $2.50 (coins only). For greater distances, the fare is $4. If you plan to do much bus travel, **buy a booklet of tickets** (15 14-zone tickets for $22 or 15 three-zone tickets for $13). Ticket booklets and packets of discounted tokens are available at the Hamilton bus terminal and at post offices. Three- and seven-day passes ($20 and $32.50, respectively) are available at the bus terminal and the visitors bureau in Hamilton.

Hamilton buses arrive and depart from the Central Bus Terminal, a small kiosk that is open weekdays 7:15–5:30, Saturday 8–5:30, and Sunday 9:15–4:45 and is the only place to buy money-saving tokens.

Buses run about every 15 minutes, except on Sunday, when they usually come every hour. Bus schedules, which also contain ferry timetables, are available at the bus terminal in Hamilton and at many of the hotels. Note that it is considered rude in Bermuda to ask a bus driver a question, such as about the fare or your destination, without first greeting him or her. If you so request, drivers will be happy to tell you when you've reached your stop.

In addition to the public buses to and from Hamilton, private minibuses serve the western end of the island and St. George. The minibus fare depends upon the destination, although you won't pay more than $3. Minibuses, which you can flag down on the road, drop passengers wherever they want to go between Somerset Bridge and Royal Naval Dockyard. They operate daily from 8:30 to 5, April through October; call for service at other times.

In the West End, Sandys Taxi Service runs a minibus between Somerset Bridge and the Royal Naval Dockyard between 8:30 and 5 Tuesday through Friday, and from 8:30 to 1 on Monday and weekends.

➤ BUS SERVICE: **Central Bus Terminal** (✉ Washington and Church Sts., Hamilton, ☎ 441/292–3854 or 441/295–4311). **Sandys Taxi Service** (☎ 441/234–2344). **St. George's Minibus Service** (☎ 441/297–8199).

BUSINESS HOURS

BANKS

Branches of the Bank of Bermuda and the Bank of Butterfield are open Monday through Thursday from 9:30 to 3, Friday from 9:30 to 4:30. Bermuda Commercial Bank (opposite Anglican Cathedral, Church St., Hamilton) operates Monday through Thursday from 9 to 3, Friday from 9 to 4:30.

MUSEUMS

Hours vary greatly, but generally museums are open Monday through Saturday from 9 or 9:30 to 4:30 or 5; some museums close on Saturday. Check with the museum for exact hours.

STORES

Most stores are open Monday through Saturday from around 9 until 5 or 5:30. Some Hamilton stores keep evening hours when cruise ships are in port. In high season (March–November) many Front Street retailers that participate in Harbour Nights are open late on Wednesday, and many street vendors sell their wares that evening only. Shops at the Royal Naval Dockyard are generally open Monday through Saturday from 10 to 5, and Sunday from 11 to 5.

C

CAMERAS, CAMCORDERS, & COMPUTERS

Always keep your film, tape, or computer disks out of the sun. Carry an extra supply of batteries, and be prepared to turn on your camera, camcorder, or laptop to prove to security personnel that the device is real. Always ask for hand inspection of film, which becomes clouded after successive exposure to airport X-ray machines, and keep videotapes and computer disks away from metal detectors.

➤ PHOTO HELP: **Kodak Information Center** (☎ 800/242–2424). *Kodak Guide to Shooting Great Travel Pictures,* available in bookstores or from Fodor's Travel Publications (☎ 800/533–6478); $16.50 plus $4 shipping.

CUSTOMS

Before departing, **register your for-eign-made camera or laptop with U.S. Customs** (☞ Customs & Duties, *below*). If your equipment is U.S.-made, call the consulate of the country you'll be visiting to find out whether the device should be registered with local customs upon arrival.

CAR RENTAL

You cannot rent a car in Bermuda. A popular, though risky, alternative is to rent mopeds or scooters (☞ Moped & Scooter Rental, *below*), which are better for negotiating the island's narrow roads.

CHILDREN & TRAVEL

CHILDREN IN BERMUDA

Be sure to plan ahead and **involve your youngsters** as you outline your trip. When packing, include things to keep them busy en route. On sightsee-ing days try to schedule activities of special interest to your children. If you are renting a car don't forget to **arrange for a car seat** when you reserve. Most hotels in Bermuda allow children under a certain age to stay in their parents' room at no extra charge, but others charge them as extra adults; be sure to **ask about the cutoff age for children's discounts.**

BABY-SITTING

For recommended local sitters, **check with your hotel desk.** The charge is usually about $17 for the first hour and $10 for each additional hour. These rates may go up after midnight and they may vary depending on the number of children. Sitters expect paid transportation.

FLYING

As a general rule, infants under two not occupying a seat fly at greatly reduced fares and occasionally for free. If your children are two or older **ask about children's airfares.**

In general the adult baggage allowance applies to children paying half or more of the adult fare. When booking, **ask about carry-on allowances for those traveling with infants.** In general, for babies charged 10% of the adult fare you are allowed one carry-on bag and a collapsible stroller, which may have to be checked; you may be limited to less if the flight is full.

According to the FAA it's a good idea to use safety seats aloft for children weighing less than 40 pounds. Air-lines, however, can set their own policies: U.S. carriers allow FAA-approved models but usually require that you buy a ticket, even if your child would otherwise ride free, since the seats must be strapped into regu-lar seats. Airline rules vary regarding their use, so it's important to **check your airline's policy about using safety seats during takeoff and land-ing.** Safety seats cannot obstruct any of the other passengers in the row, so get an appropriate seat assignment as early as possible.

When making your reservation, **request children's meals or a free-standing bassinet** if you need them. The latter are available only to those seated at the bulkhead, where there's enough legroom. Remember, however, that bulkhead seats may not have their own overhead bins, and there's no storage space in front of you—a major inconvenience.

CONSUMER PROTECTION

Whenever possible, **pay with a major credit card** so you can cancel pay-ment, provided that you can provide documentation, if there's a problem. This is a good practice whether you're buying travel arrangements before your trip or shopping at your destina-tion.

If you're doing business with a partic-ular company for the first time, **contact your local Better Business Bureau and the attorney general's offices** in your state and the com-pany's home state, as well. Have any complaints been filed?

THE GOLD GUIDE / SMART TRAVEL TIPS

Finally, if you're buying a package or tour, always **consider travel insurance** that includes default coverage (☞ Insurance, *below*).

➤ LOCAL BBBs: **Council of Better Business Bureaus** (✉ 4200 Wilson Blvd., Suite 800, Arlington, VA 22203, ☎ 703/276–0100, FAX 703/525–8277).

CRUISING

Cruising to Bermuda combines the benefits of an inclusive package—all your transportation, meals, and lodging are usually included in the cruise fare with a typical land package (the ship acts as your hotel while you explore the island). Not all cruises to Bermuda are the same, however; **check where you will dock in Bermuda.** The traditional port is Hamilton, the capital and the most commercial area on the island. If you like to shop, most stores are here. Many ships tie up at St. George's, where you walk off the vessel into Bermuda's equivalent of Colonial Williamsburg, a charming town of 17th-century buildings, narrow lanes, and a smattering of small boutiques. The West End, Bermuda's third port of call, is fast becoming the preferred place to be. Its Royal Naval Dockyard, an erstwhile shipyard that was the British Royal Navy's headquarters until March 1995, has been beautifully restored as a minivillage with shops, restaurants, a maritime museum, an art gallery, and a crafts market. There is a marina with rental boats, submarine cruises, parasailing excursions, and a snorkeling area, and there are occasional special events.

To get the best deal on a cruise, **consult a cruise-only travel agency.** Weeklong cruises to Bermuda leave from New York, Boston, and other East Coast U.S. ports. For a complete rundown on the ships, *see* Chapter 2.

CUSTOMS & DUTIES

When shopping, **keep receipts** for all of your purchases. Upon reentering the country, **be ready to show customs officials what you've bought.** If you feel a duty is incorrect, appeal the assessment. If you object to the way your clearance was handled, get the inspector's badge number. In either case, first ask to see a supervisor, then write to the port director at the address listed on your receipt. Send a copy of the receipt and other appropriate documentation. If you still don't get satisfaction you can take your case to customs headquarters in Washington.

ENTERING BERMUDA

On entering Bermuda, you can bring in duty-free up to 50 cigars, 200 cigarettes, and 1 pound of tobacco; 1 quart of wine and 1 quart of liquor; 20 pounds of meat; and other goods with a total maximum value of $30. You may not import plants, fruit, vegetables, or animals without an import permit from the Department of Agriculture, Fisheries and Parks. Remember, though, that merchandise and sales materials for use at conventions must be cleared with the hotel concerned before you arrive.

➤ INFORMATION: **Department of Agriculture, Fisheries and Parks** (✉ HM 834, Hamilton HM CX, ☎ 441/236–4201, FAX 441/236–7582).

ENTERING THE U.S.

You can bring home $400 worth of foreign goods duty-free if you've been out of the country for at least 48 hours and haven't already used the $400 allowance or any part of it in the past 30 days.

If you are 21 and older you can bring back 1 liter of alcohol duty-free. In addition, regardless of your age, you are allowed 200 cigarettes and 100 non-Cuban cigars. (At press time, a federal rule restricting tobacco access to persons 18 years and older did not apply to importation.) Antiques, which the U.S. Customs Service defines as objects more than 100 years old, enter duty-free, as do original works of art done entirely by hand, including paintings, drawings, and sculpture.

You can also send packages home duty-free: up to $200 worth of goods for personal use, with a limit of one parcel per addressee per day (and no alcohol or tobacco products or perfume worth more than $5); label the package PERSONAL USE, and attach a list of its contents and their retail value. Do not label the package UNSOLICITED GIFT, or your duty-free exemption will drop to $100. Mailed items do not affect your duty-free allowance on your return.

➤ INFORMATION: **U.S. Customs Service** (Inquiries, ✉ Box 7407, Washington, DC 20044, ☎ 202/927–6724; complaints, ✉ Office of Regulations and Rulings, 1301 Constitution Ave. NW, Washington, DC 20229; registration of equipment, ✉ Resource Management, 1301 Constitution Ave. NW, Washington, DC 20229, ☎ 202/927–0540).

ENTERING CANADA

If you've been out of Canada for at least seven days you may bring in C$500 worth of goods duty-free. If you've been away for fewer than seven days but more than 48 hours, the duty-free allowance drops to C$200. If your trip lasts 24–48 hours, the allowance is C$50. You may not pool allowances with family members. Goods claimed under the C$500 exemption may follow you by mail; those claimed under the lesser exemptions must accompany you.

Alcohol and tobacco products can be included in the seven-day and 48-hour exemptions but not in the 24-hour exemption. If you meet the age requirements of the province or territory through which you reenter Canada you may bring in, duty-free, 1.14 liters (40 imperial ounces) of wine or liquor *or* 24 12-ounce cans or bottles of beer or ale. If you are 16 or older you may bring in, duty-free, 200 cigarettes and 50 cigars; these items must accompany you.

You can send an unlimited number of gifts worth up to C$60 each duty-free to Canada. Label the package UNSOLICITED GIFT—VALUE UNDER $60. Alcohol and tobacco are excluded.

➤ INFORMATION: **Revenue Canada** (✉ 2265 St. Laurent Blvd. S, Ottawa, Ontario K1G 4K3, ☎ 613/993–0534, 800/461–9999 in Canada).

ENTERING THE U.K.

From countries outside the EU, including Bermuda, you can import, duty-free, 200 cigarettes or 50 cigar, 1 liter of spirits or 2 liters of fortified or sparkling wine or liqueurs, 2 liters of still table wine, 60 milliliters of perfume, 250 milliliters of toilet water, plus £136 worth of other goods, including gifts and souvenirs.

➤ INFORMATION: **HM Customs and Excise** (✉ Dorset House, Stamford St., London SE1 9NG, ☎ 0171/202–4227).

D
DISABILITIES & ACCESSIBILITY

ACCESS IN BERMUDA

The Bermuda Chapter of the Society for the Advancement of Travel for the Handicapped produces information sheets on accessibilty for travelers with disabilities in Bermuda. You can also obtain this information by contacting any Bermuda Department of Tourism office. Public buses in Bermuda are not equipped for wheelchairs; however, the Bermuda Physically Handicapped Association (BPHA) has a volunteer-operated bus with a hydraulic lift. Arrangements for its use must be made in advance by contacting Mr. Keith Simmons (☞ *below*). Note that you may have to be patient if more than a few handicapped travelers are visiting Bermuda at once.

➤ LOCAL RESOURCES: Bermuda Chapter of the **Society for the Advancement of Travel for the Handicapped** (SATH; ✉ 347 5th Ave., Suite 610, New York, NY 10016, ☎ 212/447–7284). **Bermuda Physically Handicapped Association** (BPHA; contact Mr. Keith Simmons, ☎ 441/295–7376).

GUIDE DOGS

If you plan to bring a guide dog to Bermuda, you must **obtain a permit in advance.** Application forms are available at all Bermuda Department of Tourism offices. Once your application is approved, the Department of Agriculture, Fisheries, and Parks will send an import permit to the traveler; the permit must accompany the dog at the time of arrival.

LODGING

The most accessible hotels are the large resorts, such as the Belmont Hotel, Elbow Beach, Marriott's Castle Harbour, the Sonesta Beach, the Hamilton Princess, and the Southampton Princess.

➤ INFORMATION: If you are looking for a vacation apartment suitable for a traveler with a disability, contact **Mrs. Ianthia Wade** (✉ "Summer

SMART TRAVEL TIPS / THE GOLD GUIDE

Haven," Box HS 30, Harrington Sound HS BX, ☎ 441/293–2099). Mrs. Wade can also assist with sightseeing arrangements.

TIPS & HINTS

When discussing accessibility with an operator or reservationist, **ask hard questions.** Are there any stairs, inside *or* out? Are there grab bars next to the toilet *and* in the shower/tub? How wide is the doorway to the room? To the bathroom? For the most extensive facilities meeting the latest legal specifications, **opt for newer accommodations,** which are more likely to have been designed with access in mind. Older buildings or ships may offer more limited facilities. Be sure to **discuss your needs before booking.**

➤ COMPLAINTS: **Disability Rights Section** (✉ U.S. Department of Justice, Box 66738, Washington, DC 20035–6738, ☎ 202/514–0301 or 800/514–0301, FAX 202/307–1198, TTY 202/514–0383 or 800/514–0383) for general complaints. **Aviation Consumer Protection Division** (☞ Air Travel, *above*) for airline-related problems. **Civil Rights Office** (✉ U.S. Department of Transportation, Departmental Office of Civil Rights, S-30, 400 7th St. SW, Room 10215, Washington, DC 20590, ☎ 202/366–4648) for problems with surface transportation.

TRAVEL AGENCIES & TOUR OPERATORS

The Americans with Disabilities Act requires that travel firms serve the needs of all travelers. That said, you should note that some agencies and operators specialize in making travel arrangements for individuals and groups with disabilities.

➤ TRAVELERS WITH MOBILITY PROBLEMS: **Access Adventures** (✉ 206 Chestnut Ridge Rd., Rochester, NY 14624, ☎ 716/889–9096), run by a former physical-rehabilitation counselor. **Hinsdale Travel Service** (✉ 201 E. Ogden Ave., Suite 100, Hinsdale, IL 60521, ☎ 630/325–1335), a travel agency that benefits from the advice of wheelchair traveler Janice Perkins. **Wheelchair Journeys** (✉ 16979 Redmond Way, Redmond, WA 98052, ☎ 206/885–2210 or 800/313–4751), for general travel arrangements.

Be a smart shopper and **compare all your options before making a choice.** A plane ticket bought with a promotional coupon may not be cheaper than the least expensive fare from a discount ticket agency. For high-price travel purchases, such as packages or tours, keep in mind that what you get is just as important as what you save. Just because something is cheap doesn't mean it's a bargain.

LOOK IN YOUR WALLET

When you use your credit card to make travel purchases you may get free travel-accident insurance, collision-damage insurance, and medical or legal assistance, depending on the card and the bank that issued it. American Express, MasterCard, and Visa provide one or more of these services, so **get a copy of your credit card's travel-benefits policy.** If you are a member of the American Automobile Association (AAA) or an oil-company-sponsored road-assistance plan, always **ask hotel or car-rental reservationists about auto-club discounts.** Some clubs offer additional discounts on tours, cruises, or admission to attractions. And don't forget that auto-club membership entitles you to free maps and trip-planning services.

DIAL FOR DOLLARS

To save money, **look into "1-800" discount reservations services,** which use their buying power to get a better price on hotels, airline tickets, even car rentals. When booking a room, always **call the hotel's local toll-free number** (if one is available) rather than the central reservations number—you'll often get a better price. Always ask about special packages or corporate rates.

When shopping for the best deal on hotels and car rentals **look for guaranteed exchange rates,** which protect you against a falling dollar. With your rate locked in you won't pay more even if the price goes up in the local currency.

➤ AIRLINE TICKETS: ☎ 800/FLY–4–LESS.

SAVE ON COMBOS

Packages and guided tours can both save you money, but don't confuse the two. When you buy a package your travel remains independent, just as though you had planned and booked the trip yourself.

JOIN A CLUB?

Many companies sell discounts in the form of travel clubs and coupon books, but these cost money. You must use participating advertisers to get a deal, and only after you recoup the initial membership cost or book price do you begin to save. If you plan to use the club or coupons frequently you may save considerably. Before signing up, find out what discounts you get for free.

➤ DISCOUNT CLUBS: **Entertainment Travel Editions** (✉ 2125 Butterfield Rd., Troy, MI 48084, ☎ 800/445–4137); $23–$48, depending on destination. **Great American Traveler** (✉ Box 27965, Salt Lake City, UT 84127, ☎ 800/548–2812); $49.95 per year. **Moment's Notice Discount Travel Club** (✉ 7301 New Utrecht Ave., Brooklyn, NY 11204, ☎ 718/234–6295); $25 per year, single or family. **Privilege Card International** (✉ 237 E. Front St., Youngstown, OH 44503, ☎ 330/746–5211 or 800/236–9732); $74.95 per year. **Sears's Mature Outlook** (✉ Box 9390, Des Moines, IA 50306, ☎ 800/336–6330); $14.95 per year. **Travelers Advantage** (✉ CUC Travel Service, 3033 S. Parker Rd., Suite 1000, Aurora, CO 80014, ☎ 800/548–1116 or 800/648–4037); $49 per year, single or family. **Worldwide Discount Travel Club** (✉ 1674 Meridian Ave., Miami Beach, FL 33139, ☎ 305/534–2082); $50 per year family, $40 single.

E

EMERGENCIES

Police, fire, or ambulance (☎ 911). **Air/Sea Rescue** (☎ 441/297–1010). The Government Emergency Broadcast Station is FM 100.1 MHz.

➤ DOCTORS AND DENTISTS: Contact the hospital or the **Government Health Clinic** (✉ 67 Victoria St., Hamilton, ☎ 441/236–0224) for referrals.

➤ HOSPITALS: **King Edward VII Memorial Hospital** (✉ 7 Point Finger Rd., outside Hamilton near the Botanical Gardens, ☎ 441/236–2345) is open 24 hours.

➤ PHARMACIES: **Bermuda Pharmacy** (✉ Near bus depot, Church St., Hamilton, ☎ 441/295–5375); open Monday–Saturday 8–6. **Clarendon Pharmacy** (✉ Clarendon Building, Bermudiana Rd., Hamilton, ☎ 441/295–9137 or 441/295–6144); open Monday–Saturday 8–6. **Collector's Hill Apothecary** (✉ South Shore Rd. and Collector's Hill, Smith's, ☎ 441/236–8664 or 441/236–9878); open Monday–Saturday 8–8, Sunday 11–7. **Hamilton Pharmacy** (✉ Parliament St., Hamilton, ☎ 441/295–7004); open Monday–Saturday 8–9. **Paget Pharmacy** (✉ Rural Hill Plaza, Middle Rd., Paget, ☎ 441/236–2681 or 441/236–7275); open Monday–Saturday 8–8, Sunday 10–6. **Phoenix Centre** (✉ 3 Reid St., Hamilton, ☎ 441/295–3838 or 441/295–0698); open Monday–Saturday 8–6, Sunday noon–6:30. **Daina Ltd. at Marriott's Castle Harbour** (✉ Paynter's Rd., Tucker's Town, ☎ 441/293–1514); open daily 8 AM–9 PM. **Robertson's Drug Store** (✉ York St. and Customs House Sq., ☎ 441/297–1736 or 441/297–1828); open Monday–Saturday 8–7:30, Sunday 4–6. **Woodbourne Chemist** (✉ Woodbourne Ave., Pembroke, on the outskirts of Hamilton, ☎ 441/295–1073 or 441/295–2663); open Monday–Saturday 8–8.

F

FERRY TRAVEL

Quick and enjoyable, ferries sail every day from the Ferry Terminal in Hamilton, with routes to Paget, Warwick, and across the Great Sound to Somerset in the West End. On weekdays, the Paget and Warwick ferries run until 11 PM; the last ferry from Hamilton to Somerset leaves at 5:20 PM; on Sunday, ferry service is limited and ends around 7 PM. A one-way fare to Paget or Warwick is $2.25, to Somerset $3.75. Bicycles can be brought aboard free, but passengers must pay $3.75 extra to take a motor scooter to Somerset; scooters are not allowed on the smaller Paget and Warwick ferries. The friendly, helpful ferry operators will answer questions about routes and schedules, and they'll even help get your bike aboard. Pick up schedules at the ferry terminal, central bus terminal, and most hotels; they're also posted at each landing.

➤ INFORMATION: **Hamilton Ferry Terminal** (☎ 441/295–4506).

G

GAY & LESBIAN TRAVEL

➤ GAY- AND LESBIAN-FRIENDLY TRAVEL AGENCIES: **Advance Damron** (✉ 1 Greenway Plaza, Suite 800, Houston, TX 77046, ☎ 713/850–1140 or 800/695–0880, FAX 713/888–1010). **Club Travel** (✉ 8739 Santa Monica Blvd., West Hollywood, CA 90069, ☎ 310/358–2200 or 800/429–8747, FAX 310/358–2222). **Islanders/Kennedy Travel** (✉ 183 W. 10th St., New York, NY 10014, ☎ 212/242–3222 or 800/988–1181, FAX 212/929–8530). **Now Voyager** (✉ 4406 18th St., San Francisco, CA 94114, ☎ 415/626–1169 or 800/255–6951, FAX 415/626–8626). **Yellowbrick Road** (✉ 1500 W. Balmoral Ave., Chicago, IL 60640, ☎ 773/561–1800 or 800/642–2488, FAX 773/561–4497). **Skylink Women's Travel** (✉ 3577 Moorland Ave., Santa Rosa, CA 95407, ☎ 707/585–8355 or 800/225–5759, FAX 707/584–5637) serves lesbian travelers.

H

HEALTH

STAYING WELL

Sunburn and sunstroke are legitimate concerns if you're traveling to Bermuda in summer. On a hot, sunny day, wear a long-sleeve shirt, a hat, and long pants or a beach wrap. These are essential for a day on a boat but are also advisable for midday at the beach. Carry sunscreen for your nose, ears, and other sensitive areas. Drink liquids and, above all, **limit the amount of time you spend in the sun** until you become acclimated.

The Portuguese man-of-war is an occasional visitor to Bermuda's waters, so **be alert when swimming,** especially in summer or whenever the water is particularly warm. They are recognizable by a purple, balloonlike float sack of perhaps 8 inches in diameter, below which dangle 20- to 60-inch tentacles armed with powerful stinging cells. Contact with these stinging cells causes immediate, severe

pain. A serious sting can put a person in shock, in which case seek medical attention immediately. Even if you don't think the sting is severe, you should still go to a doctor. In the meantime—or if getting to a doctor will take a while—liberally treat the affected area with ammonia. Although usually encountered in the water, Portuguese man-of-wars may also wash up on shore, and if you spot one on the sand, steer clear—the sting is just as severe when they're out of the water.

Divers' alert: **Do not fly within 24 hours of scuba diving.**

MEDICAL PLANS

No one plans to get sick while traveling, but it can happen, so **consider signing up with a medical-assistance company.** Members get doctor referrals, emergency evacuation or repatriation, 24-hour telephone hot lines for medical consultation, cash for emergencies, and other personal and legal assistance. Coverage varies by plan, so **review the benefits carefully.**

➤ MEDICAL-ASSISTANCE COMPANIES: **International SOS Assistance** (✉ Box 11568, Philadelphia, PA 19116, ☎ 215/244–1500 or 800/523–8930; ✉ 1255 University St., Suite 420, Montréal, Québec H3B 3B6, ☎ 514/874–7674 or 800/363–0263; ✉ 7 Old Lodge Pl., St. Margarets, Twickenham TW1 1RQ, England, ☎ 0181/744–0033). **MEDEX Assistance Corporation** (✉ Box 5375, Timonium, MD 21094-5375, ☎ 410/453–6300 or 800/537–2029). **Traveler's Emergency Network** (✉ 3100 Tower Blvd., Suite 1000B, Durham, NC 27707, ☎ 919/490–6055 or 800/275–4836, FAX 919/493–8262). **TravMed** (✉ Box 5375, Timonium, MD 21094, ☎ 410/453–6380 or 800/732–5309). **Worldwide Assistance Services** (✉ 1133 15th St. NW, Suite 400, Washington, DC 20005, ☎ 202/331–1609 or 800/821–2828, FAX 202/828–5896).

I

INSURANCE

Travel insurance is the best way to **protect yourself against financial loss.** The most useful policies are trip-cancellation-and-interruption, default, medical, and comprehensive insurance.

Without insurance you will lose all or most of your money if you cancel your trip, regardless of the reason. It's essential that you **buy trip-cancellation-and-interruption insurance,** particularly if your airline ticket, cruise, or package tour is nonrefundable and cannot be changed. When considering how much coverage you need, look for a policy that will cover the cost of your trip plus the nondiscounted price of a one-way airline ticket, should you need to return home early. Also **consider default or bankruptcy insurance,** which protects you against a supplier's failure to deliver.

Medicare generally does not cover health-care costs outside the United States, nor do many privately issued policies. If your own policy does not cover you outside the United States, **consider buying supplemental medical coverage.** Remember that travel health insurance is different from a medical-assistance plan (☞ Health, *above*).

Citizens of the United Kingdom can buy an annual travel-insurance policy valid for most vacations during the year in which it's purchased. If you are pregnant or have a preexisting medical condition, make sure you're covered.

If you have purchased an expensive vacation, particularly one that involves travel abroad, comprehensive insurance is a must. **Look for comprehensive policies that include trip-delay insurance,** which will protect you in the event that weather problems cause you to miss your flight, tour, or cruise. A few insurers sell waivers for preexisting medical conditions. Companies that offer both features include Access America, Carefree Travel, Travel Insured International, and Travel Guard (☞ *below*).

Always **buy travel insurance directly from the insurance company**; if you buy it from a travel agency or tour operator that goes out of business you probably will not be covered for the agency or operator's default, a major risk. Before you make any purchase, **review your existing health and home-owner's policies** to find out whether they cover expenses incurred while traveling.

➤ U.S. TRAVEL INSURERS: **Access America** (⊠ 6600 W. Broad St., Richmond, VA 23230, ☎ 804/285–3300 or 800/284–8300). **Carefree Travel Insurance** (⊠ Box 9366, 100 Garden City Plaza, Garden City, NY 11530, ☎ 516/294–0220 or 800/323–3149). **Near Travel Services** (⊠ Box 1339, Calumet City, IL 60409, ☎ 708/868–6700 or 800/654–6700). **Travel Guard International** (⊠ 1145 Clark St., Stevens Point, WI 54481, ☎ 715/345–0505 or 800/826–1300). **Travel Insured International** (⊠ Box 280568, East Hartford, CT 06128–0568, ☎ 860/528–7663 or 800/243–3174). **Travelex Insurance Services** (⊠ 11717 Burt St., Suite 202, Omaha, NE 68154-1500, ☎ 402/445–8637 or 800/228–9792, FAX 800/867–9531). **Wallach & Company** (⊠ 107 W. Federal St., Box 480, Middleburg, VA 20118, ☎ 540/687–3166 or 800/237–6615).

➤ IN CANADA: **Mutual of Omaha** (⊠ Travel Division, 500 University Ave., Toronto, Ontario M5G 1V8, ☎ 416/598–4083, 800/268–8825 in Canada).

➤ IN THE U.K.: **Association of British Insurers** (⊠ 51 Gresham St., London EC2V 7HQ, ☎ 0171/600–3333).

L
LODGING

APARTMENT & VILLA RENTALS

If you want a home base that's roomy enough for a family and comes with cooking facilities, **consider a furnished rental.** In Bermuda there are also housekeeping cottages and apartments available (☞ Chapter 5). Some furnished rentals can save you money, whereas others are luxury properties, economical only when your party is large.

Home-exchange directories list rentals (often second homes owned by prospective house swappers), and some services search for a house or apartment for you (even a castle if that's your fancy) and handle the paperwork. Some send an illustrated catalog; others send photographs only of specific properties, sometimes at a charge. Up-front registration fees may apply.

➤ RENTAL AGENTS: **Europa-Let/
Tropical Inn-Let** (✉ 92 N. Main St.,
Ashland, OR 97520, ☎ 541/482–
5806 or 800/462–4486, FAX 541/
482–0660). **Property Rentals International** (✉ 1008 Mansfield Crossing
Rd., Richmond, VA 23236, ☎ 804/
378–6054 or 800/220–3332, FAX
804/379–2073). **Rent-a-Home International** (✉ 7200 34th Ave. NW,
Seattle, WA 98117, ☎ 206/789–9377
or 800/488–7368, FAX 206/789–
9379).

M

MAIL

Airmail letters and postcards to the
United States and Canada require 60¢
postage per 10 grams, and 75¢ per 10
grams to the United Kingdom.

RECEIVING MAIL

If you have no address in Bermuda,
you can **have mail sent care of General Delivery** (General Post Office,
Hamilton HM GD, Bermuda).

MONEY

The Bermudian dollar is on par with
the U.S. dollar, and the two currencies
are used interchangeably. You can use
American money anywhere, but
change is often given in Bermudian
currency. Try to **avoid accumulating
large amounts of local money,** which
is difficult to exchange for U.S. dollars in Bermuda and expensive to
exchange in the United States. Canadian and British currency must be
converted.

In Bermuda, most shops and some
restaurants accept credit cards, but
the majority of hotels on the island
insist on other forms of payment,
such as cash or traveler's checks, so
**check in advance whether your hotel
takes credit cards.** Some take personal
checks by prior arrangement (a letter
from your bank is sometimes requested).

ATMS

Before leaving home, **make sure that
your credit cards have been programmed for ATM use in Bermuda.**
Note that Discover is accepted mostly
in the United States. Local bank cards
often do not work overseas or may
access only your checking account;
**ask your bank about a MasterCard/
Cirrus or Visa debit card,** which works

like a bank card but can be used at
any ATM displaying a MasterCard/
Cirrus or Visa logo. These cards, too,
may tap only your checking account;
check with your bank about their
policy.

➤ ATM LOCATIONS: **Cirrus** (☎ 800/
424–7787). A list of **Plus** locations is
available at your local bank.

COSTS

Since Bermuda imports everything
from cars to cardigans, prices are
high. A common complaint is the
high cost of a vacation on the island.
At an upscale restaurant, for example,
be prepared to pay as much for a
meal as you would in New York,
London, or Paris: on average, $60 to
$80 per person, $120 with drinks and
wine. There are other options, of
course. The island is full of coffee
shops, where you can eat with locals
hamburgers and french fries for about
$7. The same meal at a restaurant
costs about $15.

A cup of coffee costs between $1.50
and $3; a mixed drink from $4 to $6;
a bottle of beer from $2.25 to $6; and
a can of Coke about $1.50. A 15-
minute cab ride will set you back
about $25 including the tip, and a
pack of Kodak 110 cartridge film
with 12 exposures costs about $4.30.
A 36-exposure roll of 35mm 100 ASA
print film costs about $8. Smokers
pay from $5 to $7 for a pack of
cigarettes.

CURRENCY EXCHANGE

For the most favorable rates, **change
money at banks.** Although fees
charged for ATM transactions may be
higher abroad than at home, Cirrus
and Plus exchange rates are excellent,
because they are based on wholesale
rates offered only by major banks.
You won't do as well at exchange
booths in airports or rail and bus
stations, in hotels, in restaurants, or
in stores, although you may find their
hours more convenient. To avoid lines
at airport exchange booths, **get a
small amount of local currency before
you leave home.**

➤ EXCHANGE SERVICES: **International
Currency Express** (☎ 888/842–0880
on the East Coast or 888/278–6628
on the West Coast for telephone
orders). **Thomas Cook Currency**

Services (☎ 800/287–7362 for telephone orders and retail locations).

TRAVELER'S CHECKS

Whether or not to buy traveler's checks depends on where you are headed. **Take cash if your trip includes rural areas** and small towns, traveler's checks to cities. If your checks are lost or stolen, they can usually be replaced within 24 hours. To ensure a speedy refund, buy your checks yourself (don't ask someone else to make the purchase). When making a claim for stolen or lost checks, the person who bought the checks should make the call.

MOPED & SCOOTER RENTAL

Because car rentals are not allowed in Bermuda, you might decide to get around by moped or scooter. Bermudians routinely use the words "moped" and "scooter" interchangeably, even though a scooter is actually a type of moped. The difference between the two is horsepower and passenger capacity. Mopeds have 3-hp engines and scooters 6-hp. Unless you request otherwise, you'll find that you'll get a 6-hp scooter if you have a passenger, or a 3-hp moped if you're going solo.

Riding a moped is not without hazards—especially for first-time riders. The often rough-surface roads are narrow, winding, and full of blind curves. Also, many Bermudians are bad drivers, and it is wise to **think twice before renting a moped,** as accidents occur frequently and are sometimes fatal. The best ways to avoid mishaps are to drive defensively, obey the 20-mph (35-km) speed limit, remember to **stay on the left-hand side of the road**—especially at traffic circles—and avoid riding in the rain and at night.

Helmets are required by law. Single- or double-seat mopeds and scooters can be rented from cycle liveries by the hour, the day, or the week. The liveries will show first-time riders how to operate the vehicles. Rates vary, but single-seat mopeds cost about $32 per day or $113 per week (plus a mandatory $12 repair waiver). The fee includes helmet, lock, key, third-party insurance, breakdown service, pickup and delivery, and a tank of gas. A $20–$50 deposit is required for the lock, key, and helmet, and you must be at least 16 and have a valid driver's license to rent. Major hotels have their own cycle liveries, and all hotels and guest houses will make rental arrangements. Many gas stations are open daily 7–7, and a few stay open until 11 PM; most are closed on Sunday. Gas for cycles runs $3–$4 per liter.

➤ RENTAL COMPANIES: **Oleander Cycles** (✉ Valley Rd., Paget, ☎ 441/236–5235; ✉ Gorham Rd., Hamilton, ☎ 441/295–0919; ✉ Middle Rd., Southampton, ☎ 441/234–0629; ✉ The Reefs, Southampton, ☎ 441/238–0222; ✉ Dockyard, Sandys, ☎ 441/234–2764). **Eve's Cycle Livery** (✉ Middle Rd., Paget, ☎ 441/236–6247). **Devil's Hole Cycles** (✉ Harrington Sound Rd., Smith's, ☎ 441/293–1280).

P

PACKING FOR BERMUDA

Bermudians are more formal than most Americans when it comes to dress. Although attire tends to be casual during the day—Bermuda shorts are acceptable, even for businessmen—cutoffs, short shorts, and halter tops are inappropriate. Swimsuits should not be worn outside pool areas or off the beach; you'll need a cover-up in the public areas of your hotel. Joggers may wear standard jogging shorts but should avoid appearing on public streets without a shirt. In the evening, many restaurants and hotel dining rooms require that men wear a jacket and tie and that women dress comparably. Recently, some hotels have been setting aside one or two nights a week for "smart casual" attire, when jacket-and-tie restrictions are loosened. For women, tailored slacks with a dressy blouse or sweater are fine, although most Bermudian women wear dresses or skirts and blouses. Bermudian men often wear Bermuda shorts (and proper knee socks) with a jacket and tie.

During the cooler months, you should bring lightweight woolens or cottons that you can wear in layers, depending on the vagaries of the weather; a few sweaters and a lightweight jacket are always a good idea, too. Regardless of the season, you should **pack a swimsuit, a cover-up, sunscreen, and sun-**

glasses, as well as an umbrella and raincoat. Comfortable walking shoes and a bag for carrying maps and cameras are a must. If you plan to play tennis, be aware that many courts require proper whites and that tennis balls in Bermuda are extremely expensive—bring your own if possible.

Bring an extra pair of eyeglasses or contact lenses in your carry-on luggage, and if you have a health problem, **pack enough medication** to last the entire trip or have your doctor write you a prescription using the drug's generic name, because brand names vary from country to country. It's important that you **don't put prescription drugs or valuables in luggage to be checked**: it might go astray. To avoid problems with customs officials, carry medications in the original packaging. Also, don't forget the addresses of offices that handle refunds of lost traveler's checks.

LUGGAGE

In general, you are entitled to check two bags on flights within the United States and on international flights leaving the United States. You can bring a third piece on board, but it must fit easily under the seat in front of you or in the overhead compartment.

If you are flying between two foreign destinations, note that baggage allowances may be determined not by piece but by weight—generally 88 pounds (40 kilograms) in first class, 66 pounds (30 kilograms) in business class, and 44 pounds (20 kilograms) in economy. If your flight between two cities abroad *connects* with your transatlantic or transpacific flight, the piece method still applies.

Airline liability for baggage is limited to $1,250 per person on flights within the United States. On international flights it amounts to $9.07 per pound or $20 per kilogram for checked baggage (roughly $640 per 70-pound bag) and $400 per passenger for unchecked baggage. Insurance for losses exceeding these amounts can be bought from the airline at check-in for about $10 per $1,000 of coverage; note that this coverage excludes a rather extensive list of items, which is shown on your airline ticket.

Before departure, **itemize your bags' contents** and their worth, and label the bags with your name, address, and phone number. (If you use your home address, cover it so that potential thieves can't see it readily.) Inside each bag, **pack a copy of your itinerary.** At check-in, **make sure that each bag is correctly tagged** with the destination airport's three-letter code. If your bags arrive damaged or fail to arrive at all, file a written report with the airline before leaving the airport.

PASSPORTS & VISAS

Once your travel plans are confirmed, **get a passport even if you don't need one to enter Bermuda**—it's always the best form of I.D. It's also a good idea to **make photocopies of the data page;** leave one copy with someone at home and keep another with you, separated from your passport. If you lose your passport, promptly call the nearest embassy or consulate and the local police; having a copy of the data page can speed replacement.

U.S. CITIZENS

Bring your passport to ensure quick passage through immigration and customs. You do not need it to enter Bermuda if you plan to stay less than six months, although you must have onward or return tickets and proof of identity (original or certified copy of your birth certificate with raised seal, a U.S. Naturalization Certificate, a U.S. Alien Registration Card, or a U.S. Reentry Permit).

➤ INFORMATION: **Office of Passport Services** (☎ 202/647–0518).

CANADIANS

Canadians do not need a passport to enter Bermuda, though a passport is helpful to ensure quick passage through customs and immigration. A birth certificate or a certificate of citizenship is required, along with a photo ID.

➤ INFORMATION: **Passport Office** (☎ 819/994–3500 or 800/567–6868).

U.K. CITIZENS

Citizens of the United Kingdom need only a valid passport to enter Bermuda for stays of up to 30 days.

➤ INFORMATION: **London Passport Office** (☎ 0990/21010) for fees and documentation requirements and to request an emergency passport.

S

To qualify for age-related discounts, **mention your senior-citizen status up front** when booking hotel reservations (not when checking out) and before you're seated in restaurants (not when paying the bill). Note that discounts may be limited to certain menus, days, or hours.

➤ EDUCATIONAL TRAVEL PROGRAMS: **Elderhostel** (⊠ 75 Federal St., 3rd floor, Boston, MA 02110, ☎ 617/426–8056).

SIGHTSEEING

BOAT TOURS

Bermuda Island Cruises operates a 200-passenger boat, which leaves Albuoy's Point in Hamilton at 7 PM on Tuesday, Wednesday, Friday, and Saturday for a "Pirate Party Cruise" ($69, includes dinner, drinks, and entertainment). Two-hour tours of Sea Gardens ($25) in glass-bottom boats leave twice daily from the ferry terminal in Hamilton. A five-hour island cruise ($60) is also available.

Bermuda Water Tours operates the 65-ft *Ovation* and the 50-ft *Bottom Peeper,* which depart daily on a variety of excursions from the dock next to the Ferry Terminal in Hamilton. A two-hour sightseeing trip in a glass-bottom boat ($30) leaves at 10, 1:30, and 6:15; a three-hour snorkeling excursion ($45) leaves at 1:15 and 3; the three-hour combination snorkeling and glass-bottom sightseeing tour ($45) leaves at 9:20 and 4. A daylong outing ($65) leaves at 9:20 and includes snorkeling, viewing fish through the boat's glass bottom, sightseeing, and time out for lunch and shopping. A three-hour barbecue dinner, glass-bottom-boat sightseeing, and stargazing cruise features live entertainment and an open bar ($65); it leaves at 5 and 6:30. A two-hour, open-bar cocktail cruise ($35) leaves at 6:30.

➤ BOAT TOURS: **Bermuda Island Cruises** (☎ 441/292–8652, FAX 441/292–5193). **Bermuda Water Tours** (☎ 441/236–1500, FAX 441/292–0801). **Butterfield Travel Ltd., Bee-**

Line Transport, and **Destination Bermuda Ltd.** (☞ Taxi & Minibus Tours, *below*).

HELICOPTER TOURS

Bermuda Helicopters Limited provides up to four passengers with tours of the dramatic southern coast, surrounding reefs, and the island itself. The rides last approximately 20 minutes and cost $85 per passenger. You can also rent the helicopter by the hour ($950).

➤ INFORMATION: **Bermuda Helicopters Limited** (⊠ Box 109, Southampton SN BX, ☎ 441/293–4800, 441/238–0551 after hours; FAX 441/295–2539).

HORSE-DRAWN CARRIAGE TOURS

You can hire carriages on Front Street in Hamilton. Rates for a one- or two-horse carriage for up to four passengers are $20 for the first 30 minutes and $20 for each additional 30 minutes; an additional $5 is charged for each adult per half hour when more than five people ride in a carriage.

➤ FOR SPECIAL ITINERARIES: **Terceira's Stables** (☎ 441/236–3014).

GARDEN TOURS

In spring, the Garden Club of Bermuda arranges tours that visit three different houses each Wednesday between 2 and 5. Admission is $10.

Free guided tours of the Botanical Gardens leave at 10:30 AM from car park by the Berry Hill Road entrance. These 75-minute tours are conducted April through October on Tuesday, Wednesday, and Friday and November through March on Tuesday and Friday. Tours can be taken at other times by special arrangement with the curator of the gardens on the condition that a donation be made to the Botanical Society.

➤ INFORMATION: **Garden Club President** (☎ 441/295–1301). **Botanical Gardens** (☎ 441/236–4201).

SNORKELING TOURS

Bermuda Barefoot Cruises aboard the 32-ft *Minnow* leave Darrell's Wharf in Warwick. Captain Shirley tours the inshore waterways before ducking into his favorite local snorkeling site in shallow waters off Somerset, where no other charters go.

Bermuda's Multihull Sailing Adventures offers the island's only regularly scheduled sail-snorkel charters. Owned and operated by the experienced Captain Kirk Ward and his wife, Joan, two vessels are available for private or regularly scheduled trips, daily at 10 and 2, April through October.

Hayward's Snorkeling and Glass Bottom Boat Cruises has one of the island's best sightseeing-snorkeling excursions ($45, including instruction and gear) aboard the 54-ft glass-bottom *Explorer*. The cruise departs from the dock adjacent to Hamilton Ferry Terminal. Special excursions are arranged during the spring migration of the humpback whales; call for prices.

Pitman's Snorkeling offers excellent sightseeing-snorkeling excursions with informative ecological lectures aboard the glass-bottom *Fathom*. The $45, four-hour outing, which includes snorkeling instruction and gear, departs every morning (May–October) from the Robinson's Marina dock.

Jessie James Snorkeling & Sightseeing Cruises offers half-day snorkeling cruises ($40) aboard its 40-passenger luxury Chris-Craft *Rambler* from Albuoy's Point in Hamilton and Darrell's Wharf and Belmont Hotel dock in Warwick. Cruises depart daily at 9:15 and 2:15.

Salt Kettle Yacht Charters Ltd. has four-hour motorboat snorkeling trips that depart Salt Kettle, Paget Monday through Saturday at 9:30 and 1:30. The price ($42 per person) includes complimentary rum swizzles, soft drinks, and use of snorkeling gear.

➤ INFORMATION: **Bermuda Barefoot Cruises** (✉ Box DV 525, Devonshire, ☎ 441/236–3498). **Bermuda's Multihull Sailing Adventures** (☎ 441/234–1434). **Hayward's Snorkeling and Glass Bottom Boat Cruises** (☎ 441/292–8652 from 9 to 5, 441/236–9894 after hours, FAX 441/236–2608). **Pitman's Snorkeling** (☎ 441/234–0700). **Jessie James Snorkeling & Sightseeing Cruises** (☎ 441/236–4804, FAX 441/236–9208). **Salt Kettle Yacht Charters Ltd.** (☎ 441/236–4863, FAX 441/236–2427).

TAXI & MINIBUS TOURS

For an independent tour of the island, a taxi is a good but more expensive alternative to a group tour. A blue flag on the hood of a cab indicates that the driver is a qualified tour guide. These cabs can be difficult to find, but most of their drivers are friendly, entertaining—they sometimes bend the truth for a good yarn—and well informed about the island and its history. Ask your hotel to arrange a tour with a knowledgeable driver.

Cabs are four- or six-seaters, and the legal rate for island tours is $20 per hour for one to four passengers and $30 per hour for five and six passengers; two children under 12 equal an adult. A 25% surcharge is added between 10 PM and 6 AM and on Sunday.

➤ INFORMATION: **Bee-Line Transport Ltd.** (✉ Box HM 2270, Hamilton HM, ☎ 441/293–0303, FAX 441/293–8015). **Bermuda Hosts Ltd.** (✉ Box CR 46, Crawl, Hamilton CR, ☎ 441/293–1334, FAX 441/293–1335). **Destination Bermuda Ltd.** (✉ Box HM 1822, Hamilton HM HX, ☎ 441/292–2325, FAX 441/292–2252). **PenbossMeyer** (✉ Box HM 510, Hamilton HM CX, ☎ 441/295–9733, FAX 441/292–8251).

WALKING TOURS

The Bermuda Department of Tourism publishes brochures detailing self-guided tours of Hamilton, St. George's, the West End, and the Railway Trail. "The Bermuda Nature Guide," also issued by the Bermuda Department of Tourism, has details about the island's flora, fauna, and pink coral sand. Available for free at all visitor service bureaus and at hotels and guest houses, these brochures also contain detailed directions for walkers and cyclists and historical notes and anecdotes.

From November through March, the Bermuda Department of Tourism coordinates 45-minute to two-hour walking tours of Hamilton's Session House, North Hamilton, St. George's, Spittal Pond Nature Reserve, the Royal Naval Dockyard, and Somerset. The tours of St. George's and most of the Royal Naval Dockyard tours take in the large number of

17th- and 18th-century buildings, while the Spittal Pond and Somerset tours focus on the island's flora. The Sessions House tour begins outside the historic Hamilton building on the corner of Parliament and Church streets every Monday at 11:15 AM. On Tuesday at 10:30 AM, amblers meet at the Cabinet office for a Heritage and Cultural Trail Walk that takes in the history and development of North Hamilton. The tour of Spittal Pond, and its endemic flora with their healing qualities, is conducted Friday at 1; meet in the east parking lot. The St. George's walk leaves from King's Square at 10:30 AM on Wednesday and Saturday. The Somerset walk departs Thursday at 10 AM from the Country Squire restaurant; a slide show is held afterward at 11:15 AM. Tours at the Royal Naval Dockyard leave from the Clocktower Building on Thursday at 2:15 PM and Sunday at 11:15 AM; the 2:15 PM Sunday walk leaves from the Craft Market. On Sunday mornings, this tour is a nature walk through woodlands, parks, bird sanctuaries, and historic cemeteries.

➤ INFORMATION: **Bermuda Department of Tourism** (☎ 441/292–0023).

STUDENTS

Like other travelers, students arriving in Bermuda must have confirmation of hotel reservations, a return plane ticket, a photo ID, and proof of citizenship, such as a passport, birth certificate, or a signed voter registration card. There are no youth hostels, YMCAs, or YWCAs on the island. During Bermuda Spring Break Sports Week (☞ Festivals and Seasonal Events *in* Chapter 1), however, special student rates are offered at some hotels and guest houses, restaurants, pubs, and nightclubs.

To save money, **look into deals available through student-oriented travel agencies.** To qualify you'll need a bona fide student ID card. Members of international student groups are also eligible.

➤ STUDENT IDs AND SERVICES: **Council on International Educational Exchange** (✉ CIEE, 205 E. 42nd St., 14th floor, New York, NY 10017, ☎ 212/822–2600 or 888/268–6245, FAX 212/822–2699), for mail orders only,

in the United States. **Travel Cuts** (✉ 187 College St., Toronto, Ontario M5T 1P7, ☎ 416/979–2406 or 800/667–2887) in Canada.

➤ HOSTELING: **Hostelling International—American Youth Hostels** (✉ 733 15th St. NW, Suite 840, Washington, DC 20005, ☎ 202/783–6161, FAX 202/783–6171). **Hostelling International—Canada** (✉ 400-205 Catherine St., Ottawa, Ontario K2P 1C3, ☎ 613/237–7884, FAX 613/237–7868). **Youth Hostel Association of England and Wales** (✉ Trevelyan House, 8 St. Stephen's Hill, St. Albans, Hertfordshire AL1 2DY, ☎ 01727/855215 or 01727/845047, FAX 01727/844126). Membership in the U.S., $25; in Canada, C$26.75; in the U.K., £9.30.

T

TAXES

Hotels add a 7.25% government tax to the bill, and most add a 10% service charge or a per diem dollar equivalent in lieu of tips. Other extra charges sometimes include a 5% "energy surcharge" (at small guest houses) and a 15% service charge (at most restaurants).

TAXIS

Taxis are the fastest and easiest way around the island—and also the most costly. Four-seater taxis charge $4.80 for the first mile and $1.68 for each subsequent mile. A three-hour trip costs $20 per hour, excluding tip. Between midnight and 6 AM, and on Sunday, a 25% surcharge is added to the fare. There is a 25¢ charge for each piece of luggage stored in the trunk or on the roof.

For information on taxi tours, *see* Sightseeing, *above.*

➤ CAB COMPANIES: **Radio Cabs Bermuda** (☎ 441/295–4141). **Bermuda Taxi Operators** (☎ 441/292–5600). For West Enders, **Sandys Taxi Service** (☎ 441/234–2344) runs island-wide from 8 AM to 11 PM.

TELEPHONES

Pay phones, identical to those found in the United States, are found on the streets of Hamilton, St. George's, and Somerset, as well as at ferry landings, some bus stops, and public beaches.

THE GOLD GUIDE / SMART TRAVEL TIPS

SMART TRAVEL TIPS / THE GOLD GUIDE

Deposit 20¢ (U.S. or Bermudian) in the meter as soon as your party answers. Most hotels charge 20¢–$1 for local calls.

Direct dialing is possible from anywhere on the island. Most hotels impose a surcharge for long-distance calls, even those made collect. Many of the small guest houses and apartments have no central switchboard; if you have a phone in your room, it's a private line from which you can make only collect, credit-card, or local calls. Some of the small hotels have a telephone room or kiosk where you can make long-distance calls.

CALLING HOME

You'll find specially marked AT&T USADirect phones at the airport, the cruise-ship dock in Hamilton, and at King's Square and Ordnance Island in St. George's. You can also make international calls with a calling card from the main post office. You can make prepaid international calls from the Cable & Wireless Office, which also has international telex, cable, and fax services Monday through Saturday, from 9 to 5.

To call the United States, Canada, and most Caribbean countries, dial 1 (or 0 if you need an operator's assistance), then the area code and the number. For all other countries, dial 011 (or 0 for an operator), the country code, the area code, and the number. Using an operator for an overseas call is more expensive than dialing direct. For calls to the United States, rates are highest from 10 AM to 7 PM and discounted from 7 PM to 11 PM; the lowest rates are from 11 PM to 7 AM. Calls to Alaska and Hawaii are not discounted. Calls to Canada are cheapest from 9 PM to 7 AM and to the United Kingdom from 6 PM to 7 AM.

➤ To Obtain Access Codes: **AT&T USADirect** (☎ 800/874–4000). **MCI Call USA** (☎ 800/444–4444). **Sprint Express** (☎ 800/793–1153).

➤ International Calls: **Main post office** (✉ Church and Parliament Sts., Hamilton, ☎ 441/295–5151). **Cable & Wireless Office** (✉ 20 Church St., opposite City Hall, Hamilton, ☎ 441/297–7000).

TIPPING

A service charge of 10% (or an equivalent per diem amount), which covers everything from baggage handling to maid service, is added to your hotel bill. Most restaurants tack on a 15% service charge; if not, a 15% tip is customary (more for exceptional service). Porters at the airport expect about a dollar a bag, while taxi drivers usually receive 15% of the fare.

TOUR OPERATORS

Buying a prepackaged tour or independent vacation can make your trip to Bermuda less expensive and more hassle-free. Because everything is prearranged, you'll spend less time planning.

Operators that handle several hundred thousand travelers per year can use their purchasing power to give you a good price. Their high volume may also indicate financial stability. But some small companies provide more personalized service; because they tend to specialize, they may also be more knowledgeable about a given area.

A GOOD DEAL?

The more your package or tour includes, the better you can predict the ultimate cost of your vacation. Make sure you know exactly what is covered, and **beware of hidden costs.** Are taxes, tips, and service charges included? Transfers and baggage handling? Entertainment and excursions? These can add up.

If the package or tour you are considering is priced lower than in your wildest dreams, **be skeptical.** Also, **make sure your travel agent knows the accommodations** and other services. Ask about the hotel's location, room size, beds, and whether it has a pool, room service, or programs for children, if you care about these. Has your agent been there in person or sent others you can contact?

BUYER BEWARE

Each year consumers are stranded or lose their money when tour operators—even very large ones with excellent reputations—go out of business. So **check out the operator.** Find out how long the company has been in business, and ask several agents about its reputation. **Don't book unless the firm has a consumer-protection program.**

Members of the National Tour Association and United States Tour Operators Association are required to set aside funds to cover your payments and travel arrangements in case the company defaults. Nonmembers may carry insurance instead. Look for the details, and for the name of an underwriter with a solid reputation, in the operator's brochure. Note: When it comes to tour operators, **don't trust escrow accounts.** Although the Department of Transportation watches over charter-flight operators, no regulatory body prevents tour operators from raiding the till. You may want to protect yourself by buying travel insurance that includes a tour-operator default provision. For more information, *see* Consumer Protection, *above.*

It's also a good idea to choose a company that participates in the American Society of Travel Agents' Tour Operator Program (TOP). This give you a forum if there are any disputes between you and your tour operator; ASTA will act as mediator.

➤ TOUR-OPERATOR RECOMMENDA-
TIONS: **National Tour Association** (✉ NTA, 546 E. Main St., Lexington, KY 40508, ☎ 606/226–4444 or 800/ 755–8687). **United States Tour Operators Association** (✉ USTOA, 342 Madison Ave., Suite 1522, New York, NY 10173, ☎ 212/599–6599, ℻ 212/599–6744). **American Society of Travel Agents** (☞ Travel Agencies, *below*).

USING AN AGENT

Travel agents are excellent resources. In fact, large operators accept bookings made only through travel agents. But it's a good idea to **collect brochures from several agencies,** because some agents' suggestions may be influenced by relationships with tour and package firms that reward them for volume sales. If you have a special interest, **find an agent with expertise in that area;** ASTA (☞ Travel Agencies, *below*) has a database of specialists worldwide. Do some homework on your own, too: Local tourism boards can provide

information about lesser-known and small-niche operators, some of which may sell only direct.

SINGLE TRAVELERS

Prices for packages and tours are usually quoted per person, based on two sharing a room. If traveling solo, you may be required to pay the full double-occupancy rate. Some operators eliminate this surcharge if you agree to be matched with a roommate of the same sex, even if one is not found by departure time.

PACKAGES

Like group tours, independent vacation packages are available from major tour operators and airlines. The companies listed below offer vacation packages in a broad price range.

➤ AIR/HOTEL: **American Airlines Fly AAway Vacations** (☎ 800/321– 2121). **Certified Vacations** (✉ 110 E. Broward Blvd., Fort Lauderdale, FL 33302, ☎ 954/522–1440 or 800/ 233–7260). **Continental Vacations** (☎ 800/634–5555). **Delta Dream Vacations** (☎ 800/872–7786). **US Airways Vacations** (☎ 800/455– 0123).

THEME TRIPS

➤ FISHING: **Fishing International** (✉ Box 2132, Santa Rosa, CA 95405, ☎ 707/539–3366 or 800/950–4242, ℻ 707/539–1320).

➤ GOLF: **ITC Golf Tours** (✉ 4134 Atlantic Ave., #205, Long Beach, CA 90807, ☎ 310/595–6905 or 800/ 257–4981). **Stine's Golftrips** (✉ Box 2314, Winter Haven, FL 33883-2314, ☎ 941/324–1300 or 800/428–1940, ℻ 941/325–0384).

➤ LEARNING: **Smithsonian Study Tours and Seminars** (✉ 1100 Jefferson Dr. SW, Room 3045, MRC 702, Washington, DC 20560, ☎ 202/357– 4700, ℻ 202/633–9250).

➤ SPAS: **Spa-Finders** (✉ 91 5th Ave., #301, New York, NY 10003-3039, ☎ 212/924–6800 or 800/255– 7727).

➤ VILLA VACATIONS: **Villas International** (✉ 605 Market St., San Francisco, CA 94105, ☎ 415/281–0910 or 800/221–2260, ℻ 415/281– 0919).

THE GOLD GUIDE / SMART TRAVEL TIPS

TRANSPORTATION

Despite its small size, Bermuda does pose some transport problems. Because rental cars are not allowed, you'll have to **travel by bus, taxi, ferry, moped, bike, or on foot.** More than 1,200 mi of narrow, winding roads and a 20-mph (35-km) speed limit make moving around the island a time-consuming process. Though the island was once famous for its "mopeds" (motorized pedal cycles), the island's rapidly increasing number of cars and overall congestion can make this mode of travel somewhat stressful, if not dangerous. Ferries, on the other hand, offer clean, relaxing jaunts and are an inexpensive way to see the island from the water. Traveling the length of this long, skinny island takes particularly long: The trip from St. George's to Hamilton takes an hour by bus, and the journey onward to the West End takes another hour, although an express bus from Hamilton to the West End takes only 40 minutes. Hiring a taxi can cut down the amount of time you spend on the road, but the cost may discourage you. Fortunately, Hamilton, St. George's, and Somerset are all manageable on foot.

TRAVEL AGENCIES

A good travel agent puts your needs first. Look for an agency that has been in business at least five years, emphasizes customer service, and has someone on staff who specializes in your destination. In addition, **make sure the agency belongs to the American Society of Travel Agents** (ASTA). If your travel agency is also acting as your tour operator, *see* Tour Operators, *above.*

➤ LOCAL AGENT REFERRALS: **American Society of Travel Agents** (ASTA, ☎ 800/965–2782 for 24-hr hot line, FAX 703/684–8319). **Alliance of Canadian Travel Associations** (⊠ 1729 Bank St., Suite 201, Ottawa, Ontario K1V 7Z5, ☎ 613/521–0474, FAX 613/521–0805). **Association of British Travel Agents** (⊠ 55–57 Newman St., London W1P 4AH, ☎ 0171/637–2444, FAX 0171/637–0713).

TRAVEL GEAR

Travel catalogs specialize in useful items, such as compact alarm clocks and travel irons, that can **save space when packing.** They also offer dual-voltage appliances, currency converters, and foreign-language phrase books.

➤ MAIL-ORDER CATALOGS: **Magellan's** (☎ 800/962–4943, FAX 805/568–5406). **Orvis Travel** (☎ 800/541–3541, FAX 540/343–7053). **TravelSmith** (☎ 800/950–1600, FAX 800/950–1656).

U

U.S. GOVERNMENT

The U.S. government can be an excellent source of inexpensive travel information. When planning your trip, **find out what government materials are available.**

➤ ADVISORIES: **U.S. Department of State** (⊠ Overseas Citizens Services Office, Room 4811 N.S., Washington, DC 20520); enclose a self-addressed, stamped envelope. **Interactive hot line** (☎ 202/647–5225, FAX 202/647–3000). **Computer bulletin board** (☎ 301/946–4400).

➤ PAMPHLETS: **Consumer Information Center** (⊠ Consumer Information Catalogue, Pueblo, CO 81009, ☎ 719/948–3334) for a free catalog that includes travel titles.

V

VISITOR INFORMATION

For general information, seasonal events, and brochures contact the state tourism offices, *below.*

➤ BERMUDA DEPARTMENT OF TOURISM: **U.S. nationwide** (⊠ 310 Madison Ave., Suite 201, New York, NY 10017-6083, ☎ 212/818–9800 or 800/223–6106, FAX 212/983–5289). **Brochures nationwide** (☎ 800/237–6832). **Atlanta** (⊠ 245 Peachtree Center Ave. NE, Suite 803, Atlanta, GA 30303-1223, ☎ 404/524–1541, FAX 404/586–9933). **Boston** (⊠ 44 School St., Suite 1010, Boston, MA 02108, ☎ 617/742–0405, FAX 617/723–7786). **Chicago** (⊠ 150 North Wacker Dr., Suite 1070, Chicago, IL 60606-1605, ☎ 312/782–5486, FAX 312/704–6996). **Los Angeles** (⊠ 269 S. Beverly Dr., Suite 448, Beverly Hills, CA 90212, ☎ 213/933–2416, FAX 213/933–2469). **Canada** (⊠ 1200 Bay St., Suite 1004, Toronto, Ontario M5R 2A5,

☎ 416/923–9600, ꊚ 416/923–4840). **U.K.** (✉ BCB Ltd., 1 Battersea Church Rd., London SW11 3LY, ☎ 0171/734–8813, ꊚ 0171/352–6501).

W
WHEN TO GO

During summer, the island teems with activities. Hotel barbecues and evening dances complement daytime sightseeing excursions, and the public beaches are always open. The pace during the off-season slows considerably. A few of the hotels and restaurants close, some of the sightseeing boats are dry-docked, and only the taxis and the St. George's minibus operate tours of the island. The majority of hotels remain open, however, slashing their rates by as much as 40% from November to March. The weather at this time of year is often perfect for golf and tennis, and visitors can still rent boats, tour the island, and take advantage of the special events and walking tours offered (☞ Festivals and Seasonal Events *in* Chapter 1).

CLIMATE

Bermuda has a remarkably mild climate that seldom sees extremes of either heat or cold. During the winter (December through March), temperatures range from around 55°F at night to 70°F in the early afternoon. High, blustery winds can make the temperature feel cooler, however, as can Bermuda's high humidity. The hottest part of the year is between May and mid-October, when temperatures range from 75°F to 85°F; 90°F is not uncommon in July and August. The summer months are somewhat drier, but rainfall is spread fairly evenly throughout the year. Bermuda depends solely on rain for its supply of fresh water, so residents usually welcome the brief storms. In August and September, hurricanes moving northward from the Caribbean sometimes batter the island.

➤ FORECASTS: **Weather Channel Connection** (☎ 900/932–8437), *95¢* per minute from a Touch-Tone phone.

Climate in Bermuda

What follows are average daily maximum and minimum temperatures for Bermuda.

Jan.	68F	20C	May	76F	24C	Sept.	85F	29C
	58	14		65	18		72	22
Feb.	68F	20C	June	81F	27C	Oct.	79F	26C
	58	14		70	21		70	21
Mar.	68F	20C	July	85F	29C	Nov.	74F	23C
	58	14		74	23		63	17
Apr.	72F	22C	Aug.	86F	30C	Dec.	70F	21C
	59	15		76	24		61	16

THE GOLD GUIDE / SMART TRAVEL TIPS

1 Destination: Bermuda

A BASTION OF BRITAIN, WITH A TROPICAL TWIST

BASKING IN THE ATLANTIC, 508 mi due east of Cape Hatteras, North Carolina, Bermuda is one of the wealthiest countries in the world—average per capita income is $20,000. Bermuda has no income tax, no sales tax, no slums, no unemployment, and no major crime problem. Don't come to Bermuda expecting a tropical paradise where laid-back locals wander around barefoot drinking piña coladas. On Bermuda's 21 square mi, you will find neither towering mountains, glorious rain forests, nor exotic volcanoes. Instead, pastel cottages, quaint shops, and manicured gardens are indicative of a more staid, suburban way of life. As a British diplomat once said, "Bermuda is terribly middle-age"—and in many ways he was right. Most of the island is residential, the speed limit is 20 mph, golf and tennis are popular pastimes, most visitors are over 40 years old, restaurants and shops are expensive, and casual attire in public is frowned upon. The population of 58,000 is 61% black and 39% white, but Bermudians speak the Queen's English in the Queen's own accent. White Bermudians, in particular, have strived to create a middle-class England of their own. And like almost all colonies, the Bermudian version is more insular, more conservative, and more English than the original. Pubs, fish-and-chips, and cricket are just outward manifestations of a fierce loyalty to Britain and everything it represents (or used to represent). A self-governing British colony, with a Parliament that dates from 1620, Bermuda loves pomp and circumstance, British tradition, and Bermudian history. Great ceremony attends the convening of Parliament; marching bands parade through the capital in honor of the Queen's official birthday; regimental bands and bagpipers reenact centuries-old ceremonies; and tea is served each afternoon.

Bermuda wears its history like a comfortable old coat—land is too valuable to permit the island's legacy to be cordoned off for mere display. A visitor need only wander through the 17th-century buildings of St. George's, now home to shops and private residences, to realize that Bermudian history remains part of the fabric of life, with each successive generation adding its own thread of achievement and color. Indeed, the island's isolation and diminutive size have forged a continuity of place and tradition almost totally missing in the United States. Walk into Trimingham's or A. S. Cooper & Son department store, and you are likely to be helped by a descendant of the original founders. The same names from history keep cropping up—Tucker, Carter, Trott—and a single lane in St. George's can conjure up centuries of memories and events. Even today, the brief love affair in 1804 between Irish poet Thomas Moore and the married Hester Tucker—the "Nea" of his odes—is gossiped about with a zeal usually reserved for the transgressions of a neighbor. Bermuda's attachment to its history is more than a product of its size, however. Through its past, Bermuda invokes its own sense of identity and reinforces its relationship with Britain. Otherwise, cast off in the Atlantic more than 3,445 mi from London (yet only 508 mi from the United States), Bermuda would probably have succumbed to American cultural influences long ago.

Since the very beginning, the fate of this small colony in the Atlantic has been linked to that of the United States. The crew of the *Sea Venture,* whose wreck on Bermuda during a hurricane in 1609 began the settlement of the island, was actually on its way to Jamestown in Virginia. Indeed, the passenger list of the *Sea Venture* reads like a veritable "Who's Who" of early American history. Aboard were Sir Thomas Gates, deputy governor of Jamestown; Christopher Newport, who had led the first expedition to Jamestown; and John Rolfe, whose second wife was Native American princess Pocahontas. In succeeding centuries, Bermuda has been a remarkable barometer of the evolving relationship between the United States and Britain. In 1775, Bermuda was secretly persuaded to give gunpowder to George Washington in return for the lifting of a trade blockade that threatened the island with starvation. In the War of 1812, Bermuda was the staging post for the British fleet's attack on Washington, D.C. With Britain facing a national crisis in 1940, the United States was given land on Bermuda to build a Naval Air Station in exchange for ships and supplies; then in 1990, British prime minister Thatcher and President Bush held talks on the island.

The fact that Bermuda—just two hours by air from New York—has maintained its English character through the years is obviously part of its appeal for the half million-plus Americans (89% of all tourists) who flock here each year. More important, however, Bermuda means sun, sea, and sand. This bastion of Britain boasts a mild climate year-round, pink beaches, turquoise waters, coral reefs, 17th-century villages, and splendid golf courses (Bermuda has more golf courses per square mile than anywhere else in the world).

Bermuda did not always seem so attractive. After all, more than 300 wrecks lie submerged on those same reefs where divers now frolic. William Strachey, secretary-elect for Virginia and a passenger on the *Sea Venture,* wrote that Bermuda was "a place so terrible to all that ever touched on them—such tempests, thunders and other fearful objects are seen and heard about those islands that they are called The Devills Islands, feared and avoided by all sea travellers above any place in the world." For the crew of the *Sea Venture,* however, the 181 small islands that compose Bermuda meant salvation. Contrary to rumor, the islands proved to be unusually fertile and hospitable, supporting the crew during the construction of two new ships, in which they departed for Jamestown on May 10, 1610.

Shakespeare drew on the accounts of the survivors in *The Tempest,* written in 1611. The wreck of the *Sea Venture* on harsh yet beneficent Bermuda—"these infortunate (yet fortunate) islands," as one survivor described them—contained all the elements of Shakespearean tragicomedy: that out of loss something greater is often born. Just as Prospero loses the duchy of Milan only to regain it and secure the kingdom of Naples for his daughter, Admiral Sir George Somers lost a ship but gained an island. Today, Bermuda's motto is "Quo Fata Ferunt" (Whither the Fates Carry Us), an expression of sublime con-

fidence in the same providence that carried the *Sea Venture* safely to shore.

That confidence has largely been justified over the years, but concerns have recently been raised about congestion, overfishing, reef damage, and a declining quality of life. Nearly 600,000 visitors a year are the golden eggs that many Bermudians feel are now killing the goose. In the face of such an influx of tourists, the behavior of some service employees, particularly bus drivers and young store clerks, has become sullen and rude. Traffic jams leading into Hamilton, the island's capital, are no longer a rarity, despite the fact that families can have only one car and car rentals are prohibited. In 1990, the government restricted the number of cruise-ship visits to four per week, citing the large numbers of passengers who add to the congestion but contribute little to the island's coffers. Instead, the Bermuda Department of Tourism hopes to attract a younger, livelier mix of tourists in an effort to change its image as a stodgy island.

When all is said and done, however, Bermuda's problems stem from a surfeit of advantages rather than a dearth, and almost every island nation would gladly inherit them. The "still-vexed Bermoothes" is how Shakespeare described this Atlantic pearl; he may have changed his tune if he had had a chance to swim at Horseshoe Bay, or hit a mashie-niblick to the 15th green at Port Royal. Who knows, instead of referring to a storm-wracked island, *The Tempest* might have been Shakespeare's reaction to a missed putt on the 18th.

— Honey Naylor

NEW AND NOTEWORTHY

By September 1998, the National Aeronautics & Space Agency will have vacated its satellite tracking facility on Bermuda. Set up in 1961, the station provided a satellite voice link to NASA headquarters. In recent years its primary job has been to support space shuttle launch phases; with new satellite technology the earth-bound tracking facility has become redundant.

The Southampton Princess Hotel has installed a $1.6 million dolphin encounter program that may well prove to be among the island's most popular attractions. The hotel, in partnership with Dolphin Quest, gives humans the opportunity to join dolphins in the water and interact with them personally, so to speak. A 3-acre lagoon on the hotel's beach is home to seven bottlenose dolphins, who appear quite delighted to interact with humans. There are separate programs for children and adults. This is Bermuda's only such program.

The Bermuda Aquarium, Museum, and Zoo has embarked on a substantial $5.2 million development program. One part is the North Rock Exhibit, a 140,000-gallon tank in the main gallery that displays Bermuda's famed living coral reefs. It covers the way corals live and grow, the fragile ecosystem of plants and animals that the reef supports, the history of the island's marine resources, and local protection measures to guard Bermuda's coral reef system. The other part of the aquarium's development plan is called Australasia, a walk-through exhibit of wildlife indigenous to Australia, New Guinea, Borneo, and Malaysia. Sundry tree kangaroos, wallabies, mousedeer, hornbills, fruit bats, Asian otters are in their natural habitats. Both new exhibits are up and running.

Following up on last year's question of whether Golden Arches would be soaring all over the island—the answer is no. There was one McDonald's, at the Naval Air Station; on certain days locals were welcome, and those with small children found it a boon. But there was also fear that the fast-food chain would proliferate. It was rumored that there would be locations at Dockyard, in St. George, and in Hamilton, as well as on St. David's Island. But McDonald's has packed up and left, and nary an arch is to be seen.

The Corporation of St. George has embarked on a $20 million, 15-year program to "enhance an already attractive town." The initial phase of the program is already visible in "new old-fashioned" lanterns and street signs. Since "the story and stories of Bermuda are best told from within St. George's," officials are planning a Heritage Centre, with introductory video or film, exhibits pertaining to the discovery and settlement of Bermuda, and the links between Bermuda and Britain, the West Indies, the United States, and Canada. A Heritage Foundation will be charged with establishing the Centre, developing fundraising options, and overseeing the preservation of buildings vital to the community. A Waterfront Promenade will permit continuous access to the waterfront from Penno's Wharf to Convict Bay, and the Market Wharf Building will be opened to allow walk-through access to the water's edge. Some of the narrow lanes will be resurfaced and, in some cases, widened.

From time to time one hears murmurings to the effect: "Please don't let them Disney-fy it."

WHAT'S WHERE

Hamilton

As the capital of Bermuda since 1815, Hamilton is the home of most of the island's government buildings; here visitors may watch Parliament in session or visit the grand City Hall, home to two major art galleries. The soaring Cathedral of the Most Holy Trinity, seat of the Anglican Church of Bermuda, is in Hamilton, as is Ft. Hamilton, a moated fortress with underground passageways. But most people know Hamilton as the hub of shopping and dining, with colorful Front Street as the main thoroughfare. The departure point for ferries heading to other parts of the island, Hamilton is one of the smallest, busiest port cities in the world.

St. George

Bermuda's original capital (from the early 17th century until 1815) is steeped in history; settled in 1609, it was the second English settlement in the New World (after Jamestown, Virginia). Today its alleys and walled lanes are packed with small museums and historical sights, starting with King's Square—where cedar replicas of the stocks, pillory, and ducking stool once used to punish criminals serve as props.

The West End

The West End of Bermuda, encompassing Somerset and Ireland islands, is a bucolic area of nature reserves, wooded areas, and beautiful bays and harbors. In addition to its natural beauty, the area's big attraction is the Royal Naval Dockyard, a former bastion of the Royal British Navy, now a major tourism center with a maritime museum and a shopping arcade.

The Parishes

Bermuda's many other parishes harbor diverse attractions: from the historic smugglers' town of Flatts Village to the coveted beaches of Paget. Scattered across the island, the parishes of Southampton, Warwick, Paget, Pembroke, Devonshire, Smith's, and Tucker's Town are best visited by bicycle or moped—but don't try to see them all in one day.

PLEASURES AND PASTIMES

Beaches

The fine, pink sand of Bermuda's beaches—a result of shell particles, calcium carbonate, and bits of crushed coral mixed with sand—gives them an ephemeral hue. This is amplified by their picturesque surroundings, which include dramatic cliff formations, coconut palms, and gently rolling dunes that slope toward the shimmering blues of the Atlantic. The island's 34 beaches range from long, unbroken expanses of shoreline such as that at Warwick Long Bay to small, secluded coves divided by rock cliffs such as those found at Whale Bay Beach and Jobson's Cove.

Cricket

To Americans, the popularity of cricket in Bermuda begins to sink in only when you consider that the annual Cup Match Cricket Festival, a two-day event, is a national holiday. Traditionally held the Thursday and Friday before the first Monday in August, Cup Match draws an average of 12,000 spectators, including zealous supporters who "decorate" the batsman by running out onto the field and slipping a little cash in his pocket. Other cricket games can be seen throughout the summer, from April through September.

Diving and Snorkeling

Reefs, shipwrecks, underwater caves, a variety of coral and marine life, and warm, clear water make Bermuda an ideal place for underwater exploration. Around Bermuda's many sheltering reefs, you might encounter parrot fish, angelfish, trumpet fish, or grouper, while divers enjoy a visibility range of 70 to 150 ft—the longest in the western Atlantic. The island's numerous shipwrecks also make great dive sites as well.

Shopping

For shoppers, Bermuda has everything from sophisticated department stores and top-quality boutiques to art galleries with works by resident artists, as well as fun products such as Outerbridge's Sherry Peppers and Bermuda rum. On the high end, European-made crystal and china, British-made clothing (especially woolen sweaters), and fine jewelry are popular (and expensive) products. On the artsy side, galleries throughout the island offer sculptures and paintings, handblown glass, handmade dolls, and other works by local artists and artisans.

Tennis

With more than 80 tennis courts in its 22 square mi, Bermuda has been a tennis capital since 1873. That was the year when Sir Bronlow Gray, the island's chief justice, introduced the game and built a grass tennis court at his Paget Parish home; the court still stands today. With its semitropical climate, Bermuda is still a perfect place to play tennis year-round, day or night (many courts are lit).

FODOR'S CHOICE

Beaches

★ The tiny adjacent beaches of **Chaplin Bay,** which almost disappear at high tide, are blissfully secluded.

★ Fine, pink sand, clear water, and a vibrant social scene make **Horseshoe Bay** a Bermudian favorite.

★ The quiet, low-key **Somerset Long Bay** is shielded by undeveloped parkland, grass, and brush.

★ **Warwick Long Bay,** the island's longest beach, has a beautiful sculpted coral outcropping that seems to balance on the surface of the water.

Favorite Outdoor Activities

★ **Offshore wreck diving** is a dramatic way to contemplate the storm-tossed past that's responsible for Bermuda's 300 wrecks.

★ For a leisurely tour of the nooks and crannies of a coral-cliff wall, try **snorkeling in Church Bay.**

★ **The Port Royal Golf & Country Club's 16th hole** sits on a treeless promontory overlooking the waters of Whale Bay.

★ The hard-packed trails that wind through **the dunes in South Shore Park** are a great place to run and ride horses.

Lodging

★ The island's original cottage colony, 100-year old **Cambridge Beaches,** remains a favorite among royalty and commoners alike. *$$$$*

★ The Relais & Châteaux **Horizons & Cottages** has the elegant feel of an 18th-century home—which, in fact, it once was. *$$$$*

★ The pink lanais of **The Reefs,** a small, casually elegant resort, are set in cliffs above Christian Bay. *$$$$*

★ **Waterloo House,** another Relais & Châteaux property, is in an early-19th-century white-column house that faces Hamilton Harbour. *$$$$*

★ The traditional, slightly formal **Princess,** in business since 1884, is regarded as the mother of Bermuda's tourist industry. *$$$–$$$$*

★ In a quiet residential area near Hamilton Harbour, the **Little Pomander Guest House** is a find for budget travelers. *$$*

★ The secluded **Pretty Penny** guest cottages have bright, colorful rooms, kitchen and dining areas, and private patios. *$$*

★ The cozy **Salt Kettle House,** with its water views, fireside lounge, and hearty English breakfast, attracts repeat visitors year after year. *$*

Restaurants

★ Superior French cuisine and a 1670 manor-house setting combine to make the **Waterlot Inn** one of the island's finest restaurants. *$$$$*

★ Nestled between high cliff rocks and a pristine beach, **Coconuts** at the Reef Resort is a lovely place to enjoy grilled fish, charbroiled steak, and, of course, coconut tart. *$$$*

★ At **Plantation,** a plant-filled, glass-enclosed atrium is the perfect setting in which to enjoy freshly caught fish and tropical specialties. *$$$*

★ **Black Horse Tavern** is the place to try curried conch stew, Bermuda lobster, amberjack, rockfish, and—a true Bermuda original—shark hash. *$$*

★ The eclectic menu at **Paw-Paws,** a bistro with a cozy dining room and outdoor seating, includes everything from homemade lobster ravioli to shark hash with Creole sauce. *$$*

★ At **Dennis's Hideaway,** you'll find the eccentric Dennis Lamb offering everything from conch fritters to mussel pie to bread-and-butter pudding, among homemade picnic tables and a yapping dog or two. *$$*

Special Moments

★ **Riding the ferry from Hamilton to Somerset,** which gives you one of the finest views of the island.

★ **Exploring the parishes on a moped,** feeling like a real onion—a Bermudian, that is—on wheels.

★ **Browsing through the Bermuda Book Store,** a musty old place with stacks of books about the island.

★ **Watching the colorfully costumed Gombey Dancers,** a troupe whose tradition blends African, West Indian, and Carribean influences.

FESTIVALS AND SEASONAL EVENTS

Precise dates and information about the events listed below are available from the Bermuda Department of Tourism (☞ Visitor Information *in* the Gold Guide).

WINTER

DEC.➤ The **Hamilton Jaycees Santa Claus Parade** brings Father Christmas to Front Street, along with bands, floats, majorettes, and other seasonal festivities. St. Nick also appears at the West End Junior Chamber Santa Claus Parade and the St. George's Junior Chamber Silver Bells Santa Comes to Town Parade. Contact the Bermuda Department of Tourism.

The **Annual Belmont Invitational Tournament for Men,** played at the Belmont Golf & Country Club, is open to professionals and amateurs. Contact Tournament Chairman (✉ Belmont Golf Club, Box HM 3266, Hamilton WK PX, ☎ 441/236–6400).

The **Bermuda Goodwill Tournament for Men** (golf) is played on four courses. Contact Tournament Director (✉ Box WK 127, Warwick, WK BX, ☎ 441/238–3118, FAX 441/238–0338).

DEC. 24➤ **Christmas Eve** is celebrated with midnight candlelight services in churches of all denominations.

DEC. 25➤ **Christmas** is a public holiday.

DEC. 26➤ **Boxing Day** is a public holiday for visiting friends and family. You'll find a variety of sports events, and the Bermuda Gombey Dancers perform around town.

DEC. 31➤ **St. George's New Year's Eve Celebration** at Ordnance Island has continuous entertainment by local musicians, food stalls, and children's rides. A midnight countdown and raising of the "onion" are followed by a fireworks display. Contact Corporation of St. George's (☎ 441/297–1532).

JAN. 1➤ **New Year's Day** is a public holiday. All sightseeing attractions and restaurants remain open.

EARLY JAN.➤ **Bermuda International Race Weekend** includes marathon and half-marathon races, fitness walks, and celebrity races featuring local notables. Most races are open to all; top international runners participate. Contact Race Committee (✉ Box DV 397, Devonshire DV BX, ☎ FAX 441/236–6086).

The **Bermuda Senior Golf Classic,** open to visitors and residents, is played on the Port Royal Golf Course, the St. George's Golf Club, and the Ocean View Golf Course. Contact Kim Swan, Tournament Chairman, Bermuda Golf Company (✉ Box GE 304, St. George's GE BX, ☎ 441/297–8148).

The **Annual Photographic Exhibition** features the work of local amateur and professional photographers. Particularly strong representation of underwa-

ter shots reveals the island's beauty beneath the surface. It is organized by the Bermuda Society of Arts in its City Hall gallery (☎ 441/292–3824).

JAN.–MAR.➤ The **Bermuda Festival** attracts internationally known artists for concerts and dance and theatrical performances. Contact Bermuda Festival Ltd. (✉ Box HM 297, Hamilton HM AX, ☎ 441/295–1291, FAX 441/295–7403); ☞ Chapter 6.

Regimental Musical Display is a captivating re-creation of a retreat ceremony that lures both locals and visitors. It is performed by the Bermuda Regiment Band and the Bermuda Isles Pipe Band with dancers in Hamilton. Contact the Regimental Band (☎ 441/238–2470).

Various **horse shows** take place around the island, including harness racing and dressage events. For specific dates and times contact Annie Sousa, Bermuda Horse & Pony Association (☎ 441/232–2162); Michael DiCosta, Horse & Pony Driving Club (☎ 441/293–4964); Eve Redford, Saddle Club of Bermuda (☎ 441/295–4558); Yvonne Hubbard, Bermuda Dressage Group (☎ 441/295–6204); or Michael Cherry, Bermuda Equestrian Federation (☎ 441/234–0485).

FEB.➤ The **Golden Rendezvous Month** includes special events designed for travelers over 50.

The **Bermuda International Open Chess Tournament,** open to visitors and residents, takes place at one of Bermuda's major hotels. Contact the Bermuda Chess Association (✉ Box HM 1705, Hamilton HM GX, ☎ 441/238–2313, FAX 441/238–8699).

The **Annual Regional Bridge Tournament** is held at a major hotel. Contact Bermuda Bridge Club (✉ 7 Pomander Rd., Paget PG 05, ☎ 441/297–7740 days, 441/236–4035 evenings).

The **Lobster Pot Pro-Amateur Golf Tournament** is an annual event played at one of the island's top courses. Contact Tournament Director (✉ Box HM 1154, Hamilton HMEX, ☎ 441/292–8822, FAX 441/292–0008).

The **Bermuda Mixed Foursomes Amateur Golf Championship,** a couples' tournament open to all golfers, is a 36-stroke play competition on St. George's Golf Course. Handicap limit: men 24, ladies 36. Entry fee $170 per team. Contact Bermuda Golf Association (✉ Box HM 433, Hamilton HM BX, ☎ 441/238–1367, FAX 441/238–0983).

The **Annual Bermuda Rendezvous Bowling Tournament,** open to all bowlers, is sanctioned by the ABC and WIBC. Cash prizes are awarded. Contact Warwick Lanes (✉ Box WK 128, Warwick WK BX, ☎ 441/236–5290).

SPRING

MAR.➢ The **Bermuda All Breed Championship Dog**

Shows and Obedience Trials draw dog lovers from far and wide to the Botanical Gardens in Paget. The same event also takes place in November. Contact Bermuda All Breed Club (✉ Box HM 23, Hamilton HM AX, ☎ 441/291–1426).

The **Bermuda Super Senior Invitational Tennis Tournament** is a USTA-sanctioned event held at the Coral Beach & Tennis Club in Paget. Contact the Bermuda Lawn Tennis Association (✉ Box HM 341, Hamilton HM BX, ☎ 441/296–0834, FAX 441/295–3056).

See a range of equestrian events at the **Bermuda Horse & Pony Association Spring Show Horse Trials,** including dressage, jumping, Western, and driving classes at National Equestrian Centre, Vesey St., Devonshire (contact Michael Cherry, ☎ 441/234–0485). **Bermuda Horse and Pony Association Trials** take place at one of the island's equestrian arenas; contact Annie Sousa (☎ 441/232–2162).

The **Bermuda Men's Amateur Golf Championship** is played at the Mid Ocean Club in Tucker's Town. Contact the Secretary, Bermuda Golf Association (✉ Box HM 433, Hamilton HM BX, ☎ 441/238–1367, FAX 441/238–0983).

The **Bermuda Cat Fanciers Association Championship Cat Show** features pedigree felines and household pets judged by All Breed American judges at various locations. Contact Morag Smith, Bermuda Cat Fanciers Association (✉ Box HM 1306, Hamilton

HM FX, ☎ 441/238–0112) or Diana Plested (☎ 441/295–5723).

MAR.➢ **Kidfest** is an annual event of family entertainment, presented in City Hall, Hamilton, that might include a variety show, musical comedy skits, Big Band music, and other family-oriented acts. Contact Kidfest (✉ Box DV 433, Devonshhire DV BX, ☎ 441/236–1085, FAX 441/236–6456).

MAR.–APR.➢ The **Palm Sunday Walk** is an annual stroll. Contact the Bermuda National Trust (☎ 441/236–6483).

Good Friday is a public holiday and traditionally a kite-flying day. Enjoy a spectacular display of locally made kites at the **Bermuda Kite Festival** at Horseshoe Bay in Southampton between 11 and 4. Contact United Bermuda Party (☎ 441/295–0729).

The **Easter Rugby Classic** features international competitions at the National Sports Club in Devonshire. Contact the National Sports Club (✉ Middle Rd., Devonshire, ☎ 441/236–6994 or 441/295–8495).

The **Bermuda Easter Lily Pro-Am Invitational Golf Tournament** for women takes place the Belmont Golf Club, St. George's Golf Club and Port Royal Golf Course. Contact the Tournament Chairman, Bermuda Golf Company (✉ Box GE 304, St. George's GE BX, ☎ 441/297–8148).

The **Bermuda Spring Break Programme,** targeting visiting American college students, was started in 1994 to replace the party-oriented College Weeks that had been held for decades. Spring Break Sports is an organized program of lacrosse, golf, tennis, and rugby; Spring Break Arts offers gallery tours and classes in watercolors, oils, and photography, as well as meet-the-artist events. Contact Wayne Smith, Bermuda Department of Tourism (✉ Global House, 43 Church Street, Hamilton HM 12, ☎ 441/292–0023).

The **Bermuda Youth Soccer Cup** attracts teams from the United Kingdom, the United States, Canada, and several Caribbean nations. Matches are played at several fields on the island. Contact Wayne Smith, Manager, Sports Promotion, Bermuda Department of Tourism (☎ 441/292–0023).

Harvard's Hasty Pudding Club has presented its satirical theatricals in Bermuda for more than 30 years; it's the club's only performance site outside the United States. Call City Hall Theatre in Hamilton (☎ 441/295–1727).

MAR.–OCT.➤ The **Beat Retreat Ceremony** is usually performed twice monthly by the Bermuda Regiment Band, the Bermuda Isles Pipe Band with Dancers, and members of the Bermuda Pipe Band. The historic ceremony is performed alternately on Front Street in Hamilton, King's Square in St. George's, and Dockyard in the West End. No performances are given in August. Contact the Bermuda Department of Tourism.

APR.➤ The **Agricultural Exhibition,** similar to a

county or state fair, takes place at the Botanical Gardens in Paget (☎ 441/236–4201).

The **Peppercorn Ceremony** celebrates—amid great pomp and circumstance—the payment of one peppercorn in rent to the government, by the Masonic Lodge of St. George No. 200 of the Grand Lodge of Scotland, for its headquarters in the Old State House in St. George's. Contact the Bermuda Department of Tourism.

The **Bermuda Open Tennis Classic** is an ATP Tour, USTA–Sanctioned Event of the world's top professional players. Tickets are available in advance through the Bermuda Tennis Foundation (✉ 69 Pitts Bay Rd., 3rd floor, Pembroke HM 08, ☎ 441/296–2554, FAX 441/296–2551).

The **Annual Fun/Run Walk Around Harrington Sound** welcomes walkers, joggers, runners, bikers, rollerbladers—whatever—to go the 7- to 8-mi distance around the sound. Contact Saundra Cowen (✉ Bermuda Zoological Society, ☎ 441/293–7074).

APR.–MAY➤ The **open houses and garden tours** sponsored by the Bermuda Garden Club give you the chance to walk through some of Bermuda's private houses and gardens that are not usually open to the public. Contact Garden Club of Bermuda (✉ Box HM 1141, Hamilton HM EX, ☎ 441/236–6425).

International Race Week pits sailors from around the world against Bermudians in a series of races on the Great Sound.

Contact Sailing Secretary, the Royal Bermuda Yacht Club (☎ 441/295–2214).

MAY➤ The **Bermuda Heritage Month** features a host of cultural, commemorative, and sporting activities. The crescendo is Bermuda Day (May 24), a public holiday that includes a parade at Bernard Park, a cycling race, a half-marathon (13 mi) for Bermuda residents only, and Bermuda dinghy races in St. George's Harbour. Contact the Department of Cultural Affairs (☎ 441/292–9447).

The eight-day **Bermuda International Film Festival** screens independent films in two local theaters. Filmmakers participate in question and answer sessions. Contact Bermuda International Film Festival Ltd. (✉ Box HM 2963, Hamilton HM MX, ☎ 441/293–3456).

The **Bermuda End-to-End Scenic Railway Trail Walk for Charities** is a terrific way to see the island and meet plenty of active residents. The 26-mi course begins in King's Square, St. George's and finishes amid a range of festive activities at the Royal Naval Dockyard. An alternate 15-mi course begins at Albouy's Point, Hamilton. Visitors may sign up 30 minutes before either starting point. Proceeds go to four local charities. Contact Karon Wolffe, Bermuda End-to-End (☎ 441/299–8824 from overseas, 441/297–9705 locally).

The **Bermuda Senior Amateur Championships for Men and Ladies,** which takes place at Belmont Golf & Country Club, requires that women be at least 50 years old and men at least 55. Contact Tom Smith, Bermuda Golf Association (⊠ Box HM 433, Hamilton HM BX, ☎ 441/238–1367, FAX 441/238–0983).

The **Annual Bermuda Open Karate Championships** invites spectators to Pembroke Sunday School to watch junior and senior competitors of all ages. Contact Bermuda Karate Institute (⊠ Box HM 2140, Hamilton HM JX, ☎ 441/292–2157).

ZooDoo Day at the Bermuda Aquarium, Natural History Museum & Zoo, has free admission, fun, games, and gift stalls, and activities for all ages. Contact Saundra Cowen (⊠ Bermuda Zoological Society, ☎ 441/293–7074).

SUMMER

JUNE➤ **Queen Elizabeth II's Birthday** is a public holiday celebrated in mid-June with military marching bands parading down Front Street in Hamilton. Contact the Bermuda Department of Tourism.

The **Open Air Pops Concerts,** presented by the Bermuda Philharmonic Society at King's Square, St. George's and Clocktower Centre at the Royal Naval Dockyard, are free and a great way to meet residents. Contact Sue Blakeley (⊠ Bermuda Philharmonic Society, Box HM 552, Hamilton HM CX, ☎ 441/238–1108 evenings, 441/295–3770 days).

A host of **sailing races** takes place in June, alter-

nating between odd- and even-numbered years. Races that attract powerhouse yachtsmen during even-numbered years include the spectacular Newport to Bermuda Ocean Yacht Race and the Onion Patch Series (contact the Royal Bermuda Yacht Club, ☎ 441/295–2214), as well as the Bermuda Ocean Race from Annapolis, Maryland (contact St. George's Dinghy & Sports Club, ☎ 441/297–1612). Events in alternate years include the Bermuda 1-2 Single-Handed Race, from Newport to Bermuda and back (contact St. George's Dinghy & Sports Club), the Marion (MA) to Bermuda Cruising Yacht Race (contact the Royal Hamilton Amateur Dinghy Club, ☎ 441/236–2250), and the Trans-At Daytona to Bermuda Yacht Race (contact St. George's Dinghy & Sports Club, *above*).

The **Bermuda Amateur Stroke Play Championship for Men and Ladies** are two simultaneous events played at the Port Royal Golf Course. Men and women play 72- and 54-hole strokes, respectively. Contact Tom Smith, Bermuda Golf Association (⊠ Box HM 433, Hamilton HM BX, ☎ 441/238–1367, FAX 441/238–0983).

JULY➤ **Marine Science Day** at the Bermuda Biological Station for Research gives you an opportunity to learn about marine research from the perspective of a mid-ocean island. Contact Alison Carlson (⊠ Bermuda Biological Station for Research, Inc., 17 Biological Station L

ane, Ferry Reach GE 01, ☎ 441/297–1880).

The **Bermuda Angler's Club International Light Tackle Tournament,** organized by the Spanish Point Boat Club, draws a large crowd to its 5 PM weigh-in. Contact R. Rego, Bermuda Angler's Club (⊠ Box HM 754, Hamilton HM CX, ☎ 441/292–5450 days, 441/236–6565 evenings).

Atlantic International Junior Championships, played at the Belmont, Mid Ocean, and Port Royal golf courses, is a 72-hole stroke play junior golf tournament. Contact Bermuda Junior Golf Association (⊠ Box WK 127, Warwick WK BX, ☎ 441/238–3118, FAX 441/238–0338).

JULY OR AUG.➤ The **Cup Match Cricket Festival** is a public holiday, with matches between East and West End cricket clubs. Held at the Somerset Cricket Club (⊠ Broome St., Sandys, ☎ 441/234–0327) or the St. George's Cricket Club (⊠ Wellington Slip Rd., St. George's, ☎ 441/297–0374), the match is one of the most festive occasions of the year, attracting thousands of fans who gather to picnic, chat, and dance.

JULY–AUG.➤ **Sea Horse Anglers' Club Annual Bermuda Billfish Tournament,** contact David Pantry (⊠ Sea Horse Anglers Club, Box HM 1847, Hamilton HM HX, ☎ 441/292–7272, FAX 441/292–7830).

AUG.➤ Landlubbers in homemade contraptions compete in the hilarious **Non-Mariners Race** on Mangrove Bay. Contact the Race Organizer (☎ 441/236–3683).

AUTUMN

SEPT.➤ **Labour Day,** a public holiday, occasions a wide range of activities, including a march from Union Square in Hamilton to Bernard Park. Local entertainers and specialty food stalls featuring local fare are included in the festivities. Contact the Bermuda Department of Tourism.

The **Annual Bermuda Triathlon** is open to visiting and local teams who compete in a 1-mi swim, 15-mi cycle, and 6-mi run. Contact the Bermuda Triathlon Association (✉ Box HM 1002, Hamilton HM DX, ☎ 441/293–2765).

OCT.➤ The **Columbus Day Regatta Weekend,** sponsored by the Royal Bermuda Yacht Club, features keel boats competing in the Great Sound. Contact the Sailing Secretary, Royal Bermuda Yacht Club (☎ 441/295–2214).

Skippy Peanut Butter K. I. C. K., a children's international karate competition, includes Form, Weapons, and Fighting. Contact Bermuda Karate Institute (✉ Box HM 2140, Hamilton HM JX, ☎ 441/292–2157).

Bermuda International Open Golf Championship for Men, played at Port Royal Golf Course, is open to professional and amateurs with a handicap of 6. Contact Tom Smith at the Bermuda Golf Association (✉ Box HM 433, Hamilton HM BX, ☎ 441/238–1367, FAX 441/238–0983).

The **King Edward VII Gold Cup International Match Race Tournament** is an exciting series of one-on-one yacht races in Hamilton Harbour that attracts top sailors from around the world. Contact the Sailing Secretary, Royal Bermuda Yacht Club (☎ 441/295–2214).

LATE OCT.➤ **Bermuda Masters International Golf Classic,** played at Port Royal and Castle Harbour golf courses. Contact Elegant Vacations (☎ 800/648–1136, FAX 404/983–8270).

NOV.➤ **Remembrance Day** is a public holiday in memory of Bermuda's and its allies' fallen soldiers. A parade with Bermudian, British, and U.S. military units, the Bermuda Police, and war veterans' organizations begins at Front Street in Hamilton. Contact the Bermuda Department of Tourism.

The **Convening of Parliament** on the first Friday of the month is preceded by the arrival of His Excellency the Governor, in plumed hat and full regalia, at the Cabinet Building on Front Street in Hamilton. You should get there by 10:30 to secure a place to stand. Contact the House of Assembly (☎ 441/292–7408).

The **Bermuda Four Ball Stroke Play Amateur Championship for Men and Ladies** are two simultaneous events at the Port Royal Golf Course. Contact Tom Smith, Bermuda Golf Association (✉ Box HM 433, Hamilton HM BX, ☎ 441/238–1367, FAX 441/238–0983).

The **World Rugby Classic** pits former international rugby players against the best players from Bermuda in a match at the National Sports Club (Middle Rd., Devonshire). Contact World Rugby Classic Ltd. (✉ Box HM 2267, Hamilton HM JX, ☎ 441/295–8495, FAX 441/291–1196).

2 Cruising to Bermuda

With its fabulous beaches, its turquoise seas, and its isolation in the Atlantic, Bermuda has long been a favorite of cruise passengers. It is understandably Britain's most famous resort island— and its oldest colony, due to the wreck of a New World–bound ship in 1609. The isle is more than 500 miles from the United States, the nearest point on the mainland being Cape Hatteras, North Carolina.

ERMUDA IS ONLY A 90-MINUTE FLIGHT from most East Coast cities, but there is nothing that quite compares to sailing up to the crown colony by ship. Most ships make seven-night loops from New York, with three nights spent at sea and four tied up in port. Three Bermuda harbors serve cruise ships: Hamilton (the capital), St. George's, and the Royal Naval Dockyard. Ships are not permitted in port on weekends. Therefore, your cruise will begin and end on a weekend and you'll be in Bermuda during the weekdays.

Concerned about overcrowding, the Bermudian government has limited the number of regular cruise-ship visits to the island. Cruise lines with weekly sailings are Celebrity Cruises, Norwegian Cruise Line, and Royal Caribbean International. Lines that call occasionally include Crystal Cruises, Seabourn Cruise Line, and Silversea Cruises. Ships calling on regular weekly visits stay in Bermuda for five days and act as your hotel. Some call at only one port—either Hamilton, St. George's, or the Dockyard—others split their time in port between Hamilton and St. George's. Ships that call only occasionally dock in Hamilton just for the day as part of a longer Caribbean or transatlantic itinerary.

The Bermuda cruise season runs from April through October.

CHOOSING A CRUISE

Because the government allows only five ships to make weekly visits, cruise line choices are more limited to Bermuda than to other cruise destinations. While the ships involved are similar in size and facilities, they vary considerably in age, amenities, on-board ambience, and cost.

The Cruise Experience

Your cruise experience will be shaped by several factors, and to determine whether a particular ship's style will suit you, you need to do a bit of research. Is a full program of organized activities scheduled each day? What happens in the evening? What kind of entertainment is offered after dark? And, some cruises being fancier than others, how often will you need to dress up for dinner?

Space and passenger-to-crew ratios are equally important. The latter indicates the number of passengers served by each crew member, and the lower the ratio, the better the level of service. The space ratio, the gross tonnage of a ship divided by its passenger capacity, allows you to compare ships' roominess. The higher the ratio, the more spacious the vessel feels: At 40:1 or higher a ship will feel quite roomy; less than 25:1 will cramp anyone's style.

Although no two cruises are quite the same, even aboard the same ship, all of the ships that sail to Bermuda on a weekly schedule fall into the semiformal or casual categories. More formal sailings are available, however, aboard cruise lines that make occasional calls (☞ Introduction, *above*).

Semiformal

Semiformal cruises are a bit more refined than their casual counterparts. Meals are served in two seatings, menu choices are plentiful, and the cuisine is on a par with that available in better restaurants. Men tend to wear a jacket and tie to dinner most nights. Adding flair to the dining room is the common practice of staffing the restaurant with waiters of one nationality. Featured dishes may be prepared tableside, and you often are able, with advance notice, to order a special diet, such as kosher, low-salt, low-cholesterol, sugar-free, or vegetarian. There is a daily program of scheduled events, but there is also time for more independent pursuits; passengers with similar interests are often encouraged to meet at appointed times for chess or checkers, deck games, and other friendly contests. Production-style shows are staged each evening, but you aren't likely to find a lively disco scene.

Casual

Casual cruises are the most popular. Shipboard dress and lifestyle are informal. Meals in the dining room are served in two seatings; menus are usually not extensive, and food is typically good but not extraordinary; your options may be limited if you have special dietary requirements. Men dress in sport shirts and slacks for dinner most nights, in jackets and ties only two or three evenings of a typical seven-day sailing. Aboard casual ocean liners, activities are more diverse than on formal and semiformal ships, and there is almost always something going on, from bingo to trivia contests. Las Vegas–style variety shows or Broadway revues headline evening entertainment. Discos bop into the wee hours.

Cost

For one all-inclusive price, a cruise gives you what many have called the trip of a lifetime. The only extras are tips, shore excursions, shopping, bar bills, and other incidentals. The axiom "the more you pay, the more you get" doesn't always hold true: While higher fares do prevail for better ships, which have more comfortable cabins, more attractive decor, and better service, passengers in the least expensive cabins eat the same food, see the same shows, and share the same amenities as those paying more than $1,000 per day for the top suite on any given ship. (A notable exception is the *Queen Elizabeth 2,* where dining room assignments are based on cabin categories.) Some people consider a larger cabin not worth the extra money, because it is used mainly for sleeping and dressing.

A handy way to compare costs of different ships is to look at the per diem—the price of a cruise on a daily basis per passenger, based on double occupancy. (For example, the per diem is $100 for a seven-day cruise that costs $700 per person when two people share the same cabin.)

For each ship described in the reviews below, average per diems are listed in three cabin categories: suites, outside cabins, and inside cabins (☞ Accommodations, *below*). These average per diems are meant for comparative purposes only; for actual cruise fares, which can vary wildly and are subject to discounting, you'll need to contact a travel agent or cruise specialist. When booking a cruise, don't forget to consider these expenditures:

Pre- and post-cruise arrangements: If you plan to arrive a day or two early at the port of embarkation, or linger a few days for sightseeing after you leave the ship, estimate the cost of your hotel, meals, car rental, sightseeing, and other expenditures. Cruise lines sell packages for pre- and post-cruise stays that may or may not cost less than arrangements you make independently, so shop around.

Airfare: Airfare and transfers are often included in the basic cruise rate; however, the cruise line chooses your airline and flight. Lines sometimes give passengers who make their own arrangements an air transportation credit of $200–$500 for Bermuda cruises. You may find a better airfare or more convenient routing, or use frequent-flyer miles.

Pretrip incidentals: These may include trip or flight insurance, the cost of boarding your pets, airport or port parking, departure tax, visas, long-distance calls home, clothing, film or videotape, and other miscellaneous expenses.

Shore excursions and expenses: Costs for ship-organized shore excursions in Bermuda begin at less than $25 for the cheapest one-hour city tour. Most snorkeling and diving trips generally cost about $40–$45. An evening out on the town, including dinner, dancing, and drinks, can run about $65.

Amusement and gambling allowance: Video games, bingo, and gambling can set you back a bundle. If you plan to bet, budget for your losses—you'll almost certainly have them. You must be over 18 to gamble on a cruise ship.

Shopping: Include what you expect to spend for both inexpensive souvenirs and pricey duty-free purchases.

On-board incidentals: Most cruise lines recommend that passengers tip their cabin steward, dining room waiter, and assistant waiter $7.50 per person, per day. Tips for bartenders and others who have helped you will vary. Also figure in bar bills and the cost of wine with meals, laundry, beauty parlor services, purchases in the gift shop, and other incidentals.

Accommodations

On most of today's one-class cruise ships no particular status or stigma is attached to your choice of cabin. Having said that, there's certainly an advantage to personally selecting the best cabin within your budget, rather than having your travel agent or cruise line representative simply book you into the next available accommodation. The earlier you book, the better the selection.

Cabin Size
The term "stateroom," used on some ships, is usually interchangeable with "cabin." Price is directly proportional to size and location, and most cabins are tiny. The higher you go in the ship, the larger the quarters tend to be; outside cabins are generally bigger than inside ones.

Suites are the roomiest and best-equipped accommodations, but even aboard the same ship, they may differ in size, facilities, and price. Steward service may be more attentive to passengers staying in suites; top suites on some ships are even assigned private butlers. Most suites have a sitting area with sofa and chairs; some have two bathrooms, occasionally with a whirlpool bath. The most expensive suites may be priced without regard to the number of passengers occupying them.

Location
On all ships, regardless of size or design, the bow (front) and stern (back) pitch up and down on the waves far more than the hull amidships (middle). Ships also experience a side-to-side motion known as roll. The closer your deck is to the true center of the ship—which is halfway between the bottom of the hull and the highest deck and midway between the bow and the stern—the less you will feel the ship's movement. Some cruise lines charge more for cabins amidships; most charge more for higher decks.

Outside cabins have portholes or windows (which cannot be opened). Upper deck views from outside cabins may be partially obstructed by lifeboats or overlook a public promenade. Because outside cabins are more desirable, newer ships are configured with mostly outside cabins or with outside cabins only. Increasingly, an outside cabin on an upper deck comes with a private veranda. Windows are mirrored in cabins that overlook a public promenade so that passersby can't see in—at least by day; after dark, you need to draw your curtains.

Inside cabins on older vessels are often smaller and oddly shaped. On newer ships, the floor plans of inside cabins are virtually identical to those of outside cabins. Providing you don't feel claustrophobic without a window—and most lines hang curtains on the wall to create the illusion of one—inside cabins are generally an excellent value.

Cruise brochures show a ship's layout deck by deck and include the approximate location and shape of every cabin and suite. Use the deck plan to make sure the cabin you pick is not near public rooms or the ship's engine, which can be noisy, and make sure that you are near stairs or an elevator if you want to avoid walking down long corridors every time you return to your cabin. If detailed layouts of typical cabins are printed, you can determine what kind of beds the cabin has, whether it has a window or a porthole, and what furnishings are provided.

Furnishings

All ocean liner cabins are equipped with individually controlled air-conditioning, limited closet space, and a private bathroom—usually closet-size, with a toilet, small shower, and washbasin. More expensive cabins, especially on newer ships, may have a bathtub. Most cabins also have a small desk or dresser, a reading light, and, on many ships, a TV and sometimes even a VCR. Except on some older ocean liners, all cabins also come with a phone.

Sharing

Most cabins are designed to accommodate two people. When more than two share a cabin, the third and fourth passengers are usually offered a substantial discount, thereby lowering the per-person price for the room for the entire group. An additional discount is sometimes offered when children share a cabin with their parents. There's usually a premium on smaller, one-person cabins—when you can find them. When none is available, as is frequently the case, passengers traveling on their own must pay a single supplement, which usually ranges from 125% to 200% of the double-occupancy per-person rate. On request, many cruise lines will match up two strangers of the same sex in a cabin at no additional surcharge.

BOOKING A CRUISE

Timing is important when booking a cruise. Since most ships sail at or near capacity, especially during high seasons, you get the greatest choice and sometimes a discount if you make a reservation six months to a year in advance. If you book close to the sailing date, your choices may be more limited, but you may get a better deal.

Using a Travel Agent

Since nearly all cruises are sold through travel agents, the agent you choose to work with can be just as important as the ship you sail on. So how do you know if an agent or agency is right for you? Talk to friends, family, and colleagues who have used an agency to book a cruise. The most qualified agents are members of CLIA (Cruise Lines International Association) and the NACOA (National Association of Cruise-Only Agencies), as well as ASTA (American Society of Travel Agents). Agents who are CLIA Accredited Cruise Counsellors or Master Cruise Counsellors have had extensive cruise and ship inspection experience;

agents who are NACOA members are also experienced cruisers. If you're undecided about a ship or line, an agent's personal account of his or her own cruise can be invaluable. However, keep in mind that agencies often have partnerships with certain cruise lines. In some cases, the agency may actually block space on a ship; in other cases, the agency only agrees to sell a certain amount of space. Either way, the agency gets a favorable rate from the cruise line; the agency can then afford to offer a "discounted" price to the public. But because agents often receive higher commissions on these cruises, they might steer you toward a cruise that might not be for you. A good travel agent puts your needs first.

Larger agencies often have more experienced cruisers on their staff and can provide the biggest discounts. Smaller agencies might have more personalized service. Whether you choose a large or small agency, a good agent will take the time to learn as much as possible about you and your cruise companion(s). An agent who asks a few cursory questions before handing you a brochure is a mere order-taker; an agent who asks you to fill out a questionnaire about your personal interests is a professional. A travel agent might not know just what ship is right for you, but a good agent will know which ones are wrong.

Of course, you want the best price. When it comes down to it, the top agencies can more or less get you the same price on most cruises, because they'll guarantee that if the cruise line lowers the price in a promotion, you'll get the deal. So look for an agency that offers this guarantee. But the overall value of your cruise depends on an agency's service, and agencies that are willing to go the extra mile for you by providing free cruise-discount newsletters, cabin upgrades, dollar-stretching advice, and 24-hour service in case of a problem are the best bet.

Cruise-Only Travel Agents
As the name implies, "cruise-only" travel agencies specialize in selling cruises. These agencies can also sell air tickets and other travel arrangements, too, as part of a cruise package. Sometimes, your choice may be limited to a package put together by the cruise line. Increasingly, though, cruise-only agencies are putting together their own custom-designed cruise vacations.

Full-Service Travel Agents
Full-service agents have broad travel experience but may be less knowledgeable about cruise lines than their cruise-only counterparts. If you know exactly what line and ship you want to sail on and are more concerned about your pre- or post-cruise land arrangements, a full-service agent may be more helpful—but keep in mind that full-service agencies may not have the same discounts as cruise-only agencies. If you choose to use a full-service agency, look for one that has a cruise desk with agents who sell only cruises. Then, you get the best of both worlds.

Spotting Swindlers
Always be on the lookout for a scam. Although reputable agencies far outnumber crooks, a handful of marketeers use deceptive and unethical tactics. The best way to avoid being fleeced is to pay for your cruise with a credit card, from deposit to full payment. That way, if an agency goes out of business before your cruise departs, you can cancel payment on services not rendered.

Here are two tip-offs that an agency may be a bad apple: It doesn't accept credit cards, and it asks for a deposit that is more than what the cruise line has requested (check the brochure). To avoid a disreputable agency, make sure the one you choose has been in business for at least five years. Check its reputation with a local Better Business Bureau or consumer protection agency before you pay any deposits. If a cruise price seems too good to be true, it could mean the agency is desperate to bring in money and may close its doors tomorrow, so don't be tempted by agencies that claim they can beat any price.

Also be wary of bait-and-switch tactics: If you're told that an advertised bargain cruise is sold out, don't be persuaded to book a more expensive substitute. Also, if you're told that your cruise reservation was canceled because of overbooking and that you must pay extra for a confirmed rescheduled sailing, demand a full refund. Finally, if ever you fail to receive a voucher or ticket on the promised date, place an inquiry immediately.

Getting the Best Cruise for Your Dollar

By selecting the right agent, you have the greatest chance of getting the best deal. But having a basic knowledge of how and why cruises are discounted can only benefit you in the end. Since your vacation experience can vary greatly depending on the ship and cruise line you sail with, it's best to pick your vessel and itinerary first, and then try to get the best price. Remember, it's only a deal if the cruise you book, no matter what the price, meets your expectations.

Like everything in retail, each cruise has a brochure list price. But like the sticker price on a new car, nobody actually pays this amount. These days, if you asked any 10 cruise passengers on any given ship what they paid, they would give you 10 different answers. Discounts from cruise lines and agencies can range from 5% on a single fare to 50% on the second fare in a cabin.

Approach deep discounts with skepticism. Fewer than a dozen cabins may be offered at the deep-discounted price, they may be inside cabins, and the fare may not include air transportation or transfers between the airport and the ship. Finally, do the math. A promotion might sound catchy, but when you divide the price by the number of days you'll be cruising and include the cost of air and accommodations, you might find that the deal of the century is quite a dud.

Deals and Discounts

SEASONAL DISCOUNTS

Cruise-brochure prices are typically divided into three categories based on the popularity of sailing dates and weather: high season, shoulder season, and low season. Before you take advantage of a low season rate, be sure to look into weather conditions in Bermuda during that time (☞ When to Go *in* the Gold Guide).

EARLY-BIRD SPECIALS

Almost all cruise lines provide a discount for passengers who book and put down a deposit far enough in advance; an additional discount may be provided if payment is made in full at the time of booking. These discounts, given to passengers who book at least six months before departure, range from 10% to 50% off of brochure rates. (Brochures are usually issued a year or more in advance of sailing dates.) Booking a popular cruise early is the best way to get the best price; there will likely be no last-minute deals on these sailings. The other advantage of booking far in advance is that you're more likely to get the cabin and meal seating you want. On most cruises, the cheapest and most expensive cabins sell out first.

LAST-MINUTE SAVINGS

In recent years, cruise lines have provided fewer and fewer last-minute deals. However, if a particular cruise is not selling well, a line might pick certain large, cruise-only travel agencies to unload unsold cabins. These deals, sometimes referred to by agents as "distressed merchandise," are typically available three weeks to three months before the cruise departs. These specials are unadvertised but might be listed in the agencies' newsletters and on their cruise telephone hot lines (☞ Agencies to Contact, *below*). Keep in mind that choice of cabin and meal seating is limited for such last-minute deals and that last-minute deals may only be available in certain regions.

MIXED BAG

Besides the major discounts mentioned above, agencies and cruise lines might attract passengers with price promotions such as "Sail for 12 Days and Pay for Only 10," "Free Hotel Stay with Your Cruise," and "Two Sail for the Price of One." Read the fine print before you book. The offer may be a bargain—or just slick advertising. How can you tell? Compare the advertised price with the standard early-booking discount, and check whether or not the promotion includes airfare. Also check on senior-citizen discounts and "cruise dollars" accrued on participating credit cards. Cruise lines that target families sometimes take on a third or fourth cabin passenger for free. Some of the best cruise prices are available on repositioning cruises.

UPGRADES

There are two types of cabin upgrades: One is guaranteed; the other is not. The first kind of upgrade is a promotional offer by the cruise line. For example, you may be offered a two-category upgrade if you book by a certain date. In this case, the cabin assignment that you receive with your documents prior to sailing should reflect your higher-level accommodations.

The second kind of upgrade is dispensed on board at the discretion of the cruise line. Like airlines, cruise lines overbook at their cheapest price in order to attract as many passengers as possible. When the number of bookings at these low rates exceeds the number of cabins available, some people are given better accommodations. How does the cruise line decide? Sometimes, passengers who booked early get priority for upgrades. At other times, passengers who booked through top-selling travel agencies are at the top of the upgrade list—which gives two more reasons to book early and book with a cruise-only agency that does a lot of business with your line.

Agencies to Contact

The agencies listed below specialize in booking cruises, have been in business at least five years, and emphasize customer service and value.

CRUISE ONLY

Cruise Fairs of America (✉ 2029 Century Park E, Suite 950, Los Angeles, CA 90067, ☎ 310/556–2925 or 800/456–4386, FAX 310/556–2254), established in 1987, has a fax-back service for information on the latest deals. The agency also publishes a free twice-yearly newsletter with tips on cruising.

Cruise Holidays of Kansas City (✉ 7000 N.W. Prairie View Rd., Kansas City, MO 64151, ☎ 816/741–7417 or 800/869–6806, FAX 816/741–7123), a franchisee of Cruise Holidays, a cruise-only agency with outlets throughout the United States, has been in business since 1988. The agency mails out a free newsletter to clients every other month with listings of cruise bargains.

Cruise Line, Inc. (✉ 150 N.W. 168th St., N. Miami Beach, FL 33169, ☎ 305/653–6111 or 800/777–0707, FAX 305/576–0073), established in 1983, publishes *World of Cruising* magazine three times a year and a number of free brochures, including "Guide to First Time Cruising," "Guide to Family Cruises," and "Guide to Cruise Ship Weddings and Honeymoons." The agency has a 24-hour hot line with prerecorded cruise deals that are updated weekly.

Cruise Pro (✉ 2527 E. Thousand Oaks Blvd., Thousand Oaks, CA 91362, ☎ 805/371–9884 or 800/222–7447; in CA, 800/258–7447; FAX 805/371–9084), established in 1983, has special discounts listed in its two-times-per-month mailings to members of its Voyager's Club ($15 to join).

CruiseMasters (✉ 300 Corporate Pointe, Suite 100, Culver City, CA 90230, ☎ 310/568–2040 or 800/242–9000, FAX 310/568–2044), established in 1987, will provide you with a personalized, bound guide to your ship's ports of call. The guide provides money-saving tips and advice on whether to opt for a prepackaged port excursion or strike out on your own. The agency's Family Cruise Club serves parents cruising with their children. A World Cruise Desk is dedicated to booking very long cruises.

Cruises, Inc. (✉ 5000 Campuswood Dr., E. Syracuse, NY 10357, ☎ 315/463–9695 or 800/854–0500, FAX 315/434–9175) opened its doors in 1981 and now has nearly 200 cruise consultants, including many CLIA Master Cruise Counsellors and Accredited Cruise Counsellors. Services provided by the agency include complimentary accident insurance for up to $250,000 per cruise, a monthly bargain bulletin ($19 a year), and a free twice-a-year cruise directory with cruise reviews, tips, and discounts.

Cruises of Distinction (✉ 2750 S. Woodward Ave., Bloomfield Hills, MI 48304, ☎ 810/332–2020 or 800/634–3445, FAX 810/333–9743), established in 1984, publishes a free 80-page cruise catalog four times a year. For a fee of $39, which is credited to your first cruise booking, you can receive notification of unadvertised specials by mail or fax.

Don Ton Cruise Tours (✉ 3151 Airway Ave., E–1, Costa Mesa, CA 92626, ☎ 714/545–3737 or 800/318–1818, FAX 714/545–5275), established in 1972, features a variety of special-interest clubs, including a short-notice club, singles club, family cruise club, and adventure cruise club. The agency is also experienced in personalized pre- and post-cruise land arrangements.

Golden Bear Travel (✉ 16 Digital Dr., Novato, CA 94949, ☎ 415/382–8900; outside CA, 800/551–1000; FAX 415/382–9086) acts as general sales agent for a number of foreign cruise ships and specializes in longer, luxury cruises. Its Cruise Value club sends members free twice-a-month mailings with special prices on "distressed merchandise" cruises that are not selling well. The agency's "Mariner Club" runs escorted cruises for passengers who would like to travel as part of a group.

Kelly Cruises (✉ 1315 W. 22nd St., Suite 105, Oak Brook, IL 60521, ☎ 630/990–1111 or 800/837–7447, FAX 630/990–1147), established in 1986, publishes a quarterly newsletter highlighting new ships and special rates. Passengers can put their name on a free mailing list for last-minute deals.

National Discount Cruise Co. (✉ 1409 N. Cedar Crest Blvd., Allentown, PA 18104, ☎ 610/439–4883 or 800/788–8108, FAX 610/439–8086) is a five-year-old cruise division launched by GTA Travel, an American Express representative that has served travelers since 1967. The cruise division specializes in high-end cruises and includes shipboard credits, which are exclusive to American Express, on most of the sailings it books. A three-times-a-year newsletter highlights the agency's latest discounts.

Vacations at Sea (⊠ 4919 Canal St., New Orleans, LA 70119, ☎ 504/482–1572 or 800/749–4950, FAX 504/486–8360), established in 1983, puts together its own pre- and post-cruise land packages and escorted land tours. The agency also publishes a free six-times-a-year newsletter with cruise reviews and discounts.

FULL SERVICE

Ambassador Tours (⊠ 120 Montgomery St., Suite 400, San Francisco, CA 94104, ☎ 415/981–5678 or 800/989–9000, FAX 415/982–3490), established in 1955, does 80% of its business in cruises. Three times a year, the agency distributes a free 32-page catalog that lists discounts on cruises and land packages, plus free monthly discount alerts.

Time to Travel (⊠ 582 Market St., San Francisco, CA 94104, ☎ 415/421–3333 or 800/524–3300, FAX 415/421–4857), established in 1935, does 90% of its business in cruises. It mails a free listing of cruise discounts to its clients three to five times a month. Time to Travel specializes in pre- and post-cruise land arrangements and claims its staff of 19 has been nearly everywhere in the world.

White Travel Service (⊠ 127 Park Rd., West Hartford, CT 06119, ☎ 860/233–2648 or 800/547–4790, prerecorded cruise hot line with discount listings ☎ 860/236–6176, FAX 860/236–6177), founded in 1972, does most of its business in cruises and publishes a free 40-page brochure listing the latest cruise discounts.

Payment

Once you have made a reservation for a cabin, you will be asked to put down a deposit. Handing money to your travel agent constitutes execution of a contract, so before you pay, review the cruise brochure to find out the provisions of the cruise contract. What is the payment schedule and cancellation policy? Will there be any additional charges before you can board your ship, such as transfers, port fees, or local taxes? If your air connection requires you to spend an evening in a hotel near the port before or after the cruise, is there an extra cost?

If possible, pay your deposit and balance with a credit card. This gives you some recourse if you need to cancel, and you can ask the credit card company to intercede on your behalf in case of problems.

Deposit

Most cruises must be reserved with a refundable deposit of $200–$500 per person, depending upon how expensive the cruise is; the balance is due 45–75 days before you sail. If the cruise is less than 60 days away, however, you may have to pay the entire amount immediately.

Cancellation

Your entire deposit or payment might be refunded if you cancel your reservation between 45 and 75 days before departure; the grace period varies from line to line. If you cancel later than that, you will forfeit some or all of your deposit (☞ Protection, *below*). An average cancellation charge is $100 one month before sailing, $100 plus 50% of the ticket price between 15 and 30 days prior to departure, and $100 plus 75% of the ticket price between 14 days and 24 hours ahead of time. If you simply fail to show up when the ship sails, you will lose the entire amount. Many travel agents also assess a small cancellation fee. Check their policy.

PROTECTION

Cruise lines sell two types of policies that protect you in the event of cancellation or trip interruption. Waivers provide a full refund if you cancel your trip for any reason, usually up to 72 hours before sailing; the cost to cover a seven-day cruise is about $75. Insurance, sold by an insurance broker and through travel agencies, protects against cancellation for specified reasons plus trip delay, interruption, medical expenses, emergency evacuation, and lost, stolen, or damaged luggage; the cost to cover a seven-day cruise is about $99. The insurance does not cover cancellations, interruptions, or delays caused by a preexisting medical condition. Keep in mind that a waiver is only available at the time of booking; insurance policies are best purchased after you have paid a significant portion of your cruise that you will lose in the case of cancellation. Neither insurance nor waivers protect you against cruise-line default. For that, you'll need special default insurance, sold only by a select number of companies, such as Travel Guard International (☞ Insurance *in* the Gold Guide). These companies also cover preexisting medical conditions.

BEFORE YOU GO

Tickets, Vouchers, and Other Travel Documents

After you make the final payment to your travel agent, the cruise line will issue your cruise tickets and vouchers for airport-ship transfers. Depending on the airline, and whether you have purchased a fly-cruise package, you may receive your plane tickets or charter flight vouchers at the same time; you may also receive vouchers for any shore excursions, although most cruise lines issue these aboard ship. Should your travel documents not arrive when promised, contact your travel agent or call the cruise line directly. If you book late, tickets may be delivered directly to the ship.

Planning for Expenses

Some ships will not cash personal checks or take certain credit cards. Check your cruise documents to determine which forms of payment are accepted aboard ship. The purser's office usually cashes traveler's checks, and on some ships you can even open an account and get cash when you need it; your withdrawals will be added to your bill along with onboard purchases, all of which you pay at the end of the cruise. Cashiers at onboard casinos also cash traveler's checks and dispense cash advances on your credit card, even if you don't intend to gamble.

ON BOARD

Checking Out Your Cabin

The first thing to do upon arriving at your cabin or suite is to make sure that it is the one you booked. If there are two twin beds instead of the double bed you wanted, or other serious problems, ask to be moved before the ship sails. Unless the ship is full, you can usually persuade the chief housekeeper or hotel manager to allow you to change cabins. It is customary to tip the stewards who assist you in moving to another cabin.

Since your cabin is your home away from home for a week, everything should be to your satisfaction. Take a good look around: Is the cabin clean and orderly? Do the toilet, shower, and faucets work? Check the telephone and television. Again, major problems should be addressed immediately. Minor concerns, such as not enough bath towels or pillows, can wait until the frenzy of embarkation has subsided.

Your dining time and seating assignment card may be in your cabin; check it, too, and immediately request changes if necessary.

Shipboard Accounts

Virtually all cruise ships operate as cashless societies where you charge onboard purchases and settle accounts at the end of the cruise with a credit card, traveler's checks, or cash. You can sign for shore excursions, gifts in the shop, wine at dinner, drinks at the bar—virtually any expense you may incur aboard ship. On some lines, an imprint from a major credit card is necessary to open an account. Otherwise, a cash deposit may be required and a positive balance maintained to keep the shipboard account open. Either way, you will want to open a line of credit soon after settling into your cabin if an account was not opened for you at embarkation. You can arrange this by visiting the purser's office in the central atrium or main lobby.

Tipping

For better or worse, tipping is an integral part of the cruise experience. Most companies pay their cruise staff nominal wages and expect tips to make up the difference. A number of lines have replaced "voluntary" tipping with a mandatory 15% service charge, which is added to every bar bill. Tipping of dining room staff and cabin stewards on these ships is still left to your discretion.

Whom to Tip

Cruise lines that encourage tipping advertise a recommended tipping policy in their brochures and even on information sheets left on your pillow (along with envelopes addressed to Steward, Waiter, Assistant Waiter, and so on). These are guidelines only; you may tip as much or as little as you wish. On most cruise ships it is customary to tip on the last night at sea. Always tip in cash, preferably in U.S. dollars. Generally, tip your regular waiter and cabin steward. On some ships you should also tip the assistant waiter, but on others waiters share tips with busboys. If the maître d' provides any special services, such as moving you to another table, he should be tipped a nominal amount, usually between $5 and $15. If you order wine with your meals, the wine steward should be tipped 15% of the total bill, unless a service charge is added automatically. You may wish to tip a bartender or steward who has been especially friendly or gracious. Do not tip any of the officers, entertainers, or cruise staff.

Dining

Restaurants

The chief meals of the day are served in the dining room. Most ships' dining rooms and kitchens are too small to serve all passengers simultaneously, so there are usually two mealtimes—early (or main) and late (or second) seatings—usually from 1½ to 2½ hours apart. Early seating for dinner is generally between 6 and 6:30, late seating between 8 and 8:30.

Most cruise ships have a Lido deck, adjacent to the swimming pool, where fast food and snacks are served cafeteria-style. Entrées available in the regular dining room may also be served here. Most Lidos are open for sunrise coffee, breakfast, morning snacks, lunch, and afternoon tea. Many ships provide self-serve coffee or tea on the Lido around the clock, as well as buffets at midnight.

Special Diets

With notification well in advance, many ships can provide a kosher, low-salt, low-cholesterol, sugar-free, vegetarian, or other special menu. However, there's always a chance that the wrong dish will somehow be handed to you. Especially when it comes to soups and desserts, it's a good idea to ask about the ingredients.

An increasing number of cruise ships offer an alternative "light" or "spa" menu based upon American Heart Association guidelines that uses less fat, leaner cuts of meat, low-cholesterol or low-sodium preparations, smaller portions, salads, fresh-fruit desserts, and healthy garnishes. Some smaller ships may not be able to accommodate special dietary needs. Vegetarians generally have no trouble finding appropriate selections on ship menus.

CRUISE SHIPS

Chart Symbols. The following symbols are used in the cabin charts that accompany each ship's evaluation. **D**: Double bed; **K**: King-size bed; **Q**: Queen-size bed; **T**: Twin bed; **U/L**: Upper and lower berths; ●: All cabins have this facility; ○: No cabins have this facility; ◑: Some cabins have this facility. Per diems listed are averages. Lower and higher fares exist.

Celebrity Cruises

MV Horizon and MV Zenith

SPECIFICATIONS

Types of ships: Cruise liners
Cruise experience: Semiformal
Years built: 1990/1992
Sizes: 46,811/47,255 tons
Numbers of cabins: 677/687 (79%/84% of them outside)
Crew: 642/657 (international; Greek officers)
Passengers: 1,354/1,374 (passenger/crew ratio of 2.1 to 1)

ITINERARY

Horizon, April through October: Six- and seven-night Bermuda loops depart New York on Sunday, calling at King's Wharf and Hamilton. **Zenith,** April through October: Seven-night Bermuda loops depart New York on Saturday, calling at Hamilton and St. George's.

SHIP'S LOG

With a navy-blue band of paint encircling their otherwise white hulls, these ships cut sharp profiles at sea. The design makes the most of natural light with well-placed oversize windows, and the interiors are indisputably gracious, airy, and comfortable. Nine passenger decks have several bars and entertainment lounges, and ample deck space. Wide corridors, broad staircases, seven elevators, and ample signage make it easy to get around. Decor is contemporary and attractive, and the artwork is pleasant rather than memorable. The *Zenith* has a slightly different layout from that of its sister ship: There are two fewer bars—though some have been enlarged—more suites, a larger health club, more deck space, and a meeting room.

Cabins are modern and quite roomy. Furnishings include a nightstand, desk, and small, glass-top coffee table. Closets are reasonably large, as are bathrooms. Bedtime readers will find the lone lamp on the nightstand insufficient, especially in rooms with double beds. All staterooms have 24-hour room service. The 20 suites are enormous, with

Bermuda Cruise Fleet

	Horizon / Zenith	Queen Elizabeth 2	Norwegian Crown	Norwegian Majesty	Song of America
Child Care	●	●	●	●	◑
Video Arcade	●	●	●	●	○
Boutiques/Gift Shops	●	●	●	●	●
Library	●	●	●	●	○
Cinema/Theater	●	●	●	○	●
Disco	●	●	●	●	●
Casino	●	●	●	●	●
Deck Sports	●	●	●	●	●
Sauna/Massage	●	●	●	●	●
Whirlpool	●	●	●	●	○
Swimming Pool	2	3	2	1	2
Walking/Jogging Circuit	●	●	●	●	●
Health Club	●	●	●	●	●
Special Dietary Options	●	●	●	●	◑
Accessibility	●	◑	●	●	◑
Sanitation Rating*	97 / 93	89	88	97	95
Passenger/Crew Ratio	2.1:1	1.5:1	2.6:1	2.1:1	2.6:1
Number of Passengers	1,354 / 1,374	1,500	1,052	1,056	1,402
Length of Cruise	7 days	5 days	7 days	7 days	7 days
Average Per Diem Rates (Outside Cabin)	$356	$432	$300	$271	$264
Cruise Experience	Semiformal	Formal–Semiformal	Casual	Semiformal	Casual
Type of Ship	Cruise liner	Classic liner	Cruise liner	Cruise liner	Cruise liner
Tonnage	46,811 / 47,255	70,327	34,250	32,400	37,584
Cruise Line	Celebrity Cruises	Cunard Line	Norwegian Cruise Line	Norwegian Cruise Line	Royal Caribbean Cruise Line

*Sanitation ratings are provided by the Vessel Sanitation Program, Centers for Disease Control. Ships are rated on water, food preparation and holding, potential contamination of food, and general cleanliness, storage, and repair. A score of 86 or higher indicates an acceptable level of sanitation. According to the center, "a low score does not necessarily imply an imminent outbreak of gastrointestinal disease." Chart ratings come from the center's June 13, 1997, report.

large sitting areas, tubs with whirlpool jets, and a private butler. The view from many outside cabins on the Bahamas Deck is partially obstructed by lifeboats.

MV Zenith and Horizon Cabins and Rates

	Beds	Phone	TV	Sitting Area	Fridge	Tub	Per Diem*
Suite	D or T/K	●	●	●	●	●	$471
Outside	D or T/K	●	●	●	○	○	$356
Inside	D or T/K	●	●	○	○	○	$278

Rates are for Bermuda itineraries. Airfare and port taxes are extra.

Outlet voltage: 110/220 AC.
Single supplement: 150%–200% of double-occupancy rate.
Discounts: A third or fourth passenger in a cabin pays reduced per diems. Children 2–12 traveling with two full-paying adults also pay reduced per diems. Children under 2 travel free. Discounts apply for booking early. Free motorcoach service is available from 15 cities.

SPORTS AND FITNESS
Health club: Bright, sunny upper-deck spa with sauna, massage, weight machines, stationary bicycles, rowing machine, stair climber, treadmill, separate mirrored aerobics area, facial/body treatments.
Walking/jogging: Unobstructed circuit on Marina Deck (5 laps = 1 mi).
Other sports: Exercise classes, putting green, shuffleboard, snorkeling, trapshooting, table tennis, two pools, three whirlpools.

FACILITIES
Public rooms: Nine bars and lounges (*Horizon*) or seven bars and lounges (*Zenith*), showroom, casino, disco, card room, library/reading room, video-game room.
Shops: Gift shop, boutique, perfume shop, cigarette/liquor store, photo shop.
Health care: Doctor and nurse on call.
Child care: Playroom; child, preteen, and teen programs supervised by counselors as needed; baby-sitting arranged with crew member.
Services: Photographer, laundry service, beauty shop/barber.
Other: Safe-deposit boxes.

ACCESSIBILITY
Four cabins with 39½″ doorways are accessible to wheelchair users. Specially equipped public elevators are 35½″ wide, but certain public areas may not be wide enough for wheelchairs. Passengers with mobility problems must provide their own small, collapsible wheelchairs and travel with an able-bodied companion.

FOR MORE INFORMATION
Celebrity Cruises (✉ 5200 Blue Lagoon Dr., Miami, FL 33126, ☎ 800/437–3111, FAX 800/437—9111.)

Cunard Line Limited

RMS Queen Elizabeth 2
SPECIFICATIONS
Type of ship: Classic liner
Cruise experience: Semiformal/Formal
Year built: 1969
Size: 70,327 tons
Number of cabins: 900 (70% of them outside)

Crew: 1,015 (international; British officers)
Passengers: 1,500 (passenger/crew ratio 1.5 to 1; varies according to cabin price)

ITINERARY
Several five-night Bermuda loops depart New York, calling at Hamilton.

SHIP'S LOG
The *Queen Elizabeth 2* looks better than it has in years, although you'll still find dings, dents, and water damage if you look carefully. Since 1994, Cunard has invested more than $65 million in this vessel. The most recent $20 million infusion fixed some of the more serious wear overlooked in 1994's $50 million refurbishment. The most impressive results are in the Queen's Grill and the new Mauretania Restaurant. Both were outfitted with new chairs and carpeting, replacing furnishings and fabrics that were stained and soiled. Bright new lighting also makes both rooms much cheerier.

As part of Cunard's goal of creating a consistently upscale fleet, the passenger capacity of the ship has also been reduced to 1,500 people. This means that all passengers can now be accommodated in a single seating—even in the Mauretania Restaurant, which previously served passengers in two seatings. So while, technically, the *QE2* remains a four-class ship in terms of dining (passengers are assigned a dining room according to cabin category), the differences are less pronounced than they were in the past.

As the only ship still sailing on regularly scheduled service across the Atlantic, the *Queen Elizabeth 2* is a link to cruising's past. Cunard is proud of this tradition and displays it prominently. The "Heritage Trail," a series of museum-quality displays added during the 1994 refit, presents artifacts from Cunard's storied history. (Did you know, for example, that the *QE2* served as a troop carrier during the Falkland Islands War?) Historical posters hang in the main stairwells. The Golden Lion, another 1994 addition, re-creates the ambience of an Old World pub. And in the Chart Room, you'll find the original piano from the *Queen Mary*—still played every night—and you can peruse the collection of laminated navigation charts from an antique chest of drawers. In fact, a sense of nautical tradition is the *QE2*'s prevailing quality—and perhaps the reason it attracts a staunchly loyal following for its world cruises and transatlantic crossings. Transatlantic sailings, in particular, attract ship buffs who are as interested in this ship's legacy and history as they are in its fine dining. These repeat passengers share stories about their many previous crossings.

The *QE2* has the most varied cabin configurations of any ship afloat. Suites accommodate up to four passengers, at no extra charge per passenger, making them more economical for a family of four than two luxury cabins. Penthouse suites, with verandas and whirlpools, are the largest, most luxurious accommodations afloat; first-class cabins (all with VCRs) compare with those of any luxury ship. Luxury cabins, except No. 8184, have private verandas. Lifeboats partially obstruct the view from some cabins on the Sports Deck, and Boat Deck cabins look onto a public promenade.

Most but not all cabins have new bathrooms. Before booking, make sure your cabin's bathroom has been renovated.

QE2 Cabins and Rates

	Beds	Phone	TV	Sitting Area	Fridge	Tub	Per Diem*
Queen's Grill	Q or T/D	●	●	●	●	●	$632
Princess/Britannia Grill	Q or T	●	●	●	●	●	$550
Caronia	Q or T	●	●	◐	◐	◐	$432
Mauretania	T or U/L	●	●	○	○	○	$290

Rates are for Bermuda itineraries. Airfare and port taxes are extra.

Outlet voltage: 110 AC.
Single supplement: 175%–200% of double-occupancy rate; several single cabins are available at $319–$655 a day.
Discounts: A third or fourth passenger in a cabin pays half the minimum fare in the cabin's restaurant grade.

SPORTS AND FITNESS

Health club: Thalassotherapy pool, inhalation room, French hydrotherapy bath treatment, computerized nutritional and lifestyle evaluation, aerobics and exercise classes, weight machines, Lifecycles, rowers, Stairmasters, treadmills, sauna, whirlpools, hydrocalisthenics, massage.
Walking/jogging: There is no unobstructed circuit.
Other sports: Putting green, golf driving range, paddle tennis, table tennis, shuffleboard, tetherball, trapshooting, volleyball, one outdoor and one indoor pool, whirlpools, sports area with separate clubhouses for adults and teens.

FACILITIES

Public rooms: Six bars, five entertainment lounges, card room, casino, chapel/synagogue, cinema, art gallery, Epson computer center, disco, executive boardroom, library/reading room, piano bar, video-game room.
Shops: Arcade with men's formal rental shop, designer boutiques (Burberry, Pringle, Wedgwood), florist, beauty salon/barber.
Health care: Doctors and nurses on call.
Child care: Playroom, wading pool, teen center, nursery staffed with British nannies, baby-sitting by counselors.
Services: Full-service laundry, dry-cleaning, valet service, laundromat, ironing room, photographer, film processing.
Other: Foreign exchange and cash center, kennel, safe-deposit boxes.

ACCESSIBILITY

Most public corridors have ramps, but many public rooms have a step or two up and down. Four cabins can accommodate wheelchair users.

FOR MORE INFORMATION

Cunard Line Limited (✉ 555 5th Ave., New York, NY 10017, ☎ 800/221–4770, FAX 212/949–0915).

Norwegian Cruise Line

MS Norwegian Crown

SPECIFICATIONS

Type of ship: Cruise liner
Cruise experience: Casual
Year built: 1988
Size: 34,250 tons

Number of cabins: 526 (78% of them outside)
Crew: 470 (Greek; Greek officers)
Passengers: 1,052

ITINERARY

Seven-night Bermuda loops depart New York on Saturday, April through October, calling at St. George's and Hamilton.

Ship's Log

The *Norwegian Crown* was ahead of its time when it was built in 1988, which keeps it contemporary today: There are fountains and a modern sculpture on deck and a miniature two-story atrium inside. An observation lounge with wraparound glass has panoramic views and the small but impressive fitness center has a Greco-Roman theme. The ship's style overall is predominantly disco-deco—plenty of chrome and brass and some simulated stained glass. The look has become a little dated in public areas, where fabrics and furnishings suffer from wear and tear. However, the exterior is better maintained: Painting, sanding, and refinishing are done as they should be. The *Norwegian Crown* is not an especially spacious ship. When it is fully loaded, lines form for buffets, while open deck chairs and tables are hard to find. The scene around the pool can be especially crowded. Cabins, on the other hand, are relatively roomy. If you choose this ship, you must book one of the suites with a bay window—they're the highlight of the ship.

MV Norwegian Crown Cabins and Rates

	Beds	Phone	TV	Sitting Area	Fridge	Tub	Per Diem*
Suite	T/D	●	●	●	●	●	$354
Outside	T	●	●	○	○	◑	$300
Inside	T/D	●	●	○	○	◑	$228

Rates are for Bermuda itineraries. Airfare and port taxes are extra.

Outlet voltage: 110/220 AC.
Single supplement: Single-occupancy cabins are bookable at no surcharge, subject to availability.
Discounts: A third or fourth passenger in a cabin pays reduced per diems. You get a discount for booking early.

Sports and Fitness

Health club: Three Cybex weight machines, five Lifecycles, three treadmills, two step machines, free weights, indoor pool, two whirlpools, massage, health bar, men's and women's saunas, full-service beauty center (herbal wraps, facials, and more).
Recreation: Table tennis, shuffleboard, exercise classes, two outdoor pools, two outdoor whirlpools, unobstructed circuits for jogging.

Facilities

Public rooms: Six bars, five entertainment lounges, casino, disco, cinema, card room, library.
Shops: Two-level shopping arcade, beauty salon/barber.
Health care: Doctor on call.
Child care: Organized youth programs with counselors during selected holidays only.
Services: Laundry service, pressing, dry cleaning, 24-hour information desk, photographer, film processing.

Accessibility

Four cabins are equipped with sit-down showers, grip bars around the shower and toilet areas, and tilting mirrors.

MV Norwegian Majesty

SPECIFICATIONS

Type of ship: Cruise liner
Cruise experience: Semiformal
Year built: 1992
Size: 32,396 tons
Number of cabins: 528 (65% of them outside)
Crew: 525 (international; Greek officers)
Passengers: 1,056 (passenger/crew ratio of 2.1 to 1)

ITINERARY

Seven-night Bermuda loops depart Boston on Sunday, May through October, calling at St. George's.

SHIP'S LOG

The *Norwegian Majesty* has a spaciousness that belies its size. On the top decks, you won't be packed in with hundreds of other passengers. If you want a quiet place to read a book, the mostly shaded outdoor promenade is the perfect place. Inside, public rooms are open and flow logically from one space to another. Overlooking the bow is a traditional steamship observation lounge with windows on three sides, and doors lead to an outdoor observation deck extending all the way to the bow. Meanwhile, amidships, the V-shape Rendezvous Bar has more intimate nooks for quiet repose. At the stern, the dining room has expansive sea views through windows on three sides (this feature is being adopted by some of the most contemporary ships).

The intimate nature of the MV *Norwegian Majesty* is enhanced by subdued lighting and decor. Wood-grain paneling set against dark-blue carpeting serves as a backdrop in many of the public rooms. And while service is more friendly than sophisticated, the staff goes the extra mile to keep you happy. All in all, it adds up to a very agreeable shipboard experience.

Like the rest of the ship, cabin decor is tasteful. Color schemes are understated earth tones complemented with wood furnishings and moldings. Each stateroom is equipped with a color TV (including CNN), five channels of music, direct-dial ship-to-shore telephones, hair dryers, security safes, and ironing boards. Suites come with complimentary robes; standard cabins have kimonos. Suites and some outside cabins also have a minibar, a queen-size bed, and bay windows. Views from many cabins on Queen's Deck are obstructed by lifeboats; cabins on Princess Deck look onto a public promenade.

MV Norwegian Majesty Cabins and Rates

	Beds	Phone	TV	Sitting Area	Fridge	Tub	Per Diem*
Suite	Q/T	●	●	●	●	○	$385
Outside	Q/T/D	●	●	○	○	○	$271
Inside	Q/T/D	●	●	○	○	○	$228

Rates are for Bermuda itineraries. Airfare and port taxes are extra.

Outlet voltage: 110 AC.
Single supplement: 150% of double-occupancy rate.
Discounts: A third or fourth passenger in a cabin pays reduced per diems. You get a discount for booking early.

SPORTS AND FITNESS

Health club: Fitness center with circuit training, weights, stair climber, stationary bikes, rowing machines, treadmills, and sauna.

Walking/jogging: Unobstructed wraparound promenade on Princess Deck.

Other sports: Pool, two whirlpools.

FACILITIES

Public rooms: Five bars, showroom, casino, disco, card room, library, meeting rooms, boardroom.

Shops: Gift shop.

Child care: Playroom, splash pool, youth program in three age groups with counselors year-round, baby-sitting arranged privately with crew member.

Services: Photographer, beauty salon/barber.

ACCESSIBILITY

The ship is fully accessible to wheelchair users, including four elevators, rest rooms on various decks, and four specially equipped staterooms.

FOR MORE INFORMATION

Norwegian Cruise Line (✉ 7665 Corporate Center Dr., Miami, FL 33126, ☎ 305/436–0866 or 800/327–7030, ℻ 305/448–6406).

Royal Caribbean Cruise Line

MS Song of America

SPECIFICATIONS

Type of ship: Cruise liner
Cruise experience: Casual
Year built: 1982
Size: 37,584 tons
Number of cabins: 701 (57% of them outside)
Crew: 535 (international; Norwegian officers)
Passengers: 1,402 (passenger/crew ratio of 2.6 to 1)

ITINERARY

Seven-night Bermuda loops depart New York on Sunday, May through October, calling at St. George's and Hamilton.

SHIP'S LOG

With its bold colors, ample chrome, and period decor, the *Song of America* exudes a 1980s flashiness. You enter into a traditional lobby appointed in warm earth tones, which contrast sharply with the halogen brightness of Royal Caribbean's megaships. Like the lobby, the magenta-themed main showroom is a far cry from the two-deck facilities on the line's biggest ships, but it stands out nonetheless for its early-1980s glass-bubble chandeliers and Victorian table lamps. A small gym has windows, but lighting is more florescent than natural. Things get a little brighter in the Oklahoma Lounge, the ships' cabaret, where in-the-round couches and groups of swivel chairs provide a visual extravaganza of red, orange, and yellow. A similar scheme prevails in the Guys and Dolls Lounge, the ship's disco. In fact, three large entertainment lounges are a lot for a ship this size.

The sunniest spot on the ship, at least indoors, is the Viking Crown Lounge, a study in turquoise, chrome, and some badly stained carpeting. The highlight of the ship's public rooms is, without a doubt, the Schooner Bar, a nautical tour de force of brown leather, brass accents, and maritime imagery. Moving outside, the *Song of America* has an expansive sundeck with plenty of chaises longues and two well-apportioned swimming pools. Seating at the Verandah Cafe, the ship's buffet restaurant, is all outside, which is appropriate because the vessel sails exclusively to warm-weather destinations.

As a middle-aged liner in its second decade of service, the *Song of America* is in basically good repair. There's no rust to be seen, but worn fabrics, furniture, and dented wall and ceiling panels in some areas of the ship are in need of refurbishment.

Cabins are on the small side; bathrooms are tiny, too. A high percentage of cabins are inside, and many accommodations have Pullman-style lower berths, particularly in standard outside cabins. Suites, however, are especially nice, with the bed at the far end of the cabin and the sitting area forward, closest to the door. It's the perfect arrangement for entertaining. Standard outside cabins are done in a soft blue; inside cabins are finished in peach. In-cabin TVs show CNN broadcasts. Suites on the Promenade Deck look onto a public area.

MS Song of America Cabins and Rates

	Beds	Phone	TV	Sitting Area	Fridge	Tub	Per Diem*
Suite	T or T/Q	●	●	●	●	●	$378
Outside	T or T/Q	●	●	○	○	○	$264
Inside	T or T/Q	●	●	○	○	○	$236

Rates are for Bermuda itineraries. Airfare and port taxes are extra.

Outlet voltage: 110/220 AC.
Single supplement: 150% of double-occupancy rate; however, less expensive singles are available if you are willing to wait for your cabin assignment until embarkation time.
Discounts: A third or fourth passenger in a cabin pays reduced per diems. You get a discount for booking early.

SPORTS AND FITNESS
Health club: Rowing machines, treadmills, stationary bikes, massage, men's and women's saunas.
Walking/jogging: Unobstructed circuits on Compass Deck and wraparound Promenade Deck.
Other sports: Aerobics, table tennis, basketball, shuffleboard, skeet shooting, two pools.

FACILITIES
Public rooms: Six bars, four entertainment lounges, casino, card room, cinema, disco.
Shops: Gift shop, drugstore, beauty salon/barber.
Health care: Doctor and two nurses on call.
Child care: Youth programs with counselors year-round, baby-sitting arranged privately with crew member if available, cribs available but must be requested at time of booking.
Services: Full-service laundry, dry-cleaning, photographer, film processing.

ACCESSIBILITY
Accessibility aboard this ship is limited. Doorways have lips, and public bathrooms are not specially equipped. Passengers with mobility problems must bring a portable wheelchair and be escorted by an able-bodied companion. Tenders are easy to board; if seas are rough, crew members will attempt to carry passengers and their wheelchairs.

FOR MORE INFORMATION
Royal Caribbean Cruise Line (✉ 1050 Caribbean Way, Miami, FL 33132, ☎ 800/255–4373 for brochures only).

3 Exploring Bermuda

Travel Bermuda's twisting roads past sherbet-colored cottages, manicured gardens heavy with tropical scents, and rocky coves embracing sapphire-colored waters. The capital of Hamilton has its bustling harbor, porcelain shops, museums, and shaded parks. And St. George's at the island's northeastern end has its historical sites. On the West End, pick your favorite deserted beach. Elsewhere on the island are Bermuda's many parishes, where you can wander along quiet streets or lose yourself on soft, pink-sand shores.

BERMUDA is nothing if not colorful. Streets are lined with hedges of hibiscus and oleander, and rolling green hills are shaded by tall palms and casuarina trees. The limestone buildings are painted in pretty pastels—pink and white seem to be most popular—and their gleaming white roofs are steeply pitched to channel the rain upon which Bermudians depend, because the island has no freshwater lakes or streams. In addition, many houses have quaint butteries, miniature cottages that were once used to keep food cool. House numbers are a relatively new phenomenon on the island, although most houses have names, such as Tranquillity, Struggle, and Last Penny. Bermuda's moon gates are another common architectural feature. You will find these Chinese-inspired freestanding stone arches, which have been popular since the late 18th century, in gardens all over the island, and Bermudians favor them as backdrops for wedding pictures.

Bermuda's early history is closely tied with that of the United States. In 1609, three ships set sail from Plymouth, England, taking passengers and supplies to the beleaguered colony of Jamestown, Virginia. One of the ships, the *Sea Venture,* captained by Sir George Somers, ran into a fierce storm and was wrecked off Bermuda's east end, near the present site of the Town of St. George (also called St. George's). Shakespeare's play *The Tempest* was based on the famous shipwreck. Somers and the *Sea Venture* are legendary on Bermuda, and you will see many references to the man and his ship.

Hamilton is of primary interest for its harbor, its shops—housed in small pastel-colored buildings—and the government buildings, where you can watch sessions of Parliament. In addition, the town is the major departure point for sightseeing boats, ferries, and the pink-and-blue buses that ramble all over the island. Don't confuse Hamilton town with the parish of the same name—Hamilton town is adjacent to Pembroke Parish.

The island's first capital was the Town of St. George on the northeastern end of the island. History mavens will find much of interest in St. George's, including several noteworthy 17th-century buildings. The island's West End is the site of the sleepy hamlet of Somerset and the Royal Naval Dockyard, a former British naval shipyard that is home to the Maritime Museum and a developing tourist center. The West End is in Sandys Parish, which can be pronounced either "Sandies" or "Sands."

Hamilton, St. George's, and Dockyard can all be explored easily on foot. The other parishes, however—that part of the island Bermudians refer to as "the country"—are best explored by moped, bicycle, or taxi. The parishes date back to 1616, when Bermuda was first surveyed and the island was divided into eight tribes or parishes, each named for an investor in the Bermuda Company, an offshoot of the Virginia Company, which controlled the island until 1684. The parishes are Sandys, Southampton, Warwick, Paget, Smith's, Hamilton, Pembroke, and Devonshire. St. George's, which was considered public land in the early days, is the ninth parish and includes the Town of St. George. Bermudians customarily identify sites on the island by the parish in which they are located: "It's in Pembroke," a resident will say, or "It's in Warwick."

The main roads connecting the parishes are self-explanatory: North Shore Road, Middle Road, South Road, and Harbour Road. Almost all traffic traversing the island's 21-mi length uses these roads, although some 1,200 smaller roads crisscross the land. You will see several "tribe roads" that date back to the initial survey of the island. Many are now no more than country lanes, and some are dead ends. As you travel around the island you'll also see small brown-and-white signs pointing to the Railway Trail. Built along the route of Bermuda's old railway line, the trail is now a peaceful route reserved for pedestrians and cyclists.

Hamilton

The island's capital is a small town on Hamilton Harbour, where sightseeing boats and ferries bob on the water waiting to take on passengers. Downtown Hamilton rises on hills above the harbor, its busy streets lined with small two- and three-story shops and office buildings painted in the requisite pastels. Many of the buildings have arcades, and narrow alleyways strung between Front and Reid streets, two of the main drags. Imagine what Front Street was like prior to 1946, when horse-drawn carriages and bicycles were the main modes of transportation, and "Old Rattle and Shake," the narrow-gauge railway that ran from East End to West End, chugged along Hamilton's main street. Several important museums and galleries are in Hamilton, though for many its main attractions are the plethora of shops selling discounted woolens, jewelry, perfumes, and electronics.

Numbers in the text correspond to numbers in the margin and on the Hamilton map.

A Good Walk

Any tour of Hamilton should begin on **Front Street** ①, a pretty thoroughfare lined with small, colorful buildings, many with balconies and arcades. The Visitors Bureau in the Ferry Terminal Building on Front Street is an appropriate place to begin a stroll through town. Turn left after leaving the bureau and cross Point Pleasant Road to reach the **Bank of Bermuda** ②, which houses displays of old Bermudian coins. For a splendid view of Hamilton Harbour, follow Point Pleasant Road to the waterside park called **Albuoy's Point** ③. From the point, retrace your steps and pass the Ferry Terminal Building. Adjacent to the terminal on Front Street you'll see sightseeing boats tied up waiting for passengers to tour the island's waterways. Just beyond the docks is a large pink building, called the No. 1 Shed, one of the island's several terminals for the elegant cruise ships that call at Bermuda.

At Heyl's Corner, at Front and Queen streets, you'll see the Birdcage, a traffic box where police occasionally direct traffic. Named for its designer, Michael "Dickey" Bird, the traffic box has been a Hamilton landmark for more than 30 years. The corner itself is named for J.B. Heyl, a southerner from the United States who came to Bermuda in the 19th century and opened an apothecary shop on this site. Continue up Queen Street to the 19th-century **Perot Post Office** ④, Hamilton's main post office. Just beyond the post office is the **Museum of the Bermuda Historical Society/Bermuda Public Library** ⑤. Continue up Queen Street, or cut through the Washington Mall, to reach **City Hall** ⑥. In addition to administrative offices, City Hall is home to a theater, the Bermuda National Gallery, and the Bermuda Society of Arts Gallery.

Behind City Hall, on Victoria Street, is **Victoria Park** ⑦, a lush 4-acre oasis with a Victorian bandstand. From the park, follow Cedar Avenue one block to see **St. Theresa's Church** ⑧, a dramatic Spanish Mission-style church not unlike some in the western United States. Retrace your steps to Victoria Park and continue walking toward Front Street. At Victoria Street, Cedar Avenue becomes Burnaby Street. Walk past the Central Bus Terminal, and turn left on Church Street. On your left you'll see the imposing **Cathedral of the Most Holy Trinity** ⑨. Just beyond the cathedral, at the corner of Church and Parliament streets, is **Sessions House** ⑩. Continue down Parliament Street to Front Street to see the **Cabinet Building** ⑪ and, in front of it, the **Cenotaph** ⑫.

Ft. Hamilton ⑬, which lies on the eastern outskirts of the capital, is a bit far to walk. It's best seen by taking a taxi or a moped.

TIMING

You can see Hamilton in less than an hour, but you should allow at least a full day to explore the museums and galleries. Die-hard shoppers will need two to three days here, or perhaps even longer. Avoid sightseeing during lunch hours, as the streets are thronged with office workers. The streets are also crowded when cruise ships are docked from late spring to early fall.

Sights to See

❸ **Albuoy's Point.** Picturesque Hamilton Harbor is dotted with tiny islands, its blue waters graced with the white sails of pleasure craft. Ferries churn from the capital to Paget, Warwick, and Somerset parishes. Ringside seats for this show are the benches beneath the trees of Albuoy's Point, a pleasant waterside park. Nearby is the **Royal Bermuda Yacht Club,** which was built in the 1930s. The idea for the yacht club was conceived in 1844 beneath the Calabash Tree at Walsingham (☞ Tom Moore's Tavern *in* The Parishes, *below*), and Prince Albert gave permission for the club to use the word "Royal" in 1845. Today, royalty, international yachting celebrities, and the local elite hobnob at the posh club, which sponsors the Newport-Bermuda Ocean Yacht Race and the Gold Cup International Match Race Tournament. Barr's Bay Park to the west of Albuoy's Point also affords a good view of the yacht club and the harbor. Just beyond Bermudiana Road on Pitts Bay Road (a continuation of Front Street), steps and a ramp lead from the street to the park's vast expanse of green grass, its vistas, and benches for sitting and taking it all in.

❷ **Bank of Bermuda.** Pigs were the only inhabitants Sir George Somers and his crew encountered when his ship, the *Sea Venture,* foundered on Bermuda's shores in 1609. Bermuda's earliest coin, called "hog money," commemorated those first residents. The coin is appropriately stamped on one side with a wild hog ringed with the words "Somer Ilands" and on the other with a replica of Sir George's ruined ship. If you are interested in coins, go up to the mezzanine of the Bank of Bermuda. British and Spanish coins, many of them ancient, are displayed in glass cases. The collection includes some pieces of "hog money," which the Bermuda Company issued in 1616. ⊠ *6 Front St.,* ☎ *441/295–4000.* ⌸ *Free.* ☉ *Mon.–Thurs. 9:30–3, Fri. 9:30–4:30.*

⑪ **Cabinet Building.** The Senate, which is the upper house of Parliament, sits in the dignified two-story Cabinet Building, surrounded by trees and gardens. Amid great ceremony, the formal opening of Parliament takes place in the Senate Chamber, traditionally on the first Friday of November. His Excellency, the Governor, dressed in a plumed hat and full regalia, arrives on the grounds in a landau drawn by magnificent black horses and accompanied by a police escort. A senior police officer, carrying the Black Rod made by the Crown jewelers, asks the Speaker of the House, elected representatives, and members of the Senate Chamber to convene. The governor makes his Throne Speech from a tiny cedar throne, dating from the 1600s, which is carved with the words "Cap Josias Forstore Govornour of the Sumer Islands Anodo 1642" (Josias Foster was governor in 1642). The portraits above the dais are of King George III and Queen Charlotte. The chamber is open

Hamilton

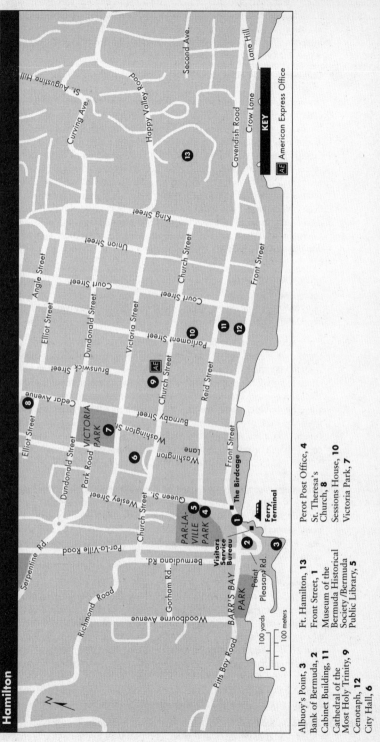

KEY

AE American Express Office

Albuoy's Point, **3**
Bank of Bermuda, **2**
Cabinet Building, **11**
Cathedral of the
Most Holy Trinity, **9**
Cenotaph, **12**
City Hall, **6**

Ft. Hamilton, **13**
Front Street, **1**
Museum of the
Bermuda Historical
Society/Bermuda
Public Library, **5**

Perot Post Office, **4**
St. Theresa's
Church, **8**
Sessions House, **10**
Victoria Park, **7**

to visitors, but come on a Wednesday if you want to watch the Senate in action; call first to find out about scheduling. Take some time to admire the **Cenotaph** out front (☞ *below*). ⊠ *Front St.,* ☎ *441/292–5501.* ☒ *Free.* ⊙ *Weekdays 9–5.*

★ ❾ **Cathedral of the Most Holy Trinity.** One of the island's most impressive structures, this is the seat of the Anglican Church of Bermuda. The cathedral is the second church to have been built on this site: Twelve years after its completion in 1872, Trinity Church was burned to the ground by an arsonist. Work began on the present church the following year, and it was consecrated in 1911. Designed in Early English style with Gothic Revival flourishes, the church is constructed of Bermuda limestone and materials imported from Scotland, Nova Scotia, France, Ireland, and Indiana. The tower rises to 143 ft, and the clerestory in the nave is supported by piers of polished Scottish granite. The four smaller columns in each aisle were added after a hurricane shook the cathedral—and its architect—during construction. The altar in the Lady Chapel is of Italian marble, and above it is a copy of Andrea del Sarto's *Madonna and Child.*

In the south transept, the Warrior Chapel was dedicated in 1977 to honor those who serve in the armed forces of the Crown, and to commemorate those who died in service to their country. The Great Warrior Window is a memorial to 85 Bermudian men who died in World War I; the flags represent military units of Bermuda and England.

The choir stalls and bishop's throne were carved from English oak, and the pulpit is a replica of the one in St. Giles Cathedral, Edinburgh. On a wall near the lectern, the Canterbury Cross, set in stone taken from the walls of Canterbury Cathedral, is a copy of one made in Kent in the 8th century. The stained-glass windows are lovely; note especially the Angel Window on the east wall of the north transept, which was made by local artist Vivienne Gilmore Gardner. After exploring the interior, take time to climb the 150-odd steps to the tower. Once at the top, you will be rewarded with spectacular views of Hamilton. ⊠ *Church St.,* ☎ *441/292–6987.* ☒ *Tower $3.* ⊙ *Mon.–Sat. 10–4.*

NEED A BREAK?　　Executives, secretaries, shoppers, and store owners flock to **The Spot** (⊠ 6 Burnaby St., ☎ 441/292–6293) for breakfast, plate lunches, burgers, sandwiches, and coffee. In business for more than 50 years, this nook serves full meals and daily specials for less than $10, and sandwiches for about $5. It's one of the best values on the island. The Spot is open Monday–Saturday 6:30 AM to 7 PM.

⑫ **Cenotaph.** This memorial to the war dead stands in front of the Cabinet Building; on Remembrance Day (November 11), the governor and other dignitaries lay wreaths at the base of the monument. The Cenotaph is a smaller version of the famous one in Whitehall, London. The cornerstone was laid in 1920 by the Prince of Wales, who, as King Edward VIII, abdicated to wed Mrs. Simpson. The Cenotaph lies between Parliament Street and Court Street. Although Court Street is safe during daylight hours, it is not advisable to wander around here at night. Bermuda does have some problems with drugs, and what traffic there is centers on Court and Victoria streets after dark.

★ ❻ **City Hall.** Set back from the street behind a lawn, fountains, and a lily pond is a large white structure topped by a weather vane that is shaped like the *Sea Venture.* This relatively new structure, built in 1960, houses City Hall. Massive cedar doors open into a large lobby with great chandeliers, high ceilings, and a portrait gallery. The large portrait of Queen Elizabeth II was painted by Curtis Hooper and unveiled on April 29, 1987, by the Duke of Gloucester. Oil paintings of Bermuda's former mayors hang here as well. Behind tall cedar doors on the right is the Coin and Note Display of the Bermuda Monetary Authority, the extensive Benbow Collection of 20th-century stamps, and occasional displays of historic Bermudiana. The City Hall Theatre often serves as a venue for musical, dance, and theatrical performances. A handsome cedar staircase leads to the second-floor exhibition galleries.

Upstairs, the East Exhibition Room houses the **Bermuda National Gallery,** the island's only climate-controlled gallery. Opened in 1992, the gallery displays European paintings from the early 16th to 19th centuries, including works by Thomas Gainsborough, Sir Joshua Reynolds, and George Romney. There are also 20th-century lithographs, oils, sculptures, and acrylics, and an extensive collection of Bermudian artists and works by painters who visited the island from the late 19th century to the 1950s.

In the West Wing of City Hall, changing exhibits are displayed in the **Bermuda Society of Arts Gallery.** The juried annual Spring, Summer, Autumn, and Winter Members' Shows attract talented local artists, who display high-quality works painted and drawn with watercolors, oils, pastels, acrylics, and charcoals; collage and sculpture are also included occasionally. The Photographic Show in January features underwater and shoreside shots. One-person shows by local and visiting artists are also held in the Society's small gallery throughout the year. ⊠ *Church St., Hamilton,* ☏ *441/292–1234 city hall, 441/295–9428 Bermuda National Gallery (East Wing), 441/292–3824 Bermuda Society of Arts Gallery (West Wing).* ⊡ *City hall free, Bermuda National Gallery $3, Bermuda Society of Arts Gallery free (donations accepted).* ☉ *City hall weekdays 9–5; Bermuda National Gallery Mon.–Sat. 10–4, Sun. 12:30–4; Bermuda Society of Arts Gallery Mon.–Sat. 10–4.*

NEED A
BREAK?

Fourways Pastry Shop (⊠ Reid St., at the entrance to Washington Mall, ☏ 441/295-3263) and the **Gourmet Store** (⊠ Windsor Pl. Mall, across Queen St. and north of the library, ☏ 441/295-4085), both operated by Fourways Inn, are great places to relax over diet-destroying pastries.

★ ⑬ **Ft. Hamilton.** On the eastern outskirts of Hamilton is this imposing old fortress, complete with a moat, 18-ton guns, and underground passageways that were cut through solid rock by Royal Engineers in the 1860s. The restored fort is one of several built by order of the Duke of Wellington. Outdated even before its completion, the fort never fired a shot in aggression. Today, you can enjoy the splendid views of the capital and the harbor from here. Accompanied by drummers and dancers, the kilted Bermuda Isles Pipe Band performs a stirring skirling ceremony on the green every Monday at noon from November through March. To get here from downtown Hamilton, head east on East Reid Street, turn left on King Street, and then right onto Happy Valley Road. ⊠ *Happy Valley Rd., Pembroke, no phone.* ⊡ *Free.* ☉ *Daily 9:30–5.*

❶ **Front Street.** Hamilton's main drag runs alongside the harbor. Front Street bustles with small cars, mopeds, bicycles, buses, pedestrians, and the occasional horse-drawn carriage. The street is lined with colorful little buildings, many with balconies and arcades that house shops and boutiques selling everything from imported woolens to perfumes and cosmetics. This is the main shopping area on the island, and shoppers will probably want to spend plenty of time—and money—here (☞ Chapter 8). The **Visitors Service Bureau,** with its friendly staff and abundance of free brochures, is in the Ferry Terminal Building on Front Street.

★ **⑤** **Museum of the Bermuda Historical Society/Bermuda Public Library.** On a visit to Bermuda, Mark Twain admired the giant rubber tree that stands on Queen Street in the front yard of the Georgian house where Bermuda's first postmaster, William Bennet Perot, and his family lived. Although charmed by the tree, which was imported from British Guiana (now Guyana) in the mid-19th century, Twain lamented that the rubber tree didn't bear fruit in the form of hot-water bottles and rubber overshoes.

Today, the Bermuda Public Library and Museum of the Bermuda Historical Society are housed in Postmaster Perot's former house. The library, which was founded in 1839, moved to its present quarters in August 1916. One early librarian was an eccentric gentleman with the Dickensian name of Florentius Frith, who rode in from the country on horseback and struck terror into the heart of anyone who interrupted his chess games to check out a book. The reference section of the library has virtually every book ever written about Bermuda as well as a collection on microfilm of Bermudian newspapers dating back to 1784. The collection of rare books contains a 1624 edition of John Smith's *Generall Historie of Virginia, New England and the Somers Isles*. In the museum's entrance hall are portraits of Sir George Somers and his wife, painted about 1605; portraits of Postmaster Perot and his wife can be seen in the back room. Notice Admiral Sir George Somers's lodestone (circa 1600), used for magnetizing compass needles, and a Bermuda map from 1622 that shows the division of the island into 25-acre shares by the original Bermuda Company. The museum also contains an eclectic collection of old English coins and Confederate money, Bermuda silver, Asian porcelains, portraits of the major investors in the Bermuda Company, and pictures of horse-and-buggy Bermuda juxtaposed with modern-day scenes. There are several cedar pieces, including two Queen Anne chairs from about 1740; a handsome grandfather clock; a Waterford chandelier; handmade palmetto hats; and a recently restored sedan chair from around 1770. Ask to see the letter from George Washington, written "to the inhabitants of Bermuda" in 1775, asking for gunpowder. ⊠ *13 Queen St.,* ☎ *441/295–2905 library, 441/295–2487 museum.* ✉ *Free (donations accepted).* ☉ *Library weekdays 9:30–6, Sat. 9:30–5; museum weekdays 9:30–3:30.*

NEED A
BREAK?

There is now a branch of the **Ice Queen** (⊠ Reid and Queen Sts., ☎ 441/292–6497), Paget's late-night burger joint, right in Hamilton, with long hours, ample seating, and a line-up of burgers, ice cream, and such.

---

④ **Perot Post Office.** Bermuda's first postage stamps originated (in 1848) in this white, two-story edifice, which dates from around 1840 and still serves as the island's main post office. Bermuda's first postmaster was William Bennet Perot. Appointed in 1818, Perot would meet arriving steamers to collect the mail, stash it in his beaver hat, and then stroll around Hamilton to deliver it. To post a letter, residents paid Perot, who hand-stamped each letter. Obviously, the postmaster had to be at his station to do this, which annoyed Perot, who preferred pottering around in the garden. Local historians credit Perot's friend, the pharmacist J.B. Heyl, with the idea for Bermuda's first book of stamps. Heyl suggested that Perot make a whole sheet of postmarks, write "Wm B. Perot" on each postmark, and sell the sheet for a shilling. People could then tear off a postmark, paste it on a letter, and post it—without having to extricate Mr. Perot from the garden shrubbery. The extremely rare Perot stamps, some of which are in the Queen's Royal Stamp Collection, are now coveted by collectors. At press time, the record price for an 1848 Perot stamp was £225,000 ($350,000). ⊠ *Queen St.,* ☏ *441/295–5151.* ▣ *Free.* ⊘ *Weekdays 9–5.*

The garden where Perot liked to pass his time is now **Par-la-Ville Park,** a pleasant spot that occupies a large portion of Queen Street. The Queen Street entrance (there's another on Par-la-Ville Road) is next to the post office. Paths wind through the luxuriant gardens, and the park benches are ideal for picnicking or enjoying a short rest. At noon you may have trouble finding a place to sit, because this is a favorite lunch spot of Hamilton office workers. If you're hungry for lunch, there's a Kentucky Fried Chicken franchise half a block along Queen Street.

❽ St. Theresa's Church. During a 1968 visit, Pope Paul VI presented Bermuda's Roman Catholic diocese with a gold and silver chalice. The chalice is housed in St. Theresa's Church, a Spanish Mission–style church that serves as head of the island's sixth Roman Catholic Church. Mass was first celebrated in here in 1932. The church is two blocks north of Victoria Park. ⊠ *Cedar Ave. and Elliot St.,* ☏ *441/292–0607.* ⊘ *Daily 7:30–7.*

❿ Sessions House. Bermuda's Parliament, the world's third-oldest, met for the first time in 1620 in St. Peter's Church in St. George's. It later moved to the State House, where deliberations were held for almost 200 years until the capital was moved to Hamilton. An eye-catching Italianate edifice, called Sessions House, is now the home of the House of Assembly (the lower house of Parliament) and the Supreme Court. The original two-story structure was built in 1819; the Florentine towers and colonnade, decorated with red terra-cotta, were added in 1887 to commemorate Queen Victoria's Golden Jubilee. The Victoria Jubilee Clock Tower made its striking debut at midnight, December 31, 1893.

In its present location, the House of Assembly meets on the second floor, where business is conducted in a style befitting such a venerable body. The Sergeant-at-Arms precedes the Speaker into the chamber, bearing a silver-gilt mace. Introduced in 1921, the mace is fashioned after a James I mace in the Tower of London. The Speaker, in wig and flowing black robe, solemnly calls the meeting to order with a cedar gavel made from an old belfry tree that has been growing in St. Peter's churchyard since before 1620. The proceedings are no less ceremonious and colorful in the Supreme Court on the lower floor, where judges in red robes and full wigs hear the arguments of barristers in black robes and wigs. Visitors are welcome to watch the proceedings in the Assembly and the Supreme Court, but you must call to find out when sessions are scheduled. ⊠ *Parliament St. between Reid and Church Sts.,* ☏ *441/ 292–7408.* ▣ *Free.* ⊘ *Weekdays 9–4:30.*

❼ Victoria Park. Amid gardens and shaded by trees, a Victorian bandstand is the focal point of the 4-acre Victoria Park. Concerts are sometimes held in the summer in the park, which was built in 1887 in honor of Queen Victoria's Golden Jubilee and opened with great fanfare in 1890. The park is perfectly safe when filled with people, but it isn't a good place to wander alone—some fairly seedy-looking characters hang out here. ⊠ *Behind City Hall on Victoria St.*

The Town of St. George

The settlement of Bermuda began on St. George's end of the island nearly 400 years ago, when the *Sea Venture* was wrecked off the coast. Much of the fun of St. George's is exploring the alleys and walled lanes that wind through the town. A tour of the town is easily managed on foot.

Numbers in the text correspond to numbers in the margin and on the Town of St. George map.

A Good Walk

Start your tour in **King's Square** ⑭, stopping first in the Visitors Bureau to pick up maps and brochures. Stroll out onto **Ordnance Island** ⑮ to see the statue of Sir George Somers and a replica of the *Deliverance II.* The **White Horse Tavern** ⑯ is a pleasant place for a lunch or refreshment stop. Just up the street is the **Bermuda National Trust Museum at the Globe Hotel** ⑰, which houses fascinating historical exhibits pertinent to American history. Across the square is **Town Hall** ⑱, with King Street running alongside it. As you walk up King Street, notice the fine Bermudian architecture of **Bridge House** ⑲. At the top of King Street, just across Princess Street, you'll come to the **Old State House** ⑳, the oldest stone house in Bermuda, and on the left you'll see **Reeve Court** ㉑, a property of the Bermuda National Trust.

Walk along Princess Street and cross Duke of York Street to **Somers Garden** ㉒ to see the putative burial site of the heart of Sir George Somers. After walking through the garden, ascend the steps to Blockade Alley, where you'll see on a hill ahead the **Unfinished Church** ㉓. To your left are Duke of Kent Street, Featherbed Alley, and the **St. George's Historical Society Museum** ㉔. Around the corner is the **Featherbed Alley Printery** ㉕. Cross Clarence Street to Church Street and then turn right on Broad Alley to reach the **Old Rectory** ㉖. Straight ahead, if "straight" even applies among these twisted alleys, is Printer's Alley, where, on January 17, 1784, Joseph Stockdale published Bermuda's first newspaper. The short street connecting Printer's Alley with Old Maid's Lane is **Nea's Alley** ㉗, which looks like something out of a tale retold by the Brothers Grimm.

Return to Church Street and enter the yard of **St. Peter's Church** ㉘, an ancient Anglican church. From the church, continue down Duke of York Street to Barber Alley, but before turning left to reach **Tucker House** ㉙ notice, on the right, **Petticoat Lane** ㉚. After visiting Tucker House, cross Water Street to Somers Wharf and stop in the **Carriage Museum** ㉛.

TIMING

Despite its small size, St. George's encompasses much of historical interest, and you should plan to spend a full day poking around in the houses and museums.

Between March and November, the government sponsors several free events, including walking tours. The island is usually not terribly crowded during the low season, so it's a good time to see the Town Crier and the Mayor of St. George's, both of whom are present. Note, however, that St. George's can be very crowded between late spring and early fall, when cruise ships dock here (as they do in Hamilton), and shoppers flood the streets near and around King's Square.

Sights to See

★ ⑰ **Bermuda National Trust Museum at the Globe Hotel.** In 1700, Governor Samuel Day built the house that is now the Bermuda National Trust Museum. For 150 years, the building served as the Globe Hotel, and, until 1995, it housed the Confederate Museum. Opened in July 1996, the Trust museum exhibits "Rogues and Runners: Bermuda and the American Civil War." Based on photos and documents from public and private collections, this exhibit tells the story of St. George's adventures as a port for Confederate blockade runners. A diorama of the town's waterfront, a model of the blockade-runner *Fergus,* and a Victorian seal press that reproduces the Great Seal of the Confederacy are on display.

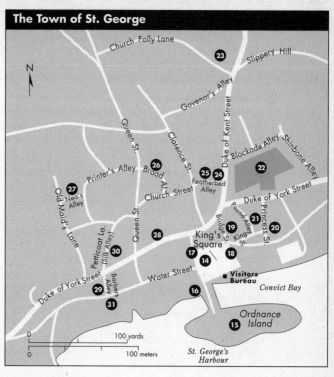

The Town of St. George

The story behind one of the museum's former displays is worth recounting. During the U.S. Civil War, Major Norman Walker, who came to Bermuda as a Confederate agent, used the building as his office. St. George's—which suffered a depression after the capital moved to Hamilton in 1815—sided with the South for economic reasons, and the town became a hotbed of blockade-running. The first woman to run the blockade was Georgiana Walker, Major Walker's pregnant wife, who risked capture by the North to join him in Bermuda. She was determined that their baby would be born on Confederate soil, underneath the Stars and Bars. In the room where she gave birth, therefore, the four-poster bed was draped with the Confederate flag, and it's said that Confederate soil was spread beneath the bed. ⊠ *Duke of York St.,* ☎ *441/297–1423.* ☞ *$4; $5 combination ticket includes admission to Tucker House and Verdmont, in Smith's Parish.* ⊙ *Mon.–Sat. 10–4, Sun. 1–4.*

⑲ Bridge House. Named for a bridge that once crossed a small tidal creek nearby, this house was built prior to 1700. The house is a fine example of Bermudian architecture, and it has served as the home of several of Bermuda's governors. Now owned by the Bermuda National Trust, it has been restored and is privately leased as several small apartments, an art studio, and a shop.

㉛ Carriage Museum. With the arrival of cars on Bermuda in 1946, horse-drawn carriages were put out to pasture, so to speak. This museum offers a fascinating look at some of the island's old carriages. Yes, there's a surrey with a fringe on top, along with isinglass curtains that roll down. Among other displays are a dignified Brougham, a six-passenger enclosed Opera Bus, and a small two-wheeler for children, called the Little Red Dog Cart. The carriages are labeled, but it's entertaining to hear the curator, Mr. Frith, describe them. The museum is at Somers Wharf, which is part of a multimillion-dollar waterfront restoration that includes several shops and the pleasant Carriage House Restaurant. St. George's passenger-ship terminal is in this area. ⊠ *Water St.,* ☎ *809/297–1367.* ⬚ *Free (donations accepted).* ◷ *Weekdays 10–5 (and occasionally Sat.).*

㉕ Featherbed Alley Printery. As quaint as its name, the Featherbed Alley Printery is in a little cottage that houses a working printing press of the ilk invented by Johannes Gutenberg in the 1450s. ⊠ *Featherbed Alley,* ☎ *441/297–0009.* ⬚ *Free.* ◷ *Mon.–Sat. 10–4.*

⑭ King's Square. Now the hub and heartbeat of St. George's, King's Square actually is comparatively new. For 200 years after the town was settled, the square was a marshy part of the harbor—the area was filled in only in the last century. Stop at the **Visitors Service Bureau** for maps, brochures, and advice.

Prominently displayed in King's Square is a cedar replica of the stocks and pillory originally used to punish criminals. Today, they serve as props for tourist photos and for special activities staged here on Wednesdays during the low season. If you decide to take the walking tour (☞ Sightseeing *in* the Gold Guide), you will be greeted in the square by the mayor of St. George's. The town crier, whose resounding voice is almost enough to wake the dead, is on hand in full colonial costume. After the official welcome, the crier bellows a few pronouncements and places any perceived malefactors in the stocks. The main event, however, is when a colonially garbed woman is branded a "gossip" and ducked in the harbor.

㉗ Nea's Alley. The 19th-century Irish poet Tom Moore lived on this street, then known as Cumberland Lane, during his four-month tenure as registrar of the admiralty court. Moore, who was endowed with considerable charm, had an impact on the island that endures to this day. He was invited to stay in the home of Admiral Mitchell, the neighbor of Mr. William Tucker and his wife, Hester—who is the "Nea" to whom Moore pours out his heart in several poems. Moore is thought to have first seen her in Cumberland Lane, which he describes in one of his odes as "the lime-covered alley that leads to thy home." However discreet Nea and Moore may have been about their affair, his odes to her were on the steamy side—much to the dismay of her husband. Although it was rather like locking the barn door after the horse has bolted, Tucker refused to allow his former friend into his house again. Some Bermudians speculate that Nea was very much in love with Tom, but that he considered her merely a pleasant *divertissement.* He returned to Ireland after his assignment, and Nea died in 1817 at the age of 31. Bermudians are much enamored of the short-lived romance between Hester and Moore, and visitors are likely to hear a good deal about it.

㉖ Old Rectory. Built around 1690 by a local pirate, George Dew, this house takes its name from a later owner, Alexander Richardson. Called the "Little Bishop," he was rector of St. Peter's from 1755 to 1805, excepting a six-year stint on St. Eustatius. Richardson's diary is filled with anecdotes about 18th-century St. George's. Traditional architectural features, such as cedar beams, chimneys, and a welcoming-arms staircase are handsome. A garden is open to the public as well. The house is now owned by the Bermuda National Trust. ⊠ *Broad Alley,* ☎ *441/ 297–0879.* ⬚ *Free (donations accepted).* ◷ *Wed. noon–5.*

⑳ Old State House. In April of each year, a curious ritual takes place in King's Square. Amid much pomp and circumstance, one peppercorn, regally placed upon a velvet pillow, is presented to the Mayor of St.

George's. The peppercorn is the annual rent paid to the town by the Masonic Lodge St. George's No. 200 of the Grand Lodge of Scotland, which has occupied the Old State House ever since the capital moved from St. George's to Hamilton in 1815. The oldest house in Bermuda, it was constructed in 1620 in what Governor Nathaniel Butler believed was the Italian style. The limestone building used a mixture of turtle oil and lime as mortar and set the style for future Bermudian buildings. Upon completion, it became home to the Parliament, which had been meeting in St. Peter's Church; dances and social gatherings were also held there. ⊠ *Princess St., no phone.* ⊠ *Free.* ⊙ *Wed. 10–4.*

★ ⑮ **Ordnance Island.** A splendid Desmond Fountain statue of Sir George Somers, titled *Land Ho!,* dominates Ordnance Island. The ducking stool on the island is a replica of the one used to dunk gossips, nagging wives, and suspected witches in the water. Demonstrations are sometimes given, although volunteers say that getting dunked is no fun, even in fun.

Also on the island is the *Deliverance II,* a replica of one of the ships built by the survivors of the wreck. After their shipwreck in 1609, Somers and his crew built two ships, the *Deliverance* and the *Patience,* to carry them to Jamestown, Virginia. Below deck, life-size mannequins in period costume are used to depict the realities of ocean travel in the 17th century—it's not the *QE2.* ⊠ *Ordnance Island, no phone.* ⊠ *$3.* ⊙ *Daily 9–4.*

③⓪ **Petticoat Lane.** Also called Silk Alley, this little street received its name in 1834 after the emancipation of Bermudian slaves. Legend has it that two freed slaves, who had always wanted petticoats like those worn by their mistresses, strolled down the lane on Emancipation Sunday amid much rustling of petticoat skirts.

㉑ **Reeve Court.** The Bermuda National Trust purchased this three-story house on Princess Street to ensure protection from development around the State House. Although the building is not open to the public, you can wander through the colonial garden to admire plantings of fruits, herbs, and a formal parterre. ⊠ *Princess St.*

㉔ **St. George's Historical Society Museum.** Furnished much as it was when it was a private home, this typical Bermudian structure from the early 1700s houses artifacts and documents pertaining to the island's earliest days. One of Bermuda's oldest pieces is a table believed to have been used as the High Court bench in the State House. The house is also filled with documents—including a doctor's bill from 1790—old letters, and displays of pewter, china, and rare books; there's even a whale-blubber cutter.

A torpedo raft is one of the relics from the U.S. Civil War. Constructed of heavy timber with projecting arms to hold torpedoes, the raft was part of a Union plan to blow up the submarine barricade in Charleston harbor. After breaking loose from its towing ship during a gale, the raft drifted for six years before washing ashore in Dolly's Bay on St. David's Island. When the captain of the towing ship later visited Bermuda, he recognized the raft and explained its purpose to the puzzled Bermudians.

On the south wall of the house is an iron grate that is said to have come from the cell where Bermuda's first Methodist missionary, the Reverend John Stephenson, was confined for preaching to slaves. The persistent missionary continued to preach from his cell to a crowd that collected outside. The cottage gardens in the back of the building are beautiful and worth a visit; there is no fee to view them. ⊠ *Featherbed Alley,* ☎ *441/297–0423.* ⊠ *$2.50, including guided tour.* ⊙ *Apr.–Dec., weekdays 10–4.*

★ ㉘ **St. Peter's Church.** The tombstones here in Bermuda's oldest church-yard tell some interesting tales, indeed—this is the resting place of governors, doctors, simple folk, and pirates. East of the church is the grave of Hester, or "Nea," marked "Mr. William Tucker's Family Vault." One of the best-known monuments stands over the grave of Richard Sutherland Dale, who died in 1815 at age 20. An American navy midshipman, Dale was mortally wounded during a sea battle with the British in the War of 1812. The monument was erected by his parents as a tribute to the St. Georgians, whose "tender sympathy prompted the kindest attentions to their son while living and honoured him when dead." In an enclosure to the west of the church is the slaves' graveyard. The ancient cedar tree, which antedates 1620, is the old belfry tree.

Because parts of St. Peter's Church date back to its construction in 1620, it holds the distinction of being the oldest continuously operating Anglican church in the Western Hemisphere. It was not the first church to stand on this site, however; it replaced a 1612 structure of posts and palmetto leaves that was destroyed in a storm. The present church was extended in 1713, and the galleries on either side were added in 1833. The oldest part of the church is the area around the 17th-century triple-tier pulpit. The dark-red cedar altar is the oldest piece of woodwork in the colony, carved under the supervision of Richard Moore, a shipwright and the first governor. The baptismal font, brought to the island by the early settlers, is about 500 years old, and the late-18th-century bishop's throne is believed to have been salvaged from a wreck. Among the treasures displayed in the vestry are a 1697 William of Orange communion set and a Charles I chalice, sent from England by the Bermuda Company in 1625.

Commemorative plaques hang on the walls here, and some of the names are wonderfully Pickwickian: One large memorial is to Governor Allured Popple. If you enter through the back door, be sure to look at the front of the church when you leave. ⊠ *Duke of York St.,* ☎ *441/297–8359.* 🖭 *Free (donations accepted).* ☉ *Daily 10–4:30.*

㉒ **Somers Garden.** After sailing to Jamestown and back in 1610, Sir George Somers fell ill and died. According to local lore, Somers told his nephew Matthew Somers that he wanted his heart buried in Bermuda, where it belonged. Matthew, who never seemed to pay much attention to his uncle's wishes, sailed for England soon afterward, sneaking Somers's body aboard in a cedar chest to avoid alarming the superstitious seamen. (Somers's body is buried near his birthplace in Dorset.) When the tomb where Somers's heart was supposedly interred was opened many years later, only a few bones, a pebble, and some bottle fragments were found—no one knows if Matthew Somers ever carried out his uncle's wishes. Nevertheless, ceremonies were held at the empty grave upon the 1920 visit of the Prince of Wales, during which the prince christened this pleasant, tree-shrouded park Somers Garden. ⊠ *Bordered by Shinbone Alley, Blockade Alley, Duke of Kent, and Duke of York Sts., no phone.* 🖭 *Free.* ☉ *Daily 9–4.*

NEED A BREAK?   Off the tourist beat, **Angeline's Coffee Shop** (⊠ Duke of York St. across and east of Somers Garden, ☎ 441/297–0959) is a popular spot for basic egg breakfasts and plate lunches. The fish sandwiches are among the island's tastiest.

---

⑱ **Town Hall.** St. George's administrative offices are housed in this two-story building that was constructed in 1808. The hall is paneled and furnished with cedar, and there's a delightful collection of photographs of former mayors. Many years ago Town Hall was the scene of a memorable con. A gentleman calling himself Professor Trott appeared in town and announced a spectacular production of *Ali Baba and the Forty Thieves*. A great crowd collected at Town Hall for the play, and thievery was duly performed: Having lured residents away from their homes, the wily "professor" made off with an iron safe. The *Bermuda Journey*, a worthwhile audiovisual presentation, is shown in the second-floor theater. ⊠ *King's Sq.*, ☎ *441/297–1642 Bermuda Journey*. 🔳 *Town hall free*, Bermuda Journey $3. ☉ *Town hall daily 9–4*; Bermuda Journey *Apr.–Oct., Mon.–Thurs. and Sat. at 11:15, 12:15, and 2:15; Nov.–Mar., Wed. and Sat. at 12:15 and 2:15.*

㉙ Tucker House. Antiques aficionados will find much of interest in this historic house, one of the showplaces of the Bermuda National Trust. Built of native limestone in 1711, the house sat close to the waterside (the area is now all built up). Henry Tucker, president of the Governor's Council, lived in the house with his family from 1775 to 1807. His grandson donated most of the furnishings, which date from the mid-18th and early 19th centuries. Much of it is cedar, but there are some handsome mahogany pieces as well: The mahogany dining table was crafted in Bermuda from a tree grown in Cuba, and an English mahogany breakfront holds a collection of Tucker family silver.

A short flight of stairs leads down to the kitchen, originally a separate building, with a doorway leading to the enclosed kitchen garden. Through the small courtyard is an archaeological exhibit that uses artifacts recovered through excavations of the site to explore the connections between the St. George and Williamsburg branches of this interesting local family.

The Tucker name has been important in Bermuda since the island's beginnings, and a number of interesting family portraits hang in the house. Henry Tucker's father and brother were both involved in the famed "Gunpowder Plot" of 1775. The Continental Congress had imposed a ban on exports to all British colonies not taking part in the revolt against England. Bermuda depended upon the American colonies for grain, so a delegation of Bermudians traveled to Philadelphia offering salt in exchange for the resumption of grain shipments. Congress rejected the salt but agreed to lift the ban if Bermuda sent gunpowder instead. A group of Bermudians, including the two Tuckers, then sneaked into the island's arsenal, stole the gunpowder, and shipped it to Boston. The ban was soon lifted.

The house sits at the corner of Barber's Alley, named for Joseph Hayne Rainey, a former slave from South Carolina whose father had bought him his freedom. At the outbreak of the Civil War, Rainey and his French wife fled to Bermuda. Renting one of the outbuildings on the Tucker property, Rainey set up shop as a barber, while his wife developed a large clientele for his dress-making business. After the Civil War, they returned to South Carolina, where he went into politics. His career advanced quickly and in 1870 Rainey became the first black man to be elected to the U.S. House of Representatives. ⊠ *Water St.*, ☎ *441/297–0545.* 🔳 *$3; $5 combination ticket includes admission to Bermuda National Trust Museum and Verdmont Museum in Smith's Parish.* ☉ *Mon.–Sat. 10–4.*

㉓ Unfinished Church. Considering how much attention and affection is lavished on St. Peter's these days, it's hard to believe that residents in the 19th century wanted to replace the old church with a new one. Work began on this church in 1874, but construction was halted when a schism developed in the church. Money for construction was later diverted to rebuild Trinity Church in Hamilton after it burned down; work on the new church in St. George's was abandoned by the turn of the century. In 1992 the Bermuda National Trust obtained a 50-year lease on the church and is repairing and stabilizing the structure. Access is subject to completion of the work. ⊠ *Up Kent St. from King's Sq. (where Kent St. becomes Government Hill Rd. at intersection of Church Folly La.)*

⑯ White Horse Tavern. For much of the 19th century, this popular waterside restaurant was the Davenport home. After his arrival in St. George's in about 1815, John Davenport opened a small dry-goods store on the square. He was able to wangle a profitable contract to supply beef to the garrison, and gold and silver began to pour in. There were no banks in Bermuda, but Davenport wasn't the trusting sort anyway. He stashed the money in a keg that he kept beneath his bed. When the keg was full, he took it down to the cellar and put another one under his bed. By the time he was an old man, Davenport would spend hours each day gloating over the kegs that now filled his cellar. After his death, it was discovered that the old miser had amassed a fortune in gold and silver worth £75,000. ⊠ *King's Sq., St. George's,* ☎ *441/297–1838.*

The West End

In contrast to Hamilton and St. George's, the West End is a rather bucolic part of Bermuda. With the notable exception of Dockyard, many of the attractions here are natural rather than manmade: nature reserves, wooded areas, and beautiful harbors and bays. In the waters off Daniel's Head, the Sea Gardens are regularly visited by glass-bottom boats from Hamilton: With its bow jutting out of the water, the coral-wrapped wreck of HMS *Vixen* is a major attraction. The ship was deliberately sunk by the British to block the channel and protect Dockyard from attack by torpedo boats. The West End is part of Sandys Parish, named after Sir Edwin Sandys, an investor in the Bermuda Company. Local lore contends that Sir George Somers took a keen interest in this region, and in the early days it was known as "Somers's seate"—hence the name of Somerset Village. Today, Somerset is a sleepy little hamlet with banks, several restaurants, a few shops, and not much else. The West End's big attraction is the Royal Naval Dockyard, a bastion of the British Royal Navy for nearly 150 years.

Numbers in the text correspond to numbers in the margin and on the West End map.

A Good Tour

The Somerset ferry from Hamilton stops at Somerset Bridge, Cavello Bay, Watford Bridge, and Dockyard. Disembark from the ferry at the Dockyard landing to begin your walk through the **Royal Naval Dockyard** ㉜ on Ireland Island, a sprawling complex with several notable attractions. Start at the former fortress that houses the **Maritime Museum** ㉝. The museum's collections are in several large stone buildings spread over six acres. Across the street from the museum is the Old Cooperage, or barrel-maker's shop. Dating from 1831, the reconstructed building houses the Neptune Cinema, which shows first-run films, as well as the Craft Market. Just across from the market is the popular Frog & Onion pub and restaurant, where you can have alfresco (or indoor) repast. To see some fine examples of Bermudian art, stop at the nearby **Bermuda Arts Centre at Dockyard** ㉞.

From here, you can travel by bicycle. Bike down the main road out of Dockyard along Ireland Island South. Turn left on Craddock Road and cycle down to see **Lagoon Park** ㉟ and the little inlet called the Crawl.

Cross over Boaz and Watford islands to Somerset Island. The largest of all these islets, Somerset Island is fringed on both sides with beautiful secluded coves, inlets, and bays. **Somerset Village** ㊱ nestles sleepily beside pretty Mangrove Bay. A short distance farther along Cambridge Road is pretty **Long Bay Park and Nature Reserve** ㊲. Continue along Cambridge Road (which becomes Somerset Road) until you see the arched gateway leading to Springfield and the **Gilbert Nature Reserve** ㊳.

Somerset Road winds around to the **Somerset Visitors Service Bureau** ㊴, where you can stop for some orientation. Nearby, high atop a promontory against a backdrop of the sea, you can see **St. James Church** ㊵. A short distance beyond the church, opposite Willowbank guest house, is the entrance to the bucolic **Heydon Trust property** ㊶. Just around the bend on your left is **Ft. Scaur** ㊷, which affords spectacular views of the Great Sound, and at the bottom of the hilly, twisting road lies spectacular **Ely's Harbour** ㊸.

Linking Somerset Island with the rest of Bermuda is **Somerset Bridge** ㊹, said to be the world's smallest drawbridge. Near the bridge is the Somerset ferry landing, where you can catch a ferry back to Hamilton. Across the bridge, Somerset Road becomes Middle Road, which leads into Southampton Parish.

TIMING

Allow at least a day for exploring this area. If you take the ferry to Somerset, look closely at the ferry schedule: The trip can take anywhere from a half hour to more than an hour, depending on which ferry you take. However, there are worse ways to while away an hour than churning across Bermuda's Great Sound. Take your bicycle or moped aboard the ferry, too, because after strolling around Dockyard you will need wheels to see other parts of the West End. Bus service is available if you don't have your own transport.

Sights to See

❸ **Bermuda Arts Centre at Dockyard.** Since its opening by Princess Margaret in 1984, this spot has been a showcase for local artists and artisans, and an excellent place to see Bermudians' work (☞ Chapter 8). Exhibits, which change frequently, include watercolors, oils, and photography. Beautifully crafted silver jewelry, hand-dyed scarves, and quilts are sold throughout the year. The selection of note cards and posters emphasizes Bermuda themes. ⊠ *Dockyard,* ☎ *441/234–2441.* ⊠ *Free (donations accepted).* ☉ *Apr.–Oct., daily 10–5; Nov.–Mar., Tues.–Sun. 10:30–4:30.*

㊸ **Ely's Harbour.** Pronounced "*ee*-lees," this small sheltered harbor, with pleasure boats dotting its brilliant turquoise waters, was once a hangout for smugglers. ⊠ *Off Middle Rd., west of Somerset Bridge.*

㊷ **Ft. Scaur.** Perched on the highest hill in Somerset, the fort was begun in 1868 and completed in the 1870s. British troops were garrisoned here until World War I, and during World War II, American forces from Battery D, 52nd Coast Artillery Battalion, were stationed here. Little remains to be seen of that now, although the 22 acres of gardens are quite pretty, and the view of the Great Sound is fantastic. Almost worth the long climb is the Early Bermuda Weather Stone, the "perfect weather indicator." The plaque reads: "A wet stone means . . . it is raining; a shadow under the stone . . . means the sun is shining; if the stone is swinging, it means there is a strong wind blowing; if the stone jumps up and down it means there is an earthquake; if ever it is white on top . . . believe it or not . . . it is snowing." ⊠ *Somerset Rd., Ely's Harbour,* ☎ *441/234–0908.* ⊠ *Free.* ☉ *Apr.–Oct., daily 7:30–4:30; Nov.–Mar., daily 7:30–4.*

50

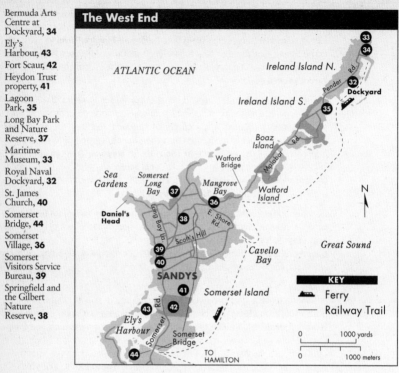

The West End

🔵 **Heydon Trust property.** A reminder of what the island was like in its early days, this quiet, peaceful property has been maintained as undeveloped open space. Among its 43 acres are citrus orchards, banana groves, flower and vegetable gardens, and bird sanctuaries. Pathways dotted with park benches wend through the preserve, affording some wonderful views of the Great Sound. If you persevere along the main path, you'll reach the tiny, rustic **Heydon Chapel**, which dates from before 1620. A rugged cross is planted in the hillside, and a welcome mat lies at the door. Inside are a few wooden pews, cedar beams, and an ancient oven and hearth in a small room behind the altar. Services are still held in the chapel, which include Gregorian chant at 3 PM Monday–Saturday. ⊠ *Somerset Rd.,* ☎ *441/234–1831.* 🎫 *Free.* ☉ *Daily dawn–dusk.*

🔵 **Lagoon Park.** Hidden in the mangroves are a lovely lagoon, footpaths, wild birds, and places to picnic. Next to the park, the Crawl is a picturesque inlet with fishing boats bobbing in the water and lobster pots on the dock. The park is always open, and there's no charge for entry. ⊠ *Lagoon Rd. off Malabar Rd.*

🔵 **Long Bay Park and Nature Reserve.** There's a great beach, shallow water, and picnic areas at this park. The Bermuda Audubon Society owns the adjacent nature reserve and its pond, which attracts migrating birds spring and fall. Peaceful as the area is now, it was the scene of one of Bermuda's most sensational murders. Skeeters' Corner, at the end of Daniel's Head Road, was the site of a cottage once owned by a couple of the same name. One night in 1878, Edward Skeeters strangled his wife and dumped her in the water. His long, rambling confession revealed that he was irked because she talked too much!

🔵 **Maritime Museum.** Opened by Queen Elizabeth II in 1975, the sprawling 6-acre Maritime Museum is housed in Bermuda's largest fort, which was built to defend the Royal Naval Dockyard. You enter the museum over a moat. Exhibition rooms are in six old magazines and munitions warehouses arranged around the parade grounds and the Keep Pond area. Several of the rather tired exhibits pertain to the *Sea Venture* and the early history of the island. Artifacts and relics from some of the approximately 300 ships wrecked on the island's reefs are exhibited; the Age of Discovery exhibit traces some of those voyages. Sailors will appreciate the Bermuda dinghies (14-ft sailboats that can carry as much as 1,000 ft of canvas) on display in the Boat Loft. You can also explore the restored ramparts to take in commanding views of the Great Sound and North Shore. Currently undergoing renovation, the 19th-century Commissioner's House, set high on a bluff, is the world's oldest cast-iron–framed residence. Home to Dockyard commissioners from 1827 to 1837, and later a barracks, the house was formally commissioned as a ship—the HMS *Malabar*—in 1919. Fundraisers for the $3 million restoration project hope to complete work on the house by late 1999.

Across the street, the **Neptune Cinema** shows first-run films and the **Craft Market** displays the works of local craftspeople and commercial artists. Jaded tourists who think of crafts as tacky souvenirs are in for a pleasant surprise. There are some delightful items on sale here, including wood carvings and miniature cedar furniture (☞ Chapter 8). ⊠ *Dockyard,* ☎ *441/234–1418 maritime museum, 441/234–3208 craft market.* ☒ *Maritime museum $7.50, craft market free.* ☉ *Both daily 10–5.*

③② **Royal Naval Dockyard.** After the American Revolution, Britain found itself with neither an anchorage nor a major ship-repair yard in the western Atlantic. When Napoleon started to make threatening noises in Europe and British ships became increasingly vulnerable to pirate attack, Britain began construction of a major stronghold in Bermuda, around 1809. The work was done by slaves and English convicts toiling under appalling conditions—thousands of workers died before the project was completed. This was a functioning shipyard for nearly 150 years; it was closed in 1951, and the Royal Navy closed operations here in 1995 after a 200-year presence.

With the opening of the **Maritime Museum** (☞ *above*) in 1975, the decision was made to transform the entire naval port into a tourist site. The Dockyard is currently under development as a minivillage, and Bermudians are justifiably proud of the project. The area includes a shopping arcade and a visitor information center in the handsome, century-old Clocktower Building, a cruise-ship terminal, a children's entertainment center, a movie theater, shops and galleries, restaurants, a marina with deepwater berths, and the submarine *Enterprise.* The former shipyard has literally blossomed, having undergone extensive landscaping to replace its vast stretches of concrete with shrubs, trees, and grassy lawns. New additions include an extension of the shopping mall, a snorkel park, and horse-drawn-carriage tours.

You can reach the Dockyard in 40 minutes from Hamilton on an express bus that leaves the capital every 15 minutes. From November through March, walking tours meet regularly (☞ Sightseeing *in* the Gold Guide), and from April through October, arrangements can be made in advance through the Royal Naval Dockyard's public relations department (☎ 441/234–1709). Hold on to your hat when you're strolling in the area—it's often very windy, particularly along the water.

In the new Victorian Mall, adjacent to the Clocktower Building is **Nan-nini's Häagen-Dazs** (☎ 441/234-2474), that staple of the sweet-tooth trade. Choose one of the 16 flavors of ice cream or nonfat soft yogurt, or enjoy a cup of freshly brewed espresso, cappuccino, or hot chocolate at a table outside. Also look for Nannini cakes and Perugina chocolates from Italy. Have a chat with owner Fosco Nannini, who weaves his share of interesting yarns.

40 **St. James Church.** The entrance to this church is marked on the main road by handsome wooden gates that were designed by a Royal Engineer in 1872; a long pathway curls past glistening white tombs in the churchyard. The first church on this site was a wood structure destroyed by a hurricane in 1780. The present church, one of the loveliest on the island, was consecrated in 1789. The tall, slender spire is a faithful replica of the 1880 spire that was hit by lightning in 1937 and sent crashing down into the church's center aisle. ⊠ *Main Rd., Somerset,* ☎ *441/234-2025.* ⊑ *Free.* ⊙ *Daily dawn–dusk.*

44 **Somerset Bridge.** Reputed to have the smallest draw in the world, this bridge opens a mere 18 inches, just wide enough to accommodate a sailboat mast.

A good place to stop for one of the best—if most expensive—lunches on the island is the casual **La Plage** restaurant at the Lantana Colony Club (⊠ Somerset Rd., ☎ 441/234-0141). Reservations are essential.

36 **Somerset Village.** A quiet retreat, this village is quite different from St. George's, Hamilton, and Dockyard. Only one road runs through it, and the few shops are mostly branches of Hamilton stores, along with two banks. In low season, tour guides concentrate on the area's history as well as its natural beauty and unusual medicinal plants. Somerset Island itself is heavily populated, laced with roads and pathways through quiet residential areas.

39 **Somerset Visitors Service Bureau.** You can get lots of information here about this area. It's open from April to November. There's also a Visitors Service Bureau at Dockyard (⊠ The Cooperage Building, ☎ 441/234-3824) that's open year-round, Monday through Saturday 9:30–2, Sunday 11–3. ⊠ *Somerset Rd.,* ☎ *441/234-1388.* ⊙ *Daily 9–3.*

38 **Springfield and the Gilbert Nature Reserve.** Set in five heavily wooded acres, Springfield is an old plantation home dating from around 1700 that the National Trust owns. Restoration was to begin in 1997 on the main house and outbuildings—the kitchen, slave quarters, and buttery—which are built around an open courtyard; unfortunately, while under renovation, the house is closed to the public.

The Gilbert Nature Reserve, named after the family that owned the property from 1700 to 1973, was acquired by the Bermuda National Trust in conjunction with the Bermuda Audubon Society. There are a number of walking trails in the reserve. ⊠ *Main Rd., Somerset,* ☎ *441/236-6483.* ⊑ *Free.* ⊙ *Daily.*

The Parishes

Bermuda's other points of interest—and there are many—are scattered throughout the island's parishes. This final section covers the length and breadth of the colony, commenting only on the major sights. Half the fun of exploring Bermuda, though, is wandering down forgotten lanes or discovering some little-known beach or cove. A moped or bicycle is ideal for this kind of travel, although most of the island is served by buses and ferries. It would be foolish, if not impossible, to try to see all the sights here in one day. The tour below, which leaves from Hamilton, can easily be broken into two halves: the first exploring parishes in the eastern part of the island, the second traveling through the western parishes. Keep in mind that you will probably end up touring the parishes piecemeal—a couple of sights here, a church there, and plenty of time at the beach in between.

Numbers in the text correspond to numbers in the margin and on the Parishes map.

A Good Tour

EASTERN PARISHES

Follow Cedar Avenue north out of Hamilton to **St. John's Church** ㊺, the parish church of Pembroke. Marsh Folly Road, which runs between the church and Bernard Park, will take you to the limestone passageway called **Black Watch Pass** ㊻. The road received its name from Black Watch Well, at the intersection of Black Watch Pass and North Shore Road. The residence of Bermuda's governor, imposing **Government House** ㊼, sits atop Langton Hill, which overlooks North Shore Road, Black Watch Well, and the sea. North Shore Road merges with Spanish Point Road near **Spanish Point** ㊽, at the tip of the peninsula, where a park affords pleasant vistas. En route to Spanish Point you pass **Admiralty House Park** ㊾, a pretty spot with several caves and sheltered coves. Head back along North Shore Road to Devonshire Parish. Ideal for cycling and quiet picnics, Devonshire is a serene part of the island, with much to offer in the way of natural beauty. Locals come to Devonshire Dock to buy fresh fish (something to bear in mind if you're staying in a housekeeping apartment). A short distance farther along North Shore Road is **Palmetto House** ㊿, an 18th-century cruciform house.

If you continue along North Shore Road, you will reach **Flatts Village** ⑤, home of the estimable **Aquarium, Museum, and Zoo** ㉒, and the small but interesting **Railway Museum and Curiosity Shop** ㉓. Continuing east, North Shore Road climbs Crawl Hill, a high point offering spectacular views over the island and sea. "Crawl" derives from the Afrikaans word *kraal,* meaning animal enclosure; on Bermuda, the word was applied to several ponds containing turtles and fish. This part of Hamilton Parish was also a site for shipbuilding during the early days of the colony.

Turn right on Trinity Church Road to see the early 17th-century **Holy Trinity Church** ㉔. Just off Trinity Church Road is Mt. Wyndham, the peak from which Admiral Sir Alexander Cochrane surveyed the British fleet prior to its attack on Washington, D.C., in 1814. Follow North Shore Road as it dips south to the **Bermuda Perfumery and Gardens** ㉕. Blue Hole Hill leads to the causeway over Castle Harbour.

Once across the causeway, you are in St. George's Parish. Take Kindley Field Road around the airport, turn left onto Mullet Bay Road, and cross Swing Bridge over Ferry Reach. The **Bermuda Biological Station for Research** ㉖ will interest you if you're keen on environmental issues.

There is **magnificent scenery** along the stretch of road that runs between Mullet Bay and the sea. A little farther east, Mullet Bay Road becomes Wellington Road, and finally Duke of York Street when you reach St. George's (☞ The Town of St. George, *above*). East of town, Duke of York Street becomes Barrack Hill Road. From the road, the views of the town, St. David's Island, and Castle Harbour are spectacular.

Barrack Hill Road turns into Cut Road, which leads all the way to **Gates Fort** ㉗, a reconstruction of an early 17th-century fort. The main camp of the *Sea Venture* survivors is believed to have been in this general area. Leaving Gates Fort via Barry Road, you'll pass Buildings Bay. One of the two ships that carried Sir George Somers and his crew to Virginia was built here in 1610, hence the bay's name.

Continue up Barry Road to the very impressive **Fort St. Catherine** ⑧. The fort overlooks St. Catherine's Beach, where the survivors from the *Sea Venture* scrambled ashore on July 28, 1609. Nearby **Tobacco Bay** ⑨ also played a prominent role in the island's history.

Retrace your route through St. George's to Swing Bridge, which connects St. George's with St. David's Island. In addition to Bermuda's airport, about 2 square mi of St. David's have for many years been occupied by a U.S. Naval Air Station, which closed operations in September 1995. In 1940, during World War II, Sir Winston Churchill agreed to give the United States a 99-year lease to operate a base on Bermuda in exchange for destroyers. The entire area taken up by the air station is now called St. David's, but construction of the base actually required linking three islands—St. David's, Longbird, and Cooper's—with landfills. One of Bermuda's oldest houses, and a must-see for visitors, is the **Carter House** ⑥, on grounds previously occupied by the air base.

Apart from the base, St. David's is a rustic spot where the inhabitants have always led an isolated life—some are said to have never visited St. George's, let alone the other end of the island. A number of residents had to be relocated when the base was built, but they refused to leave St. David's. Therefore, a section of the island called "Texas" was purchased by the government, which built cottages there for the displaced islanders. The area is just off the naval base; you can see Texas Road at the tip of the island near the lighthouse. When **St. David's Lighthouse** ⑥ is open, you can see spectacular views of the surroundings from inside.

Head back across the causeway and turn left on Wilkinson Avenue. A network of caves, caverns, and subterranean lakes runs beneath the hills in this part of the island. Two of them are on the property of the nearby Grotto Bay Beach Hotel & Tennis Club (☞ Chapter 5). Just south of the hotel are the **Crystal Caves** ⑥, the most impressive of the caves that are open to the public.

Harrington Sound Road runs along the strip of land between the Sound and Castle Harbour. At Walsingham Lane, you'll see a white sign for the restaurant called **Tom Moore's Tavern** ⑥. Harrington Sound Road leads southward to the amber-color **Leamington Caves** ⑥.

Farther south on Harrington Sound Road is **Tucker's Town** ⑥, where you'll find the exclusive Mid Ocean Club and a community of well-heeled Bermudians. Below the clubhouse on the south shore are the **Natural Arches** ⑥, one of the island's oldest and most photographed attractions. A chain of islands dots the channel into the harbor between St. David's and Tucker's Town Bay. In the colony's early days, these islands were fortified to protect Castle Harbour from possible enemy attack. Soon after his arrival in 1612, Governor Moore built his first and best fort on **Castle Island** ⑥.

Back on Harrington Sound Road, the **Devil's Hole Aquarium** ⑥ is touted as Bermuda's first tourist attraction, dating from the mid-19th century. Take steep Knapton Hill Road, which leads westward to South Shore Road and **Spittal Pond** ⑥, a lovely nature park. West of Spittal Pond on South Shore Road is the turnoff to Collector's Hill, which is a very steep climb indeed. The hill is named for Gilbert Salton, a 19th-century customs collector who lived in a house near the top; the house has long since disappeared. At the very top of Collector's

Hill is **Verdmont** ⑦, Bermuda's finest historic house. Return to South Shore Road and follow it west to the 18-acre **Palm Grove** ⑦, whose gardens are a singular delight of Devonshire Parish.

WESTERN PARISHES

The western group of parishes begins with Paget, south of Hamilton town. Brighton Hill Road, just west of Palm Grove, runs north to Middle Road and the **Old Devonshire Church** ⑦, the parish's biggest attraction. Turn left off Middle Road onto Tee Street, and then right onto Berry Hill Road. One mile farther on the left is the turnoff to Point Finger Road and the **Botanical Gardens** ⑦, a landscaped park laced with roads and paths. A few minutes away by moped are the offices of the **Bermuda National Trust** ⑦, a prestigious preservation organization. From the Trust offices, go west on Harbour Road, and near the Lower Ferry Landing is **Clermont** ⑦, a historic house that is not open to the public.

If you're on foot, turn left on Valley Road to reach the late-18th-century **St. Paul's Church** ⑦. If you are riding a moped, take Chapel Road and turn east on Middle Road to Valley Road, or walk the bike up the narrow one-way stretch of hill past the SPCA headquarters on the left. St. Paul's sits on the edge of **Paget Marsh** ⑦, notable for its natural splendors. From St. Paul's, head west into Warwick Parish along Middle Road. Just after the intersection with Ord Road (opposite the Belmont Hotel, Golf & Country Club), look to your left to see **Christ Church** ⑦. Turn left off Middle Road onto Camp Hill Road, which winds down to the south-shore beaches. Along the way is Warwick Camp, built in the 1870s to guard against any enemy landing on the beaches. The camp was used as a training ground and rifle range during World War I. In 1920, Pearl White of *The Perils of Pauline* fame came to Bermuda to shoot a movie, bringing along an entourage that included lions, monkeys, and a host of other exotic fauna. Scenes for the film were shot on Warwick Bay, below the rifle range. Most Bermudians had never seen either a lion or a movie star, and great crowds collected to watch the filming.

Some of the island's prettiest beaches are just off South Shore Road; two of them are at Warwick, as is peaceful, green **Astwood Park** ⑦. Two miles west along South Shore Road is the turnoff for Lighthouse Road, which takes you to **Gibbs Hill Lighthouse** ⑧ and unsurpassed views of the island.

If you're still feeling adventurous, head west, turn left off Middle Road onto Whale Bay Road (just before the Port Royal Golf & Country Club), and go down the hill to **Whale Bay Fort** ⑧. Continuing west, a small road just before Somerset Bridge has the odd name of **Overplus Lane** ⑧, which harks back to the 17th century. Across Somerset Bridge is the West End, which is covered in the exploring section immediately above. If you are traveling by bike or by moped, you can catch a ferry from Somerset Bridge back to Hamilton. Otherwise, take your choice of Middle, Harbour, or South Shore Road to find your way back to the capital.

TIMING

The parishes, outside of Hamilton and St. George's (Somerset is a rural community), are considered by Bermudians to be "out in the country." These parts of the island are less congested than the towns; however, it should be noted that the area just to the east of the capital—especially the traffic circle where Crow Lane intersects with the Lane and Trimingham Road—is very busy during morning and afternoon rush hours. Those unaccustomed to riding on mopeds and driving on the left should take particular care at the traffic circles, especially during rush hours.

Sights to See

EASTERN PARISHES

㊾ Admiralty House Park. In the 19th century, this pretty spot was the estate of John Dunscombe. Dunscombe, who later became lieutenant governor of Newfoundland, sold the property in 1816 to the British military, which decided to build a house for the commanding British admiral of the naval base at Dockyard. The house was reconstructed several times over the years, notably in the 1850s by an eccentric admiral with a weakness for subterranean tunnels—he had several caves and galleries cut into the cliffs above the sea. The house was closed when the Royal Navy withdrew in 1951 and was later demolished. All that remains of the complex is the ballroom. Within the park, Clarence Cove offers a sheltered beach and pleasant swimming. ⊠ *Off North Shore Rd. at merge with Spanish Point Rd., Pembroke Parish.*

㊿ Aquarium, Museum, and Zoo. The aquarium has always been a pleasant, if not awe-inspiring diversion, but thanks to an ambitious $5.2 million expansion project it has become awesome, indeed. The state-of-the-art North Rock Exhibit, opened in late 1996 in the main gallery, is a 140,000-gallon tank that displays Bermuda's famed living coral reefs. A crystal-clear acrylic wall that curves overhead gives you the impression of actually being underwater with all manner of sea creatures.

Among the zoo's displays are a beehive, octopuses, and a touch pool in the Invertebrate House, and a reptile walkway that gives you a close look at alligators and Galápagos tortoises. There is a children's Discovery Room with activities pertaining to Bermuda. And the natural history museum has a geology display with explanations of Bermuda's volcanic origins, information about humpback whales that migrate past the island, and a deep-sea exhibit that documents the half-mile dive of marine biologist Dr. William Beebe in the early 1930s. A new, walkthrough Australasian Exhibit contains wildlife indigenous to Australia, New Guinea, Borneo, and Malaysia. ⊠ *Flatts Village, Smith's Parish,* ☎ *441/293–2727.* ☞ *$8.* ☉ *Daily 9–5 (last admission at 4:30).*

㊲ Astwood Park. Bermuda's beaches tend to elicit the most effusive travel-writing clichés—simply because they are so good. A 3-mi chain of sandy beaches, coves, and inlets begins at Warwick Long Bay and extends to Horseshoe Bay in the east (☞ Chapter 7). Just east of Warwick Bay, Astwood Park is a lovely public park with picnic tables and two beaches. The larger of the two beaches—the one to the left as you face the park—is ideal for snorkeling. ⊠ *Off South Shore Rd., Warwick and Southampton Parishes.*

NEED A BREAK?   **Bailey's Ice Cream Parlour & Food D'Lites** (⊠ Blue Hole Hill, ☎ 441/293-9333) has 40 varieties of freshly made natural ice cream, as well as shakes, sodas, yogurts, and sorbets. For something a bit stronger, cross the road for a rum swizzle and a "swizzleburger" at the **Swizzle Inn** (⊠ Blue Hole Hill, Hamilton Parish, ☎ 441/293-9300).

㊶ Bermuda Biological Station for Research. In 1903—long before the environment became the hot topic that it is today—scientists here began conducting research on marine life. Facilities include ships for ocean research, 13 laboratories, a 250-seat lecture hall, and a 20,000-volume library. Research programs here focus on environmental issues such as global change and the health of Bermuda's reefs. Extensive research has been conducted here on acid rain. Guided tours of the grounds and laboratory are conducted Wednesday at 10 AM (only), beginning in the main building. ⊠ *17 Biological La., Ferry Reach, St. George's Parish,* ☎ *441/297–1880.* ☞ *Free (donations accepted).*

OFF THE
BEATEN PATH **BERMUDA GOLF ACADEMY –** As you're tooling west along Middle Road about a mile past the South Road intersection, watch for Granaway Heights Road on the left across from a pond. Slow down and prepare for a left turn onto Industrial Park Road for the Academy. You'll want to come here for the 320-yard driving range, practice greens, 40 practice bays, and, of course, lessons, videotaping, and club repair and rental. But there is also a small restaurant that serves light meals and has the Golf Channel running continuously, and a playground for the children. ⊠ *Industrial Park Rd., Southampton Parish,* ☎ *441/238-8800.* ☉ *Daily 9 AM–11 PM.*

74 **Bermuda National Trust.** The nonprofit organization that oversees the restoration and preservation of many of the island's gardens, open spaces, and historic buildings has its offices in Waterville, a rambling 18th-century house built by the Trimingham family. The drawing and dining rooms are open to the public during normal business hours. Waterville also houses the Trustworthy gift shop, which sells handmade crafts, novelties, and Trust logo items. The Trust is a solid source of information about the island. ⊠ *29 The Lane, Paget Parish,* ☎ *441/236-6483.* ⌧ *Free (donations accepted).* ☉ *Bermuda National Trust weekdays 9–5, gift shop Mon.–Sat. 10–4.*

55 **Bermuda Perfumery and Gardens.** In 1929, the Lili Perfume Factory began extracting natural fragrances from the island's flowers, and the enterprise blossomed into the present perfumery and tourist attraction. Guided tours are conducted of the factory, which is in a 200-year-old cottage with cedar beams, but the biggest draw is the aromatic nature trail that you can walk on your own. A complimentary map helps you sniff your way around the oleanders, frangipani, jasmine, orchids, and passionflowers that are the raw material for the factory. The adjoining Calabash Gift Shop carries a large selection of soaps and toiletries. ⊠ *212 North Shore Rd., Hamilton Parish,* ☎ *441/293-0627.* ⌧ *Free.* ☉ *Apr.–Oct., Mon.–Sat. 9–5, Sun. 10–4; Nov.–Mar., Mon.–Sat. 9–4:30.*

OFF THE
BEATEN PATH **BERMUDA TRIANGLE BREWERY –** Yes, indeed, microbrewing has arrived in Bermuda. There is no bar here, or eatery, or even a place to sit for that matter. Touring the brewery and sampling the fruits of its vats are what the place is all about. When we tasted, there were four brews available: Wild Hogge Amber Ale, Spinnaker Beer, Full Moon Pale Ale ("brewed only under the peak of the lunar orbit"), and Hammerhead Stout. Free tours are offered weekdays at 4 PM April–October and Saturday at noon and 3 year-round. ⊠ *Industrial Park Rd., Southampton Parish,* ☎ *441/238-2430.*

46 **Black Watch Pass.** The Public Works Department excavated about 2.5 million cubic ft of solid limestone during construction of the awesome passageway that leads from Hamilton to North Shore Road. This pass took its name from the **Black Watch Well.** During a severe drought in 1849, the governor ordered a well dug on government ground to alleviate the suffering of the poor in the area. Excavated by a detachment of the famed Black Watch regiment, the well is marked by a commemorative plaque and shaded by a tiered concrete slab. The site is not particularly inspiring, however, and only the most dedicated well-wishers will want to make the pilgrimage to see it. ⊠ *Black Watch Pass and North Shore Rd., Pembroke Parish.*

73 **Botanical Gardens.** A fragrant haven for the island's exotic subtropical plants, flowers, and trees—and for whoever enjoys them—the park has within its 36 acres a miniature forest, an aviary, a hibiscus garden

58

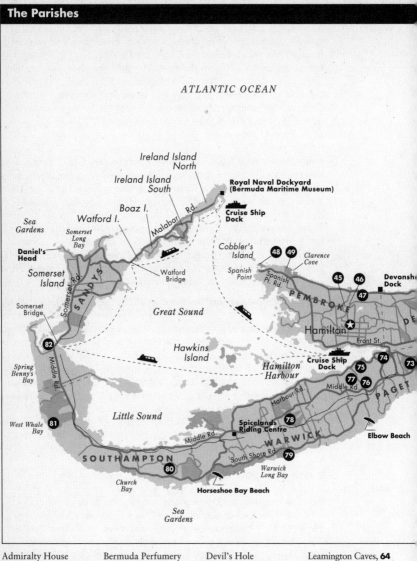

ATLANTIC OCEAN

Ireland Island
North

Ireland Island
South

Boaz I.

Watford I.

Royal Naval Dockyard
(Bermuda Maritime Museum)

Cruise Ship
Dock

Malabar Rd.

Sea
Gardens

Somerset
Long
Bay

Daniel's
Head

Cobbler's
Island

48 49

Clarence
Cove

Spanish
Point

Spanish
Pt. Rd.

45 46
47

Devonsh
Dock

Somerset
Island

Watford
Bridge

SANDYS

Somerset Rd.

Great Sound

PEMBROKE

DE

Somerset
Bridge

Hamilton

Front St.

Spring
Benny's
Bay

Middle Rd.

Hawkins
Island

Hamilton
Harbour

Cruise Ship
Dock

75
77 76

74

Middle Rd.

73

PAGET

West Whale
Bay

81

Little Sound

Spicelands
Riding Centre

78

Harbour Rd.

Elbow Beach

Middle Rd.

WARWICK

South Shore Rd.

79

Warwick
Long Bay

SOUTHAMPTON

80

Church
Bay

Horseshoe Bay Beach

Sea
Gardens

82

Overplus Lane

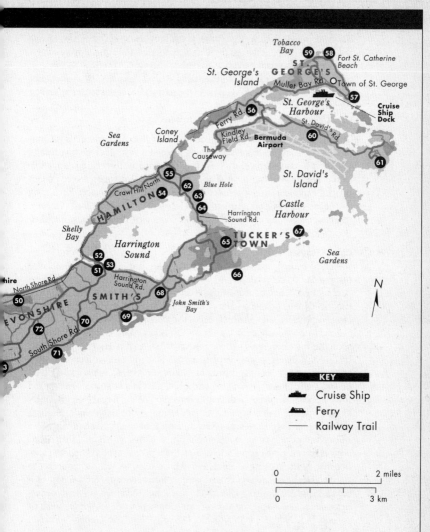

St. David's
Lighthouse, **61**
St. John's Church, **45**
St. Paul's Church, **76**
Spanish Point, **48**
Spittal Pond, **69**
Tobacco Bay, **59**

Tom Moore's
Tavern, **63**
Tucker's Town, **65**
Verdmont, **70**
Whale Bay Fort, **81**

(with more than 150 species of the flower), and a special Garden for
the Blind, which is filled with the scent of sweet geranium, lemon, lavender, and spices. Seventy-five-minute walking tours of the gardens leave
the visitor center at 10:30 on Tuesday, Wednesday, and Friday (Tuesday and Friday only from November through March). To arrange
tours at other times, talk to the curator of the gardens or make a donation to the Botanical Society. Information is available in the visitor
center, where there are also gift and tea shops. Offices of the Agriculture Department are also on the grounds.

The pretty white house on the grounds of the Botanical Gardens is **Camden,** the official residence of Bermuda's premier. A large two-story house,
Camden is more typical of West Indian estate architecture than traditional Bermudian building. The house is open for tours, except when
official functions are scheduled. ⊠ *Point Finger Rd., Paget Parish,* ☎
441/236–4201 botanic garden, 441/292–5501 Camden House. ⊠ *Free.*
☉ *Botanic garden daily dawn–dusk, Camden House Tues. and Fri.
noon–2.*

★ ⑥⓪ **Carter House.** Christopher Carter, one of three men left behind when
the *Deliverance* and the *Patience* sailed for Jamestown in 1610, was
offered St. David's Island in 1612 as a reward for revealing the "Ambergris Plot." Before the ships returned to Bermuda, it seems, one of
the three men, Edward Chard, found 80 pounds of ambergris (a pre-
cious sperm-whale product used for perfumes) washed up on the
beach. In collusion with Carter and another man, Chard planned to
smuggle the ambergris off the island (when a ship arrived) and sell it
in London at enormous profit. At the last minute, however, Carter
squealed on his coconspirators to Governor Moore, who had arrived
in 1612 with new settlers. Instead of St. David's Island, Carter opted
for Cooper's Island, which is also now part of the naval base. Built by
Carter's descendants in 1640, Carter House is one of the oldest houses
in Bermuda. The stone-and-cedar house has been refurbished with new
floors and period furnishings, including a 17th-century bedding chest,
a mortar and pestle, and an 18th-century tavern table. At press time,
because of the closing of the Naval Air Station, on whose grounds the
house sits, the house was closed, and its future was uncertain. Ms. Florence Lins, a volunteer caretaker of the house, keeps up with devel-
opments and is happy to answer questions about it. ⊠ *On grounds of
former U.S. Naval Air Station, St. David's Island, St. George's Parish;
call Florence Lins,* ☎ *441/297–1376.*

⑥⑦ **Castle Island.** According to an oft-told tale, two Spanish ships appeared
outside the channel in 1613 and attempted to attack the colony. Two
shots were fired from the fort: One fell into the water, and the other
hit one of the ship's hulls. The Spaniards fled, unaware that the fortress
had expended two-thirds of its stock of ammunition—the colonists had
less than a barrel of gunpowder and only one cannonball left. ⊠
Smith's Parish.

⑦⑧ **Christ Church.** This one-story gray-stone church with four soaring towers was built in 1719. It is reputedly the oldest Presbyterian house of
worship in any British colony or dominion. Services are held Sunday.
⊠ *Devonshire Parish.*

⑦⑤ **Clermont.** Bermuda's first tennis court was on the grounds of the imposing house, also noted for its fine woodwork, that was once the residence of Sir Brownlow Gray, Chief Justice of Bermuda. During a visit
from New York in 1874, Miss Mary Outerbridge learned to play here.
Upon her return to the United States, she asked the Staten Island
Cricket Club to build a court; armed with her racquet and a book of

THE BERMUDA RAILWAY

From the collection of Colin A. Pomeroy

THE HISTORY of the Bermuda Railway is as fascinating as it is brief. Along with horse-drawn carriages, boats, and bicycles, Old Rattle and Shake was the primary means of transportation on the island from 1931 to 1948. As early as 1899, the Bermuda Public Works Department bandied about proposals for a railroad. In 1922, over the objections of livery stable owners, the Bermuda Parliament finally granted permission for a standard-gauge line to run from Somerset to St. George's.

The laying of the tracks was a formidable undertaking, requiring the construction of long tunnels and swing bridges. By the time it was finished, the railway had cost investors $1 million. Mile for mile it was the most expensive railroad ever built, and the construction, which proceeded at a somnolent 2½ miles per year, was the slowest ever recorded. Finally, on October 31, 1931, the little train got its roaring start with festive opening ceremonies at Somerset Bridge.

First-class passengers sat in wicker chairs; second-class cars were outfitted with benches. An American visitor reported in glowing terms of her first train ride in Bermuda, waxing lyrical about rolling cedar-covered hills, green velvet lawns, and banks of pink oleanders. Certainly, it was a vast improvement over the 19th-century horse buses that lumbered from Somerset to St. George's, carrying freight as well as passengers. Not everyone was happy, however. One writer groused that the train was "an iron serpent in the Garden of Eden."

Old Rattle and Shake began going downhill during World War II. Military personnel on the island put the train to hard use, and it proved impossible to obtain the necessary maintenance equipment. At the end of the war, the government acquired the distressed railway for $115,000. Automobiles came to Bermuda in 1946, and train service ended in 1948, when the government sold the railway in its entirety to British Guiana (now Guyana).

Today's secluded, 18-mile Bermuda Railway Trail runs the length of the island along the route of the old Bermuda Railway. Restricted to pedestrians, horseback riders, and cyclists, the trail is a delightful way to see the island, away from the traffic and noise of the main roads. The Bermuda Department of Tourism's "The Bermuda Railway Trail Guide," available at all Visitors Service Bureaus, includes seven walking tours, ranging from about two to four hours, and an outline of what you can expect to see along the way. (For more information about sights along the way, turn to the "Off Bermuda's Beaten Track" portrait *in* Chapter 9.) Note that many of the trails are isolated, and none is heavily trafficked. Although Bermuda has no major crime problem, unpleasant incidents can occur; women travelers especially should avoid striking out on remote trails alone. Apart from reasons of safety, the Railway Trail is much more enjoyable shared with a companion.

rules, she introduced tennis to America. This house is not open to the public. ⊠ *On Harbour Rd. (to left as you head west), Paget Parish, between Lovers and Highwood Las.*

62 **Crystal Caves.** In 1907, while playing ball, two boys made a startling discovery. When the ball disappeared down a hole, the boys burrowed after it and found themselves in a vast cavern 120 ft underground, surrounded by fantastic stalagmite and stalactite formations. Today, the approach is along a wet, sloping walkway and a wooden pontoon bridge across the underground lake. After explaining the formation of stalactites and stalagmites, a tour guide uses a lighting system to make silhouettes. People who suffer from claustrophobia will probably want to skip the caves, as space can be quite tight. ⊠ *8 Crystal Caves Rd., off Wilkinson Ave., Hamilton Parish,* ☎ *441/293–0640.* ☞ *$4.* ⊘ *Apr.–Oct., daily 9:30–4:30; Nov.–Mar., daily 9:30–3:30.*

68 **Devil's Hole Aquarium.** In 1830, a Mr. Trott built a wall around his fish pond—manifestly to prevent people from fishing in it—and, naturally, was besieged with questions about what he was hiding. In 1843, yielding to the curiosity of the Bermudians, Mr. Trott permitted people to view his fish pond—for a fee. These days, the deep pool contains about 400 sea creatures, including giant grouper, sharks, and huge turtles. You can play at fishing, using baited—but hookless—lines. ⊠ *Harrington Sound Rd., Smith's Parish,* ☎ *441/293–2072.* ☞ *$7.* ⊘ *Daily 10–4:30.*

51 **Flatts Village.** One of the earliest settlements on the island, Flatts occasionally hosted the House of Assembly, although much of the village's activities involved flouting the law rather than making it. Hoping to avoid customs officers, Bermudians returning from the West Indies would sometimes sail into the village in the dead of night to unload their cargoes. ⊠ *Smith's Parish.*

★ **58** **Ft. St. Catherine.** Apart from Dockyard, this restored fortress is the most impressive on the island. It has enough cannons, tunnels, and ramparts to satisfy the most avid military historian. One of a host of fortifications constructed in St. George's, the original fort was begun around 1613. It was remodeled and enlarged at least five times, and work continued on it until late in the 19th century. As you travel through the tunnels, you'll come across some startlingly lifelike figures tucked into niches. Several dioramas depict the island's development, and an audiovisual presentation describes the building and significance of the fort. There is also a small but elaborate display of replicas of the Crown jewels of England. ⊠ *Barry Rd., St. George's Parish,* ☎ *441/297–1920.* ☞ *$2.50.* ⊘ *Daily 10–4.*

57 **Gates Fort.** St. George's has always had the greatest concentration of fortifications on the island. Gates Fort is a reconstruction of a small militia fort dating from the 1620s. Don't expect turrets, towers, and tunnels, however; there is little to see here apart from the sea. The fort and Gates Bay, which it overlooks, were named for Sir Thomas Gates, the first of the survivors of the *Sea Venture* to reach dry land. Upon doing so, he is reputed to have shouted, "This is Gates, his bay!" Public speaking was obviously not his forte, although Gates was by profession a politician—he later became governor of Virginia. ⊠ *Cut Rd., St. George's Parish, no phone.* ☞ *Free.* ⊘ *Daily 10–4.*

★ **80** **Gibbs Hill Lighthouse.** The second cast-iron lighthouse ever built soars above Southampton Parish. Designed in London and opened in 1846, the tower stands 117 ft high and 362 ft above the sea. Originally the light was produced by a concentrated burner of four large, circular wicks. Today, the beam from the 1,000-watt bulb can be seen by ships 40 mi

In case you want to see the world.

At American Express, we're here to make your journey a smooth one. So we have over 1,700 travel service locations in over 120 countries ready to help. What else would you expect from the world's largest travel agency?

do more

AMERICAN EXPRESS

http://www.americanexpress.com/travel

Travel

In case you want to be welcomed there.

We're here to see that you're always welcomed at establishments everywhere. That's why millions of people carry the American Express® Card – for peace of mind, confidence, and security, around the world or just around the corner.

do more

AMERICAN EXPRESS

Cards

In case you're running low.

We're here to help with more than 118,000 Express Cash locations around the world. In order to enroll, just call American Express before you start your vacation.

do more

And just in case.

We're here with American Express® Travelers Cheques and Cheques *for Two*.® They're the safest way to carry money on your vacation and the surest way to get a refund, practically anywhere, anytime. Another way we help you...

do more

AMERICAN
EXPRESS

Travelers
Cheques

out to sea, and by planes 120 mi away at 10,000 ft. You can climb to the top of the lighthouse, although this is not a trip for anyone who suffers from vertigo. It's a long haul up 185 spiral stairs, but you can stop to catch your breath at platforms along the way, where photographs and drawings of the lighthouse are displayed. At the top you can stroll on the balcony for a spectacular view of Bermuda, but the wind may snatch you bald-headed, and the tower is known to sway in high winds. ✉ *Lighthouse Rd., Southampton Parish,* ☎ *441/238–0524.* 🎫 *$2.* ⏲ *Daily 9–4:30.*

NEED A BREAK? A charming place to relax and take in the island vistas is the **Lighthouse Tea Room** (☎ 441/238–8679) in the Gibbs Hill Lighthouse keeper's cottage. A selection of tasty sweet cakes and a lineup of imported English pasties, meat pies, and sausage rolls are all satisfying choices for breakfast, lunch, or afternoon tea.

㊼ **Government House.** Overlooking North Shore Road, Black Watch Well, and the sea, the residence of the governor is not open to the public. The 45 acres of land were purchased when the capital was transferred from St. George's to Hamilton in 1815. A simple two-story house served as the governor's home until the present, rather austere mansion was completed in 1892. Various royals and other distinguished visitors planted the trees and shrubs on the pretty, landscaped lawns. Among the guests who have been entertained in Government House were Sir Winston Churchill, President Kennedy, and, more recently, Queen Elizabeth II and Prince Philip, Prince Charles, Margaret Thatcher, and George Bush. The mansion was also the scene of the 1973 assassination of Governor Richard Sharples and his aide, Captain Hugh Sayers. ✉ *Pembroke Parish.*

(54) **Holy Trinity Church.** Built in 1623 as one long room with a thatched roof, Holy Trinity is said to be the oldest Anglican church on Bermuda. The church has been much embellished over the past 372 years, but the original building remains at its core. The small graveyard is encircled by palms, royal poinciana, and cherry trees. ✉ *Church Bay, Harrington Sound, Hamilton Parish, no phone.* ⏲ *Open to public for services only.*

(64) **Leamington Caves.** An amber-tinted Statue of Liberty is among the fanciful formations of stalagmites and stalactites, though by and large these caves are smaller and less impressive than Crystal Caves. Aboveground, the Plantation restaurant (☞ Chapter 4) serves some of the island's best food—worth a trip whether you visit the caves or not. If you have lunch at the Plantation, a meal of $10 or more will gain you entry to the caves. ✉ *Harrington Sound Rd., Hamilton Parish,* ☎ *441/293–1188.* 🎫 *$4.* ⏲ *Mid-Feb.–late Nov., Mon.–Sat. 10–4.*

(66) **Natural Arches.** Carved over the centuries by the wind and ocean, two limestone arches rise 35 ft above the beach. Look for the signs pointing to Castle Harbour Beach and the Natural Arches near the end of South Shore Road. ✉ *Smith's Parish.*

(72) **Old Devonshire Church.** A church has stood on this site since 1612, although the original was replaced in 1716. That replacement church was almost wholly destroyed in an explosion on Easter Sunday in 1970, and the present church is a faithful reconstruction. A small, simple building of limestone and cedar, it looks much like an early Bermuda cottage. The three-tier pulpit, the pews, and the communion table are believed to be from the original church. Some pieces of church silver date back to 1590 and are said to be the oldest on the island. A cedar chest, believed to have once held the church records, dates from the early 17th century. Other pieces that have survived include an old cedar

armchair, a candelabra, a cross, and a cedar screen. ⊠ *Middle Rd., Devonshire Parish,* ☎ *441/236–3671.* 🎟 *Free.* ☉ *Daily 9–5:30.*

㉒ Overplus Lane. The name of this lane harks back to the 17th century when Richard Norwood divided the island into shares and tribes. He allotted 25 acres to each share, and 50 shares to each tribe. When the survey was completed, 200 acres (too small to form a tribe) remained unallotted and were listed as "overplus." Governor Tucker directed the surveyor to keep an eye peeled for an attractive chunk of territory that could be designated as the surplus land. Norwood recommended a piece of real estate in the western part of the island, whereupon the governor claimed it and built a fine house on it. Upon hearing of the governor's action, the Bermuda Company lodged a complaint, forcing Tucker to return to London to sort everything out. The surplus land was eventually divided into seven parts, with Tucker retaining the section on which his house sat; the remainder was given to the church. ⊠ *Sandys Parish.*

㉗ Paget Marsh. Protected by the Bermuda National Trust, this lovely marsh contains cedars and palmettos, endangered plants, and a mangrove swamp. ⊠ *Middle Rd., Paget Parish,* ☎ *441/236–6483.*

★ **㉑ Palm Grove.** On the grounds of this private estate, there is a pond within which is a relief map of the island—each parish is divided by carefully manicured grass sections. Desmond Fountain statues stand around the edge, peering into the pond's depths. ⊠ *South Shore Rd., across from Brighton Hill, Smith's Parish, no phone.* 🎟 *Free.* ☉ *Mon.–Thurs. 9–5.*

㊿ Palmetto House. In the 18th century, when this cruciform house was built, cross-shaped houses were thought to ward off evil spirits. Three rooms, furnished in period antiques, can be see on a house tour. The house is now owned by the Bermuda National Trust and is open to the public on a limited basis. In **Palmetto Park,** you can pick up one of the North Shore stretches of the Railway Trail. ⊠ *North Shore Rd., Devonshire Parish,* ☎ *441/236–6483.* 🎟 *Free.* ☉ *Call for hrs.*

㊾ Railway Museum and Curiosity Shop. The old Aquarium Station of the island's erstwhile standard-gauge railroad houses a tiny museum cluttered with photos, signs, wicker chairs from the first-class compartment, and other memorabilia. "Old Rattle and Shake," as the railway was known, is so fondly remembered by Bermudians you'll wonder why the line was shut down. Rarely shown footage of the railway in operation was recently installed. ⊠ *37 North Shore Rd., Hamilton Parish,* ☎ *441/293–1774.* 🎟 *Free (donations accepted).* ☉ *Weekdays 10–4 and some Sat.; ring bell and curator will let you in if she's home.*

㊱ St. David's Lighthouse. Built in 1879 of Bermuda stone and occupying the highest point on Bermuda's eastern end, the lighthouse rises 208 ft above the sea. Although only about half the height of Gibbs Hill Lighthouse in Southampton Parish, it nevertheless has spectacular views: From the balcony you can see St. David's and St. George's, Castle Harbour, and the reef-fringed south shore. The lighthouse is not always open; check with the Department of Agriculture and Fisheries (☎ *441/236–4201*) for hours. ⊠ *St. George's Parish.*

NEED A
BREAK?

Right on the water near St. David's Lighthouse, the **Black Horse Tavern** (⊠ Clarkes Hill, ☎ 441/293-9742) is a casual spot that's popular with locals. Seafood is the specialty, fish sandwiches are delicious, and shark hash and curried conch stew are also on the menu. There are outdoor picnic tables as well as indoor dining. It's closed Monday.

45 **St. John's Church.** The first church on this site was built in 1621; the present church was consecrated in 1826 as the parish church of Pembroke. During a funeral in 1875, the churchyard was the scene of a verbal duel between the Anglican rector and a Wesleyan minister. The Anglican church insisted that all burial services in parish churchyards be conducted by the rector, but the Wesleyans challenged the church in the case of a deceased woman named Esther Levy. Claiming he'd been asked by her friends to perform the funeral service, a Wesleyan minister appeared in the churchyard despite the efforts of the Anglican rector to stop him. Simultaneous services were held over poor Mrs. Levy's body, with the minister and the adamant Anglican trying to outshout each other. The rector subsequently filed charges of trespassing against the Wesleyan, and the celebrated case went before the Supreme Court. The jury found for the rector, and fined the minister one shilling. ⊠ *St. John's Rd., Pembroke Parish,* ☎ *441/292-0299.* ▣ *Free.* ☉ *Daily 8–5:30.*

76 **St. Paul's Church.** Around the turn of the century, the "Paget Ghost" began to be heard in and around St. Paul's. Nothing could be seen, but the mysterious sound of tinkling bells was plainly audible, coming from several directions. The ghost became quite famous, and a veritable posse—armed with firearms and clubs—gathered to find it; vendors even set up refreshment stands. Finally, a visiting American scientist proclaimed that the tinkling sound came from a rare bird, the fililo. According to the scientist, the fililo was a natural ventriloquist, which explained why the sound jumped around. No one ever saw the fililo, however, and no one saw the ghost either—it disappeared as mysteriously as it had materialized. The present church was built in 1796 to replace an earlier church on this site. ⊠ *Middle Rd., Paget Parish,* ☎ *441/236-5880.* ▣ *Free.* ☉ *Weekdays 8–4:30, Sat. by appointment, Sun. 7:30–1.*

48 **Spanish Point.** The survivors of the wrecked *Sea Venture* thought they found evidence here of an earlier visit by the Spanish. Apparently they were right: Historians now believe that Captain Diego Ramirez landed here in 1603. There is a small park for picnicking, a sheltered bay for swimming, public facilities, and a lovely view of Somerset across the sound. Here you can also see the remains of a 19th-century floating dock from Dockyard, which looks a bit like a dinosaur's skeleton. Unfortunately, some rather seedy characters hang out here, so do not come alone. In summer, lots of people camp here, and the noise level can be far from peaceful. Cobbler's Island, across Cobbler's Cut from Spanish Point, has a grisly history—executed slaves were exhibited here as a warning to others of the consequences of disobedience. ⊠ *Pembroke Parish.*

★ **69** **Spittal Pond.** A showcase of the Bermuda National Trust, this nature park has 60 acres you can roam, although you're requested to keep to the walkways. More than 25 species of waterfowl winter here between November and May. On a high bluff overlooking the ocean, Spanish Rock stands out as an oddity. Early settlers found a rock crudely carved with the date 1543 and other markings that were unclear. It is now believed that a Portuguese ship was wrecked on the island in 1543, and that her sailors built a new ship on which they departed. The carvings are thought to be the initials RP (for *Rex Portugaline,* King of Portugal), and the cross to be a badge of the Portuguese Order of Christ. The rock was removed to prevent further damage by erosion, and the site is marked by a bronze casting of the original carving. A plaster-of-paris cast of the Spanish Rock is also on display at the Bermuda Historical Society Museum in Hamilton. ⊠ *South Shore Rd., Smith's Parish, no phone.* ▣ *Free.* ☉ *Daily dawn–dusk.*

⑤⑨ Tobacco Bay. In 1775, gunpowder bound for Boston was secretly loaded on this bay (☞ Tucker House *in* the Town of St. George, *above*). Nowadays there are changing facilities and a refreshment stand on its fine beach. Nearby St. Catherine's Beach is a pleasant place for a swim and quiet contemplation of the events of July 28, 1609. ⊠ *St. George's Parish.*

⑥③ Tom Moore's Tavern. Now a popular restaurant, the house was originally the home of Samuel Trott, who constructed it in the 17th century and named it Walsingham. (The harbor nearby was named for Robert Walsingham, a sailor on the *Sea Venture* who apparently became enamored of the bay.) The house is surrounded by woods that are much the same as they were three centuries ago. When Tom Moore, the Irish poet, arrived in Bermuda in 1804, the house was occupied by a descendant of the original owner (also named Samuel Trott) and his family. The Trotts befriended the poet, who became a frequent visitor to the house. In Epistle V, Moore immortalized the Trott Estate's Calabash Tree, under which he liked to write his verses. In 1844, the idea for the Royal Bermuda Yacht Club (☞ *above*) was conceived under the very same tree. ⊠ *Walsingham La. and Harrington Sound Rd., Hamilton Parish,* ☎ *441/293–8020.*

⑥⑤ Tucker's Town. In 1616, Governor Daniel Tucker, for whom the town was named, wanted to abandon St. George's in favor of a new settlement here on the shores of Castle Harbour. A few streets were laid out and some cottages were built, but the plan was eventually shelved. For 300 years Tucker's Town remained a small fishing and farming community; cotton was grown for a while, and a few whaling boats operated from here. Dramatic change overtook the community soon after World War I, however. Seeking to raise the island's appeal in order to attract passengers on its luxury liners to Bermuda, a steamship company called Furness, Withy & Co. purchased a large area of Tucker's Town for a new country club. The result was the exclusive Mid Ocean Club, with its fine golf course; the Castle Harbour Resort, now run by Marriott, adjoins the club. Members of the club started building residences nearby, and the Tucker's Town boom began. Today, only members of the club can buy a house in the area, and private residences have been known to sell for more than $3 million. ⊠ *Smith's Parish.*

★ ⑦⓪ Verdmont. It may have been prominent shipowner John Dickinson who built this house around 1710. At the end of the War of Independence, Verdmont was the home of John Green, an American Loyalist who fled to Bermuda from Philadelphia. Green married the stepdaughter of Dickinson's granddaughter Elizabeth, and he was appointed judge of the Court of Vice Admiralty. Green was also a portrait painter, and the family portraits by him remain in the house. The house resembles a small English manor house and has an unusual double roof and four large chimneys—each of the eight rooms has its own fireplace. Elegant cornice moldings and paneled shutters grace the two large reception rooms downstairs, originally the drawing room and formal dining room. The sash windows reflect a style that was fashionable in English manors.

Although it contains none of the original furnishings, Verdmont is a treasure house of Bermudiana. Some of the furniture is mahogany imported from England—there is an exquisite early 19th-century piano—but most of it is fine 18th-century cedar, crafted by Bermuda cabinetmakers. In particular, notice the desk in the drawing room, the lid and sides of which are made of single planks. Also displayed in the house is a china coffee service, said to have been a gift from Napoleon to President Madison. The president never received it: The ship bearing it across the Atlantic was seized by a Bermudian privateer and brought to Bermuda. Look carefully, too, at the handmade cedar staircase, with its handsomely turned newels and posts. The newel posts on each landing have removable caps to accommodate candles in the evening. Upstairs is a nursery: It's easy to imagine a child at play with the antique toys or napping in the cedar cradle. The last occupant of Verdmont was an eccentric woman who lived here for 75 years without installing electricity or any other modern trappings. After her death, her family sold the house to the Bermuda Historic Monuments Trust—the forerunner of the Bermuda National Trust—which opened it as a museum in 1956. ⊠ *Collector's Hill, Smith's Parish,* ☎ *441/236–7369.* ⊠ *$3; $5 combination ticket allows admission to Bermuda National Trust Museum and Tucker House in St. George's.* ⊙ *Tues.–Sat. 10–4.*

NEED A BREAK?	The popular **Speciality Inn** (⊠ South Shore Rd., foot of Collector's Hill, ☎ 441/236-3133) is a simple place that serves pasta, pizza, sandwiches, soups, shakes, ice cream, and good breakfasts.

㉛ Whale Bay Fort. Overgrown with grass, flowers, and subtropical plants, this small, 19th-century battery offers little in the way of a history lesson, but it does overlook a secluded pink-sand beach, gin-clear water, and craggy cliffs. The beach is accessible only on foot, but it's a splendid place for a swim. Bear in mind that you have to climb back up the hill to your moped or bike. ⊠ *In Southampton Parish, turn off Middle Rd. to Whale Bay Rd.; road ends and fort is at bottom of steep hill in Sandys Parish.*

4 Dining

In moments of candor, islanders will confide that Bermudian cuisine is really a collection of dishes showing English, American, and West Indian influences. But whatever the origins of the recipes, the island's cuisine begins and ends with Bermudian ingredients—and therein lies the island's culinary identity. Still, dining on the island is for the most part non-Bermudian, which you'll find when you step into a local French café or Japanese sushi bar.

WITH ABOUT 150 RESTAURANTS from which to choose—nearly seven per square mile—you will have little trouble gaining those few extra holiday pounds. Italian cuisine predominates, but there are also Indian, Greek, Chinese, English, French, and Mexican restaurants within walking distance of one another in the island's capital. Much harder to swallow than the average spoonful of fish chowder, though, are the prices. Bermuda has never tried to gain a reputation for affordability, and restaurateurs haven't sought to change that. There are the odd greasy spoons that serve up standard North American fare for a decent price, but by and large you should prepare for something of a shock when perusing the bills of fare.

What you won't find on Bermuda are McDonald's, Burger King, or any of their ilk—for now. Apart from a lone Kentucky Fried Chicken outlet, which snuck in several years ago, the fast-food chains have been barred by Bermuda's government. That might change in the next couple of years. After Bermuda's last premier, Sir John Swan, saw his independence plans rejected in a referendum, he resigned, promptly applied for, and was given permission to, open a McDonald's outlet. Though it won't become a reality for at least a while, many fear it will be the "foot in the door." At press time, rumors of a Taco Bell were swirling around the island.

Ironically, true Bermudian cuisine is nearly as elusive as a rumor. Dishes that pass for "local" are generally variations on standards one finds throughout the islands—conch stew, fish chowder, and the like—although Bermuda's mussel pie is found practically nowhere else in the islands. That doesn't make them any less delicious, however. Local fish is usually available—try it panfried and topped with local bananas fried in black rum—and Bermuda spiny lobster, seasonally available from September through March, is succulent. Other must-tries are fish chowder laced with locally brewed sherry peppers and dark rum, available at most restaurants; shark hash, for which a trip to the Black Horse Tavern in St. David's is called for; and codfish and potato breakfast—boiled salt cod served with boiled potatoes, egg, and topped with tomato sauce, banana, and avocado slices. Try the Halfway House in Flatts Village for this Sunday morning favorite.

Dining in Bermuda is typically expensive. Don't be surprised if dinner for two at one of the very top places—the Newport Room or Fourways Inn, for example—puts a $200–$300 dent in your pocket. And a 15% service charge is almost always added to the bill "for your convenience." Between the Newport Room and the KFC, there are a myriad of dining opportunities and some truly innovative menus. And many lodgings offer a choice of meal plans, which can provide significant savings (☞ Chapter 5). Be sure to ask about these when booking your room.

As with most things in Bermuda, dining tends to be rather formal. For men, jackets won't ever be out of place and are required in most upscale restaurants. Credit cards are generally accepted, though some smaller taverns and lunch spots take only cash and traveler's checks.

CATEGORY	COST*
$$$$	over $50
$$$	$35–$50
$$	$20–$35
$	under $20

per person, excluding drinks and service (a 15% service charge is sometimes added)

HAMILTON

Asian

$$ ✕ Bombay Bicycle Club. The culinary scene of any British colony would be woefully incomplete without a curry house. Named after a private gentlemen's club in the waning days of the Raj, this burgundy-hued restaurant captures the flavor of the subcontinent without becoming a caricature. All the traditional Indian favorites are offered here and prepared remarkably well. Order the *peeaz pakora* (onion fritters) and mulligatawny soup as starters; then opt for the *jhinga vindaloo* (shrimp in hot curry), *mutton saagwala* (braised lamb in creamy spinach), or anything from the clay tandoor oven. *Nan, paratha,* and *papadum* are terrific breads and snacks to accompany the meal. Ask about the discounted dinner menus, or stop by on a weekday for the $11.95 buffet lunch. Takeout is available. ⊠ *Reid St., Hamilton,* ☎ *441/292–0048 or 441/292–8865. AE, DC, MC, V.*

$$ ✕ Chopsticks. An alternative to New Queen (☞ *below*) at the east end of Hamilton, this Chinese restaurant features an intelligent mix of Szechuan, Hunan, and Cantonese favorites. Chef Luk's best Chinese selections include jumbo shrimp with vegetables in black bean sauce, hoisin hot chicken, and lemon chicken. Thai chefs bring a taste of their home country, with such favorites as *Pla Pae Sa* (boneless fish fillet steamed on a bed of cabbage and celery with ginger, sweet pepper, scallions, red chilies, and cilantro) and beef *Panang* (cooked in coconut sauce, curry paste, and lime leaves). All dishes are made to order, people with special diets can specify exactly what they want, and MSG can be omitted. Specially priced dinner menus are available for $15.50 or $21.95, plus gratuities, during the low season from November through March. Takeout is available. ⊠ *Reid St. E, Hamilton,* ☎ *441/292–0791. MC, V.*

$$ ✕ New Queen. This Chinese restaurant is an old favorite of Bermudians, who flock here for the hot and spicy fare. The emphasis is on the food rather than the decor, but the interior is attractive, clean, and subdued. Try the Szechuan duck, steamed until tender, then pressed with black mushrooms and potato flour, deep-fried, and served with a peppery mushroom sauce. Another great choice is *wor suit* chicken—boneless chicken pressed with minced meat, lightly battered and fried, and served on a bed of vegetables. Takeout is available. ⊠ *Par-la-Ville Rd., Hamilton,* ☎ *441/295–4004 or 441/292–3282. AE, DC, MC, V.*

Bermudian

$ ✕ MacWilliams. When you're shopping in Hamilton and you're hit with the hungries, consider this no-frills eatery for delicious homestyle cooking. From short ribs and macaroni and cheese to barbecued chicken and peas and rice, from lasagna to fried shrimps and scallops, it's all here—the kind of food you'd find in the home of a Bermudian. Breakfast brings fluffy omelets and blueberry or strawberry pancakes, and Sunday brunch means you can order that local institution, the Bermuda codfish breakfast. ⊠ *Pitts Bay Road, Hamilton,* ☎ *441/295 5759. AE, MC, V.*

British

$$ ✕ Colony Pub. A favorite meeting place for some of Hamilton's business and government communities, this cozy steak house is one place where you can gain an understanding of how Bermuda works. Tourists are readily accepted by the lunching locals, although more as honored

Hamilton Dining

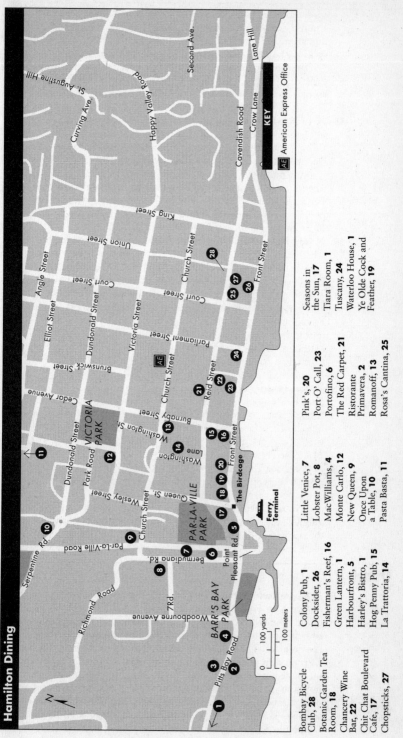

KEY

AE American Express Office

Bombay Bicycle Club, **28**
Botanic Garden Tea Room, **18**
Chancery Wine Bar, **22**
Chit Chat Boulevard Cafe, **17**
Chopsticks, **27**

Colony Pub, **1**
Docksider, **26**
Fisherman's Reef, **16**
Green Lantern, **1**
Harbourfront, **5**
Harley's Bistro, **1**
Hog Penny Pub, **15**
La Trattoria, **14**

Little Venice, **7**
Lobster Pot, **8**
MacWilliams, **4**
Monte Carlo, **12**
New Queen, **9**
Once Upon a Table, **10**
Pasta Basta, **11**

Pink's, **20**
Port O' Call, **23**
Portofino, **6**
The Red Carpet, **21**
Ristorante Primavera, **2**
Romanoff, **13**
Rosa's Cantina, **25**

Seasons in the Sun, **17**
Tiara Room, **1**
Tuscany, **24**
Waterloo House, **1**
Ye Olde Cock and Feather, **19**

spectators than participants. Part of the Princess Hotel, the pub is redolent of Britain and the history of this tiny island. Rich shades of brown and green and plenty of polished brass give the place a clublike atmosphere. The meat-oriented menu features locker-aged Angus steaks and USDA prime roast rib of beef. The 10-ounce salmon fillet promises to satisfy fish lovers. For lighter fare, start with the fresh fruit plate with sorbet, then follow it up with the daily pasta special. ⊠ *Princess Hotel, Hamilton,* ☎ *441/295–3000. AE, DC, MC, V.*

$$ ✕ **Ye Olde Cock and Feather.** One of the busiest spots along Front Street in Hamilton, this is a favorite meeting place for locals. Patrons sit either in a room that is a cross between a British pub and a Key West–style tropical outpost or on the upstairs balcony overlooking the harbor. Food is served pub-style, but the eclectic menu spans several cuisines and continents, from Portuguese red bean soup to steak-and-kidney pie to the Bermuda Triangle: fish, chicken, and cream cheese with jalapeño peppers. Live entertainment is featured nightly April through November. ⊠ *Front St., Hamilton,* ☎ *441/295–2263. MC, V.*

$–$$ ✕ **Hog Penny Pub.** Veterans of a London pub crawl might wonder whether, in fact, they did cross the Atlantic when they arrive in this atmospheric watering hole off Front Street. Die-hard aficionados of British cooking (if such animals actually exist) will be rewarded with Yorkshire pudding, shepherd's pie, steak-and-kidney pie, steak in ale, and bangers and mash (sausages and mashed potatoes). There's even a small sampling of curries. You'll find good fun as well as good food in this dark, cozy den, where sunburned strangers mingle freely and entertainment is offered nightly. Once a thickly smoky place, the Hog Penny Pub has markedly improved its ventilation. ⊠ *Burnaby Hill, Hamilton,* ☎ *441/292–2534. AE, DC, MC, V.*

$ ✕ **Botanic Garden Tea Room.** One of Bermuda's most pleasant traditions is afternoon tea at Trimingham's department store in Hamilton. A good place to escape the shopping scene, the tea room also serves light lunches. Look for crab, tuna, or chicken salad, large-bun sandwiches, lasagna, and fruit plates. ⊠ *Front St., Hamilton,* ☎ *441/295–1183. No credit cards.*

$ ✕ **Docksider.** This Front Street hangout claims to have the widest selection of draft beers on the island, which says a lot about its priorities and those of its young clientele. However, that's no reason to steer clear of the fish-and-chips or the hamburgers. The club sandwiches are a good bet, too, although taste just won't matter once you've drunk your way through the bar's array of European brews. Frequented by locals, it's a popular place at night. ⊠ *Front St., Hamilton,* ☎ *441/292-4088. AE, MC, V.*

French

$–$$ ✕ **Monte Carlo.** Some of Bermuda's best meals are served at this cheerful southern French restaurant behind City Hall in Hamilton. Beams of old Bermuda cedar add local color to the many copied Impressionist works painted on the walls and china and copper pans hanging over the fireplace. The lunchtime pasta selection is broad, but the emphasis is on a sprightly collection of hot and cold appetizers—fresh tuna marinated in oil and herbs of Provence and served with caper sauce is outstanding, as are sautéed scallops served with spinach and a light orange sauce. For dinner, favorite entrées include bouillabaisse Marseillaise—a feast of fish and shellfish in a delicious broth—and veal scaloppine Riviera served with sun-dried tomatoes, roast peppers, and sweet Vermouth. A special lighter menu (with lighter prices) includes pasta, gourmet pizza, vegetable lasagna, and crepes. The dessert trolley has wonderful cakes and outstanding *tiramisù.* ⊠ *Victoria St., Hamilton,* ☎ *441/295–5453 or 441/295–5442. AE, MC, V.*

$$$ ✕ **Waterloo House.** A private house a century ago, this restaurant and small hotel on Hamilton Harbour serves Bermudian and Continental cuisine. You can dine either on the waterside patio or in the elegant dining room, where deep raspberry walls, rich chintzes, and elegant sconces set the mood. The restaurant usually offers a daily special or two, but don't overlook the menu items, especially the appetizer of delicately seasoned snails served inside new potatoes, the lobster salad, and the tender lamb. Service is outstanding. ⊠ *Pitts Bay Rd., Pembroke, Hamilton,* ☎ *441/295–4480. Jacket and tie. AE, MC, V.*

International

$$$$ ✕ **Tiara Room.** This gourmet restaurant in Bermuda's historic Princess Hotel (☞ Chapter 5) has honed the art of serving fine Continental cuisine with a theatrical flair. The dining room has a fresh look, with clean lines and bright colors (mostly mauve), but the highlight remains the stunning view of Hamilton Harbour. Whenever possible, dishes are finished table-side, often flambéed dramatically. Rack of lamb is always an excellent choice, likewise cherries Jubilee. ⊠ *Princess Hotel, Hamilton,* ☎ *441/295–3000. Jacket and tie. AE, DC, MC, V.*

$$$ ✕ **Harbourfront.** Few eateries on Front Street have as much variety as this busy one, where sushi is served alongside Continental and Mediterranean specialties. Sit on the porch or at a table behind the large glass doors and watch the action along Front Street and the harbor as you choose from the extensive menu. At lunchtime, this is the place to come for a good burger or salad. For dinner, start with fried calamari or carpaccio, or calamari followed by lobster, rack of lamb, or any of the excellent pastas. The small sushi bar is worth trying. ⊠ *Front St., Hamilton,* ☎ *441/295–4207. AE, DC, MC, V.*

$$$ ✕ **Once Upon a Table.** Hailed by many Bermudians as the island's finest restaurant, this 18th-century island house, complete with fine china and crystal, is distinctly romantic, with an abundance of pretty flowers and Victorian memorabilia. From the menu, consider the rack of lamb, roast duckling, or grilled fresh yellowfin tuna with tomato confit, spring onions, and dill. A fixed-price menu, featuring local specialty items for $43 to $46.50, includes an appetizer, entrée, dessert, and coffee. For instance, the Sunday night fixed menu offers fish chowder, conch stew, mussels, fish, curried conch, green paw paw (papaya) pie, and loquat ice cream. Low-cholesterol dishes are always available. ⊠ *Serpentine Rd., Hamilton,* ☎ *441/295–8585. Jacket required. AE, DC, MC, V. No lunch.*

$$$ ✕ **Romanoff.** Elegant European meals served in a theatrical Russian setting are the specialty of this restaurant run by Anton Duzevic. Deep-red walls decorated with faux-naif landscape paintings provide a dramatic backdrop for the vodka and black caviar that Duzevic himself presents to each diner. Stick to the well-known dishes or select a seafood special from the cart that is wheeled around the tables. ⊠ *Church St., Hamilton,* ☎ *441/295–0333. Reservations essential. Jacket and tie. AE, DC, MC, V.*

$$ ✕ **Chancery Wine Bar.** Though the menu here changes monthly, it is always among the island's most innovative. This spot is a perennial favorite with locals, particularly at lunchtime—when workers head for the umbrella-topped outdoor tables in an enclosed, white-gravel-covered courtyard. Inside, there's a wine-cellarlike room with a vaulted ceiling, and the upstairs wine bar serves some excellent wines by the glass. ⊠ *Chancery La., off Front St., Hamilton,* ☎ *441/295–5058. Reservations essential. AE, MC, V.*

$$ ✕ **The Red Carpet.** This tiny restaurant is very popular at lunch, especially among local politicians and businesspeople who flock here to savor the traditional yet creatively prepared Italian and French fare. The clever use of mirrors creates an illusion of space, while plentiful brass gives the place a stylish look. Among the culinary highlights are veal, fish dishes, and tortellini stuffed with veal and served with light tomato sauce. ⊠ *Armoury Bldg., Reid St., Hamilton,* ☎ *441/292–6195. AE, MC, V.*

$ ✕ **Pink's.** This deli in the heart of Hamilton is certain to make your day—or at least your lunch. Salads range from tabbouleh to tarragon chicken and pasta, and sandwich combinations are inventive. Also consider Pink's country pâté. Arrive early for lunch on weekdays to avoid the crowd. ⊠ *55 Front St., Hamilton,* ☎ *441/295–3524. No credit cards. Closed Sun. No dinner.*

$–$$ ✕ **Seasons in the Sun.** This restaurant and deli serves "natural foods" (no red meat) like marinated, grilled tofu sandwiches, and fresh salmon salad on pita. Organic brown rice, hummus, tabbouleh, grilled eggplant, and tomato and mozzarella salad make this brightly lit café a favorite among the health-conscious. A juice bar serves beverages made of freshly squeezed carrots, apples, oranges, bananas, and/or strawberries. There is even a selection of organic beer, wine, and coffee. Come for breakfast, lunch, dinner, or Saturday brunch. ⊠ *Bermudiana Arcade, Queen St., Hamilton,* ☎ *441/295–9587. MC, V. Closed Sun.*

$ ✕ **Chit Chat Boulevard Cafe.** Seven different food stations allow you to walk around and graze as food is prepared on the spot. Choose from an ever-changing menu of pasta and pizza made from scratch, freshly baked bread, salad and sandwich bars, made-to-order crepes, potato pancakes with various toppings, and rotisserie chicken, lamb, or beef. Along with freshly squeezed juices, beverages include wine, beer, and brewed-to-order coffees in trendy flavors. ⊠ *Gnd. floor, Bermudiana Arcade, Queen St., Hamilton,* ☎ *441/292–3400. AE, MC, V.*

Italian

$$$ ✕ **Little Venice.** Bermudians head for this trattoria when they want more from Italian cooking than pizza. Little Venice can be expensive, but the food is good enough to command higher prices, and the service is expert. Try snails in tomato sauce, an abundant plate of antipasto, or shrimp in white wine, herb, and garlic sauce. Salads are first-rate, particularly the Caesar, and spinach salad is topped with Gorgonzola croutons. All pastas are commendable, especially the *ravioli bicolore,* two-color pasta filled with seafood and mushrooms in a sauce of fresh tomatoes, white wine, asparagus, and scallops. For dessert, *pannacotta* (Bavarian cream with fresh berries and strawberry coulis) is sublime. ⊠ *Bermudiana Rd., Hamilton,* ☎ *441/295–8279. Reservations essential. AE, DC, MC, V.*

$$ ✕ **Harley's Bistro.** Popular with Hamilton businesspeople, this poolside eatery overlooking Hamilton Harbour serves up northern Italian fare—either indoors or alfresco. Pizzas with standard toppings, the expected lineup of pasta dishes (try the lobster ravioli), and more expensive veal and fish dishes are consistently good. At lunch you can enjoy interesting salads and large sandwiches. ⊠ *The Princess Hotel, Hamilton,* ☎ *441/295–3000. AE, DC, MC, V.*

$$ ✕ **Portofino.** Busy at lunch and dinner, this popular Italian restaurant is often noisy, particularly when the separate bar-waiting area is full of those who don't have reservations. If pizza's your game, a wide array of toppings is available (phone 15 minutes ahead if you want a pie to go). Sirloin steak *pizzaiola* (with olives, anchovies, capers, and tomato sauce) is also quite good, as is calamari fried in a delicate batter. For a bit of undersea adventure consider octopus cooked in red sauce with olives and capers and served over risotto. Homemade pasta and other risotto specials are excellent. ⊠ *Bermudiana Rd., Hamilton,* ☎ *441/*

292–2375 or 441/295–6090. Reservations essential. AE, MC, V. No lunch weekends.

$$ ✕ **Ristorante Primavera.** An understated elegance pervades this pleasing Mediterranean dining room in the west end of Hamilton, where you'll sit under a cleverly designed ceiling of grape vines and lattice. The menu is extensive, and all dishes are made to order. Spectacular starters are Carpaccio Primavera—thin slices of beef tenderloin with parmesan cheese and olive oil on arugula—and scampi and scallops innamorati—sautéed in cognac, paprika, and shallots. The well-seasoned *zuppa di pesce* (fish soup) is a wonderful combination of scallops, clams, salmon, rock fish, and mushrooms. You can also choose from a variety of consistently good pastas—*triangolo di paste* is a combination of three different pastas with three different sauces. ⊠ *Pitts Bay Rd., Hamilton,* ☎ *441/295–2167. AE, MC, V. No lunch weekends.*

$$ ✕ **Tuscany.** This spot is a hit with the island's chefs on their night off—not to mention everyone else. The balcony overlooks Front Street and has views of Hamilton Harbour; inside, a mural of the Tuscan countryside dominates one wall. The service in this owner-run restaurant is efficient and unusually friendly. The pizzas are top ranking, particularly the *4 Stagioni* (4 seasons) with tomato, mozzarella, artichoke hearts, and asparagus. Penne *terra mare* with baby shrimp, zucchini, and tomato as well as scaloppine cacciatore are also superb. ⊠ *Front St., Hamilton,* ☎ *441/292–4507. AE, MC, V.*

$–$$ ✕ **La Trattoria.** Tucked in a Hamilton alley, this no-nonsense trattoria has red-check tablecloths and the familiar feel of a mom-and-pop establishment. Recommended entrées are ravioli stuffed with ricotta cheese in tomato cream sauce, and fillet of fish with baby shrimp sautéed in white wine with oregano, garlic, and tomato. Or you may want to try one of the unusual pizzas, such as arugula and prosciutto. The early dinner special menu ($14.75) includes appetizer, main course, dessert, and coffee, and is available between 6 and 7. ⊠ *Washington La., Hamilton,* ☎ *441/295–1877. AE, DC, MC, V.*

$ ✕ **Pasta Basta.** Two restaurants—Pasta Basta in Hamilton and Pasta Pasta in St. George's—share the same menu and decor. Both are Bermudian favorites, with their brightly painted interiors, colorful tables and chairs, and lively (if slightly institutional) atmosphere. Food is tasty and well prepared, and an ever-changing menu of simple northern Italian cuisine provides good value. Try penne with chicken and pepper sauce, classic or vegetable lasagna, orecchiette with pesto and potato, Caesar salad, or any of the daily specials. No liquor is served in either restaurant, and smoking is not permitted. ⊠ *1 Elliot St. W, Hamilton,* ☎ *441/295–9785;* ⊠ *York St., St. George's,* ☎ *441/297–2927. Reservations not accepted. No credit cards.*

Mexican

$ ✕ **Rosa's Cantina.** The island's only Tex-Mex eatery has a festive, lively atmosphere, and a predictable decor of sombreros, serapes, and south-of-the-border bric-a-brac. Despite its monopoly on the cuisine, the food here is consistently good. Nachos Unbelievable (melted cheese, refried beans, beef, onions, tomatoes, peppers, jalapeño peppers, and guacamole), fajitas, and burritos are popular favorites. Food here is generally not too spicy, although most anything can be made extra-hot. Rosa's has a loyal local following and is always filled with a crowd of Bermudians and vacationers. On balmy evenings, it's fun to sit on the balcony overlooking bustling Front Street. ⊠ *121 Front St., Hamilton,* ☎ *441/295–1912. AE, MC, V.*

Seafood

$$ ✕ **Fisherman's Reef.** Above the Hog Penny Pub, this upscale restaurant with a nautical motif draws a crowd of locals for seafood and steak lunches and dinners. The fish chowder is excellent, as is the St. David's conch chowder. Of the wide selection of seafood entrées, the best are Bermuda lobster (in season), wahoo Mangrove Bay (seasoned and broiled with slices of Bermuda onions and banana), and the Cajun-style, baked, or panfried local catch of the day. Fresh local mussels are delicious either in curry sauce or baked with tomatoes and cheese. ✉ *Burnaby Hill, off Front St., Hamilton,* ☎ *441/292–1609. AE, DC, MC, V. No lunch weekends.*

$$ ✕ **Lobster Pot.** Bermudians swear by this place, which dishes out some of the best versions of island standards, including local lobster (from September through March), Maine lobster, and a host of other local shellfish and fish. Special Lobster Pot snails are delicious in their buttery secret sauce. Apropos its specialty, the restaurant's boat-related decor includes shining brass instruments and sun-bleached rope. ✉ *Bermudiana Rd., Hamilton,* ☎ *441/292–6898. AE, DC, MC, V. Closed Sun.*

$$ ✕ **Port O' Call.** For lunch or dinner, this delightfully intimate restaurant is one of Hamilton's most popular eateries. Many choose to begin with escargots. Fresh local fish such as wahoo, tuna, grouper, and snapper is cooked perfectly, and the sauces are pure silk. Try panfried grouper with a sauce of white wine, mussels, shrimps, and mushrooms, or one of the tempting daily specials. A delicious end to a meal here is the Amaretto parfait. Early-bird specials, served 5–6:15 daily, are $19.95 for soup or salad, entrée, dessert, and coffee. ✉ *87 Front St., Hamilton,* ☎ *441/295–5373. AE, DC, MC, V. Closed Sun.*

THE TOWN OF ST. GEORGE

British

$$$ ✕ **Carriage House.** Hearty English food is the daily bread of this attractive slice of the Somers Wharf restoration. With its exposed brick walls, the interior looks rather like the exterior; try to secure a table by a window so you can watch the action on the harbor. Dinner can be pricey, especially if you choose the Bermuda Triangle—shrimp, filet mignon, and chicken breast, each prepared with its own sauce—but many offerings are reasonable. This is the place to tuck into roast prime rib of beef, cut to order in front of you, but don't overlook the fresh Bermuda fish when it's on the menu. A generous gourmet buffet is served on Sundays, including unlimited champagne. Lunch and afternoon tea with all the trimmings are served daily. ✉ *Somers Wharf, St. George's,* ☎ *441/297–1270. Jacket required. AE, DC, MC, V.*

$$ ✕ **Pub on the Square.** After a morning of wandering in St. George's, this pub on King's Square is perfect for a slaking pint of English beer. The draft beer is better than anything that comes from the kitchen, although hamburgers and fish-and-chips are reasonably prepared. Warehouse brick and plenty of dark wood give the pub a warm atmosphere. ✉ *King's Sq., St. George's,* ☎ *441/293–9704. AE, MC, V.*

$$ ✕ **Wharf Tavern.** Like most dockside restorations in Bermuda, this English-style watering hole is nondescript, with a stale atmosphere—but the chance to sit on the porch or on the wharf and take in the activity on St. George's Harbour draws a crowd. The mainstays are a varied selection of pizzas and burgers of typical pub quality, along with the mixed grill: lamb chop, steak, chicken breast, and sausage. Service is often slow. ✉ *Somers Wharf, St. George's,* ☎ *441/297–1515. MC, V.*

$$ ✕ **White Horse Tavern.** Set on the water's edge overlooking the harbor, the White Horse has a great location and a light, airy atmosphere.

Carriage
House, **3**

Pasta Pasta, **1**

Pub on the
Square, **5**

Wharf
Tavern, **2**

White Horse
Tavern, **4**

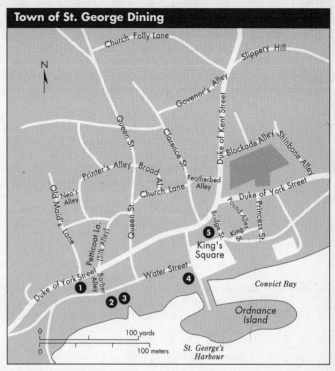

Town of St. George Dining

A Ploughman's Lunch—a baguette with cheese and a pickle—is typical of English pub fare. More exciting choices include spinach salad, herb-encrusted salmon with mushrooms, and the chef's choice curry of the day. Bring your patience along with your appetite—service can be slow. ⊠ *King's Sq., St. George's,* ☎ *441/297–1838. MC, V.*

Italian

$ ✕ **Pasta Pasta.** This ristorante shares its menu and decor with Pasta Basta in Hamilton. *See* Hamilton, *above,* for the full review. ⊠ *York St., St. George's,* ☎ *441/297–2927. Reservations not accepted. No credit cards.*

OUTSIDE HAMILTON AND ST. GEORGE

Asian

$$$ ✕ **Mikado.** This entertaining restaurant in Marriott's Castle Harbour Resort brings Japanese cooking to very English Bermuda. The decor reflects the elegantly simplistic Japanese style, so you literally cross a cultural line when you step onto the tea garden–style wooden bridge to enter Mikado. As at many Japanese-style steak houses, the enjoyment comes less from the food than from the flash of twirling knives, slapping mallets, and airborne salt and pepper shakers—no less than culinary judo. Although à la carte dining is available, you're better off with one of the complete dinners: a shrimp or scallop appetizer with ginger sauce, *miso* or *tori* soup, a seafood or beef entrée, salad, steamed rice, vegetables, and Japanese tea. The sushi bar here was the island's first, and locals continue to favor it. ⊠ *Marriott's Castle Harbour Resort, Tucker's Town,* ☎ *441/293–2040. Reservations essential. AE, DC, MC, V.*

Bermudian

$$$ ✕ **Plantation.** This comfortable, upbeat establishment is often at the top of locals' lists of "truly Bermudian" restaurants. Island rattan, flickering candles, and a glass-enclosed atrium filled with plants give the restaurant a cool, exotic ambience that works well with its tropical fare. Preparations that focus on freshly caught seafood are beautifully presented and consistently good. From the varied list of appetizers, try brie filled with rosemary and walnuts and baked in puff pastry. One maincourse standout is Bermuda wahoo sautéed with shrimp and asparagus in butter sauce. Save room for pears poached in port and served with berry sorbet. A four-course special dinner ($43) consists of selected menu items. The restaurant is closed annually in January and part of February for refurbishing. ⊠ *Bailey's Bay, Hamilton Parish,* ☎ *441/293–1188. AE, MC, V.*

$$ ✕ **Black Horse Tavern.** A menacing shark, jaws agape, hangs on a whiteplaster wall, along with an assortment of other mounted fish from local waters. In this otherwise tranquil setting, islanders fill the casual dining room and six outside picnic tables to savor the culinary magic of chef Bernel Pitcher. Curried conch stew with rice is a favorite, as are Pitcher's straightforward renderings of amberjack, rockfish, shark, tuna, wahoo, and—in season—Bermuda lobster. For lunch, the fish sandwich is a taste sensation. The chef's most popular specialty, shark hash, is an island original. Just keep in mind that the kitchen has trouble keeping it in stock. ⊠ *St. David's Island,* ☎ *441/293–9742 or 441/297–1991. AE, MC, V. Closed Mon.*

$$ ✕ **Dennis's Hideaway.** Eccentric, piratical in appearance, Dennis Lamb hunches over his pots discussing just about everything from plumbing and the government to the fate of man. These days his son, Sea Egg, does most of the cooking, but Dennis still potters around the kitchen. His Hideaway is little more than a ramshackle pink structure with a scattering of homemade picnic tables and a few yapping dogs—it is decidedly grubby—but it serves what may be Bermuda's best local food. If you want to make Dennis's day, order his "fish dinner with the works"—$32.50 for a feast of shark hash on toast, conch fritters, mussel stew, conch stew, fish chowder, fried fish, conch steak, shark steak, shrimp, scallops, and perhaps a bit of mussel pie. He may even include some bread-and-butter pudding for good measure. ⊠ *Cashew City Rd., St. David's,* ☎ *441/297–0044. Reservations essential. No credit cards.*

$$ ✕ **Loyalty Inn.** This converted old Bermuda house overlooking scenic Mangrove Bay at the island's western end is known for its fresh fish. Homemade soups are delicious, especially the Portuguese red bean and the Bermuda fish chowder. The lunch menu includes delicious fried fish sandwiches, codfish cakes, curried mussel pie, burgers, and salads (try the Caesar). Notable dinner entrées include sautéed fresh fish of the day with almonds and nut butter sauce; Seafood Sensation, a savory combination of local fish, shrimp, and scallops in white wine cream sauce served over rice; and shrimp Provençale, which is prepared at the table with great fanfare. Local lobster is served in season. ⊠ *Mangrove Bay, Somerset Village,* ☎ *441/234–0125. AE, MC, V.*

$ ✕ **Green Lantern.** For a taste of local flavor at breakfast, lunch, or dinner, this casual, friendly spot is a fine choice. Consider the fish chowder, or fish-and-chips (the house specialty), or broiled chicken, fish, or pork chops, with a side of peas and rice. You'll find Green Lantern about a 20-minute stroll (or quick taxi ride) from the ferry dock, just outside the city of Hamilton. ⊠ *Serpentine Rd. between Pitts Bay Rd. and Rosemont Ave., Pembroke,* ☎ *441/295–6995. MC, V. No dinner Wed.*

British

$$$ ✕ **Henry VIII.** As popular with locals as it is with tourists from nearby Southampton resorts, lively Henry effects an Old England look that stops just short of "wench" waitresses and contrived Tudor styling. A mix of English and Bermudian favorites includes classics like mussel pie and lighter options like steamed mussels in wine. Fish chowder is wonderful, as are the very British beef and steak-and-kidney pies; lamb is always cooked to perfection. And save room for bread-and-butter pudding and chocolate truffle cake. After dinner, join the local crowd in the bar for the entertainments of visiting comedians and singers, or island acts like calypso singer Hubert Smith. ⊠ *South Shore Rd., Southampton,* ☎ *441/238–1977. AE, DC, MC, V.*

$$ ✕ **Somerset Country Squire.** Overlooking Mangrove Bay in the West End, this typically English tavern is all dark wood and good cheer, with a great deal of malt and hops in between. Much of the food isn't good enough to warrant a special trip across the island, but you won't be disappointed if you do stop by. One exception is the Bermuda fish chowder, undoubtedly some of the island's best, and worth a long journey. Steak-and-kidney pie is fine, but curried mussel pie is much better. ⊠ *Mangrove Bay, Somerset,* ☎ *441/234–0105. AE, MC, V.*

$–$$ ✕ **Port Royal Golf Course.** The white dining room with light wicker furniture on the 19th hole of the Port Royal Golf Course has large plate-glass windows. A club sandwich with English beer is the standard order here, but don't hesitate to order something more sophisticated from the main menu—the food is quite good. This is one of the few restaurants on the island to offer breakfast, lunch, and dinner. ⊠ *Port Royal, Southampton,* ☎ *441/234–5037. MC, V.*

$ ✕ **Lighthouse Tea Room.** At the base of the famous Gibbs Hill Lighthouse in Southampton, a selection of delicious teas, properly brewed, and English favorites like quiche, smoked trout, and pork pie with chutney make this a charming spot to rest after the big climb. Breakfast (sausage, eggs, and crumpets, anyone?) is also served. ⊠ *Lighthouse Hill, Southampton,* ☎ *441/238–8679. AE, MC, V.*

French

$$$$ ✕ **Horizons.** The dining room at Horizons cottage colony in Paget is one of the island's most elegant, and reservations are difficult to secure on short notice. Occupying what once was a private house, this Relais & Châteaux property attracts an upscale crowd. And even though the impeccably trained staff is taught to make this an unforgettable dining experience, the menu speaks for itself. At the top of the appetizer list are a cheese terrine with cranberry sauce and a crepe filled with chicken and Mornay sauce. Among entrées, lamb with garlic sauce and beef Wellington with Madeira sauce are highly recommended. A fixed-price meal—$50, plus 15% gratuity—includes appetizer, soup, entrée, salad, dessert, and coffee. ⊠ *South Shore Rd., Paget,* ☎ *441/236–0048. Reservations essential. Jacket and tie. No credit cards. No lunch.*

$$$$ ✕ **Waterlot Inn.** This Bermudian treasure resides in a graceful, two-story manor house that dates from 1670. Service is impeccable: The dining room staff has just enough island exuberance to take the edge off its European-style training. Outstanding appetizers are a chilled carpaccio of beef tenderloin accompanied by basil vinaigrette and pine nuts, and grilled eggplant layered with herbs and ricotta and Asiago cheeses. A crisp Caesar salad is prepared tableside. Waterlot continues to serve one of the best fish chowders on the island, and the pan-fried Bermuda fish on braised cabbage with juniper berry sauce is superb. Another favorite is herb-crusted rack of lamb. Dessert lovers

Dining Outside Hamilton and St. George

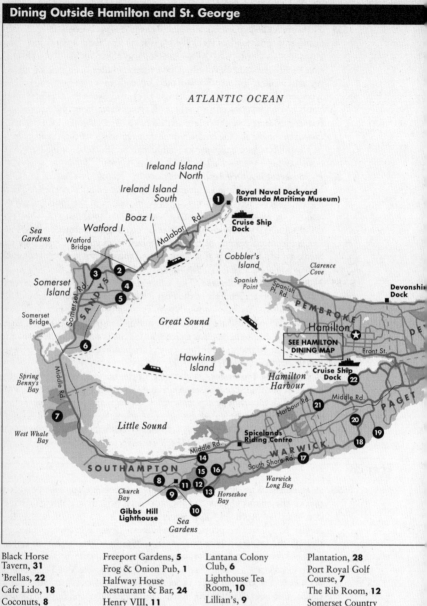

ATLANTIC OCEAN

Ireland Island North

Ireland Island South

Boaz I.

Watford I.

Sea Gardens

Watford Bridge

Malabar Rd.

1 Royal Naval Dockyard (Bermuda Maritime Museum)

Cruise Ship Dock

Cobbler's Island

Clarence Cove

Spanish Point

Spanish Pt. Rd.

Devonshire Dock

PEMBROKE

DEV

Somerset Island

SANDYS

Somerset Rd.

3
2
4
5

Great Sound

Hawkins Island

Hamilton

SEE HAMILTON DINING MAP

Front St.

Somerset Bridge

6

Middle Rd.

Hamilton Harbour

Cruise Ship Dock
22

Spring Benny's Bay

7

West Whale Bay

Little Sound

Harbour Rd.

21

Middle Rd.

PAGET

20

Spicelands Riding Centre

Middle Rd.

14

19

18

SOUTHAMPTON

15 **16**

South Shore Rd.

WARWICK

17

Warwick Long Bay

8

Church Bay

11

9

12

13 Horseshoe Bay

Gibbs Hill Lighthouse

10

Sea Gardens

Black Horse Tavern, **31**
'Brellas, **22**
Cafe Lido, **18**
Coconuts, **8**
Dennis's Hideaway, **32**
Fourways Inn, **21**

Freeport Gardens, **5**
Frog & Onion Pub, **1**
Halfway House Restaurant & Bar, **24**
Henry VIII, **11**
Horizons, **20**
Il Palio, **3**
The Inlet, **25**

Lantana Colony Club, **6**
Lighthouse Tea Room, **10**
Lillian's, **9**
Loyalty Inn, **4**
Mikado, **30**
Newport Room, **15**
Norwood Room, **19**
Paw-Paws, **17**

Plantation, **28**
Port Royal Golf Course, **7**
The Rib Room, **12**
Somerset Country Squire, **2**
Specialty Inn, **23**
Swizzle Inn, **26**

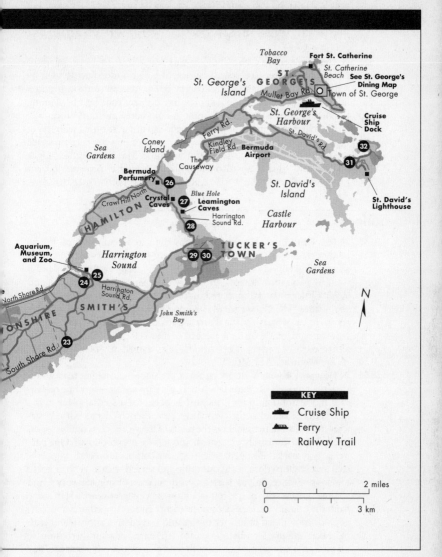

look for fresh fig tart with homemade pistachio ice cream, and frozen honey-nougat terrine with lavender sauce. ✉ *Middle Rd., Southampton,* ☎ *441/238–0510. Jacket and tie. AE, DC, MC, V. Closed Jan.– Feb. No lunch.*

$$$ ✕ **Lantana Colony Club.** Come to this resort near the western tip of the island for French classical cuisine of a high order. Surrounded by a forest of palm, hibiscus, and cherry trees, you can settle in for an à la carte lunch or a four-course prix-fixe dinner. Your best bet among the first courses is poached salmon in Pommerey mustard sauce over linguine. Among entrées, bay scallops and asparagus stir-fried with spring vegetables and basmati rice, and wahoo with orange peppercorn sauce are hard to beat. For dessert, try the Grand Marnier soufflé. "Light and healthy" dishes are also available. ✉ *Somerset Bridge, adjacent to ferry stop,* ☎ *441/234–0141. Reservations essential. Jacket and tie. AE, MC, V.*

International

$$$$ ✕ **Fourways Inn.** This restaurant has risen to preeminence on the island in recent years, as much for its lovely 18th-century surroundings as anything coming out of the kitchen. The decor evokes the air of a wealthy plantation home, with plenty of expensive china, crystal, and silver. Order mussels simmered in lobster sauce, or any of the sautéed veal dishes. The Caesar salad is a good choice, too, but leave enough room for strawberry soufflé. For a slightly different cocktail, try a Fourways Special, made with the juice of Bermuda loquats and other fruits, and a dash of bitters. ✉ *1 Middle Rd., Paget,* ☎ *441/236–6517. Jacket required. AE, MC, V.*

$$$$ ✕ **Newport Room.** With its nautical presence—glistening teak and a variety of models of victorious America's Cup yachts—this fine restaurant in the Southampton Princess has occupied a special place in the hearts of the island's elite for many years. French cuisine with American and Bermudian touches is the focus of the world-class dining room. Each dish is beautifully presented, and service is exceptional. One particularly remarkable appetizer consists of a combination of shrimp, lobster, and scallops flamed at your table and served with angel hair pasta and lobster sauce. Salads, such as a combination of spinach, sorrel, and summer greens with grapefruit in a hibiscus vinaigrette, are a step away from the traditional. Especially noteworthy entrées are salmon and sturgeon fillets sautéed in lobster butter and served on a shrimp and crab pancake, and double fillet of venison presented in a soft herb mousse on pumpkin and turnip puree, with wild cherry and juniper sauce. For dessert, the Grand Marnier soufflé or crêpes suzette (for two) are memorable. ✉ *South Shore Rd., Southampton,* ☎ *441/238–8167. Jacket and tie. AE, DC, MC, V. Closed some winter months; call for information. No lunch.*

$$$$ ✕ **Norwood Room.** Don't be put off by the fact that this restaurant in the Stonington Beach Hotel is run by students of the Hospitality and Culinary Institute of Bermuda: Under the supervision of their mentors, they offer superb food and service. The oversize training kitchen uses local ingredients and European culinary techniques to create a range of bright, fresh tastes. Mahimahi served in a ginger sauce with tiger shrimps, and seafood Norwood—a melee of shrimp, scallops, crab, and fish in a cream sauce—are two particularly fine dishes. Enjoy a preprandial cocktail at the sunken bar overlooking the swimming pool. ✉ *South Shore Rd.,* ☎ *441/236–5416. Jacket and tie. AE, DC, MC, V.*

$$$ ✕ **Cafe Lido.** On the beachfront terrace at the Elbow Beach Hotel, with waves breaking just below, this is one of the island's most romantic settings. The creative appetizer list includes marinated salmon with risotto pancake, and avocado with tomato, fresh mozzarella cheese, and a basil-vegetable dressing. Main-course winners are angel hair pasta with arugula, pine nuts, and roasted peppers, as well as grilled salmon with creamy watercress sauce. Coconut mousse with fruit and vanilla sauce and the hazelnut eclair are both unforgettable endings. ⊠ *Elbow Beach Hotel, off Shore Rd., Paget,* ☎ *441/236–9884. Reservations essential. AE, DC, MC, V.*

$$$ ✕ **Coconuts.** Nestled between high cliff rocks and a pristine beach on
★ the southern coast at the Reefs resort (☞ Chapter 5), this outdoor restaurant is one of the best spots for that table overlooking the ocean, made even more dramatic at night with floodlights. A fixed price of $44, excluding 15% gratuity, includes an appetizer, soup, salad, entrée, dessert, and coffee. The annually changing menu features freshly grown produce, and the ever-present signature Bermuda fish chowder appears on the list of creative appetizers. You will never go wrong with the grilled fresh fish of the day entrée, and charbroiled steak is cooked to perfection. The coconut tart with coconut ice cream is a perfect way to end a meal here. A simpler lunch menu includes daily specials, burgers, sandwiches, and good salads. ⊠ *South Shore Rd., Southampton,* ☎ *441/ 238–0222. Reservations essential. AE, MC, V. Closed Nov.–Apr.*

$$$ ✕ **The Rib Room.** Overlooking the Southampton Princess Golf Course in what has the appearance of a conservative country club dining room, this is the best place on the island for grilled meats and barbecued ribs. Service is superior. The house specialty, hickory-smoked prime rib, is cooked to perfection and served in its juices with traditional Yorkshire pudding. Lamb chops are superlative, as is rotisserie-cooked half chicken. Appetizers and salads are offered buffet-style, and Bermuda fish chowder is always a sensation. ⊠ *Southampton Princess Hotel, South Shore Rd., Southampton,* ☎ *441/238–8000. AE, MC, V. No lunch.*

$$$ ✕ **Tom Moore's Tavern.** In a house that dates from 1652, this restaurant in Bailey's Bay clearly enjoys its colorful past. Irish poet Tom Moore visited friends here frequently in 1804 and wrote odes under the nearby calabash tree. Today, fireplaces, casement windows, and shipbuilders' cedar joinery capture a sense of history that in no way interferes with the cuisine—it is fresh, light, and innovative. Broiled Bermuda lobster (in season) and fresh Bermuda fish sautéed with lemon butter and pine nuts both stand out, as does boneless quail stuffed with goose liver, morels, and truffles in puff pastry. The soufflés are always superb, as is the chef's pastry; both change daily. You will dine in one of five cozy rooms or, weather permitting, alfresco on a terrace that overlooks Walsingham Bay. ⊠ *Bailey's Bay, Hamilton Parish,* ☎ *441/293–8020. Jacket required. AE, MC, V. No lunch. Closed part of Jan.; call for information.*

$$$ ✕ **Windsor.** This elegant dining room in Marriott's Castle Harbour Resort overlooks the resort and serves international dishes with a strong European underpinning. The menu may not be especially innovative, but you can enjoy a good meal here. Meat lovers in particular will be happy: Filet mignon and roast lamb loin with black bean sauce are cooked to perfection. Fish lovers should try grilled swordfish with fresh papaya salsa, or smoked salmon stuffed with mango mousse. With its unhurried atmosphere, live piano music, and harbor views, the Windsor makes for a fine night out. ⊠ *Castle Harbour Resort, Tucker's Town,* ☎ *441/293–2040. Reservations essential. Jacket required. AE, DC, MC, V. No lunch.*

$$ ✕ **'Brellas.** Overlooking Hamilton Harbour from a hillside in Paget, this outdoors-only restaurant on a plant-filled terrace, open in good weather from May to early October, serves food that brightens even the less-than-dazzling days. The cold fruit soup and Bermuda fish

chowder are excellent; recommended entrées include fresh Bermuda fish and roast lamb with delicately steamed vegetables. Both are served with cassava pie—a traditional meat pie made for special holidays in Bermuda. ⊠ *Newstead Hotel, Harbour Rd., Paget,* ☎ *441/236–6060. Reservations essential. AE, MC, V.*

$$ ✕ **Frog & Onion Pub.** With its vaulted limestone ceilings and thick walls, the former warehouse of the Royal Naval Dockyard is a most fitting place for this nautically decorated eatery and its large game room for pool players. The food caters to every taste, running the gamut from hearty English pub fare to delicious European dishes to a selection of fresh local fish plates. Pub favorites are bangers and mash, Argus Bank fish sandwich, salmon and smoked-trout fish cakes, and the Frog & Onion Burger, which is topped with fried onions and bacon. A children's menu is available at lunchtime. ⊠ *The Cooperage Building, Royal Naval Dockyard, Ireland Island,* ☎ *441/234–2900. MC, V.*

$$ ✕ **Halfway House Restaurant & Bar.** On the roadside in Flatts Village, this bright and airy restaurant attracts its share of residents and visitors, who enjoy the cheery (but sometimes slow) service. The breakfast menu features a lineup of homemade coffee rolls and scones alongside delicious omelets, pancakes, and fresh fruit. Daily specials include homemade soups, pasta, curry, and seafood dishes. Look for Bermuda fish chowder, Portuguese red bean soup, and steak sandwiches. A traditional Bermuda breakfast—codfish with potatoes, banana, avocado, and tomato sauce—served every Sunday morning is delicious. ⊠ *North Shore Rd., Smith's,* ☎ *441/295–5212. MC, V.*

$$ ✕ **The Inlet.** With beautiful views over Harrington Sound, this Palmetto Hotel restaurant is filled with sunlight and fresh air. None of the dishes is likely to find its way into a gourmet magazine, but the quality is consistently good and the selection broad. Popular choices are roast rack of lamb with blueberry sauce, and a steak dinner. ⊠ *Palmetto Hotel, Flatts Village,* ☎ *441/293–2323. AE, MC, V.*

$$ ✕ **Paw-Paws.** This bistro has seating outdoors on a patio overlooking busy South Shore Road or in a cozy dining room with colorful wall murals of Italian garden scenes. The varied and unusual menu features Bermudian, European, and North American dishes. For starters try the Danish specialty of deep-fried Camembert with lingonberries and fried parsley, or Bermuda fish chowder. Ravioli *d'homard et saumon* (homemade lobster ravioli with strips of smoked salmon) and grilled jumbo shrimp stuffed with crabmeat and served with piquant sauce are not-to-be-missed main courses. A special local menu offers panfried codfish cakes and shark steak served with creole sauce. The lunchtime menu includes soups, sandwiches (try the favorite Bermudian fried fish on your choice of bread), and salads (like assorted mixed greens with fresh fruit, smoked salmon, and grilled chicken). The numerous desserts come from an adjacent bakery shop. Paw-Paws serves breakfast as well, including a traditional Bermuda codfish breakfast with all the trimmings on Sundays. ⊠ *South Shore Rd., Warwick,* ☎ *441/236–7459. MC, V.*

$$ ✕ **Swizzle Inn.** People come to this place as much to drink as to eat. Just west of the airport near the Bermuda Perfume Factory, the inn created one of Bermuda's most hallowed (and lethal) drinks—the rum swizzle. Sit in the shadowy bar—plastered with business cards from all over the world—sipping one of these delightful concoctions, or sit on the porch and watch the mopeds whiz by. If you get hungry, try a "swizzleburger" (a hamburger gussied up with bacon and cheese) or a delicious Bermuda fish sandwich. The nightly special might be an English standard such as shepherd's pie or liver and onions. ⊠ *Blue Hole Hill, Bailey's Bay,* ☎ *441/293–9300. AE, MC, V.*

$$ ✕ **Wickets Brasserie.** Prints of the game of cricket decorate the walls of this restaurant, whose fare will suit just about any palate. Bermuda fish chowder is a reasonable starter; chicken Caesar salad with fresh Parmesan cheese croutons is tasty and light. At the other end of the spectrum are hot roast beef sandwiches and Swiss cheese and bacon burgers. The soup-and-salad-bar combination is a relative bargain. Top off the meal with key lime pie or a piece of Oreo chocolate cheese cake. Dinner is served only when the hotel is full. ✉ *Southampton Princess Hotel, South Shore Rd., Southampton,* ☎ *441/238–8000. Reservations essential. AE, MC, V.*

Italian

$$$ ✕ **Il Palio.** A ship's spiral staircase leads upstairs from the bar to the dining room at this West End restaurant, where you'll find some of the island's best pizza. Antipasto and pasta dishes are also good, such as spaghetti with nicely seasoned tomato sauce blended with capers, black olives, and anchovies, or homemade cannelloni stuffed with spinach and meat. An outstanding meat dish is Scaloppine Vesuvio— veal sautéed with white wine and topped with prosciutto and mozzarella cheese. The fresh fish fillet sautéed with capers, garlic, pine nuts, and a dash of tomato sauce is another treat. For dessert there are profiteroles and owner Fosco Naninni's Panettone Surprise—Italian-style raisin bread filled with chocolate and vanilla ice cream. A special takeout menu is available. ✉ *Main Rd., Somerset,* ☎ *441/234–1049 or 441/234–2323. DC, MC, V. Closed Mon.*

$$$ ✕ **Lillian's.** Part of the Sonesta Beach Hotel & Spa (☞ Chapter 5), this windowless art nouveau restaurant serves northern Italian cuisine, which only adds to its non-Bermudian feel. Start with vegetable lasagna or lobster polenta with grilled calamari. Then try chicken breast with Gorgonzola-stuffed ravioli, sun-dried tomatoes, spinach, and walnut cream sauce. Roast rack of lamb with seared eggplant is also a good bet. Dress is semiformal, and the atmosphere can be somewhat stuffy. ✉ *Sonesta Beach Hotel & Spa, Southampton,* ☎ *441/238–8122. AE, DC, MC, V.*

$$ ✕ **Tio Pepe.** You needn't spend much money for a satisfying meal at this Italian restaurant with a Mexican name. Photocopied menus and red and green decor create an easygoing atmosphere ideal for bathers returning from a day at Horseshoe Bay Beach. Try spicy eggplant baked in tomato sauce and cheese for appetizer, followed by a small pizza or pasta dish, and reserve a table in advance. ✉ *South Shore Rd., Southampton,* ☎ *441/238–1897 or 441/238–0572. AE, MC, V. Closed Mon. Nov.–Mar.*

$ ✕ **Speciality Inn.** A favorite with locals, this south-shore restaurant is cheerful and clean, with low prices that reflect its sparse decor. Try the fish chowder or red bean soup. Otherwise, the cooking is just what you would expect of a family-style Italian restaurant. ✉ *Collectors Hill, Smith's,* ☎ *441/236–3133. MC, V.*

Seafood

$$$ ✕ **Whaler Inn.** Fresh seafood is purchased from local fishermen and flown in several times a week from New England, making the menu selections here pleasing and plentiful. The St. David's Kettle—lobster, clams, mussels, shrimp, and fish in a tomato sauce blended with sherry peppers, black rum, and Chardonnay—is a pleasing dish, as is the Bermuda Triangle—three fresh fish fillets with tomato, citrus, and dill sauce. Desserts here are stupendous; chocolate cake with a rich icing steals the show. Perched above the rocks and surf at the Southampton Princess (☞ Chapter 5), this seafood house has one of the most dra-

matic settings on the island. ⊠ *Southampton Princess Hotel, South Shore Rd., Southampton,* ☎ *441/238–0076. AE, DC, MC, V.*

$$ ✕ **Freeport Gardens.** If you are looking for good, locally caught fish, this is the place to come. The fish platter and the combination seafood platter with scallops, shrimp, and fish are not presented with great flair, but they are delicious, and fish sandwiches are unforgettable. The panfried or broiled Bermuda rockfish is particularly good. If you don't like fruits of the sea, choose from a range of pizzas with all the usual trimmings, hamburgers, or an assortment of sandwiches. For dessert, you might be offered freshly baked apple pie, strawberry short cake, or lemon chiffon pie. If you want a hearty breakfast before touring Ireland Island, tuck into a Spanish omelet or waffles with bacon. ⊠ *Pender Rd., Dockyard, Sandys,* ☎ *441/234–1692. AE, MC, V.*

5 Lodging

If all the accommodations available on Bermuda were reviewed here, this book would barely qualify as carry-on luggage. The 42 that we cover include a huge array of full-service resort hotels, cottage colonies, small inns, guest houses, and housekeeping apartments.

ERMUDA IS PROBABLY MOST FAMOUS for its beach-
front cottage colonies—freestanding cottages clustered
around a main building housing a restaurant, a
lounge, and an activities desk. Many properties, especially these cottage
colonies, are sprawling affairs set in extensive grounds and connected
by walkways and steps. At some of the smaller guest houses and housekeeping apartments, you must carry your own luggage on the long walk
to your room. If you have a disability or would rather not climb hills,
you may be happier at a conventional hotel with elevators and corridors.

Like everything else in Bermuda, lodging is expensive. Rates at Bermuda's
luxury resorts are comparable to those at posh hotels in New York,
London, and Paris. These prices would be easier to swallow if you received first-class service in return. However, such features as 24-hour
room service and same-day laundry service are rare.

You can shave about 40% off your hotel bill by visiting Bermuda in
low or shoulder seasons. The trick is trying to pin down the dates. Low
season runs roughly from November through March; however, each
property sets its own schedule, which may even change from year to
year. Some hotels begin high season rates on April 1, others April 15,
and a few kick in as late as May 1. Your best bet is to call and ask
about low- and shoulder-season rates.

As temperatures rarely dip below 60°F during the winter, low-season
weather is ideal for tennis, golf, and shopping—although the water is
a bit chilly for swimming. New in Bermuda: Most hotels offer a "temperature guarantee" in March—if the temperature dips below 68° on
a given day, you receive a 10% reduction on your room rate, as well
as discounts or free tickets to numerous sights around the island. Low-
season packages are attractively priced, and a host of government-spon-
sored special events (many of which are free) are staged for tourists.
Some hotels and smaller properties close each year during January and/or
February to refurbish and prepare for the high season.

The greatest concentration of accommodations is along the south shore,
in Paget, Warwick, and Southampton parishes, where you'll find the best
beaches. If shopping is your bag, however, you might prefer one of the
hotels that are a stone's throw from the main shopping area in Front
Street in Hamilton, or one of the numerous Hamilton Harbour properties, which are a 5- to 10-minute ferry ride from the capital. The West
End is a bit remote, but it is ideal for boaters, fishermen, and those who
want to get away from it all. And the ferry does travel regularly across
the Great Sound to Hamilton. The East End has its share of nautical pursuits, too, but its major attraction is the charming historic town of St.
George. In truth, the island is so small that it's possible to see and do
everything you want, regardless of where you unpack your bag.

Whether or not they are officially classified as cottage colonies, a large
number of guest accommodations are in cottages—most of them pink
with white trim and gleaming white tiered roofs. There are some
sprawling resorts, but no high rises and no neon signs. An enormous
property like the Southampton Princess is hard to miss, but many hotels and guest houses are identified only by small, inconspicuous signs
or plaques. The island is noted for its lovely gardens and manicured
lawns, and the grounds of almost every hotel and cottage are filled with
subtropical trees, flowers, and shrubs.

Typical Bermuda-style architecture is a limestone house, usually painted
a pastel color, with a white tiered roof and likely a white stone chim-

ney. Many houses have exterior stairs that make a gesture like welcoming arms—banisters curving outward at the base like open arms. Tray ceilings, which are shaped like inverted trays, are quite common in Bermuda, as are "knee-high fireplaces," which are built up from the floor, about knee-high.

Return visitors to the island will appreciate the annual improvements that are made to most properties. The Hotels Refurbishment (Temporary) Customs Duty Relief Bill of 1991 substantially reduced the duty on goods imported to the island, and hotels and guest house owners have taken advantage of it to further upgrade their facilities.

A 7.25% Government Occupancy tax is tacked on to all hotel bills, and a service charge is levied: Some hotels calculate a service charge as 10% of the bill, whereas others charge a per diem amount. All guests are required to make a two-night deposit two to three weeks before their arrival. Those accommodations that don't take credit cards for the deposit—and many do not—accept personal checks. Virtually every hotel on the island offers at least one vacation package—frequently some kind of honeymoon special—and many of these are extraordinarily good deals. It's worth learning about the various policies and programs at the properties that interest you before booking.

Bermuda traditionally was not a family destination, but that has changed. Hotels, guest houses, and cottage colonies welcome families with children, and most have day care and children's activities programs. Most of the hotels—including the Belmont Hotel, Golf & Country Club, the Elbow Beach Hotel, the Grotto Bay Beach Hotel & Tennis Club, the Southampton Princess, Willowbank, and most of the smaller properties—have supervised programs for children, some of which are part of attractive packages. Many hotels on the island can arrange for baby-sitters.

Most lodgings have a choice of meal plans, and the rates vary according to the meal plan you choose. Under an American Plan (AP), breakfast, lunch, and dinner are included in the hotel rate. A modified American Plan (MAP) covers breakfast and dinner. A Bermuda Plan (BP) includes only a full breakfast, while a breakfast-only Continental Plan (CP) means pastries, juice, and coffee. The rates quoted below are based on the European Plan (EP), which includes no meals at all.

Many hotels also have a variety of "dine-around" plans that allow you to eat at other restaurants on the island as part of the meal plan. The Princess and the Southampton Princess offer a Royal Dine-Around program year-round, which allows you to eat at any of the several Princess restaurants. Horizons, Newstead, and Waterloo House have similar dine-around arrangements, as do the six properties in the Bermuda Collection (Ariel Sands, Cambridge Beaches, Lantana, the Reefs, Stonington Beach, and the Pompano). Hotel and cottage colony dinners are usually formal: Men are asked to wear jackets and ties, and casual but neat dress is suggested for women. Many hotels will pack a picnic lunch for you if you want to get out and about.

Bermuda's Small Properties Ltd. is a group of small hotels and guest houses that share a toll-free information/reservations line and a fax number. The properties include Angel's Grotto, Greenbank, Longtail Cliffs, Marley Beach Cottages, Pretty Penny, and Grape Bay Cottages. To reserve at any of these properties, call 800/637–4116 or fax 441/236–1662.

Cottage colonies and hotels offer entertainment at least one night a week in high season, on which they stage everything from calypso to classical music. Barbecues and dinner dances are also popular. Afternoon tea

Hotel Facilities

	Access for Disabled	On The Beach	Swimming Pool	Restaurant	Cable T.V.	Fitness Facilities	Golf Nearby	Tennis Courts	Conference Fac.	Accept Children	Children's Prog.	Access To Spa	On-Site Water-Sports	Accept Credit Cards	Air-Conditioned	Entertainment	Boat Dock/Marina
Angel's Grotto	•				•		•			•			•	•	•		
Ariel Sands Beach Club	•	•	•	•			•	•	•		•	•		•	•	•	
Aunt Nea's Inn at Hillcrest							•			•					•		
Barnsdale Guest Apartments			•		•					•				•	•		
Belmont Hotel	•		•	•			•	•	•	•				•	•	•	•
Cambridge Beaches		•	•	•			•	•	•	•		•	•		•		•
Edgehill Manor			•		•		•			•					•		
Elbow Beach Hotel	•	•	•	•	•		•	•	•	•	•	•	•	•	•	•	
Fourways Inn			•	•	•		•		•						•		
Grape Bay Cottages		•				•				•				•	•		
Greenbank Cottages							•			•			•	•	•		
Grotto Bay Beach Hotel	•		•	•	•	•	•	•		•	•		•	•	•	•	•
Harmony Club			•	•	•		•	•						•	•	•	
Horizons & Cottages			•	•			•	•		•					•	•	
Lantana Colony Club			•	•			•	•	•	•			•	•	•	•	•
Little Pomander Guest House	•				•		•			•			•	•	•		•
Longtail Cliffs	•		•		•		•			•				•	•		
Loughlands Guest House			•				•	•		•				•	•		
Marley Beach Cottages		•	•		•					•			•	•	•		
Marriott's Castle Harbour	•	•	•	•	•	•	•	•	•	•				•	•	•	•
Newstead			•	•			•	•		•				•		•	•
Oxford House					•		•			•				•	•		
Palm Reef	•		•	•		•	•		•					•	•	•	
Palmetto Hotel & Cottages			•	•			•		•	•				•	•	•	•
Paraquet Guest Apartments				•	•		•			•					•		
Pink Beach Club & Cottages		•	•	•			•	•	•	•				•	•	•	

	Access for Disabled	On The Beach	Swimming Pool	Restaurant	Cable T.V.	Fitness Facilities	Golf Nearby	Tennis Courts	Conference Fac.	Accept Children	Children's Prog.	Access To Spa	On-Site Water-Sports	Accept Credit Cards	Air-Conditioned	Entertainment	Boat Dock/Marina
Pompano Beach Club		•	•	•		•	•	•	•	•			•	•	•	•	•
Pretty Penny			•				•			•				•	•	•	
Princess, Hamilton	•		•	•	•	•	•	•	•	•		•	•	•	•	•	•
The Reefs	•	•	•	•		•	•	•		•		•	•	•	•		
Rosedon			•							•					•		
Royal Palms Hotel			•	•	•					•				•	•		
St. George's Club	•	•	•	•			•	•	•	•			•	•	•	•	
Salt Kettle House							•			•			•				•
Sky Top Cottages							•			•			•				
Sonesta Beach Resort Bermuda	•	•	•	•	•	•	•	•	•	•	•	•	•	•	•	•	
Southampton Princess	•		•	•	•	•	•	•	•	•	•	•	•	•	•	•	•
Stonington Beach Hotel		•	•	•	•		•	•	•				•	•	•	•	
Surf Side Beach Club		•	•	•	•		•			•	•		•	•	•		
Waterloo House			•	•				•	•				•	•	•		
Whale Bay Inn					•		•			•					•		
Willowbank		•	•	•			•		•	•	•			•	•		

is served daily in keeping with British tradition, and a rum-swizzle party is usually held on Monday night. Featuring the Bermudian beverage of choice, these parties present a pleasant opportunity to welcome new arrivals, get acquainted—and, of course, knock back some rum. Guest houses and housekeeping apartments do not have regularly scheduled entertainment, although informal gatherings are not uncommon.

Most large hotels have their own water-sports facilities where you can rent Windsurfers, Sunfish, paddleboats, and other equipment. Even the smallest property, however, can arrange sailing, snorkeling, scuba, and deep-sea fishing excursions, as well as sightseeing and harbor tours. The Coral Beach & Tennis Club and the Mid Ocean Club are posh private clubs, where an introduction by a member is necessary to gain access to their excellent beach, tennis, and golf facilities. However, many hotels have arrangements with one or the other to allow guests certain club privileges.

Unless otherwise noted, rooms in all lodgings below are equipped with private bathrooms.

CATEGORY	COST*
$$$$	over $200
$$$	$125–$200
$$	$90–$125
$	under $90

All prices are for a standard double room for two (EP) during high season, excluding 7.25% tax and 10% service charge (or equivalent).

Resort Hotels

$$$$ 🏨 **Belmont Hotel, Golf & Country Club.** Occupying 110 acres between Harbour and Middle roads, this large pink hotel was built at the turn of the century and has a distinctly British personality. As its name suggests, it's also a sports-minded resort: Golf and tennis pros are on hand, and tournaments are often played here. Golf and tennis are free to hotel guests, though there is a mandatory $38 golf cart rental fee and a $5-per-hour fee for night tennis. Hotel guests also play free on the miniature golf course and the floodlit putting green. The enormous lobby, decorated with chandeliers and fresh flowers, bustles with the golf groups that frequent the hotel. Rooms are average in size (bathrooms are quite small), but their large windows admit plenty of light and create a sense of spaciousness. Mahogany Queen Anne furniture is mixed with wicker, carpets are dusty pink, and the bedspreads and drapes are in bright tropical floral patterns. With views over the harbor and the resort's gardens and pool—one of the largest on the island—the rooms on the fourth floor are probably the best. The Hamilton ferry stops at the Belmont Wharf, and though it's a long haul up the hill from the wharf to the hotel, a shuttle bus makes the trip regularly. ⊠ *Box WK 251, Warwick WK BX,* ☎ *441/236–1301, 800/225–5843 in U.S. and Canada,* ℻ *441/236–6867. 149 rooms, 1 suite. BP, EP, MAP. Restaurant, bar, saltwater pool, 18-hole golf course, miniature golf, putting green, 3 tennis courts, shops. AE, DC, MC, V.*

$$$$ 🏨 **Elbow Beach Hotel.** Major changes have taken place at Bermuda's oldest (since 1908) seaside resort. Since it took over the hotel in early 1996, Rafael Hotels Ltd. has spent $24 million in renovations on the 52-acre resort. The beach, for which the hotel is named, is now dressed with cabanas, a restaurant, and beachfront rooms. The head gardener conducts walking tours through the hotel gardens and lawns, where a three-hole putting green and croquet green have been added. The main building is a five-story structure with a white-column facade. Behind it is a lobby of palatial proportions paved with green marble and Oriental area rugs. Walls are paneled with white oak, and six giant crystal chandeliers hang over a gilt table. Guest rooms are large, decorated in muted shades of green, pink, and cream, and fabrics are top quality. Each has an in-room safe, umbrella, terry robes, and slippers. The nearly 300 rooms, suites, and junior suites are spread between the main building and outlying multi-unit lanais (here in Bermuda a lanai is a cottage, often beachfront, with sliding glass doors that open onto a patio) and duplex cottages. Most accommodations have a balcony or patio and a spectacular ocean view (land-side rooms have neither). In high season, theme parties and barbecues are held frequently. There is an $8-per-hour fee for tennis courts ($3 racket rental, $12 for night play). A Kid's Club provides daily activities for children up to age 12 whose parents are registered guests. ⊠ *Box HM 455, Hamilton HM BX,* ☎ *441/236–3535, 800/223–7434 in U.S. and Canada,* ⅃X *441/236–8043. 223 rooms, 75 suites. BP, MAP. 4 restaurants, 3 bars, pool, beauty salon, hot tub, 5 tennis courts, exercise room, beach, motorbikes, shops, children's programs, playground. AE, DC, MC, V.*

$$$$ ⊞ **Marriott's Castle Harbour Resort.** Bordered by Harrington Sound on one side and the Castle Harbour golf course on the other, this whitewashed hilltop resort is an impressive sight from the air. If "castle" conjures up images of King Ludwig, though, leave them at home. This is a big, busy, modern hotel that caters more to vacationers than groups and conventions. The original Castle, which opened in 1931, was built by Furness, Withy & Co. as a hotel for steamship passengers traveling between U.S. and British ports. Two wings are now connected to the original building by glass-enclosed skywalks: the two-story Golf Club wing and the nine-story Harbour View wing, which descends in terraces to the water. Rooms throughout the hotel are identical, with upholstered wing-back chairs, windows dressed in ruffled valances, and heavy drapes with matching quilted bedspreads; many also have balconies. The resort's beach on Castle Harbour is small, but the one on the south shore is the island's largest private beach. The resort also has three pools, including an Olympic-length lap pool and a cascading pool. Tennis courts are $10 an hour (plus $6 for racket rental), but the real draw is the adjacent 18-hole Castle Harbour golf course—one of the best courses on the island. ⊠ *Box HM 841, Hamilton HM CX,* ☎ *441/293–2040, 800/228–9290 in U.S.,* ⅃X *441/293–8288. 375 rooms, 27 suites. MAP, BP, EP. 3 restaurants, 3 bars, 3 pools, 18-hole golf course, 6 tennis courts, health club, motorbikes, laundry service, dry cleaning, concierge. AE, DC, MC, V.*

$$$$ ⊞ **Sonesta Beach Resort Bermuda.** A sloping, serpentine drive leads through landscaped lawns to this hotel, the only one on the island where you can step directly from your room onto a sandy south-shore beach. Set on a low promontory fringed by coral reefs, the six-story modern building has a stunning ocean view and direct access to three superb natural beaches. Somewhat impersonal in service and style, the Sonesta caters to guests who want an action-packed vacation: An activities director coordinates bingo games, theme parties, movies, water sports, and other diversions. A glass-enclosed entranceway leads to the enormous lobby (where there is a separate registration area for the large groups that often check in here). Guest rooms and suites are decorated in blond wooden furnishings upholstered with peach and green fabrics. A shuttle takes you to the hotel's beach at Cross Bay, but beach lovers should insist on a Bay Wing minisuite that opens onto a private sandy beach. All rooms on the 25-acre property have balconies, but standard rooms in the main building have land views only. South Side Scuba Watersports has an outlet at the hotel where you can rent scuba and snorkel gear. One of the island's best-equipped health spas is here

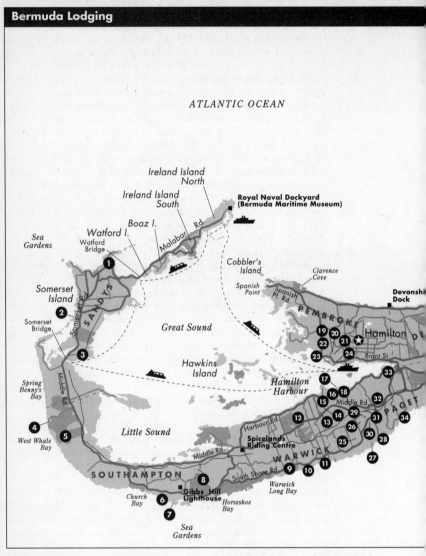

Angel's Grotto, **37**
Ariel Sands Beach Club, **35**
Aunt Nea's Inn at Hillcrest, **41**
Barnsdale Guest Apartments, **31**
Belmont Hotel, Golf & Country Club, **12**
Cambridge Beaches, **1**
Edgehill Manor, **22**
Elbow Beach Hotel, **27**
Fourways Inn, **13**

Grape Bay Cottages, **34**
Greenbank Cottages, **15**
Grotto Bay Beach Hotel & Tennis Club, **40**
Harmony Club, **32**
Horizons & Cottages, **25**
Lantana Colony Club, **3**
Little Pomander Guest House, **33**
Longtail Cliffs, **9**

Loughlands Guest House & Cottage, **29**
Marley Beach Cottages, **10**
Marriott's Castle Harbour Resort, **39**
Newstead, **18**
Oxford House, **20**
Palm Reef, **17**
Palmetto Hotel & Cottages, **36**
Paraquet Guest Apartments, **30**
Pink Beach Club & Cottages, **38**

Pompano Beach Club, **4**
Pretty Penny, **14**
The Princess, **23**
The Reefs, **6**
Rosedon, **21**
Royal Palms Hotel, **19**
St. George's Club, **42**
Salt Kettle House, **16**
Sky Top Cottages, **26**
Sonesta Beach Resort Bermuda, **7**

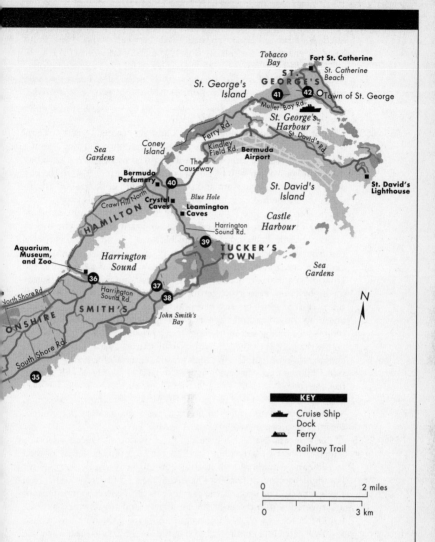

Southampton
Princess, **8**
Stonington Beach
Hotel, **28**
Surf Side
Beach Club, **11**
Waterloo House, **24**
Whale Bay Inn, **5**
Willowbank, **2**

(extra charge), and four-, five-, or six-day spa packages include room, meals, and a range of spa offerings. A variety of other packages is offered. A shuttle bus also transports guests between the hotel and South Road, at the top of the hill. ✉ *Box HM 1070, Hamilton HM EX,* ☎ *441/238–8122, 800/766–3782 in U.S.,* ☏ *441/238–8463. 365 rooms, 34 suites. MAP (EP and BP on request). 3 restaurants, 5 bars, in-room safes, minibars, indoor and outdoor pools, hot tub, massage, spa, steam room, 6 tennis courts, exercise room, motorbikes, shops, playground, concierge. AE, DC, MC, V.*

$$$–$$$$ 🏨 **Grotto Bay Beach Hotel & Tennis Club.** Set among 21 acres of gardens only a mile from the airport, this intimate hotel draws a young crowd for its relaxed atmosphere and its proximity to an enclosed bay that's riddled with romantic coves and natural caves. Also in the bay are a fish-feeding aquarium and two illuminated underground attractions: the Cathedral Cave for swimming, and Prospero's Cave, which can be seen on a guided tour. The hotel itself consists of a main building and 11 three-story lodges dotting a hill that slopes to the waters of Ferry Reach. Each lodge contains between 15 and 30 sunny rooms featuring light woods and fabrics, private balconies or patios, and views of the water. Although the lodges don't have elevators, the ground-floor units are accessible by wheelchair, but request a room near the lobby building to make getting around easier. There are also three suites, each of which has two bedrooms, three bathrooms, a living room, and a balcony. The hotel has its own sightseeing excursion boat and offers scuba diving and snorkeling from a private deep-water dock. Just below the pool is the beach, whose small causeway attracts a colorful congregation of fish. During high season, entertainment is held poolside. Children's activities are held in season. ✉ *11 Blue Hole Hill, Hamilton Parish CR 04,* ☎ *441/293–8333 or 800/582–3190,* ☏ *441/ 293–2306. 198 rooms, 3 suites. BP, EP, MAP. Restaurant, 2 bars, pool, 4 tennis courts, health club, shuffleboard, beach, motorbikes, playground, business services, meeting room. AE, MC, V.*

$$$–$$$$ 🏨 **The Princess.** Named in honor of Princess Louise, Queen Victoria's
★ daughter who visited the island in 1883, this large pink landmark opened in 1884 and is credited with starting Bermuda's tourist industry. There is a slightly formal atmosphere here, and the staff provides swift, courteous service. The walls at the entrance to the Tiara Room restaurant are covered with pictures of the politicians and royals who have visited the hotel, as well as other memorabilia from the hotel's rich past. Ideally located on Hamilton Harbour, the hotel caters to businesspeople (personal voice mail is available), convention groups, and others who want to be near downtown Hamilton. Plush, colorful upholstery, bedspreads, and drapes are used throughout the hotel, and most rooms and suites have balconies. There are several categories of large and sumptuous suites. The Princess Club's amenities include Continental breakfast and showers and changing facilities for travelers with late flights who want to swim after morning checkout. A ferry makes regular runs across the harbor to the Southampton Princess (☞ *below*), which has a golf course and other sports facilities (all cost extra). The Hamilton Princess has no beach (although you may use the Southampton Princess's), but there are stretches of lawn and terraces above the dock area with deck chairs for relaxing and sunning. The Jabulani Reportory Company performs in the hotel's Gazebo Lounge (a dinner-and-show package, with dinner in the Colony Pub, is $54; show only, $25). The Royal Dine-Around plan between the two Princess hotels offers a choice of nine restaurants—from casual to formal—with menus catering to many tastes. ✉ *Box HM 837, Hamilton HM CX,* ☎ *441/ 295–3000, 800/223–1818 in U.S., 800/268–7176 in Canada;* ☏ *441/295–1914. 413 rooms, 60 suites. BP, EP, MAP. 3 restaurants, 2*

bars, in-room safes, minibars, 2 pools (1 saltwater), beauty salon, spa, putting green, tennis court, health club, beach, motorbikes, shops, concierge. AE, DC, MC, V.

$$$–$$$$ ☆ **Southampton Princess.** This hotel is much larger and livelier than
★ its older sister, the Princess in Hamilton. It's not the place for a quiet retreat, but its planned activities, such as theme parties, bingo, aerobics, cooking demonstrations, and tennis matches do have their appeal. For families, it offers the island's best children's program, which includes parties and baby-sitting services, and children under 16 stay and eat free if parents are on a MAP. The six-story, ultramodern main building, which dominates a hilltop near Gibbs Hill Lighthouse, contains several of the island's best restaurants: The 300-year-old Waterlot Inn restaurant (☞ Chapter 4) occupies a dockside spot on the north side, and the Whaler Inn beach club is perched above the surf at South Shore Beach. A jitney churns over hill and dale to connect them all, and a regiment of staffers is on hand to assist you if you get lost. Rooms vary in size, but they are all decorated in soft coral colors and light woods, with plenty of marble in the spacious bathrooms. The oceanfront deluxe rooms are the nicest; if possible, avoid rooms on the first three floors of the west and north wings, which overlook rooftops. Some of the elegant suites have kitchens and custom-made furniture. Perks in the 55-room Newport Club include private check-in/out, complimentary Continental breakfast, and a private lounge. Fees for using the health club, sauna, and indoor pool are $10 daily ($15 per couple) or $20 weekly ($30 per couple); greens fees for the 18-hole golf course are $32, plus $28 for a mandatory cart, and tennis costs $10 an hour ($6 an hour for racket rental). The Secret Garden skin clinic and hair studio (a separate concession) is one of the island's best, with British-trained beauty therapists giving a full range of European skin treatments, massages, and reflexology. The excellent Dolphin Quest program, in a 3-acre, open-to-the-sea lagoon, allows you to interact with friendly bottlenose dolphins. Hotel guests pay $75, non-guests $85; and in both cases admission is by lottery. ✉ Box HM 1379, Hamilton HM FX, ☎ 441/238–8000, 800/223–1818 in U.S., 𝔽𝔸𝕏 441/238–8968. 598 rooms, 36 suites. MAP. 6 restaurants, 4 bars, minibars, no-smoking rooms, indoor pool, outdoor pool, beauty salon, 18-hole golf course, 11 tennis courts, boccie, croquet, health club with spa facilities, beach, motorbikes, shops, nightclub, concierge. AE, DC, MC, V.

Small Hotels

$$$$ ☆ **Harmony Club.** Nestled in lovely gardens, this two-story pink-and-white hotel—the island's only all-inclusive resort—was built in the 1930s as a home. The adult-oriented hotel has a couples-only policy, but a couple can be two aunts, two friends, or any other combination. The base rate covers everything, including round-trip airport transfers, meals, alcohol, and even two-seater scooters. Part of the meal package can include a dine-around plan at the Little Venice restaurant (☞ Chapter 4) in Hamilton. The hotel, which is refurbished annually, has a spacious reception area with Bermuda cedar paneling, and a club lounge with a large-screen TV and an assortment of games, including cards, darts, and backgammon. A complimentary bottle of champagne comes with all rooms, which are spacious and luxuriously decorated with Queen Anne furnishings. All but 12 of the rooms have a patio or balcony. The hotel is not on the water, but it's only about a five-minute scooter ride to the south-shore beaches. There is a host of activities in high season, from informal barbecues to formal dances and complimentary use of the golf course at the Belmont Hotel, Golf & Country Club. Entertainment changes nightly—offerings range from calypso-limbo dancing to solo singers and band performances to informative slide shows about the island. ✉ *Box PG 299, Paget PG BX,* ☎ *441/236–3500, 888/427–6664 in U.S.,* 🖷 *441/236–2624. 68 rooms. AP. Restaurant, bar, pool, hot tub, sauna, putting green, 2 tennis courts, motorbikes. AE, DC, MC, V.*

$$$$ 🏨 **Pompano Beach Club.** Expect a friendly, personal welcome when you arrive at this informal seaside hotel, owned and managed by the American-born Lamb family. On the western end of the island adjacent to the Port Royal Golf Course, this was the island's first fishing club before it opened as a small hotel in 1956. It still appeals to golfers, water-sports enthusiasts, and anyone in search of a quiet, remote getaway. The main building is a crescent-shape, split-level structure of pink and white stone, containing the main dining room, a British-style pub, a cozy lounge that overlooks the ocean, and an oceanfront fitness center. Spread across a luxuriant hillside are the annually refurbished rooms and one-bedroom suites, all with balconies or patios and ocean views. "Superior" rooms are the best value, not only because they are larger than the suites, but also because you wake in the morning to a splendid ocean view through the bedroom window (suites have an ocean view through the living room window). "Deluxe" rooms, which are even more spacious (for only a few dollars more), have sitting room areas and larger, more private balconies as well as ocean views. Perched on a hill adjacent to the main building are an attractive pool and a small conference center. You will also find an oceanfront shuffleboard court; two hot tubs, one with a view of the sea; a small, natural beach where at low tide you can stroll 250 yards into waist-high ocean waters; and two man-made sunbathing beaches clinging to the hillside. The Pompano's water-sports facility has Sunfish, Windsurfers, paddleboats, motorized lounges, and small glass-bottom boats for rent May through October. The restaurant, from which there are spectacular views of the sunset, serves fine food both inside and alfresco on the terrace. ✉ *36 Pompano Beach Rd., Southampton SB 03,* ☎ *441/234–0222, 800/343–4155 in U.S.,* 🖷 *441/234–1694. 34 rooms, 20 suites. BP, MAP. Restaurant, bar, refrigerators, pool, 2 outdoor hot tubs, exercise room, meeting room. AE, MC, V.*

$$$$ 🏨 **The Reefs.** The pink lanais of this small, casual and elegant resort
★ are set in cliffs above the beach at Christian Bay, adjacent to the Sonesta Beach Hotel & Spa. The pace here is sedate. If you are looking for action, look to the sports-oriented Sonesta, Elbow Beach, or Southampton Princess resorts. In a pink Bermuda cottage that serves as a clubhouse, a registration area opens onto a spacious, comfortable lounge, where a pianist or guitarist entertains nightly. Beyond the lounge is the main dining room, where you often can dance after dinner. Another restaurant is the waterside Coconuts (☞ Chapter 4), which is popular for casual lunches and candlelight dinners under the stars. Two guest rooms are in the clubhouse, but the best rooms are in the lanais around the pool and on the hillside above the sandy beach. Of the lanais, the ones near the beach are the most expensive. The Longtail suite is enormous and has a large whirlpool bath. Brightly colored fabrics and rattan predominate in the guest rooms; bathrooms are small but have marble double vanities and an adjoining dressing area. All rooms have balconies and ocean views. In addition to the lanais, there are eight secluded cottages, one a three-bedroom, three-bathroom unit. Changing rooms near the beach are available for travelers with late flights who want to swim after morning checkout. Reefs guests have access (for a fee) to the spa at the Sonesta, and the Reefs has a small exercise room near the beach. ✉ *56 South Rd., Southampton, SN 02,* ☎ *441/238–0222, 800/742–2008 in U.S. and Canada,* 🖷 *441/238–8372. 58 rooms, 1 suite, 8 cottage suites. BP, MAP. 2 restaurants, 2 bars, in-room safes, pool, 2 tennis courts, beach, motorbikes. AE, MC, V.*

$$$$ 🔟 **Stonington Beach Hotel.** The training ground for students of the Hospitality and Culinary Institute of Bermuda, this south-shore hotel has one of the friendliest, hardest-working staffs on the island. Just 10 minutes from Hamilton, Stonington Beach has a warm, gracious atmosphere, an excellent formal restaurant, and one of the island's best beaches. And unlike other major south-shore properties that tack service charges on to your bill, gratuities here are included in room rates. Set in two-story terraced lodges leading to the beach, the hotel has identical rooms done in handsome woods and attractive fabrics, with elegant heavy drapes and matching quilted bedspreads; all have balconies and ocean views. The spacious hotel lobby gains much of its character from its beamed ceiling and large windows with graceful fanlights. The Regency furnishings, well-stocked bookshelves, fireplace, and large-screen TV in the adjoining library make it a comfortable place to relax. Weekly champagne receptions are held, and classical music is played in the attractive Norwood Dining Room. Use of tennis courts is free. ⊠ *Box HM 523, Hamilton HM CX,* ☎ *441/236–5416, 800/447–7462 in U.S. and Canada,* 🗚 *441/236–0371. 64 rooms. BP, MAP. Restaurant, bar, in-room safes, refrigerators, pool, 2 tennis courts, beach, motorbikes, library. AE, DC, MC, V.*

$$$$ 🔟 **Waterloo House.** A preferred stopping place for businesspeople
★ from all over the world, this quiet Relais & Châteaux retreat has a long history. A pink archway and steps leading to the flower-filled patio from Pitts Bay Road were later additions to a house that predates 1815, when it was renamed in honor of the defeat of Napoleon. The white-columned house faces the harbor, and a spacious harborside terrace dotted with umbrellas and tables is used for outdoor dining and entertainment— live performers play harp, piano, jazz, and calypso on various nights. Beautiful cut-flower arrangements fill the stately lounge, which is tastefully decorated with oil paintings, antiques, chintz drapes, and a large fireplace. Though some rooms are in the pink two-story stone buildings beside the pool and patio, most are in the main house. Terraces and water views complement the rooms' soothing decor: Matching hand-screened European and British chintzes are used in quilted bedspreads, dust ruffles, draperies, and valances; antique prints of country scenes, flowers, and Audubon sketches complement antique furnishings. Luxurious bathrooms have whirlpools, heated towel racks, and adjoining dressing areas. Complimentary cocktail and picnic cruises on the property's endearing tug-style boat provide views of Bermuda's outer islands. Waterloo's MAP allows dine-around privileges at the sister properties of Horizons & Cottages and Newstead (☞ *below*); the short golf course at Horizons is also open to guests, as are all facilities at the Coral Beach & Tennis Club; transportation is provided. ⊠ *Box HM 333, Hamilton HM BX,* ☎ *441/295–4480, 800/468–4100 in U.S.,* 🗚 *441/295–2585. 28 rooms, 6 suites. BP, MAP. Restaurant, bar, pool. AE, MC, V.*

$$$–$$$$ 🔟 **Newstead.** This renovated manor house could accommodate only
★ 12 people when it opened to guests in 1923. Since then the elegant harborside hotel has expanded considerably, with brick steps and walkways now leading to several poolside units and cottages. Set amid tall trees and a profusion of flowering shrubs and plants, the main house and cottages are typically Bermudian—in fact, some of the cottages were originally private residences. You'll find handsome wingback chairs, traditional furnishings, fresh flowers, and a fireplace in the spacious drawing room; live musicians play harp, piano, calypso, and jazz in the lounge, which has large windows overlooking the harbor. (In October, the lounge is a great vantage point for the Gold Cup sailboat races.) The large guest rooms have framed prints, fresh flowers, and polished mahogany campaign chests with brass drawer pulls; sliding

glass doors open onto balconies. Though the hotel has no beach, it does have two private docks for deep-water swimming in the harbor, and guests have use of the facilities at the Coral Beach & Tennis Club on the south shore, about 10 minutes away by cab. Men's and women's changing rooms by the pool allow you to go straight from swimming to the Hamilton ferry at Hodsdon's Landing. Tennis on Har-Tru courts costs $3.50 an hour, and tennis whites are preferred. Guests on MAP may participate in the dine-around plan with sister properties Waterloo House (☞ *above*) and Horizons (☞ *below*). ⊠ *Box PG 196, Paget PG BX,* ☎ *441/236–6060, 800/468–4111 in U.S.,* ℻ *441/236–7454. 50 rooms, 2 suites. BP, MAP. Restaurant, bar, pool, putting green, 2 tennis courts, dock. AE, MC, V.*

$$$–$$$$　🏨 **Rosedon.** Notable for its spacious veranda and white iron furniture, this stately Bermuda manor attracts a diverse crowd for its ambience, service, and proximity to Front Street shops. The four spacious rooms in the main house have leaded-glass doors; all other rooms are in two-story buildings arranged around a large heated pool in gardens filled with exotic plants. All rooms have balconies or patios and cheerful decor. Though there is no restaurant, breakfast, sandwiches, and light meals are served either in your room or under umbrellas by the pool, and afternoon tea is served in the large lounges in the main house, where films are shown nightly and there is an honor bar. The hotel has no beach, but guests have access to Elbow Beach Hotel's beach and tennis courts at a reduced rate; complimentary transportation is provided for the 10- to 15-minute drive. ⊠ *Box HM 290, Hamilton HM AX,* ☎ *441/295–1640, 800/742–5008 in U.S. and Canada,* ℻ *441/295–5904. 43 rooms. BP, EP. 2 lounges, in-room safes, refrigerators, pool, laundry service. AE, MC, V.*

$$$–$$$$　🏨 **Willowbank.** On six acres of landscaped gardens overlooking Ely's Harbour and the ocean, this former estate was converted to a family-style hotel by a Christian trust. Morning devotions are held in a lounge for those who wish to attend, and grace is said before meals, which are announced by an ancient ship's bell and served family-style. There is no proselytizing, however, and no pressure to participate in religious activities. The hotel is simply a serene alternative to the glitzy resorts: the focus is on rest, relaxation, and renewal. With their cedar paneling and fireplaces, the two large lounges in the main building are the focal point for quiet conversations and afternoon tea. There are also the library and the Loaves and Fishes dining room, where guests meet for fellowship. Guests may have liquor in their rooms, but there is no bar. Guest rooms, in one-story white cottages, are large and simply furnished—they have neither phones nor TVs. Rooms with an ocean or harbor view are the most desirable and expensive. The hotel has a free summer children's program that includes, among other things, crafts workshops and trips around the island. No service charge is added to the bill and tipping is not expected, but the staff is friendly and helpful nonetheless. ⊠ *Box MA 296, Sandys MA BX,* ☎ *441/234–1616 or 800/752–8493,* ℻ *441/234–3373. 64 rooms. MAP. Restaurant, 2 lounges, pool, 2 tennis courts, 2 beaches. MC, V.*

$$$　🏨 **Palmetto Hotel & Cottages.** Set amid tall shade trees on the banks of Harrington Sound, this casually elegant property was once a home. The main building is a sprawling two-story pink-and-white structure typical of Bermuda. Adjoining the small reception area is the Ha'Penny, a very British pub. Afternoon tea is served in a small but attractive lounge with a tile floor, Oriental area rug, cushy furnishings, and green plants. There are 24 rooms in the main building, but the 16 cottage rooms on the banks of the sound are the most luxurious. All rooms have balconies, and many have a good view of the water. The beach is small, but the hotel provides complimentary bus fare to a south-shore beach.

In addition, you can swim or snorkel off the hotel's private dock. ⊠ *Box FL 54, Flatts FLBX,* ☎ *441/293–2323, 800/982–0026 in U.S., 800/893–3603 in Canada;* FAX *441/293–8761. 42 rooms. BP, MAP. Restaurant, bar, pool, beach, dock. AE, MC, V.*

$$$ ☎ **Royal Palms Hotel.** Richard Smith and his sister Susan Weare, whose parents own and operate nearby Oxford House, have transformed this grand home into a hotel with the atmosphere of a country inn. It's on a quiet residential street near Hamilton, and Front Street's shops are a short walk away. The house, which dates from 1903, is aptly named, surrounded as it is by tall palms and lush gardens. Many guests like to relax and read around the outdoor pool. The terrace, with its comfortable white wicker furniture, is another favorite spot for reading and enjoying quiet conversation, as well as outdoor summer dining. The hotel has polished wood floors and Oriental rugs in some rooms, and wall-to-wall carpeting in others; drapes and bedspreads are in matching fabrics. Some rooms connect to others, which suits families and groups; several have kitchens. Three rooms were added in 1997. Ascots restaurant is quite popular with locals. A generous complimentary breakfast is served. ⊠ *Box HM 499, Hamilton HM CX,* ☎ *441/ 292–1854, 800/678–0783 in U.S., 800/799–0824 in Canada;* FAX *441/ 292–1946. 14 rooms, 1 suite. CP; supplementary dinner plan available. Restaurant, lounge, pool. AE, MC, V.*

$$–$$$ ☎ **Palm Reef.** Adjacent to Darrell's Wharf, and a five-minute ferry ride from Hamilton, this somewhat modest hotel is a good buy in a great location for travelers who are willing to eschew some of the amenities available in grander properties. Built as a manor house in the late 1800s, it was converted to a hotel shortly after the turn of the century. In fact, many Bermudians still call it "the Inverurie," as the hotel was called until it closed in 1990. It reopened as the Palm Reef in 1991. The spacious, well-lit lobby, with its high ceiling and winding staircase leading to the mezzanine, opens onto a lounge and dining room, both of which have huge windows with spectacular views of the harbor and Hamilton. Furnishings throughout are of white wicker and rattan; fabrics are in soft pastel prints. Deluxe rooms (there are no suites) have balconies and small dressing areas. The least expensive, somewhat less desirable rooms have no view of the water. The dining room is open for all three meals, and if you participate in the MAP dine-around plan (at the Harbourfront, Little Venice, and La Trattoria), you will receive complimentary admission to Le Club nightclub in Hamilton. There is usually the manager's rum swizzle party on Mondays; afternoon tea is complimentary. ⊠ *Box HM 1189, Hamilton HM EX,* ☎ *441/236– 1000 or 800/221–1294,* FAX *441/236–6392. 60 rooms. EP, BP, MAP. Restaurant, lounge, heated pool, tennis court. AE, MC, V.*

Cottage Colonies

$$$$ ☎ **Ariel Sands Beach Club.** This most informal of the cottage colonies surrounds Cox's Bay in Devonshire Parish; it's adjacent to the Palm Grove estate (☞ The Parishes *in* Chapter 3) and not far from the Edmund Gibbons Nature Reserve. The picturesque sandy beach has a variety of small shells, and a graceful statue of Ariel perches on a rock in the sea. The snorkeling is superb, with many species of fish seeking refuge in the normally quiet cove area just off the beach; the Olympic-size, ocean-side natural pool—wonderful for lap swimming—contains a variety of fish found just offshore. Another smaller saltwater pool is adjacent to the beach. The one-story, salmon-color limestone clubhouse, designed Bermudian cottage–style, contains a cozy lounge and a dining room with an ocean view. Many Bermudians enjoy the quiet atmosphere here and can be found sipping a cocktail in the bar after a game of tennis, or savoring international cuisine alfresco on the terrace or in the main dining room. A grand piano, a fireplace, hardwood floors, and Oriental rugs give the resort an air of distinction. The large patio is ideal for outdoor dining, dancing, and barbecuing in season. There are two two-bedroom cottages with living rooms and fireplaces; you can hire a butler and private chef to serve you here. Three one-bedroom suites and 40 bedrooms are set in the sloping, immaculately kept, tree-shaded grounds. All rooms have an ocean view. Ariel Sands is owned by actor Michael Douglas, whose mother's family is prominent in Bermuda. It is a member of the Bermuda Collection group, so MAP guests can take advantage of dine-around options. ⊠ *Box HM 334, Hamilton HM BX,* ☎ *441/236–1010, 800/468–6610 in U.S.,* FAX *441/236–0087. 48 rooms with bath. BP, MAP. Restaurant, bar, 2 saltwater pools, freshwater pool, putting green, 3 tennis courts, exercise room, volleyball, beach, children's programs (summer only), business services, meeting rooms. AE, MC, V.*

$$$$ 🏨 **Cambridge Beaches.** This top resort near Somerset Village in the West
★   End (☞ Chapter 3) occupies a beautifully landscaped peninsula edged with private coves and five pink-sand beaches. The island's original cottage colony (it opened at the turn of the century), it remains a favorite among royals and international celebrities. Many guests return year after year, attracted by the elegance, superior water-sports facilities, and unsurpassed pink-sand beaches. Registration is in a Bermuda-style clubhouse with large, handsomely furnished lounges. Candlelight dining and dancing take place in the lower-level restaurant and on the terrace, which has a splendid view of Mangrove Bay. A wide range of accommodations is available—the entire peninsula is dotted with cottages—and prices vary considerably. On the high end, Pegem is a 300-year-old, two-bedroom Bermuda cottage with a cedar-beam ceiling, English antiques, a den, and a sunporch. On the other end of the spectrum, the least expensive units are those that have land rather than water views. The decor differs from cottage to cottage, but antiques and fireplaces are common. Many units have whirlpools; suites have bidets as well. Rooms are refurbished annually. In 1997, a two-level leisure facility opened with an indoor pool and solarium, exercise pool with current, whirlpool and hot tub, gym, exercise rooms, and restaurant and juice bar. The spa—the space it used to occupy in the main building is to be a restaurant—is on the ground floor of the leisure facility, equipped with six treatment rooms, sauna, steam, hair and beauty facilities, and professional European staff. Don't fret about being far from Front Street: A complimentary shopping launch makes trips three times a week from the resort's private dock. Ferry tokens are complimentary in the off-season. Other exclusive boat trips include snorkeling trips to St. George's and a cruise to a nightclub. The marina offers the largest selection of water-sport equipment on the island—Windsurfers, Boston Whalers, three types of sailboats, snorkel equipment, canoes, and kayaks. Scuba instruction and trips are also available. Children must be supervised at all times, and those under five are allowed in the dining room only by special arrangement. ⊠ *Somerset MA 02,* ☎ *441/234–0331, 800/468–7300 in U.S.,* FAX *441/234–3352. 62 rooms, 20 suites. MAP. 2 restaurants, 2 bars, saltwater pool, spa, putting green, 3 tennis courts, croquet, exercise room, 6 beaches. No credit cards.*

$$$$ 🏨 **Fourways Inn.** About a five-minute walk from the ferry landing and a five-minute ride to south-shore beaches, this small luxury hotel has a sedate, formal ambience and a central location. The architecture is typically Bermudian: The main building is a former family home that dates from 1727; the five cottages, set in a profusion of greenery and flowers, each contain a poolside suite and a deluxe upper-floor room. Marble floors and marble bathrooms are common throughout, and plenty of flowers give the rooms a bright freshness. In addition, each room has a balcony or terrace and large closets paneled with full-length mirrors. Amenities in the suites include bathrobes and slippers. You receive a complimentary fruit basket on arrival, and homemade pastries and the morning paper are delivered daily to your door. The hotel serves a sumptuous Sunday brunch. ⊠ *Box PG 294, Paget PG BX,* ☎ *441/236–6517, 800/962–7654 in U.S.,* FAX *441/236–5528. 5 rooms, 5 suites. CP. Restaurant, bar, minibars, kitchenettes, heated pool, business services. AE, MC, V.*

$$$$ ⊞ **Horizons & Cottages.** Oriental rugs, polished wood floors, cathedral
★ ceilings, and knee-high open fireplaces are elegant reminders of the 18th century, when the main house in this resort was a home. A Relais & Châteaux property, the cottage colony is continually upgraded to maintain its high standards. Horizons Restaurant (☞ Chapter 4) is a chic place for intimate candlelight dining; in pleasant weather, tables are set on the terrace. Menus are created under the guidance of renowned chef Steve Blumenthal. And the hotel has dine-around arrangements with sister properties Waterloo House and Newstead (☞ *above*). Guest cottages dot the terraced lawns, and each cottage has a distinct personality and decor: Most have two or three rooms and a large common room with a fireplace, library, and shelves of board games. Some rooms have white wicker furnishings, others have a traditional European flavor, and all have terraces. Most cottages also have a kitchen, where a maid prepares breakfast before bringing it to your room. The hotel has no beach of its own, but guests may use the facilities of the Coral Beach & Tennis Club, within walking distance along South Road. ⊠ *Box PG 198, Paget PG BX,* ☎ *441/236–0048, 800/468–0022 in U.S.,* FAX *441/236–1981. 42 rooms, 5 suites. BP, MAP (combination also available). Restaurant, pool, 9-hole golf course ($4 fee), 3 tennis courts, in-room safes. No credit cards.*

$$$$ ⊞ **Lantana Colony Club.** A short walk from the Somerset Bridge ferry landing in the West End, this cottage colony is known for its lavish gardens, delightful topiary, and impressive, museum-quality objets d'art. Several life-size sculptures by Desmond Fountain are placed throughout the grounds, including a delightful rendering of a woman seated on a bench reading a newspaper. The solarium dining area in the main house is dazzling, with hanging plants and Venetian, frosted-glass wall lamps. All accommodations are spacious, airy suites in a variety of configurations: lanais, split-levels, garden cottages, and family cottages with two bedrooms, two bathrooms, and a living-dining room. All units have sliding glass doors that open onto private balconies or patios; some have cedar doors, beams, trim, and vivid Souleaido prints. Waterfront suites have Mexican tile floors on the lower level, carpeting in the sleeping area, refrigerators, and wet bars; water-view suites have fireplaces, separate men's and women's dressing areas, and kitchens. About half of the suites are in garden settings; one of those is a cottage where guests may use the owner's private pool. The small private pink-sand beach overlooks the Great Sound, and boats are available to guests to explore the coastline and pristine harbors of Somerset. Many locals and visitors to the island come to have lunch at the waterside restaurant—by boat or moped—but reservations are advised. ⊠ *Box SB 90, Somerset Bridge SB BX,* ☎ *441/234–0141, 800/468–3733 in U.S., 800/463–0036 in Canada;* FAX *441/234–2562. 56 suites, 6 cottages. BP, MAP. 2 restaurants, 2 bars, heated pool, putting green, 2 tennis courts, croquet, shuffleboard, beach. AE, MC, V.*

$$$$ ⊞ **Pink Beach Club & Cottages.** With its two pretty pink beaches, this secluded, relaxing colony is a favorite of international celebrities. The location is ideal—10 minutes from the airport and 15 minutes by foot or moped from the shops of Front Street. Opened as a cottage colony

in 1947, the main house has a clubby ambience, reflected in its dark-wood paneling, large fireplace, and beamed ceilings. Paved paths wend their way throughout the 16½ acres of attractively landscaped gardens, leading to the beaches and 25 pink cottages. This is the island's largest cottage colony. Some cottages contain a single unit, while others comprise several units, and accommodations range from single rooms to two-bedroom suites with two bathrooms and twin terraces; most have ocean views. Each spacious unit has maple furnishings upholstered in conservatively colored fabrics, double or king-size beds, and sliding glass doors that open onto a balcony or terrace. Bathrooms have double sinks. The best accommodations are, of course, those near the beach. A Continental breakfast is served in-room. High season, guests dine in a casual poolside setting six nights a week. ⊠ *Box HM 1017, Hamilton HM DX,* ☎ *441/293–1666, 800/355–6161 in U.S. and Canada,* ⨳ *441/293–8935. 6 rooms, 87 suites. BP, MAP. Restaurant, bar, freshwater pool, 2 tennis courts, 2 beaches. AE, MC, V.*

$$$$ ▥ **St. George's Club.** Within walking distance of King's Square in St. George's, this residential resort and hotel adjoins an 18-hole golf course designed by Robert Trent Jones. The sleek, three-story main building contains the office, the Margaret Rose restaurant, a pub, and a convenience store where you can buy everything from champagne to suntan lotion. In two-story, one- and two-bedroom white cottages sprinkled over 18 acres, the individually decorated apartments are huge and filled with sunlight. In some, pale yellow walls are offset by bright accent pieces and fabrics in muted colors. In others, sweeping bold designs draw upon the entire spectrum of colors. Each apartment has a full kitchen with dishwasher, fine china, and crystal. Bathrooms are large and lined with marble; some have double Jacuzzis in dramatic settings. ⊠ *Box GE 92, St. George's GE BX,* ☎ *441/297–1200,* ⨳ *441/297–8003. 69 suites. EP. 2 restaurants, bar, 3 pools (1 heated), 18-hole golf course, putting green, 3 lighted tennis courts. AE, DC, MC, V.*

Housekeeping Cottages and Apartments

$$$–$$$$ ▥ **Marley Beach Cottages.** Scenes from the films *Chapter Two* and *The*
      ★   *Deep* were filmed here, and it's easy to see why—the setting is breathtaking. Near Astwood Park on the south shore, the resort sits high on a cliff overlooking a lovely beach and dramatic reefs; a long path leads down to the sand and the sea. If you plan to stay here, pack light—there are a lot of steep steps, and you may have to carry your luggage. The price is steep for one couple, but this is an excellent choice for two couples vacationing together (if you don't mind preparing your meals). There is ample space here, and splitting the cost brings it down to a moderate price for each pair. Each cottage contains a suite and a studio apartment, which can be rented separately or together, by families or friends. This is not a good place for children, as there is little to occupy them except the pool and the beach. Units are individually decorated; all have large rooms, superb ocean views, private porches or patios, phones, TVs, and fully equipped kitchens with microwave and coffeemaker. The Heaven's Above and Seasong deluxe suites are spacious; each has two wood-burning fireplaces, tile floors, upholstered rattan furniture, and ample kitchen facilities. Groceries can be delivered, and daily maid service is provided. ⊠ *Box PG 278, Paget PG BX;* ☎ *441/236–1143, ext. 42; 800/637–4116 in U.S.;* ⨳ *441/236–1984. 7 suites, 6 studios. EP. Pool, whirlpool, beach. AE, MC, V.*

$$$ ▥ **Grape Bay Cottages.** These two—almost identical—cottages sit within a whistle of the soft sands of Grape Bay beach. Beach Crest and Beach Home are two-bedroom cottages with open fireplaces, hardwood floors, phones, and big, full-size kitchens. The comfortable furnishings

include king-size beds with sturdy, attractive wicker headboards. You can't step directly from door to beach, but the stroll down to it takes little more than three minutes. If there is a difference in the two cottages, it's only that Beach Home is perhaps 30 seconds closer to the beach. This is a very quiet, secluded location, ideal for beach lovers who like to cook, shift for themselves, and do serious sand-and-surf time. The cottages are a bit costly for one person, or even one couple, but for two couples traveling together and sharing expenses this is an imminently affordable choice. And the neighborhood is a good one; the beach house of the American consulate, whose residence is on the drive leading to the cottages, is next door to Beach Home cottage. A grocery store and cycle shop are nearby. ⊠ *Box PG 137, Paget, PG BX,* ☎ *441/236–1194, 800/637–4116 in U.S.,* ℻ *441/236–1662. 2 housekeeping cottages. EP. AE, MC, V.*

$$$ 🏠 **Longtail Cliffs.** Don't be put off by the small office and the concrete parking lot that serves as the front yard of this motel-like establishment. Although it may not have the personality or splendid beach views of other cottages, its relatively flat setting makes it much more suitable for older people or anyone opposed to climbing. Housed in a modern, two-story building, guest apartments are large, light, and airy, with balconies and spectacular ocean views. Each has two bedrooms and two spacious bathrooms decorated with brightly colored tiles. A small but well-equipped kitchen comes with a microwave oven, coffeemaker, iron, and ironing board. Italian tile floors grace the living areas and are accented by Oriental rugs and high-quality furniture. Many units have beamed ceilings and some have fireplaces (for aesthetic purposes only). There's a coin-operated laundry, cable TV, and a gas barbecue grill for cookouts. Despite its location on the south shore, the complex does not have a beach; however, it is adjacent to Astwood Cove. ⊠ *Box HM 836, Hamilton HM CX,* ☎ *441/236–2864 or 441/236–2822, 800/637–4116 in U.S.,* ℻ *441/236–5178. 12 2-bedroom, 2 bath apartments, 1 1-bedroom apartment with bath. EP. Pool. AE, MC, V.*

$$$ 🏠 **Surf Side Beach Club.** This is another option for couples looking to share a space on the south shore. The bright reception area with upholstered chairs is sizable enough to be used as a lounge. Cottages are on terraced levels, each with a view of the ocean and the long stretch of sandy beach below—just a hop, skip, and a jump away. There are spacious studios and suites; each has a fully equipped kitchen (with microwave), cable TV, telephone, and porch. All are decorated with light wood furnishings, brightly colored island fabrics, and wall-to-wall carpeting; some have tile floors. You can cook on your own barbecue grills or dine at a poolside coffee shop (open April–October, room service at extra charge). Weekly rum swizzle parties are held for guests. ⊠ *Box WK 101, Warwick WK BX,* ☎ *441/236–7100 or 800/553–9990,* ℻ *441/236–9765. 10 apartments, 23 studios, 2 penthouse units. EP. Coffee shop, pool, sauna, exercise room, bicycles, coin laundry. AE, MC, V.*

$$–$$$ 🏠 **Angel's Grotto.** Some 30 years ago this was a swinging nightclub
★ and one of the hottest spots on the island. Now, it's a quiet residential apartment house close to Devil's Hole Aquarium on the south shore of Harrington Sound. Proprietor Daisy Hart and her hardworking staff took top Department of Tourism honors in 1996 for these charmingly decorated apartments. Curtains and spreads are in cool, pretty pastels; all rooms have TVs, radios, and phones, and kitchens are fully equipped. In 1996, new carpeting and air conditioners were installed. There is no beach, but the pink sands of John Smith's Bay on the south shore are a five-minute walk away; other south-shore beaches are less than 10 minutes away by moped. Most guests are couples; the secluded Honeymoon Cottage is particularly appealing if you want privacy. The two-

bedroom, two-bath apartment in the main house is a good buy for two couples traveling together. A large patio is ideal for cocktails in the evening, and there is also a barbecue. Deep-water swimming is possible in Harrington Sound. ⊠ *Box HS 81, Smith's HS BX,* ☎ *441/293–1986, 800/637–4116 in U.S.,* ℻ *441/293–4164. 7 apartments. EP. AE, MC, V.*

$$ 🖻 **Greenbank Cottages.** On a quiet dead end less than a minute's walk from the Salt Kettle ferry landing, these green, one-story cottages nestle among tall trees beside Hamilton Harbour. Small and family-oriented, they are not grand, but you can count on plenty of personal attention from the Ashton family. In the 200-year-old main house, the guests' lounge has attractive throw rugs, hardwood floors, a TV, and a grand piano. There are four rental units with kitchens in the main house; all other units are self-contained, with fully equipped kitchens, private entrances, and shaded verandas. The waterside cottages are the best choice, especially Salt Winds: The views of the harbor from the bed, dining table, and kitchen are lovely. Rooms are simply furnished. There is a private dock suitable for deep-water swimming, and the beaches are less than 10 minutes away by taxi or moped. One of the island's best water-sport facilities—Salt Kettle Boat Rentals—is on the property, so access to snorkeling spots is easy. ⊠ *Box PG 201, Paget PG BX,* ☎ *441/236–3615, 800/637–4116 in U.S.,* ℻ *441/236–2427. 3 rooms, 8 apartments. CP, EP. AE, MC, V.*

$$ 🖻 **Paraquet Guest Apartments.** These apartments (pronounced "para-keet") are in an ideal location—a mere five-minute walk from Elbow Beach. Ideal for budget travelers, they are spartan but spic-and-span, spacious and well lit, with TVs, clock radios, and small refrigerators. Nine units have kitchens. Rooms are done in simple, functional furnishings reminiscent of a motel. Efficiency units have full baths, while the rest have only shower baths. The three units in the Paraquet Cottage share a patio. There is a market nearby for supplies, and the fine restaurants at Horizons and the Stonington Beach Hotel are within walking distance. ⊠ *Box PG 173, Paget PG BX,* ☎ *441/236–5842,* ℻ *441/236–1665. 12 rooms. EP. Restaurant. No credit cards.*

$$ 🖻 **Pretty Penny.** A three-minute walk from the ferry dock at Darrell's
★   Wharf and 10 minutes by scooter from the south-shore beaches, this upscale lodging has one of the friendliest, most helpful staffs on the island. The grounds are small and offer no good views, but guest cottages are surrounded by trees and shrubs. Each room is brightened by a colorful tile floor and has a dining area and private patio. A small kitchen area has a microwave oven, refrigerator, and cupboards well stocked with china, cooking utensils, and cutlery. Each apartment has an iron and ironing board; TVs can be rented. The Shilling, a room in a quaint cottage across from the main building, is a charmer. A playground, replete with trampoline, has been added near the Play Penny, which is tucked away in the rear. ⊠ *Box PG 137, Paget PG BX,* ☎ *441/236–1194, 800/637–4116 in U.S.,* ℻ *441/236–3290. 9 apartments. EP. Pool, playground. AE, MC, V.*

$–$$ 🖻 **Barnsdale Guest Apartments.** Budget travelers who want to be near south-shore beaches and the ferry to Hamilton would do well to consider the small apartments in this two-story yellow house. In a residential neighborhood very close to a grocery store, the apartments are in a garden with an orchard of loquat, banana, orange, and peach trees, which you are encouraged to sample. All are clean and neat studio efficiency units, each with a private entrance. Annually spruced up, each room is tastefully decorated and sleeps up to four guests on pullout sofa beds. All have a fully equipped kitchen, TV, iron, and ironing board. Apartment 5 is delightful, with a light, airy feeling—but it's next to the pool area, which can become noisy. An outdoor barbecue gives you a chance to escape from the kitchen and enjoy those balmy Bermuda evenings. ⊠ *Box DV 628, Devonshire DV BX,* ☎ *441/236–0164,* FAX *441/236–4709. 7 efficiency studio apartments. EP. Pool. AE, MC, V.*

$–$$ 🏠 **Sky Top Cottages.** This aptly named hilltop property has spectacu-
★ lar views of the island's southern coast and the azure ocean beyond. It's best to have wheels (or great lungs) to negotiate the steep grade. Runners and walkers will appreciate its proximity to Elbow Beach, one of the best stretches of sand for a workout. Neat sloping lawns, care- fully tended gardens, paved walks bordered by seasonal flowers, and a nearby citrus grove provide a pleasant setting for studios and one- bedroom apartments. John and Andrea Flood, who purchased the property in late 1996, have installed new kitchens in each apartment. The individually decorated units have attractive prints and carefully coordinated colors. Studio apartments have shower baths, and one- bedroom apartments have full baths. The very private one-bedroom apartment Frangipani is furnished in white wicker and rattan and has an eat-in kitchen, king-size bed, and sofa bed. Honeysuckle is a three- level apartment with a sitting room, kitchen, dining room, and a bed- room with king-size bed and bathroom upstairs. All units have phones, TVs, irons and ironing boards, and clock radios. Barbecue grills are available for guests' use. ⊠ *Box PG 227, Paget PG BX,* ☎ *441/236– 7984,* FAX *441/232–0446. 11 apartments. EP. MC, V.*

$ 🏠 **Whale Bay Inn.** Golfers approaching the 14th hole of the Port Royal Course are sometimes baffled to find golf balls other than their own dotting the green. Little do they know that it's a mere chip shot from the front lawn of this inn, and some guests can't resist the challenge to play through. If you want to be near Hamilton's shops you will be better served elsewhere, but if you are looking for an area with un- crowded, peaceful beaches this West End property is the place to be. Whale Bay Beach is a short walk away; the beaches of Church Bay, for some of the island's best snorkeling, Horseshoe Bay, and Somer- set Long Bay are easily reached by moped. The ocean is visible beyond beds of flowers and the rolling lawn that surrounds the Bermuda-style pink building. Guest rooms are contemporary, with rattan and muted prints. All five ground-floor units have a bedroom, phone, and private entrance. Four of the five have both a double and a single bed; one has a double bed and a sofa bed. The two end units have larger bathrooms and are better suited to families. Small, modern kitchens are equipped with microwave ovens, two-burner stoves, refrigerators, cutlery, cof- feemakers, dinnerware, and cooking utensils. Annual work includes painting and freshening of the rooms. Groceries can be delivered from nearby markets. ⊠ *Box SN 544, Southampton SN BX,* ☎ *441/238– 0469,* FAX *441/238–1224. 5 apartments. EP. Beach. No credit cards.*

Guest Houses

$$ 🏠 **Aunt Nea's Inn at Hillcrest.** Formerly called Hillcrest Guest House, this erstwhile plain-and-simple place has metamorphosed into an ut- terly charming bed-and-breakfast. Furnishings and fabrics are all new and include handsome four-posters, sleigh beds, and testers—the room just off the registration area has a huge bed with lighting recessed in its tester. All rooms have cedar chests and cheval mirrors. Breakfast is served at a table with white iron chairs. A swimming pool is planned for the 1998 season. Set back from quaint Nea's Alley in St. George's behind a gate and manicured gardens, the yellow double-gallery house dates from the 18th century. The house is far from Hamilton and many of the beaches, but nearby Tobacco Bay Beach and the adjoin- ing secluded coves are some of the island's best snorkeling spots. The St. George's golf course is almost within putting distance. ⊠ *Box GE*

96, St. George's GE BX, ☎ 441/297–1630, ℻ 441/297–1908. *10 rooms. No credit cards.*

$$ ▣ **Edgehill Manor.** Atop a high hill surrounded by gardens and shrubs, this large colonial house is within easy walking distance of downtown Hamilton and less than 15 minutes by scooter from the best south-shore beaches. The staff is friendly and helpful, and you are guaranteed plenty of personal attention. In the morning, you can feast on home-baked muffins and scones in the cheery breakfast room, which is decorated with white iron chairs, glass-top tables, and vivid wallpaper. Guest rooms are individually decorated with French provincial furniture, colorful quilted bedspreads, large windows, and terraces. A large poolside room has a kitchen and is suitable for families. Anyone traveling alone on a tight budget should ask for the small ground-level room that has a kitchen and private terrace. ✉ *Box HM 1048, Hamilton HM EX,* ☎ *441/295–7124,* ℻ *441/295–3850. 9 rooms. CP. Pool. No credit cards.*

$$ ▣ **Little Pomander Guest House.** In a quiet residential area near Hamil-
★ ton Harbour, this is a find if you are seeking lower-cost accommodation near Hamilton. In a charming cottage on Hamilton Harbour, rooms are decorated with plump pastel-color comforters, and the shams, dust ruffles, drapes, headboards, and shower curtains are made of matching fabrics. All units have microwaves, phones, and refrigerators. Guests congregate at sunset on the waterside lawn to enjoy views of Hamilton Harbour and often stay to cook dinner on the barbecue grill. For a $10 fee, you can play tennis across the road at the Pomander Tennis Club. Continental breakfast is served family-style to guests in a sunny room where tables are set with china in a blue-and-white floral design. ✉ *Box HM 384, Hamilton HM BX,* ☎ *441/236–7635,* ℻ *441/236–8332. 5 rooms with bath CP, 3 apartments. EP. AE, MC, V.*

$$ ▣ **Oxford House.** This is the closest you can get to downtown Hamil-
★ ton without pitching a tent—it's less than a five-minute walk from the shops, ferries, and buses. Recipient in 1996 of the Department of Tourism's highest award in its category, this family-owned and -operated two-story establishment is popular with all age groups and is an excellent choice for shoppers. Just off the small entrance hall, a fireplace, crisp linen tablecloths, pastel-color curtains, and handsome Chippendale chairs lend warmth to the breakfast room, where guests sample scones, English muffins, fresh fruit in season, and cereal in the morning. The bright, airy rooms (doubles, triples, and quads) are individually decorated with bold fabrics. Two rooms have full baths, whereas the rest have showers only. A small bookcase in the upstairs hall is crammed with paperbacks and serves as a guests' library. ✉ *Box HM 374, Hamilton HM BX,* ☎ *441/295–0503 or 800/548–7758 in U.S.,* ℻ *441/295–0250 or 800/272–2306 in Canada. 12 rooms. CP. AE, MC, V.*

$–$$ ▣ **Loughlands Guest House & Cottage.** Built in 1920, this stately white mansion on a hill above South Road is loaded with fine antiques and European china. Lladro figurines grace the mantelpiece in the formal parlor, antique grandfather clocks stand in corners, and handsome breakfronts display Wedgwood china and Baccarat and Waterford crystal. Less than a five-minute walk from Elbow Beach, the guest house offers welcome amenities such as a guest refrigerator and a Continental breakfast of cereals, fruit juice, prunes, croissants, danish pastries, and coffee, all served in the enormous dining room. Although the guest rooms are not filled with fascinating objets d'art and may tend to be somewhat worn, they are a good deal for budget travelers. No two are alike—there are singles, doubles, triples, and quads—and most include large comfortable chairs and cotton spreads. A large cottage near the main house has additional rooms. ⊠ *79 South Rd., Paget PG 03,* ☎ *441/236–1253. 18 rooms with bath, 6 with shared bath. CP. Pool, tennis court. No credit cards.*

$ ▣ **Salt Kettle House.** Set behind a screen of palm trees on a bay ad-
★ joining Hamilton Harbour and just a two-minute walk from the Salt Kettle ferry that goes to Hamilton, this small, secluded guest house attracts repeat visitors year after year and is popular with boating enthusiasts. Just to the left of the entrance is a cozy lounge with a fireplace where guests gather for cocktails and conversation. A hearty English breakfast is served family-style in the adjacent dining room, which has water views. Two guest rooms are in the main house, and an adjoining apartment has a double bedroom, bathroom, living room, and kitchen. The best accommodations are in the four waterside cottages, which have shaded patios and lounge chairs, bed/sitting rooms, and kitchens. The Starboard, which accommodates four people, is a two-bedroom, two-bathroom unit with a living room, fireplace, and kitchen. Guest rooms are small, but the decor is charming, and owner Mrs. Hazel Lowe makes improvements every year. You can swim in a cove outside. ⊠ *10 Salt Kettle Rd., Paget PG 01,* ☎ *441/236–0407,* FAX *441/236–8639. 3 rooms in main house; 1 cottage accommodates 4 guests; 3 cottages each accommodate 2 guests. BP. Lounge. No credit cards.*

6 Nightlife and the Arts

The relatively small island of Bermuda hasn't spawned a rich arts scene or wild nightlife. In high season, however, hotels and cottage colonies do put on their entertainments—barbecues, steel bands, and dinner dancing. And there are always the local pubs for a little diversion.

NIGHTLIFE

Because Bermuda has no casinos and only a few nightclubs and discos, you'll find most of the action in pubs and lounges, hotel bars and local hangouts. Some places close off-season, so check *This Week in Bermuda* and *Preview of Bermuda,* free publications available in all hotels and tourist information centers, for the latest information about what's on each night. As a general rule, men should wear a jacket and tie to clubs; for women the dress code is casual chic. Pubs and discos begin to fill up around 9:30 or 10.

The music scene is dominated by local acts and bands playing the island's hotel and pub circuits. Occasionally, outside performers are billed, particularly during the **Bermuda Festival** (☞ The Arts, *below*). The island's longtime superstar, **Gene Steede**—a guitarist, singer, and comedian who has been described as Tony Bennett, Harry Belafonte, and Johnny Carson rolled into one—performs now mostly for private functions. Nonetheless, his performances are well worth catching should the opportunity present itself. Other popular entertainers to watch for are the **Coca-Cola Steel Band** and the **Bermuda Strollers. Jimmy Keys** is a popular pianist-comedian who holds court at the Southampton Princess Hotel's Neptune Lounge. **Sharx** is a rock band, and the **Travellers** straddle country and rock music.

Around 3 AM, when bars and discos close, head for the **Ice Queen** (⊠ Middle Rd., Paget, ☎ 441/236–3136). The place is like a drive-in movie without the movie—the parking lot is just jammed with cars and mopeds. The main attraction is the $2.75 burgers, which taste terrific after a night on the town. Order them from the take-out window and take them to the beach, where drunk and disorderly crowds won't bother you. It is open from 11 AM, which also makes it a good stop for an ice-cream-cone break.

As you'd guess from its name, **After Hours** (⊠ 117 South Rd., past intersection with Middle Rd., Paget, ☎ 441/236–8563) is another late-night spot. It opens at midnight and serves good curries, hamburgers, and sandwiches until 4 AM.

Bars and Lounges

If you like to toss a few back in a hard-core bar, **Casey's** (⊠ Queen St., across from the Little Theatre, Hamilton, ☎ 441/293–9549) is just that—a narrow room with a jukebox and a few tables. The place is by no means fancy or touristy, and it really packs 'em in, especially Friday nights. Casey's is open 10–10 every day except Sunday. In the Bailey's Bay area, between Hamilton and St. George, the **Swizzle Inn** (⊠ Middle Rd., Hamilton Parish, ☎ 441/293–9300)—where the motto is "Swizzle Inn, swagger out"—is strictly for the young. It comes with a dartboard, a jukebox that plays soft and hard rock, and business cards from all over the world tacked on the walls, ceilings, and doors.

Flanagan's Irish Pub & Restaurant (⊠ Front St., Hamilton, ☎ 441/295–8299) is a great bar where local groups entertain every night after 10. **Ye Olde Cock & Feather** (⊠ Front St., Hamilton, ☎ 441/295–2263), which draws both locals and tourists, has happy hour Monday through Saturday from 5 to 7, live music Friday and Saturday nights, and a jam session on Sundays. **Docksider Pub & Restaurant** (⊠ Front St., Hamilton, ☎ 441/292–4088) attracts a young crowd with live entertainment. **Robin Hood** (⊠ Richmond St., Hamilton, ☎ 441/295–3314) is popular at night for pub fare, pizza, and patio dining under the stars.

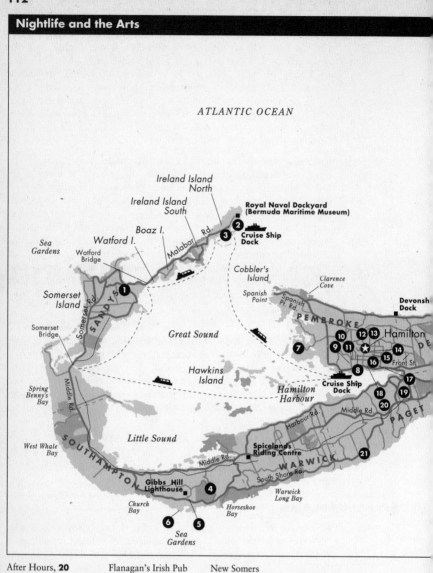

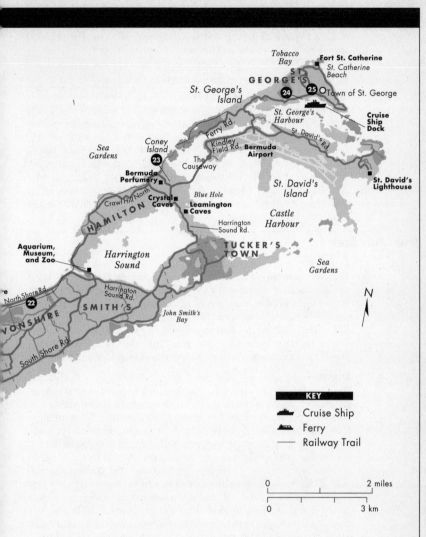

The **Colony Pub** (⊠ The Princess, 76 Pitts Bay Rd., Hamilton, ☎ 441/295–3000), where the lights are low and the piano music soft and soothing, is a popular meeting place for young professionals. The yachting crowd gathers at the **Wharf Tavern** (⊠ Somers Wharf, St. George's, ☎ 441/297–1515) for rum swizzling and nautical talk.

The **Neptune Club** at the Southampton Princess Hotel (⊠ South Shore Rd., Southampton, ☎ 441/238–8000) is wildly popular because of its British comedian-pianist Jimmy Keys, whose hilarious show airs nightly except Sunday. There is always local or visiting entertainment scheduled at the ever-popular watering hole, **Henry VIII** (⊠ South Shore Rd., Southampton, ☎ 441/238–1977). **Spazzizi's** (⊠ Elbow Beach Hotel, South Shore Rd., Paget, ☎ 441/236–3535) offers nightly entertainment by local performers. **Loyalty Inn** (⊠ Somerset Village, ☎ 441/234–0125) is a very casual neighborhood bar, where laid-back locals sometimes dare to do a karaoke bit. There's no cover, and dinner and snacks are served nightly.

The Club Scene

Calypso

The **Clayhouse Inn** (⊠ North Shore Rd., Devonshire, ☎ 441/292–3193) packs in locals and tourists for a rowdy show involving limbo dancers, the Bermuda Strollers, the Coca-Cola Steel Band, and an occasional top-name entertainer. Shows are at 10:15 Monday through Thursday; about $23 covers the entry fee plus two drinks. A range of entertainment is laid on for the weekend. Calypso bands from the Clayhouse Inn often provide entertainment at the various hotels during high season.

Discos

The Club (⊠ Bermudiana Rd., Hamilton, ☎ 441/295–6693) is a sophisticated nightspot. By day, it caters to a business crowd and can be rented for private meetings; special menus are available. When meetings are not being held, lunch and dinner are served, and cocktail happy hours from 5 to 7 keep the place hopping. With dancing every night until 3, this is a favorite nightspot among locals and visitors, who appreciate its comfort and elegance. There is no cover charge. **The Oasis** (⊠ Emporium Bldg., Front St., Hamilton, ☎ 441/292–4978 or 441/292–3379) is a hot spot for "Hot Rock" and disco dancing and a slightly younger crowd that gladly pays the $15 cover charge. There is dancing nightly from April through October in the chic **Palm Court** at the Sonesta Beach Hotel & Spa (⊠ Off South Rd., Southampton, ☎ 441/238–8122).

Folk

The only place to hear folk music is at the **Bermuda Folk Club**'s monthly get-togethers, which usually take place at 8:15 on the first Saturday of the month at the **Old Colony Club** (⊠ Trott Rd., Hamilton, ☎ 441/293–9241). Local and visiting musicians provide the entertainment and cover any number of musical styles besides folk. Drinks have happy-hour prices; the cover is $5. For information, write to the Bermuda Folk Club (⊠ Box WK 158, Warwick, WK BX).

Jazz

Hubie's Bar (⊠ Angle St., Hamilton, ☎ 441/293–9287), off Court Street, attracts jovial locals and visitors who appreciate good live jazz, which is played only on Friday 7–10. It's best to take a cab to this club, since the area can be dangerous at night. There is no cover charge.

Pop

Lights are low and the live music is loud at sophisticated **Club 21** (⊠ 16 Ireland Island, Sandys, Dockyard, ☎ 441/234–7037 or 441/234–2721). High-season shows are Tuesday through Saturday at 9:30 and

11:30, and there are Sunday jam sessions from 9 PM to 2 AM. Lots of action and a fun-loving crowd make this a popular place for locals and visitors. Cover charge is $12.

THE ARTS

All **Bermuda Department of Tourism** offices give away copies of their "Bermuda Calendar of Events" brochure. The informative *Bermuda* ($3.95), a quarterly magazine, describes upcoming island events and runs feature articles on what visitors can do. *The Bermudian* ($4) is a glossy monthly magazine that also has a calendar of events. Some hotels carry the TV station that broadcasts a wealth of information about sightseeing, restaurants, cultural events, and nightlife on the island. **Radio VSB**, FM 1450, gives a lineup of events on its Community Calendar daily at 11:15 AM. Or you can **dial 974** for a phone recording that details information about nature walks, tours, cultural events, afternoon teas, and seasonal events. The island is so small, however, that virtually everyone knows what's going on.

Because the arts scene in Bermuda is not extensive, many of the events and performing groups listed below operate on a casual or part-time basis. If you see a bulletin board, inspect it for posters describing events. **City Hall Theatre** (⊠ City Hall, Church St., Hamilton) is the major venue for a number of top-quality cultural events each year, although performances and productions are staged elsewhere on the island, as well. Contact the **Box Office** (Visitors Service Bureau, ☎ 441/295–1727) for reservations and information about all cultural events on the island. American Express, MasterCard, and Visa are accepted at the theater and the box office.

Some good amateur acting is done by members of the **Bermuda Musical & Dramatic Society,** whose plays are scheduled throughout the year in their Daylesford headquarters one block north of City Hall. A Christmas pantomime at City Hall is always a sellout, as are most other performances. Contact the box office for reservations and information (⊠ Daylesford, Dundonald St., Hamilton, ☎ 441/292–0848 or 441/295–5584).

In January and February, the **Bermuda Festival** brings internationally renowned artists to the island for a series of performances. The 2½-month program includes classical and jazz concerts and theatrical performances. The 1997 program included the British pianist David Owen Norris, the Vienna Boys Choir, and the Joshua Redman Jazz Quintet, just to name a few. Most shows take place in City Hall, and ticket prices range from $20 to $35. For information and reservations, contact Bermuda Festivals, Ltd. (⊠ Box HM 297, Hamilton HM AX, ☎ 441/295–1291, FAX 441/295–7403) or the Bermuda Department of Tourism.

If you want to meet local painters and see some of their work, the members of the **Bermuda Society of Arts** will welcome you to the Harbour Gallery (⊠ Front St. W., Hamilton, ☎ 441/296–2232), where Irish coffee is sometimes served in the evening.

Concerts

Beat Retreat Ceremony and **Regimental Musical Display** are separate performances by the Bermuda Regiment Band and the Bermuda Isles Pipe Band with Dancers, arranged by the Bermuda Department of Tourism once or twice a month, except in August. They perform on Front Street in Hamilton, King's Square in St. George's, or the Royal Naval Dockyard on Ireland Island.

The **Bermuda Philharmonic Society** presents several programs through-out the year, including classical music concerts by the full Philharmonic and by soloists. Students of the Menuhin Foundation, established in Bermuda by violin virtuoso Yehudi Menuhin, sometimes perform with the orchestra; visiting musicians often play in these events. Concerts take place in the Cathedral of the Most Holy Trinity in Hamilton (☞ Chapter 3), King's Square in St. George's, or at the Royal Naval Dockyard.

The **Gilbert & Sullivan Society of Bermuda** puts on a musical each year, usually in October. In addition to Gilbert and Sullivan operettas, the group occasionally does Broadway shows.

Dance

One of the many Bermuda Gombey troupes performs each week as part of the off-season (November–March) festivities organized by the Bermuda Department of Tourism. Gombey (pronounced "gum-bay") dancing is a blend of African, West Indian, and Caribbean Indian in-fluences. The Gombey tradition in Bermuda dates from the mid-18th century, when costumed slaves celebrated Christmas by singing and marching through the streets. The masked male dancers move to the accompaniment of skin-covered drums and the shrill, whistle-blown commands of the captain of the troupe. The ritualistic, often frenetic movements of the dancers, the staccato drum accompaniment, and the whistle commands are passed from generation to generation. Dancers wear colorful costumes that include tall headdresses decorated with peacock feathers and tiny mirrors. On all major holidays different troupes of Gombeys dance through the streets to many of the hotels, attract-ing crowds of followers. It's traditional to toss coins at the feet of the dancers.

The **Bermuda Civic Ballet** performs classical ballet at various venues dur-ing the year. Internationally known artists sometimes appear as guests.

The **National Dance Theatre of Bermuda** presents a blend of classical, modern, and jazz dancing. Performances are staged at various places throughout the year.

Movies

Bermuda has four cinemas showing first-run movies: Two are in Hamil-ton, one is in St. George's, and the fourth is in the West End. Check the listings in the *Royal Gazette* for movies and show times.

Neptune Cinema (✉ The Cooperage, Dockyard, ☎ 441/291–2035) is a 118-seat cinema that typically shows feature films at 7:30 and 9:30 nightly, with matinees at 2:30 Friday, Saturday, and Sunday.

The Little Theatre (✉ Queen St., Hamilton, ☎ 441/292–2135) is a 173-seat theater across the street from Casey's Bar. Show times are usually 2:15, 7, and 9:30.

Liberty Theatre (✉ Union and Victoria Sts., Hamilton, ☎ 441/291–2035) is a 270-seat cinema in an unsavory section of Hamilton. The area immediately outside the theater is safe during the day, but you should not loiter in this neighborhood after dark. Show times are usu-ally 2:30, 5:30, 7:30, and 9:30 daily, and 2:30 and 7:30 on Sunday.

New Somers Theatre (✉ York St., St. George's, ☎ 441/297–2821) is a 248-seat cinema at the entrance to the town of St. George's, just below the St. George's Club. Show times are usually 7 and 9 Monday through Thursday, with an additional viewing time scheduled Friday through Sunday.

Theater

Dinner theater has become popular over the past few years in Bermuda. The **Jabulani Repertory Company** (☎ 441/295–3000) stages a lineup of contemporary plays Wednesday through Saturday nights at the Hamilton Princess. Tickets for the show are $25. The hotel offers a dinner-theater package ($54), with dinner in one of the hotel's restaurants.

Bermuda is the only place outside the United States where Harvard University's **Hasty Pudding Theatricals** performs. For almost 30 years, the satirical troupe has entertained the island during Bermuda College Weeks (March–April). Produced by the estimable Elsbeth Gibson, an American-born actress-producer who lives in Bermuda, each show incorporates political and social themes and issues of the past year. Hasty Pudding Theatricals are staged at the **City Hall Theatre** (☞ *above*); ticket prices are about $20.

7 Beaches, Outdoor Activities, and Sports

Bermuda's beaches—fine-grain sand tinted pink with shells, marine invertebrates, and crushed coral—are surrounded by dramatic cliff and rock formations, shaded with coconut palms, or complemented by dunes that slope gently toward the shimmering turquoise and purple tones of the Atlantic Ocean. More than any other factor, climate is what makes Bermuda so ideal for sports—both in the water and out.

LONG BEFORE YOUR JET TOUCHES DOWN in Bermuda, the island's biggest asset becomes breathtakingly obvious—the crystal-clear, aquamarine water that frames the tiny, hook-shaped atoll. So clear is the seawater that in 1994 the Bermuda government nixed a plan by local scuba-diving groups to create a unique dive site by sinking an abandoned American warplane in 30 ft of water off the island's East End, near the airport and fairly close to the end of the runway. The government feared the plane would be easily visible from above—to arriving passengers—and could cause undue distress. That clarity of water makes Bermuda one of the world's great spots for scuba diving and snorkeling. Clear as it is, the water wasn't lucid enough to make Bermuda's treacherous reefs visible to the hundreds of ship captains who smashed their vessels on them over the centuries.

Thanks to Bermuda's position close to the Gulf Stream, the water stays warm year-round, although Bermudians consider anything below 75°F frigid. In summer, the ocean is usually above 80°F, and even warmer in the shallows between the reefs and shore. In winter, the water temperature only occasionally drops below 70°F, but it seems cooler because the air temperature is usually in the mid-60s. Lack of business, more than a drop in water temperature, is responsible for the comparative dearth of winter water-sports activity. (For the most part, dive shops are closed.) Winter does tend to be windier, which means that water conditions can be less than ideal. Rough water creates problems anchoring or stabilizing fishing and diving boats, and visibility underwater is often clouded by sand and debris. A wet suit is recommended if you plan to spend an extended period of time in the water.

High season runs from April through October, when fishing, diving, and yacht charters fill up quickly. Most boats carry fewer than 20 passengers, so it's advisable to sign up early. March through April and October through November are shoulder seasons; December through February is the off-season, when many operators close to make repairs and perform routine maintenance. During these months, a few operators stay open on a limited basis, scheduling charters only when there are enough people to fill a boat; if too few people sign up, a charter is usually canceled. For this reason, water-sports enthusiasts need to be flexible in winter.

Bermudians take their sports seriously. The daily paper's sports section is full of local coverage. Cricket and soccer grab most of the headlines, but road running, golf, field hockey, rugby, and a host of other island activities also get their share of space. Bermudian soccer players delight crowds in English leagues; Bermudian sailors hold their own in world competition, as do runners, equestrians, and swimmers. The island is also a golf and tennis paradise. With more than 70 courts and eight courses packed onto its 20 square mi it's hard to believe there would be any room left for horseback riding, cycling, running, or playing squash.

Take advantage of your hotel's activities director or your ship's cruise director—he or she can make arrangements for you long before you arrive. **"What to Do in Bermuda,"** a 39-page publication and the separate 7-page brochure, **"Information and Price Sheet for What to Do,"** have extensive information on the island's sports facilities and special events. Both are available free from the Bermuda Department of Tourism (☞ Visitor Information *in* the Gold Guide).

BEACHES

Most people would agree that the typical south-shore beach is more scenic than those on the north side—fine pinkish sand, coral bluffs topped with summer flowers, gentle, pale-blue surf moving past the barrier reefs offshore. The water at south-shore beaches tends to be a little rougher when the winds are from the south and southwest. It is along this coast, too, that waves continuously roll in and break on the sandy shoreline even when breezes are gentle. Many visitors join locals in the popular pastime of body surfing. Most Bermudian beaches are relatively small compared with ocean beaches in the United States, ranging from about 15 yards to a half-mile or so in length. In winter, when the weather is more severe, beaches may erode—even disappear—only to be replenished as the wind subsides in the spring.

The Public Transportation Board provides a free "Bermuda's Guide to Beaches and Transportation," available in all visitor centers and most hotels. A combination bus-ferry schedule and map, the guide shows locations of beaches and how to reach them. Information about the submarine *Enterprise,* taxis, and moped rentals is also included.

Few Bermudian beaches offer shade, but some have palm trees and thatched shelters. The sun can be intense, so bring hats and plenty of sunscreen. Umbrellas can be rented at some beaches. Below are reviews of the major beaches on the island that are open to the public. South-shore hotels that own private beaches are reviewed in Chapter 5.

North-Shore Beaches

Shelly Bay Beach. As at Somerset Long Bay, the water at this beach near Flatts is well protected from strong southerly winds. In addition, a sandy bottom and shallow water make this a good place to take small children. Shelly Bay also has shade trees—something of a rarity at Bermudian beaches. Drawbacks include a children's playground behind the beach, which attracts hoards of youngsters on weekends and during school holidays, and the traffic noise from busy North Shore Road, which is nearby. ⊠ *North Shore Rd., Hamilton Parish. Bus 10 or 11 from Hamilton.*

Somerset Long Bay. Popular with Somerset locals, this beach is on the quiet northwestern end of the island—far from the airport, the bustle of Hamilton, and major tourism hubs. In keeping with the area's rural atmosphere, the beach is low-key and unprepossessing. Undeveloped parkland shields the beach from light traffic on Cambridge Road. The main beach is crescent-shape and long by Bermudian standards—nearly ¼ mi from end to end. In contrast to the great coral outcroppings common on the south shore, grass and brush make up the main backdrop here. Although exposed to northerly storm winds, the bay water is normally calm and shallow—ideal for children. However, the bottom is rocky and uneven. ⊠ *Cambridge Rd., Sandys. Bus 7 or 8 from Hamilton.*

Tobacco Bay Beach. The most popular beach near St. George's—about 15 minutes northwest on foot—this small north-shore beach is huddled in a coral cove similar to those found along the south shore. Tobacco Bay has a beach house with a snack bar, equipment rentals, toilets, showers, and changing rooms. From the bus stop in the town of St. George, the beach is a 10-minute hike, or flag down one of St. George Minibus Service's vans and ask to be taken to the beach ($2 per person). ⊠ *Coot Pond Rd., St. George's,* ☎ *441/297–2756. Bus 1, 3, 10, or 11 from Hamilton.*

South-Shore Beaches

Chaplin and Stonehole Bays. In a secluded area east of Horseshoe Bay (☞ *below*), these tiny adjacent beaches almost disappear at high tide. Stonehole's most distinguishing feature is a high coral wall that reaches across the beach to the water, perforated by a 10-ft-high, arrowhead-shape hole. Like Horseshoe Bay, the beach fronts South Shore Park. ⊠ *Off South Rd., Southampton. Bus 7 from Hamilton.*

Elbow Beach Hotel. The $5 fee for nonguests is a measure to keep this portion of the beach relatively uncrowded, even on weekends. (Nonguests must call first.) One of the best places to relax on the island, the hotel beach provides umbrellas and chaises. Swimming and body surfing are just a few steps away from the chaises. Cafe Lido sells refreshments; toilet facilities are available. A free public beach is adjacent, but it can become very crowded and noisy on summer weekends. The entrance to this side is about a half-mile east of the hotel. A lunch wagon offers fast food and cold soft drinks. ⊠ *Off South Rd., Paget,* ☎ *441/ 236–3535. Bus 2 or 7 from Hamilton.*

Horseshoe Bay Beach. Horseshoe Bay has everything you would expect of a Bermudian beach: A ⅓-mi crescent of pink sand, clear water, a vibrant social scene, and an uncluttered backdrop provided by South Shore Park. This is one of the island's most popular beaches, a place where adults arrive with coolers and teenagers come to check out the action. The presence of lifeguards in summer—the only other beach with lifeguards is John Smith's Bay—and a variety of rentals, a snack bar, and toilet facilities add to the beach's appeal; in fact, it can become uncomfortably crowded here summer weekends. Parents should keep a close eye on their children in the water: The undertow can be strong, especially when the wind is blowing. ⊠ *Off South Rd., Southampton,* ☎ *441/238–2651. Bus 7 from Hamilton.*

John Smith's Bay. Backed by houses and South Road, this beach consists of a pretty strand of long, flat, open sand. The presence of a lifeguard in summer makes this an ideal place to bring children. As the only public beach in Smith's Parish, John Smith's Bay is also popular among locals. ⊠ *South Rd., Smith's. Bus 1 from Hamilton.*

Warwick Long Bay. Very different from covelike Chaplin, Stonehole, and Horseshoe bays, this beach has the longest stretch of sand—about ½ mi—of any beach on the island. Its backdrop is a combination of very steep cliffs and low grass- and brush-covered hills. The beach is exposed to some strong southerly winds, but the waves are rarely large because the inner reef is close to shore. An interesting feature of the bay is a 20-ft coral outcrop less than 200 ft offshore that looks like a sculpted boulder balancing on the surface of the water. The frequent emptiness of South Shore Park, which surrounds the bay, heightens the beach's appealing isolation and serenity. ⊠ *Off South Rd., Southampton. Bus 7 from Hamilton.*

OUTDOOR ACTIVITIES AND SPORTS

Keep in mind that you can arrange sporting activities (tee times, for example) yourself, or through your hotel or ship activities director.

Bicycling

Bermuda is not the easiest place in the world to bicycle. Be prepared for some tough climbs—the roads running north–south across the island are particularly steep and winding—and the wind can sap even the strongest rider's strength, especially along South Road in Warwick

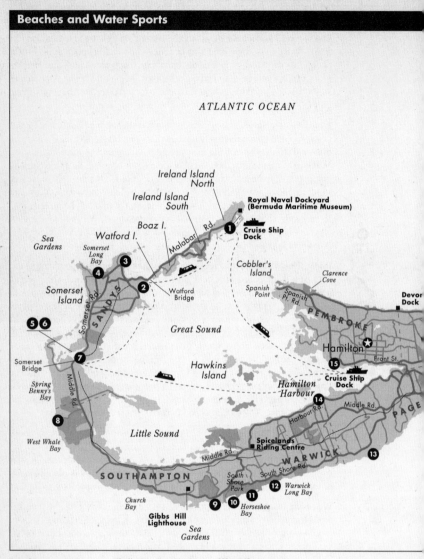

Beaches

Chaplin Bay and
Stonehole Bay, **11**
Elbow Beach
Hotel, **13**
Horseshoe Bay
Beach, **10**
John Smith's Bay, **17**

Shelly Bay Beach, **16**
Somerset Long Bay, **4**
Tobacco Bay
Beach, **19**
Warwick
Long Bay, **12**

Water Sports

Bermuda Waterski
Centre, **5**
Blue Hole Water
Sports (at Grotto Bay
Beach Hotel), **18**
Blue Water Divers
Ltd., **6**
Dive Bermuda, **1**
Fantasea Diving, **14**
Greg Hartley's Under
Sea Adventure, **2**

Mangrove Marina, **3**
Nautilus Diving, **9, 15**
Pitman's
Snorkeling, **7**
Pompano Beach Club
Watersports Centre, **8**
Salt Kettle Yacht
Charters, **16**
Wake Up Ski
School, **15**

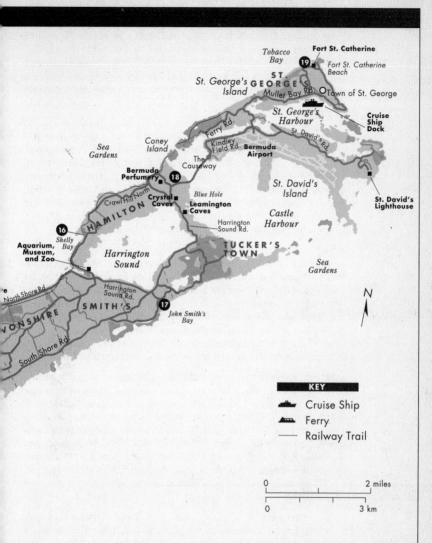

Tobacco Bay

Fort St. Catherine

19

Fort St. Catherine Beach

ST GEORGE'S

St. George's Island

GEORGE'S

Mullet Bay Rd. O Town of St. George

St. George's Harbour

Cruise Ship Dock

St. David's Rd.

Sea Gardens

Coney Island

Ferry Rd.

Kindley Field Rd.

Bermuda Airport

The Causeway

Bermuda Perfumery

18

HAMILTON

Crawl Hill North

Blue Hole

Crystal Caves

Leamington Caves

Harrington Sound Rd.

St. David's Island

St. David's Lighthouse

Castle Harbour

16

Shelly Bay

Aquarium, Museum, and Zoo

Harrington Sound

TUCKER'S TOWN

Sea Gardens

N

North Shore Rd.

Harrington Sound Rd.

SMITH'S

17

John Smith's Bay

ONSHIRE

South Shore Rd.

KEY

🚢 Cruise Ship

⛴ Ferry

— Railway Trail

0   2 miles

0   3 km

and Southampton parishes. Bermudian roads are narrow, with heavy traffic (especially near Hamilton during rush hours) and no shoulder. Most motorists are courteous to cyclists and stay within 10 mph of the 20-mph speed limit. Despite the traffic, bicycle racing is a popular sport in Bermuda, and club groups can regularly be seen whirring around the island on evening and weekend training rides. Bermudian roads are no place for novice riders, however; helmets are strongly recommended and parents should think twice before allowing preteen children to hop on a bike.

Bermuda's premier cycling and walking route, the Railway Trail (☞ Chapter 3), requires almost no road riding. Restricted to pedestrian and bicycle traffic, the trail is mostly paved, and it runs intermittently for almost the length of the island along the route of the old Bermuda Railway. The Bermuda Department of Tourism publishes "The Bermuda Railway Trail Guide," a free pamphlet that features a series of short exploring tours along the trail. The pamphlet is available at all Visitors Service Bureaus and the Department of Tourism.

Tribe roads—small side roads that are often unpaved—are also good for exploring, but don't be surprised if many of these roads, which date back to the earliest settlement of Bermuda, are dead ends. Well-paved South Road has relatively few climbs and some excellent ocean views, although it is one of Bermuda's most heavily traveled thoroughfares. The "Bermuda Handy Reference Map," also available at visitors service bureaus, is quite good, but even better is the *Bermuda Islands Guide,* a paperback available at the Bermuda Book Store in Hamilton. It is a detailed atlas showing every thoroughfare, lane, and alleyway.

In Bermuda, bicycles are called pedal or push bikes, to distinguish them from the more common motorized two-wheelers. Many of the cycle liveries around the island also rent 3-speed and 10-speed pedal bikes, but they can be difficult to find—it makes sense to reserve a bike a few days in advance. Rental rates are $10 to $15 a day. Contact **Eve's Cycle Livery** (⌧ Middle Rd., Paget, ☎ 441/236–6247) and **Oleander Cycles** (⌧ Valley Rd., Paget, ☎ 441/236–5235; ⌧ Gorham Rd., Hamilton, ☎ 441/295–0919; ⌧ Middle Rd., Southampton, ☎ 441/234–0629).

Boating and Sailing

On Bermuda you can either rent your own boat or charter a boat with a skipper. Rental boats, which are 18 ft at most, range from sailboats (typically tiny Sunfish) to motorboats (13-ft Boston Whalers), in addition to kayaks and pedal boats. Some of these vessels are ideal for exploring the coves and harbors of the sounds, or, in the case of motorboats, dropping anchor and snorkeling around the shorelines, which are abundant with different coral and colorful fish. In **Great Sound,** several small islands, such as **Hawkins Island** and **Darrell's Island,** have tiny secluded beaches and coves that are usually empty during the week. If the wind is fresh, and it is blowing in the right direction, the islands are about a half hour's sail from Hamilton Harbour or Salt Kettle. These beaches are wonderful places to picnic, although some are privately owned and visitors are not always welcome. Check with the boat-rental operator before planning an island outing.

The trade winds pass well to the south of Bermuda, so the island does not have predictable air currents. Channeled by islands and headlands, the wind direction around **Hamilton Harbour, the Great Sound,** and **Mangrove Bay** changes regularly. The variability of the winds has undoubtedly aided the education of Bermuda's racing skippers, who are traditionally among the world's best. To the casual sailor, however, wind changes can be troublesome, although you can be fairly confident you won't be becalmed: The average summer breeze is 7–10 knots, often out of the south or southwest. Mangrove Bay is often protected and is the ideal place for novice sailors and pedal boaters; a range of boats is available from Mangrove Marina. If you're looking for a taste of open water in summer, head for Pompano Beach Club Watersports Centre on the western ocean shore. For Great Sound and Somerset shoreline boating, go to the Royal Naval Dockyard and rent sailboats or motorboats.

Boat Rentals

Rates for small powerboats start at about $75 for four hours, up to $170 for a full day; sailboat rentals begin at $90 for four hours, or $115 to $170 for a full day. A credit card number or a refundable deposit of about $70 is usually required. Sailboats and powerboats can be rented at **Blue Hole Water Sports,** at Grotto Bay Beach Hotel & Tennis Club (⊠ 11 Blue Hole Hill, Hamilton Parish, ☎ 441/293–2915 or 441/293–8333, ext. 37), and **Windjammer Water Sports** (⊠ Dockyard Marina, Royal Naval Dockyard, ☎ 441/234–1343, FAX 441/234–3241). Rentals are also available at **Mangrove Marina** (⊠ Cambridge Rd., Sandys, ☎ 441/234–0914 or 441/234–0331, ext. 295), **Pompano Beach Club Watersports Centre** (⊠ 36 Pompano Rd., Southampton, ☎ 441/234–0222), and **Salt Kettle Yacht Charters** (⊠ Off Harbour Rd., Salt Kettle Rd., Paget, ☎ 441/236–4863 or 441/234–8165, FAX 441/236–2427).

Charter Boats

More than 20 large power cruisers and sailing vessels, piloted by local skippers, are available for charter. Ranging from 30 to 60 ft long, charter sailboats can carry up to 30 passengers, with overnight accommodations available in some cases. Meals and drinks can be included on request, and a few skippers have dinner cruises for the romantically inclined. Rates generally range between $375 and $425 for a three-hour cruise, or $650 to $1,000 for a full-day cruise, with additional per-person charges for large groups. Where you go and what you do—exploring, swimming, snorkeling, cruising—is up to you and your skipper. In most cases, cruises travel to and around the islands of Great Sound. Several charter skippers advertise year-round operations, but the off-season (December through February) schedule can be haphazard. Skippers devote periods of the off-season to maintenance and repairs or close altogether if bookings lag. Be sure to book well in advance; in the high season, do so before arriving on the island.

Sailboat charter firms include Capt. Kirk Ward's **Native Tours** (☎ 441/234–8149 or 441/234–1434), David Ashton's **Salt Kettle Yacht Charters** (☎ 441/236–4863 or 441/236–3612), Capt. Ed Williams's **Starlight Sailing Cruises** (☎ 441/292–1834), Percy Smith's **Perrah Yacht Charters** (☎ 441/295–0060), and Michael Voegeli's **Ocean Wind Sail Charters** (☎ 441/238–0825 or 441/234–8547, FAX 441/238–1614).

Powerboat charters are available through Capt. Douglas Shirley's **Bermuda Barefoot Cruises** (☎ 441/236–3498), **Tam Marina** (☎ FAX 441/236–0127), and **Salt Kettle Yacht Charters** (☎ 441/236–4863 or 441/236–3612).

Diving

Bermuda has all the ingredients necessary for classic scuba diving—reefs, wreckage, underwater caves, a variety of coral and marine life, and clear, warm water. Although diving is possible year-round (you must bring your own gear in winter when dive shops are closed), the best months are May through October, when the water is calmest and warmest. No prior certification is necessary; novices can learn the basics and dive in water up to 25 ft deep on the same day. Three-hour resort courses ($85–$110), which teach the basics in a pool, on the beach, or off a dive boat and culminate in a reef or wreck dive, are offered by **Fantasea Diving** (⊠ Darrell's Wharf, Harbour Rd., Paget, ☎ 441/236–6339), **Nautilus Diving** (⊠ Princess Hotel, Hamilton, ☎ 441/295–9485; ⊠ Southampton Princess Hotel, off South Rd., Southampton, ☎ 441/238–2332), **Blue Water Divers Ltd.** (⊠ Robinson's Marina, Somerset Bridge, Sandys, ☎ 441/234–1034, FAX 441/234–3561), and **Dive Bermuda** (⊠ Dockyard Terrace, Royal Naval Dockyard, Sandys, ☎ 441/234–0225).

The easiest day trips, offered by Nautilus Diving Ltd., involve exploring the south-shore reefs that lie inshore. These reefs may be the most dramatic in Bermuda: In places, the ocean-side drop-off exceeds 60 ft, and the coral is so honeycombed with caves, ledges, and holes that exploratory possibilities are infinite. Despite concerns in recent years about dying coral and fish depletion, most of Bermuda's reefs are still in good health—anyone eager to swim with multicolored schools of fish or the occasional barracuda will not be disappointed. In the interest of preservation, however, the removal of coral or coral objects is illegal.

Dive shops around Bermuda prominently display a map of the outlying reef system and its wreck sites. Only 38 of the past three centuries' wrecks are marked: the larger wrecks that are still in good condition. The nautical carnage includes some 300 wreck sites in all—an astonishing number—many of which are well preserved. As a general rule, the more recent the wreck or the more deeply submerged it is, the better its condition. Most of the well-preserved wrecks are to the north and east, and dive depths range between 25 and 80 ft. Several wrecks off the western end of the island are in relatively shallow water—30 ft or less—making them accessible to novice divers and even snorkelers. The major dive operators for wrecks on the western side of the island are Blue Water Divers Ltd. and Dive Bermuda. A one-tank dive costs $40 to $55; for introductory divers, the price range is $85 to $100. Two-tank dives for experienced divers cost $65 to $80. With two tanks, you can explore two or more wrecks during the same four-hour outing. Rates usually include all equipment—mask, fins, snorkel, scuba apparatus, and wet suit (if necessary). Some operators also offer night dives.

Helmet Diving

A different, less technical type of diving popular in Bermuda is "helmet diving," offered between mid-April and mid-November. Although helmet diving cruises last three hours or more, actual underwater time is about 25 minutes. During this time, underwater explorers, wearing helmets that are fed air through hoses leading to the surface, walk along the sandy bottom in about 10–12 ft of water, depending on the tide. Underwater videos and portraits are available for an extra charge. A morning or afternoon tour costs about $50 for adults, $40 for children 12 and under, and includes wet suits when the water temperature is less than 80°F. Contact **Greg Hartley's Under Sea Adventure** (⊠ Watford Bridge, Sandys, ☎ 441/234–2861).

Fishing

Fishing in Bermuda falls into three basic categories: shore or shallow-water fishing, reef fishing, and deep-sea fishing. No license is required, although some restrictions apply, particularly regarding the fish you can keep (for instance, only Bermudians with commercial fishing li-

Pick up
the phone.

Pick up
the miles.

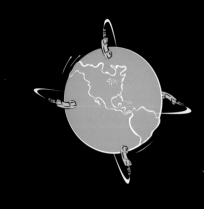

Use your MCI Card® to make an international call from virtually anywhere in the world and earn frequent flyer miles on one of seven major airlines.

Enroll in an MCI Airline Partner Program today. In the U.S., call **1-800-FLY-FREE.** Overseas, call MCI collect at **1-916-567-5151.**

1. To use your MCI Card, just dial the WorldPhone access number of the country you're calling from.
   (For a complete listing of codes, visit www.mci.com.)
2. Dial or give the operator your MCI Card number.
3. Dial or give the number you're calling.

# American Samoa	633-2MCI (633-2624)		# Guyana	177
# Antigua	#2		# Haiti (CC) ÷	193
(Available from public card phones only)			Haiti IIIC Access in French/Creole	190
# Argentina (CC)	0800-5-1002		Honduras ÷	122
# Aruba ÷	800-888-8		# Jamaica ÷	1-800-888-8000
# Bahamas	1-800-888-8000		(From Special Hotels only)	873
# Barbados	1-800-888-8000		# Mexico	
# Belize	557 from hotels		Avantel (CC)	91-800-021-8000
	815 from pay phones		Telmex ▲	95-800-674-7000
# Bermuda ÷	1-800-888-8000		Mexico IIIC Access	91-800-021-1000
# Bolivia ♦	0-800-2222		# Netherlands Antilles (CC) ÷	001-800-888-8000
# Brazil (CC)	000-8012		Nicaragua (CC)	166
# British Virgin Islands ÷	1-800-888-8000		(Outside of Managua, dial 02 first)	
# Cayman Islands	1-800-888-8000		Nicaragua IIIC Access in Spanish	★2 from any public payphone
# Chile (CC)			# Panama	108
To call using CTC ■	800-207-300		Military Bases	2810-108
To call using ENTEL ■	800-360-180		# Paraguay ÷	008-112-800
# Colombia (CC) ♦	980-16-0001		# Peru	0-800-500-10
Columbia IIIC Access in Spanish	980-16-1000		# Puerto Rico (CC)	1-800-888-8000
# Costa Rica ♦	0800-012-2222		# St. Lucia ÷	1-800-888-8000
# Dominica	1-800-888-8000		# Trinidad & Tobago ÷	1-800-888-8000
# Dominican Republic (CC) ÷	1-800-888-8000		# Turks & Caicos ÷	1-800-888-8000
Dominican Republic IIIC Access in Spanish	1121		# Uruguay	000-412
# Ecuador (CC) ÷	999-170		# U.S. Virgin Islands (CC)	1-800-888-8000
El Salvador ♦	800-1767		# Venezuela (CC) ÷ ♦	800-1114-0
# Grenada ÷	1-800-888-8000			
Guatemala (CC) ♦	9999-189			

Is this a great time, or what? :-)

Urban planning.

CITYPACKS

The ultimate guide to the city—a complete pocket guide plus a full-size color map.

www.fodors.com

censes are permitted to take lobsters) and the prohibition against spear guns. In recent years, some concern has been expressed about the decline in the number of reef and shore fish in Bermudian waters. New government measures to restore fish populations have had an adverse impact on some commercial operations, but sportfishing has been largely unaffected.

Reef Fishing

Three major reef bands lie at various distances from the island: The first is anywhere from a half mile to 5 mi offshore; the second, the Challenger Bank, is about 12 mi offshore; the third, the Argus Bank, is about 30 mi offshore. As a rule, the farther out you go, the larger the fish—and the more expensive the charter.

Most charter fishing captains go to the reefs and deep water to the southwest and northwest of the island, where the fishing is best. Catches over the reefs include snapper, amberjack, grouper, and barracuda. Of the most sought-after deep-water fish—marlin, tuna, wahoo, and dolphin—wahoos are the most common and dolphin the least. Trolling is the usual method of deep-water fishing, and charter-boat operators offer various tackle setups, with test-line weights ranging from 20 to 130 pounds. The boats, which range between 31 and 55 ft long, are fitted with a wide array of gear and electronics to track fish, including depth sounders, global positioning systems, loran systems, video fish finders, radar, and computer scanners. All boats must pass annual safety inspections, which are of the standard required by the U.S. Coast Guard.

Half-day or full-day charters are offered by most operators, but full-day trips offer the best chance for a big catch because the boat can reach waters that are less frequently fished. Rates are about $600 per boat for a half-day (four hours), and $850 per day (eight hours). Many captains encourage clients to participate in the catch-and-release program to maintain the abundant supply of fish, but successful anglers certainly can keep fish if they like.

The Bermuda Department of Tourism runs the free **Game Fishing Tournament** between April 1 and November 1; it is open to all anglers. Catches of any of 26 game varieties can be registered with the Department, and prizes are awarded. Charter bookings can be arranged through two organizations: **Bermuda Sport Fishing Association** (⌧ Creek View House, 8 Tulo La., Pembroke Parish HM02, ☎ 441/295–2370) and the smaller **St. George's Game Fishing Association** (⌧ Box 107GE, St. George, ☎ 441/297–8093; speak with Capt. Joe Kelley). In addition, several independent charter boats operate out of Hamilton Harbour as well as harbors in Sandys at the western end of the island. For more information about chartering a fishing boat, obtain a copy of the "Information and Price Sheet for What to Do" from the Bermuda Department of Tourism.

Shore Fishing

The principal catches for shore fishers are pompano, bonefish, and snapper. Excellent sport for saltwater fly-fishing is the wily and strong bonefish, which is found in coves, harbors, and bays—almost anywhere it can find food and shelter from turbulent water. Among the more popular spots for bonefish are **West Whale Bay** and **Spring Benny's Bay**, which have large expanses of clear, shallow water protected by reefs close inshore. Good fishing holes are numerous along the south shore, too. Fishing in the waters of the **Great Sound** and **St. George's Harbour** can be rewarding, but enclosed **Harrington Sound** is less promising. Ask at local tackle shops about the latest hot spots and the best baits to use.

Rod and reel rentals for shore fishing are available for about $15 to $20 a day ($20–$30 deposit or credit card impression required) from **Dockyard Boat Rentals** (⊠ Dockyard Marina, Royal Naval Dockyard, ☎ 441/234–0300), **Mangrove Marina** (⊠ Cambridge Rd., Somerset, ☎ 441/234–0914), **Salt Kettle Yacht Charters** (⊠ Off Harbour Rd., Salt Kettle Rd., Paget, ☎ 441/236–4863), and **Windjammer Water Sports** (⊠ Dockyard Marina, Royal Naval Dockyard, ☎ 441/234–1343 or 441/234–0250; ⊠ Cambridge Beaches, Sandys, ☎ 441/234–3082; ⊠ Lantana Colony Club, Sandys, ☎ 441/234–0504.). Rental prices usually include a tackle box and bait. Rental arrangements can also be made through hotel activities directors.

Golf

Bermuda is justifiably renowned for its golf courses. The scenery is spectacular, and the courses are challenging. However, you should not expect the manicured, soft fairways and greens typical of U.S. courses. Just as courses in Scotland have their own identity, the same is true of courses on this Atlantic isle. Bermudian courses are distinguished by plenty of sand, firm fairways and greens, relatively short par-fours, and wind—*especially* wind. Elsewhere, golf courses are usually designed with the wind in mind—long downwind holes and short upwind holes. Not so on Bermuda's eight courses, where the wind is anything but consistent or predictable. Quirky air currents make a Bermudian course play differently every day. On some days, a 350-yard par-four may be drivable; on other days, a solidly hit drive may fall short on a 160-yard par-three. Regardless, the wind puts a premium on being able to hit the ball straight and grossly exaggerates any slice or hook.

The island's water supply is limited, so irrigation is minimal and the ground around the green tends to be quite hard. For success in the short game, therefore, you need to run the ball to the hole, rather than relying on high, arcing chips, which require plenty of club face under the ball. Typically, Bermudian greens are elevated and protected by sand traps rather than thick grass. Most traps are filled with the soft limestone sand and pulverized pieces of pink shells that grow on the offshore reefs. Such fine sand may be unfamiliar to you, but it tends to be consistent from trap to trap and from course to course.

Greens are usually seeded with Bermuda grass and then over-seeded with rye. That means that you will putt on Bermuda grass in warmer months (March through November) and on rye when the weather cools and the Bermuda grass dies out. Greens are reseeded anytime from late September to early November, according to the weather. (Castle Harbour Golf Club's greens are reseeded in early January.) Some courses use temporary greens for two to four weeks; others keep the greens in play while reseeding and resurfacing. Greens in Bermuda tend to be much slower than the bent-grass greens prevalent in the United States, and putts tend to break less.

Another characteristic of Bermudian courses is the preponderance of rolling, hummocky fairways, making a flat lie the exception rather than the rule. Little effort has been made to flatten the fairways, because much of the ground beneath the island's surface is honeycombed with caves; bulldozer and backhoe operators are understandably uneasy about doing extensive landscaping.

The Bermuda Department of Tourism has a publication, the "Golf Guide," which has descriptions of golf courses, including addresses, phone numbers and prices.

How should golfers prepare for a Bermuda trip? In anticipation of the wind, practice hitting lower shots—punching the ball or playing it farther back in the stance may be helpful. Working on chip-and-run shots (a seven iron is ideal for this), especially from close-cropped lies, should also help. You can save yourself some strokes, too, by practicing iron shots from awkward hillside lies. On the greens, a long, firm putting stroke may save you from the bugaboo that haunts many first-time visitors: gently stroked putts dying short of the hole or drifting off-line with the grain of the Bermuda grass. As Allan Wilkinson, the former professional at the Princess Golf Club, has said, "In Bermuda, ya gotta slam 'em into the back of the cup."

Tournaments for pros, seniors, juniors, women, and mixed groups fill Bermuda's golfing schedule from February through December. The highlight of the golf year is the **Bermuda Open** in early October, which attracts a host of professionals and amateurs. Handicap limits are usually imposed for the more serious tournaments, and entry fees range between $100 and $150 (not all events are open to non-Bermudian players). A schedule with entry forms is available from the **Bermuda Golf Association** (⊠ Box HM 433, Hamilton HM BX, ☎ 441/238–1367, FAX 441/238–0983). A low-key event for golfers of all abilities is the **Bermuda Amateur Golf Festival,** a two-week affair in late February that gives players a chance to compete on several of the island's courses. Greens fees are reduced for festival participants, and several hotels offer reduced package rates. For more information, contact the Bermuda Amateur Golf Festival (⊠ Robustelli Sports Marketing, 460 Summer St., Stamford, CT 06901, ☎ 203/352–0500) or Bermuda Department of Tourism. Another easygoing tournament in mid-February is the **Valentine's Mixed Foursomes Invitational,** for which tournament/hotel packages are also available. For information or entry forms, contact the Tournament Chairman (⊠ Bermuda Golf Company, Box GE 304, St. George's GE BX, ☎ 441/297–8067).

Lessons, available at all courses, usually cost $35–$60 for a half hour, and club rentals range between $15 and $40. Caddies are a thing of the past, except at the Mid Ocean Club. Below are reviews and ratings of Bermuda's eight golf courses. The ratings, devised and administered by the United States Golf Association (USGA), "represent the expected score of an expert amateur golfer based upon yardage and other obstacles." For example, a par-72 course with a rating of 68 means that a scratch golfer would hit a four-under-par round—and ordinary hackers would probably score a little better, too. Ratings below are given for the blue tees (championship), white tees (men's), and red tees (women's).

Belmont Hotel, Golf & Country Club
Length: 5,777 yards from the blue tees
Par: 70
Rating: blue tees, 68.9; white tees, 67.9; red tees, 69.1

Of Bermuda's eight courses, the layout of the public Belmont Hotel, Golf & Country Club is perhaps the most maddening. The first two holes, straight par-fours, are a false preview of what lies ahead—a series of doglegs and blind tee shots. Playing with an experienced Belmont player who knows where to hit drives on such blind holes as the 6th, 11th, and 16th, and how best to play a dogleg hole such as the 8th, can help a newcomer trim six or more shots from a round. Despite the layout, Belmont remains one of Bermuda's easier courses, and it is ideal for inexperienced players. Belmont is an inland course and has few ocean panoramas. Instead, most holes overlook pastel houses with white roofs, a few of which have taken a beating from errant golf balls. A new irrigation system has improved the course dramatically in recent years. Fairway grass tends to be denser—and the clay soil moister—than the grass on the close-cropped, sandy fairways typical of other Bermudian courses. The rough, too, is generally deeper, snaring any wild tee shots. For this reason, and because Belmont is a short course (only one par-four is more than 400 yards), it makes sense to use a three or five wood, or even a low iron, from the tee. Belmont's chief drawback, especially on the weekend, is slow play—weekend rounds of five hours or more are common.

Highlight hole: The par-five 11th has a severe dogleg left, with a blind tee shot—Belmont in a nutshell. A short but straight drive is the key; trying and failing to cut the corner can be disastrous. The approach to the green is straight, although a row of wispy trees on the left awaits hooked or pulled shots. ⌧ *Belmont Rd., Warwick,* ☎ *441/236–6400,* FAX *441/236–6867. Greens fees: $85 for the public (includes mandatory cart).*

Castle Harbour Golf Club
Length: 6,440 yards from the blue tees
Par: 71
Rating: blue tees, 71.3; white tees, 69.2; red tees, 69.2

The only flat areas on the course, it seems, are the tees. The first tee, a crow's-nest perch by the clubhouse, offers an indication of things to come: Looking out over the fairway, with the harbor beyond, is like peering onto a golf course from a 20th-story window. Wind can make this course play especially long. Although most par-fours feature good landing areas despite all the hills, holes such as the 2nd, 16th, and 17th require players to drive over fairway rises. A wind-shortened drive can mean a long, blind shot to the green. Carrying the rise, on the other hand, can mean a relatively easy short shot, especially on the 2nd and 17th holes. Elevated greens are a common feature of Castle Harbour. The most extreme example is the 190-yard, par-three 13th, with the green perched atop a steep, 100-ft embankment. Balls short of the green inevitably roll back down into a grassy basin between the tee and the green. On the other hand, sand traps at Castle Harbour are mercifully few and far between by Bermudian standards; 10 holes feature two or fewer bunkers around the green.

Castle Harbour is one of Bermuda's most expensive courses; however, the money is clearly reinvested in the course. Greens are well maintained—firm, consistently cropped, and generally faster than most other Bermudian greens. The course also rewards golfers with several spectacular views, such as the hilltop panorama from the 14th tee, where blue water stretches into the distance on three sides.

Highlight hole: The 235-yard, par-three 18th is the most difficult finishing hole on Bermuda, especially when the wind is blowing from the northwest. On the right are jagged coral cliffs rising from the harbor; on the left are a pair of traps. When the course was revamped a few years ago, a small, flower-lined pond was added on the front right of the green, making this hard hole even harder. ⌧ *Marriott's Castle Harbour Resort, Paynters Rd., Tucker's Town,* ☎ *441/293–2040, ext. 6869;* FAX *441/293–1051. Greens fees: $110, plus $22 per person for cart Mar. 1–Nov. 1; $65, plus $22 per person for cart rest of yr ($76 with cart after 4:30 Apr. 3–Oct. 30). Shoe rentals: $8. Club rentals: $26.*

Mid Ocean Club
Length: 6,512 yards from the blue tees
Par: 71
Rating: blue tees, 72; white tees, 70; red tees, 73.6

It isn't Bermuda's oldest course—that honor belongs to Riddell's Bay—and other Bermudian courses are equally difficult, but the elite Mid Ocean Club is generally regarded as one of the top 50 courses in the world. Quite simply, this course has charisma, embodying everything that is golf in Bermuda—tees on coral cliffs above the ocean, rolling fairways lined with palms and spice trees, doglegs around water, and windswept views. It is rich in history, too. At the dogleg fifth hole, for example, Babe Ruth is said to have splashed a dozen balls in Mangrove Lake in a futile effort to drive the green. The course rewards long, straight tee shots and deft play around the green, while penalizing—often cruelly—anything less. The fifth and ninth holes, for example, require that tee shots (from the blue tees) carry 180 yards or more over water. And while length is not a factor on two fairly short par-fives, the 471-yard 2nd and the 487-yard 11th, accuracy is: Tight doglegs ensure that any wayward tee shot ends up in trees, shrubbery, or rough. However, the course may have mellowed with age: Having lost hundreds of trees to a tornado in 1986, and again to Hurricane Emily in 1987, the tight, tree-lined fairways have become more open, and the rough is less threatening.

Highlight hole: The 433-yard fifth is a par-four dogleg around Mangrove Lake. The elevated tee overlooks a hillside of flowering shrubbery and the lake, making the fairway seem impossibly far away. Big hitters can take a shortcut over the lake (although the green is unreachable, as the Babe's heroic but unsuccessful efforts attest), but anyone who hits the fairway has scored a major victory. To the left of the green, a steep embankment leads into a bunker that is among the hardest in Bermuda from which to recover. ⊠ *Mid Ocean Dr., off South Shore Rd., Tucker's Town,* ☎ *441/293–0330,* ℻ *441/293–8837. Greens fees: $140 ($70 when accompanied by a member). Nonmembers must be introduced by a club member; nonmember starting times available Mon., Wed., and Fri., except public holidays. Caddies: $25 per bag (tip not included). Cart rental: $40.*

Ocean View Golf & Country Club

Length: 3,000 yards (nine holes) from the blue tees
Par: men, 35; women, 37
Rating: none

Extensive work on the Ocean View Golf & Country Club was completed in 1994, with some $3 million having been spent by the Bermuda Government to improve the course after many years. Besides refurbishing the course—which has magnificent views of the island's north shore—a new clubhouse with a good restaurant and bar, locker rooms, and a new driving range were built. Founded in the 1940s, the nine-hole course gradually fell into neglect until badly needed improvements brought it up to the standards of the island's other courses. Ocean View's popularity has increased since the improvements, and it is busy throughout the week and on the weekends; plan ahead for tee times. Several holes challenge and intrigue: The first is a tough par-five that is a tight driving hole, with a 40-ft coral wall on one side and views of the north shore on the other. The sixth is a difficult par-four because of its elevated green; the ninth is a par-three with water guarding the front of the green, so shooting with accuracy is the key.

Highlight hole: The green on the 187-yard, par-three ninth hole is cut out of a coral hillside that is beautifully landscaped with attractive plants. It is a demanding tee shot, and club selection can be tricky, particularly when strong winds are blowing from north or west. ⊠ *Off North Shore Rd., Devonshire,* ☎ *441/295–9093,* ℻ *441/295–9097. Greens fees: $32 for 18 holes, plus $34 for cart rental; $22 for 9 holes, plus*

$17 for cart rental; $6 for hand cart. (Reduced fees when playing with a member or after 4.

Port Royal Golf Course
Length: 6,565 yards from the blue tees
Par: men, 71; women, 72
Rating: blue tees, 72; white tees, 69.7; red tees, 72.5

Such golfing luminaries as Jack Nicklaus rank the Port Royal Golf Course among the world's best public courses. A favorite with Bermudians as well, the course is well laid out, and the greens fees are modest. By Bermudian standards, Port Royal is also relatively flat. Although there are some hills, on the back nine in particular, the course has few of the blind shots and hillside lies that are prevalent elsewhere. Those holes that do have gradients tend to run either directly uphill or downhill. In other respects, however, Port Royal is classically Bermudian, with close-cropped fairways, numerous elevated tees and greens, and holes raked by the wind, especially the 8th and the 16th. The 16th hole, one of Bermuda's most famous, is frequently pictured in magazines. The green sits on a treeless promontory overlooking the blue waters and pink-white sands of Whale Bay, a popular boating and fishing area. When the wind is blowing hard on shore, as it frequently does, a driver may be necessary to reach the green, which is 163 yards away. One complaint often raised about Port Royal is the condition of the course, which can become chewed up by heavy usage—more than 55,000 rounds a year.

Highlight hole: Like the much-photographed 16th hole, the 387-yard, par-four 15th skirts the cliffs along Whale Bay. Changes to the course were made in 1995, making the par-three holes 8 and 16 longer; hole 11 now doglegs to the right and has a new green; number 13 plays a light dogleg to the left, with mounds and bunkers down the left-hand side. In addition to the ocean view, the remains of Whale Bay Battery, a 19th-century fortification, lie between the fairway and the bay. Only golf balls hooked wildly from the tee have any chance of a direct hit on the fort. The wind can be brutal on this hole. ⊠ *Off Middle Rd., Southampton,* ☎ *441/234–0974,* 🅵🅰🆇 *441/234–3562. Golf time can be reserved four days in advance through an automated system:* ☎ *441/ 295–6500. Greens fees: $65 weekdays, $70 weekends and holidays; discount rates after 4; 5-day Golf Package weekdays only, $260, greens fees only. Cart rental: $17 per person for 18 holes; $9 for hand cart. Club rental: $20. Shoe rental: $10.*

Princess Golf Club
Length: 2,684 yards from the blue tees
Par: 54
Rating: none

The Princess Golf Club unfolds on the hillside beneath the Southampton Princess. The hotel has managed to sculpt a neat little par-three course from the steep terrain, and players who opt to walk around will find their mountaineering skills and stamina severely tested. The vertical drop on the first two holes alone is at least 200 ft, and the rise on the fourth hole makes 178 yards play like 220. Kept in excellent shape by an extensive irrigation system, the course is a good warm-up for Bermuda's full-length courses, offering a legitimate test of wind and bunker play with a minimum of obstructions and hazards. Ocean views are a constant feature of the front nine, although the looming presence of the hotel does detract from the scenery.

Highlight hole: The green of the 174-yard 16th hole sits in a cup ringed by pink oleander bushes. The Gibbs Hill Lighthouse, less than a mile away, dominates the backdrop. ✉ *Southampton Princess, South Rd.,* ☎ *441/238–0446,* ℻ *441/238–8245. Greens fees: $57 per person with mandatory cart ($52 for hotel guests). Shoe rentals: $6.*

Riddell's Bay Golf and Country Club
Length: 5,588 yards from the blue tees
Par: men, 69; women, 71
Rating: blue tees, 66.9; white tees, 66.1; red tees, 70.6

Built in 1922, the Riddell's Bay Golf and Country Club is Bermuda's oldest course. In design, however, it more nearly approximates a Florida course—relatively flat, with wide, palm-lined fairways. You don't need to be a power hitter to score well here, although the first four holes, including a 427-yard uphill par-four and a 244-yard par-three, might suggest otherwise. The par-fours are mostly in the 360-yard range, and the fairways are generously flat and open. Despite the course's position on a narrow peninsula between Riddell's Bay and the Great Sound, water comes into play only on holes 8 through 11. With the twin threats of wind and water, these are the most typically Bermudian holes on the course, and accuracy off the tee is important. This is especially true of the par-four eighth, a 360-yard right dogleg around the water. With a tail wind, big hitters might try for the green, but playing around the dogleg on this relatively short hole is the more prudent choice. As at the Belmont course, a few tees are fronted with stone walls—an old-fashioned touch that harks back to the old courses of Great Britain. Like Mid Ocean's, Riddell's is a private club that is open to the public only at certain times, but the clubby atmosphere is much less pronounced here.

Highlight hole: The tees on the 340-yard, par-four 10th are set on a grass-topped quay on the harbor's edge. The fairway narrows severely after about 200 yards, and a drive hit down the right-hand side leaves a player no chance to reach the green in two. Two ponds guard the left side of a sloped and elevated green. The hole is rated only the sixth most difficult on the course, but the need for pinpoint accuracy probably makes it the hardest to par. ✉ *Riddell's Bay Rd., Warwick,* ☎ *441/238–1060,* ℻ *441/238–8785. Greens fees: $55 weekdays, $70 weekends ($35 weekdays, $45 weekends and holidays when accompanied by a member). Cart rental: $40 (for 2 people); $5 for hand cart.*

St. George's Golf Club
Length: 4,043 yards from the blue tees
Par: 63
Rating: blue tees, 62.8; white tees, 61.4; red tees, 62.8

Built in 1985, St. George's Golf Club dominates a secluded headland at the northeastern end of the island. The 4,043-yard course is short, but it makes up for its lack of length with sharp teeth. No course in Bermuda is more exposed to wind, and no course has smaller greens—some are no more than 25 ft across. To make matters trickier, the greens are hard and slick from the wind and salty air. Many of the holes have commanding views of the ocean, particularly the 8th, 9th, 14th, and 15th, which run along the water's edge. Wind—especially from the north—can turn these short holes into club-selection nightmares. Don't let high scores here ruin your enjoyment of some of the finest views on the island. The course's shortness and the fact that it gets little play midweek make St. George's Golf Club a good choice for couples or groups of varying ability.

Highlight hole: Pause to admire the view from the par-four 14th hole before you tee off. From the elevated tee area, the 326-yard hole curls around Coot Pond, an ocean-fed cove, to the green on a small, treeless peninsula. Beyond the neighboring 15th hole is old Fort St. Cather-

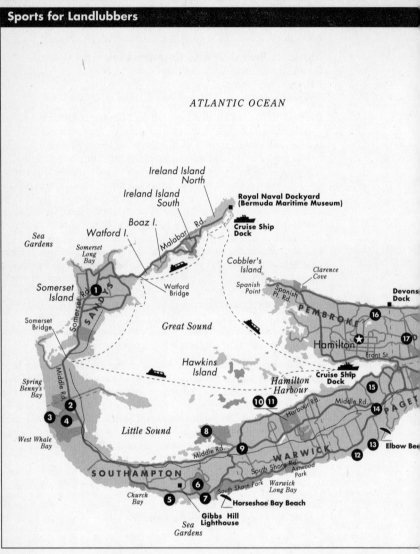

ATLANTIC OCEAN

Ireland Island
North

Ireland Island
South

Boaz I.

Watford I.

Malabar Rd.

**Royal Naval Dockyard
(Bermuda Maritime Museum)**

**Cruise Ship
Dock**

Sea
Gardens

Somerset
Long
Bay

Somerset
Island

SANDYS

Somerset Rd.

Watford
Bridge

Somerset
Bridge

Cobbler's
Island

Spanish
Point

Spanish Pt. Rd.

Clarence
Cove

**Devons
Dock**

PEMBROKE

16

17

Hamilton

Front St.

Great Sound

Hawkins
Island

Spring
Benny's
Bay

Middle Rd.

2

3   4

West Whale
Bay

Little Sound

Hamilton
Harbour

**Cruise Ship
Dock**

10 11

15

14

PAGET

8

9

Middle Rd.

13   **Elbow Bee**

SOUTHAMPTON

Middle Rd.

Harbour Rd.

WARWICK

South Shore Rd.

Astwood
Park

12

Church
Bay

5   6   7

South Shore Park

Warwick
Long Bay

Horseshoe Bay Beach

Sea
Gardens

**Gibbs Hill
Lighthouse**

Bicycling
Eve's Cycle Livery, **14**
Oleander
Cycles, **2,16**

Golf Courses
Belmont Hotel Golf
& Country Club, **10**
Castle Harbour Golf
Club, **23**
Mid Ocean Club, **22**
Ocean View Golf &
Country Club, **18**

Port Royal Golf &
Country Club, **4**
Princess Golf Club, **6**
Riddell's Bay Golf &
Country Club, **8**
St. George's Golf
Club, **26**

**Tennis and Squash
Courts**
Belmont Hotel, Golf
& Country Club, **11**
Bermuda Squash
Club, **21**
Coral Beach & Tennis
Club, **12**
Elbow Beach
Hotel, **13**

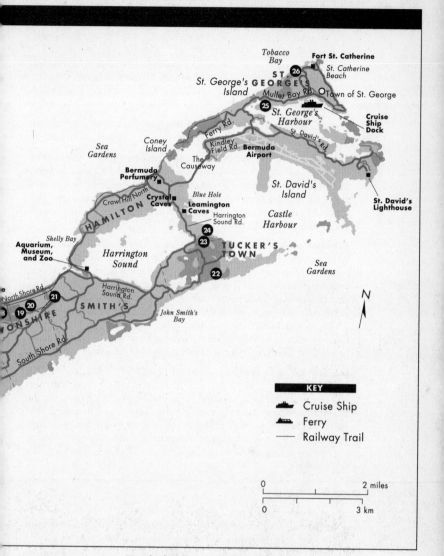

Tobacco Bay
Fort St. Catherine
St. Catherine Beach
St. George's Island
St. George's Island
St. GEORGE'S
㉖
Mullet Bay Rd.
Town of St. George
㉕
St. George's Harbour
Cruise Ship Dock
Ferry Rd.
St. David's Rd.
Sea Gardens
Coney Island
Kindley Field Rd.
Bermuda Airport
The Causeway
Bermuda Perfumery
St. David's Island
St. David's Lighthouse
Blue Hole
HAMILTON
Crawl Hill North
Crystal Caves
Leamington Caves
Harrington Sound Rd.
㉔
Castle Harbour
Aquarium, Museum, and Zoo
Shelly Bay
㉓
TUCKER'S TOWN
Harrington Sound
Sea Gardens
㉒
North Shore Rd.
㉑
SMITH'S
Harrington Sound Rd.
㉒
㉒
㉒
㉒
DEVONSHIRE
㉒
㉒
㉒
John Smith's Bay
South Shore Rd.
N

KEY
⛴ Cruise Ship
⛴ Ferry
— Railway Trail

0   2 miles
0   3 km

Government Tennis Stadium, **16**
Marriott's Castle Harbour Resort, **24**
Port Royal Course, **3**
Sonesta Beach Hotel & Spa, **5**
Southampton Princess Hotel, **7**

Horseback Riding
Lee Bow Riding Center, **17**
Spicelands Riding Centre, **9**

Spectator Sports
Bermuda Equestrian Federation, **19**
National Sports Club, **20**
St. George's Cricket Club, **25**
Somerset Cricket Club, **1**

ine's, and beyond that lies the sea. With a tail wind, it's tempting to hit for the green from the tee, but Coot Pond leaves no room for error. ⊠ *1 Park Rd., St. George's,* ☎ *441/297–8067, 441/295–5600 (tee times and information), 441/297–8148 (pro's office), or 441/297–8353 (pro shop);* FAX *441/297–2273. Greens fees: $43; $21 after 3, Apr.–Oct.; $16 after 2, Nov.–Mar. Cart rental: $34; $7 for hand cart.*

Horseback Riding

Bermuda has strict regulations regarding horseback riding, particularly on public beaches. Visitors may only rent horses for supervised trail rides.

Because most of the land on Bermuda is residential, opportunities for riding through the countryside are few. The chief exception is **South Shore Park,** between South Road and the Warwick beaches. Sandy trails, most of which are open only to riders or people on foot, wind through stands of dune grass and oleander and over coral bluffs. (Horses are not allowed on the beaches.)

The **Spicelands Riding Centre** (⊠ Middle Rd., Warwick, ☎ 441/238–8212 or 441/238–8246) is the largest riding facility on the island. The center's most popular trail ride is the 1½-hour south-shore breakfast ride, departing at 6:45 AM; Continental breakfast is included in the $50 fee (cash discount given on all rides). From December 1 through March 31, Bermuda's off-season, you can ride along the beach. The daily 10 and 11:30 AM and 3 and 6 PM trail rides ($40) are leisurely one-hour treks. Evening rides at 6 ($40) are also offered weekly May through September; call for schedules. Spicelands also offers instruction in its riding ring.

Lee Bow Riding Centre (⊠ Tribe Road 1, off Middle Rd., Devonshire, ☎ 441/236–4181), a smaller stable than Spicelands Riding Centre, offers trail rides through the island's countryside and to places along the beautiful northern coast. One-hour rides ($20) are on a request-only basis. The British-qualified riding instructor gives lessons for up to three people, at $20 per half hour, or $30 per hour. Children's riding camps are offered during the summer, Christmas, and Easter breaks for about $175 a week.

Jogging and Running

Many of the difficulties that cyclists face—hills, traffic, and wind—also confront runners in Bermuda. The presence of pedestrian sidewalks and footpaths along roadsides, however, does make the going somewhat easier. Runners who like firm pavement will be happiest on the Railway Trail (☞ Bicycling, *above*) or on South Road, a popular route. For those who like running on sand, the trails through **South Shore Park** are relatively firm, while the island's beaches obviously present a much softer surface. **Horseshoe Beach** and **Elbow Beach** are frequented by a large number of serious runners during the early morning and after 5 PM. Another beach for running is ½-mi **Warwick Long Bay,** the longest uninterrupted stretch of sand on the island; the sand is softer here than at Horseshoe and Elbow, so it is difficult to gain good footing, particularly at high tide. By using South Shore Park trails to skirt coral bluffs, runners can create a route that connects several beaches, although trails in some places can be winding and uneven.

The big running event on the island is the **Bermuda International Marathon, Half Marathon and 10K Race,** held in mid-January. The race attracts world-class distance runners from several countries, but it is open to everyone. For information, contact the Race Committee (⊠ Box DV 397, Devonshire DV BX, ☎ 441/236–3629). The association can also provide information on other races held throughout the year.

Another event for fitness fanatics is the **Bermuda Triathlon** in late September. Held in Southampton, the event combines a 1-mi swim, a 15-mi cycling leg, and a 6-mi run. For information, contact the Bermuda Triathlon Association (⌧ Box HM 1002, Hamilton HM DX, ☏ 441/ 293–2765). Less competitive—and certainly less strenuous—are the 2-mi **"fun runs,"** sponsored by the Mid-Atlantic Athletic Club (⌧ Box HM 1745, Hamilton HM BX, ☏ 441/293–8103, FAX 441/293–4089), held every Tuesday evening from April through October. Runs begin at 6 PM in front of Camden House on Berry Hill Road, Botanical Gardens. No entry fee is charged. Additional information about jogging and running is available from the Bermuda Track & Field Association (⌧ Box DV 397, Devonshire DV BX, ☏ 441/295–8574).

Parasailing

Parasailing concessions operate in the **Great Sound** and **Castle Harbour**. The cost is about $45 per person, and the ride lasts approximately 10 minutes. Couples who wish to sail through the sky under a parachute should call **Skyrider Bermuda** (⌧ Dockyard Marina, Royal Naval Dockyard, ☏ 441/234–3019). Skyrider uses a double chair; the cost is $40 per person for about six minutes.

Snorkeling

The clarity of the water, the stunning array of coral reefs, and the shallow resting places of several wrecks make snorkeling in the waters around Bermuda—both close inshore and offshore—particularly rewarding. Snorkeling is possible year-round, although a wet suit is advisable for anyone planning to spend a long time in the water in winter, when the water temperature can dip into the 60s. During the winter, too, the water tends to be rougher, often restricting snorkeling to the protected areas of Harrington Sound and Castle Harbour. Underwater caves, grottoes, coral formations, and schools of small fish are the highlights of these areas. When Bermudians are asked to name a favorite snorkeling spot, however, **Church Bay** in Southampton (at the western end of the south-shore beaches) is invariably ranked at or near the top of the list. A small cove cut out of the coral cliffs, this picturesque bay is full of nooks and crannies in the coral, and the reefs are relatively close to shore. Snorkelers should exercise caution here, as they should everywhere along the south shore, as the water can be rough. Other popular snorkeling areas close inshore are the beaches of **John Smith's Bay** at the eastern end of the south shore, and **Tobacco Bay** at the eastern end of the north shore. Despite its small size, **West Whale Bay** is also worth a visit.

Having a boat at your disposal can improve your snorkeling experience immeasurably. Otherwise, long swims are necessary to reach some of the best snorkeling sites, while other sites are inaccessible from anything but a boat. Small boats can be rented by the hour, half day, or day (☞ Boat Rentals, *above*). As the number of wrecks attests, navigating around Bermuda's reef-strewn waters is no simple task, especially for inexperienced boaters. If you rent a boat yourself, stick to the protected waters of the sounds, harbors, and bays, and be sure to ask for an ocean navigation chart. (These point out shallow waters, rocks, and hidden reefs.) For trips to the reefs, let someone else do the navigating—a charter-boat skipper or one of the snorkeling-cruise operators. Some of the best reefs for snorkeling, complete with shallow-water wrecks, are to the west. Where the tour guide or skipper goes, however, often depends on the tide, weather, and water conditions. For snorkelers who demand privacy and freedom of movement, a boat charter (complete with captain) is the only answer, but the cost is considerable—$650 a day for a party of 18. By comparison, half-day snorkeling on regularly scheduled cruises generally costs $40–$65, including equipment and instruction.

Snorkeling equipment is available for rental at most major hotels; the **Grotto Bay Beach Hotel & Tennis Club, Sonesta Beach Hotel & Spa,** and **Southampton Princess** have dive operators on site. Rates for mask, flippers, and snorkel are usually $10 a day, with rates decreasing when a rental is longer; deposits or credit card impressions are required. Equipment, including small boats and underwater cameras, can also be rented at several marinas. To rent equipment at the island's western end, go to **Mangrove Marina** (✉ Cambridge Rd., Somerset, ☎ 441/234–0914), **Pompano Beach Club Watersports Centre** (✉ Pompano Beach Club Rd., Southampton, ☎ 441/234–0222), or **Windjammer Water Sports** (✉ Dockyard Marina, Royal Naval Dockyard, ☎ 441/234–1343), all of which also rent small boats. In the central part of the island, rent boats and gear at **Salt Kettle Yacht Charters** (✉ Off Harbour Rd., Salt Kettle Rd., Paget, ☎ 441/236–4863 or 441/236–3612). **Horseshoe Bay Beach** (☎ 441/238–2651) also rents equipment.

Snorkeling Cruises

Snorkeling cruises, which are offered from April to November, may be too touristy for many visitors. Some boats carry up to 40 passengers to snorkel, and focus mostly on their music and bars (complimentary beverages are usually served on the return trip from the reefs). The smaller boats, which limit capacity to 10 to 16 passengers, offer more personal attention and focus more on touring and visiting beautiful snorkeling areas. To make sure you choose a boat that's right for you, ask for all the details before booking. Many of the boats offer private charters to groups; these can be arranged easily. Half-day snorkeling tours cost between $40 and $65.

Two of the best half-day snorkeling trips (or longer for special charters) are offered by **Hayward's Snorkeling & Glass Bottom Boat Cruises** (✉ Dock adjacent to Hamilton Ferry Terminal, ☎ 441/292–8652, 441/236–9894 after hours), and **Pitman's Snorkeling** (✉ Robinson's Marina, Somerset Bridge, ☎ 441/234–0700); both relate interesting historical and ecological information about the island in addition to visiting the pristine offshore snorkeling areas, often at shipwreck sites.

Personal attention is given by Captain Douglas Shirley, who operates **Bermuda Barefoot Cruises** (✉ Box DV 525, Devonshire, ☎ 441/236–3498). His 32-ft *Minnow* leaves Darrell's Wharf in Warwick and tours the inshore waterways before ducking into a favorite local snorkeling site where no other tour boats go—in shallow waters off Somerset, where less strong swimmers can opt to walk around. Captain Shirley also arranges private charters to the south-shore reef and other destinations. Captain Kirk Ward's **Native Tours** (☎ 441/234–8149 or 441/234–1434) is the only operation offering regularly scheduled sailing-snorkeling trips to the outer reefs aboard a 47-ft catamaran. **Bermuda Water Tours Ltd.** (✉ Dock adjacent to Hamilton Ferry Terminal, ☎ 441/295–3727) operates two boats out of Hamilton. Half-day cruises are also available from **Salt Kettle Yacht Charers** (✉ Off Harbour Rd., Salt Kettle Rd., Paget, ☎ 441/236–4863 or 441/236–3612) and **Jessie James Cruises** (✉ 48 Par-la-Ville Rd., Suite 366, Hamilton HM 11, ☎ 441/236–4804).

Squash

The **Bermuda Squash Club** (✉ Middle Rd., Devonshire; contact Jane Palker, ☎ 441/292–6881) makes its four courts and new gym available to nonmembers of all ages and standards between 11 AM and 11

PM by reservation. A $5 fee per person buys 40 minutes of play during the day, or $6.50 at peak times (noon–2 and 4:40–9); rackets and balls can be borrowed. A $5 per play guest fee is charged, but temporary memberships can be arranged if you plan to play several times. Visitors may be teamed up with a local partner; timed matches and competitions can be organized, too. Softball players will enjoy the two English courts (larger than U.S. courts) at the **Coral Beach & Tennis Club** (⊠ South Rd., Paget, ☎ 441/236–2233). Introduction by a member is required at Coral Beach. In April, the Bermuda Squash Racquets Association (☎ 441/292–6881) sponsors the **Bermuda Open Squash Tournament,** in which top international players compete.

Tennis

Bermuda has a tennis court for every 600 residents, a ratio that even the most tennis-crazed countries would find difficult to match. Many are private, but the public has access to more than 70 courts in 20 locations island-wide. Courts are inexpensive and seldom full. Hourly rates for nonguests are about $10 to $15. Bring along a few fresh cans of balls, because balls in Bermuda cost $6 to $7 per can—about three times the rate in the United States. Among the surfaces used in Bermuda are Har-Tru, clay, cork, and hard composites, of which the relatively slow Plexipave composite is the most prevalent. Considering Bermuda's British roots, it's surprising that there are no grass courts on the island.

Wind, heat (in summer), and humidity are the most distinguishing characteristics of Bermudian tennis. From October through March, when daytime temperatures rarely exceed 80°F, play is comfortable throughout the day. In summertime, however, the heat radiating from the court (especially hard-surface ones) can make play uncomfortable between 11 and 3. At such times, the breezes normally considered a curse in tennis can become a cooling blessing. Early morning or evening tennis presents players with an entirely different problem, when tennis balls grow heavy with moisture from Bermuda's humid sea air, always at its wettest early and late in the day. On clay courts, the moist balls become matted with clay, making them even heavier.

In strong winds, inland courts are preferable; these include the clay and all-weather courts at the **Government Tennis Stadium** (⊠ 2 Marsh Folly, Pembroke, ☎ 441/292–0105) and the clay courts at the **Coral Beach & Tennis Club** (⊠ Off South Rd., Paget, ☎ 441/236–2233 or 441/236–6495), where introduction by a member is required. Despite their position at the water's edge, the Plexipave courts of the **Southampton Princess Hotel** (⊠ South Rd., Southampton, ☎ 441/238–1005) are reasonably well shielded from the wind (especially from the north), although the breeze can be swirling and difficult. High on a bluff above the ocean, the courts at the **Sonesta Beach Hotel & Spa** (⊠ Off South Rd., ☎ 441/238–8122) offer players one of the more spectacular settings on the island, but the courts are exposed to summer winds from the south and southwest. Other hotels with good tennis facilities open to the public are the **Elbow Beach Hotel** (⊠ South Shore, Paget, ☎ 441/236–3535), with five courts, and **Marriott's Castle Harbour Resort** (⊠ Paynters Rd., Hamilton Parish, ☎ 441/293–2040), with six cork courts. All of the above facilities, except Marriott's Castle Harbour, have some floodlit courts for night play, as does the **Belmont Hotel, Golf & Country Club** (⊠ Belmont Rd., Warwick, ☎ 441/236–1301). The four clay courts at the **Port Royal Course** (⊠ Southampton, ☎ 441/234–0974) are $8 during daylight hours. Two courts are lighted for night play; an additional fee of $2–$6 is usually charged to play under lights.

Most tennis facilities offer lessons, ranging from $20 to $30 for 30 minutes of instruction, and racket rentals for $4–$6 per hour or per play, depending on the policy.

Tournaments

Tennis tournaments are played year-round, although most of the major ones are in the fall and winter. Included among them are the March and April **All Bermuda Tennis Club Members' Tournament,** a closed competition on clay courts to which visitors are welcome (⊠ Government Tennis Stadium, Pembroke Parish, ☎ 441/292–0105); April's **Bermuda Open,** an ATP Tour, USTA-Sanctioned Event of the world's top professionals played on clay courts at the Coral Beach & Tennis Club (☎ 441/236–2233), another closed competition to which visitors are welcome; May's **Heineken Open,** played at the Government Tennis Stadium and open to visitors; June's **Pomander Gate Tennis Club Open,** a competition on hard courts for visitors and locals (⊠ Pomander Rd., Paget, ☎ 441/236–5400); September's **Grotto Bay Open,** an 11-day tournament open to visitors, played on hard courts at the Grotto Bay Beach Hotel & Tennis Club (⊠ Hamilton Parish, ☎ 441/293–8333, ext. 1914); October's **All Bermuda Tennis Club Open,** played at the Government Tennis Stadium and open to visitors; and November's **Bermuda Lawn Tennis Club Invitational,** a closed competition played at the Coral Beach & Tennis Club (Paget, ☎ 441/236–2233). For more information about these and other tournaments, contact the Bermuda Lawn Tennis Association (⊠ Box HM 341, Hamilton HM BX, ☎ 441/296–0834, ℻ 441/295–3056).

Waterskiing

Winds on the island vary considerably, making it difficult to predict when the water will be calmest, although early morning and evening breezes are often the lightest. The best time for this sport is May through October. Head for the Warwick, Southampton, or Somerset shoreline of the **Great Sound** when the winds are coming from the south or southwest. In the event of northerly winds, however, it's best to stick to the protected areas in **Hamilton Harbour** and **Harrington Sound. Castle Harbour** and **Ferry Reach** are also good areas to waterski, depending on the wind strength and direction.

If possible, make friends with a Bermudian who has a boat; otherwise, contact **Blue Hole Water Sports** (⊠ Grotto Bay Beach Hotel & Tennis Club, 11 Blue Hole Hill, Hamilton Parish, ☎ 441/293–2915), **Bermuda Waterski Centre** (⊠ Robinson's Marina, Somerset Bridge, Sandys, ☎ 441/234–1964), or **Wake Up Ski School** (⊠ Princess Hotel, Pembroke, ☎ 441/234–8924). Rates fluctuate with fuel costs but average $55 per half hour, $100 per hour, lessons included.

Windsurfing

The **Great Sound, Elbow Beach, Somerset Long Bay, Shelly Bay,** and **Harrington Sound** are the favorite haunts of board sailors in Bermuda. For novices, the often calm waters of Mangrove Bay and Castle Harbour are probably the best choice. The Great Sound, with its many islands, coves, and harbors, is good for board sailors of all abilities, although the quirky winds that sometimes bedevil yachts in the sound obviously affect sailboards as well. When the northerly storm winds blow, the open bays on the north shore are popular among wave-riding enthusiasts. Only experts should consider windsurfing on the south shore. Wind, waves, and reefs make the south shore so dangerous that rental companies are prohibited from renting boards there. Experienced board sailors who want to meet local windsurfers can call **Hubert**

Watlington at **Sail On** (⊠ Old Cellar, off Front St., Hamilton, ☎ 441/ 295–0808), a former Olympic competitor who is an integral part of this sailing circuit.

Even the most avid board sailors should rent sailboards rather than bring their own. Transporting a board around the island is a logistical nightmare: There are no rental cars on Bermuda, and few taxi drivers are willing to see their car roofs scoured with scratches in the interest of sport. Rental rates range between $15 and $25 an hour, and between $60 and $90 a day; special long-term rates can be negotiated with some shops. Contact **Blue Hole Water Sports** (⊠ Grotto Bay Beach Hotel & Tennis Club, 11 Blue Hole Hill, Hamilton Parish, ☎ 441/293–2915; ⊠ Marriott's Castle Harbour, Paynter's Rd., Hamilton Parish, ☎ 441/293–2040), **Mangrove Marina** (⊠ Cambridge Rd., Sandys, ☎ 441/234–0914 or 441/234–0331, ext. 295), or **Pompano Beach Club Watersports Centre** (⊠ 36 Pompano Rd., Pompano Beach Club, Southampton, ☎ 441/234–0222). If you're just getting started, **Mangrove Marina** provides 90 minutes of instruction for $40. Land simulators and equipment are included in the lessons.

World-Class and Local Tournaments

Bermuda is a great place for sports enthusiasts seeking relief from an overdose of baseball, football, and basketball—sports that mean little to Bermudians. In addition to golf and tennis, the big spectator sports here are cricket, rugby, soccer, field hockey, and yacht racing.

The **World Rugby Classic** in October brings some of the formerly top players, now retired, to the island for a week of top play and partying. In September, the fabled **Mid Ocean Club** hosts a Merrill Lynch Shoot-Out, which has featured such top names in golf as Corey Pavin and Ray Floyd in a perfectly relaxed setting. Top runners flock to the island in January for the **International Marathon** and 10k. And prestigious summer sailing events include the Newport-to-Bermuda race and the Omega Gold Cup. The Bermuda Department of Tourism can provide exact dates and information about all major sporting events.

Cricket

Cricket is the big team sport in summer, and the **Cup Match Cricket Festival** is *the* event on Bermuda's summer sports calendar. In late July or early August, at the **Somerset Cricket Club** (⊠ Broome St., off Somerset Rd., ☎ 441/234–0327) or the **St. George's Cricket Club** (⊠ Wellington Slip Rd., ☎ 441/297–0374), teams from around the island compete. Although cricket is taken very seriously, the event itself is a real festival, attended by thousands of colorful picnickers and party-goers. An entry fee is charged. The regular cricket season runs from April through September.

Field Hockey

Hockey games between local teams can be seen at the **National Sports Club** (⊠ Middle Rd., Devonshire, ☎ 441/236–6994) on weekends from October through April.

Horse Racing

Equestrian events are held throughout the year at the **Bermuda Equestrian Federation** (⊠ Vesey St., Devonshire, ☎ 441/234–0485, FAX 441/234–3010). Harness races take place twice monthly from September through April (call Annie Sousa, ☎ 441/238–2110, for information). The horsey set also turns out in October for the FEI/Samsung Dressage Competition and Show Jumping events. For additional information write to the Bermuda Equestrian Federation, Box DV 583, Devonshire DV BX.

Rugby

Bermuda's rugby season runs from September to April. November brings the **World Rugby Classic.** Held at the **National Sports Club** (⌧ Middle Rd., Devonshire, ☎ 441/236–6994), the competition attracts teams from the United States, Great Britain, France, New Zealand, and Australia, as well as Bermuda. Tickets cost about $10. During the rest of the season, matches between local teams can be seen on weekends at the National Sports Club.

Soccer

In late March or early April, teams from countries around the Atlantic, including the United States, Canada, Great Britain, and several Caribbean nations, compete for the **Bermuda Youth Soccer Cup.** Teams play in three age divisions, and games are held on fields around the island. Contact the Bermuda Department of Tourism or the nearest Visitors Service Bureau.

Yachting

Bermuda has a worldwide reputation as a yacht-racing center. Spectators, particularly those on land, may find it difficult to follow the intricacies of a race or regatta, but the sight of the racing fleet, with brightly colored spinnakers flying, is always striking. The racing season runs from March to November. Most races are held on weekends in the Great Sound, and several classes of boats usually compete. The racing can be seen at a distance from Spanish Point and the Somerset shoreline. Anyone who wants to get a real sense of the action, however, should be aboard a boat near the race course.

In June, Bermuda is the finish for oceangoing yachts in three major races beginning in the United States: the **Newport–Bermuda Ocean Yacht Race,** the **Marion to Bermuda Race,** and the **Bermuda Ocean Race** from Annapolis, Maryland. Of these, the Newport–Bermuda Race usually attracts the most entries, but all provide the spectacular sight of the island's harbors and yacht-club docks filled with yachts, which usually range in length from about 30 to 80 ft. For those more interested in racing than seeing expensive yachts, the **Omega Gold Cup International Match Race Tournament** is the event to see. Held in October in Hamilton Harbour, the tournament pits visiting top sailors—many of whom are America's Cup Match Racing skippers—against Bermudians in one-on-one races for prize money.

8 Shopping

If you're looking for colorful street markets where you can haggle over the price of low-cost goods and souvenirs, find another island. Bermuda's sophisticated department stores and boutiques purvey top-notch, top-price merchandise. The quality of wares is quite good, and if you keep that in mind, you'll find that Bermuda does offer substantial savings on many items, particularly British-made clothing.

By Honey
Naylor

IF YOU'RE ACCUSTOMED TO SHOPPING** in Saks Fifth Avenue, Neiman-Marcus, and Bergdorf-Goodman, the prices in Bermuda's elegant shops won't come as a surprise. In fact, the prices on many items in Bermuda's stores are discounted, but a $600 dress discounted by 20% is still $480. Bermuda shopkeepers have felt the effect of the growing number of discount stores in the United States. It would be wise to check discount prices before you leave home and to compare them with Bermudian prices on items that interest you. Remember that Bermuda, unlike most U.S. states, has no sales tax, which means that the price on the tag is the price you pay.

Woolens and cashmere are good buys, especially after Christmas and in January when many stores offer substantial discounts. Naturally, Bermuda shorts are hot items, as are kilts, but bargains on these are a rarity. Only products actually made in Bermuda (and antiques more than 100 years old) can be sold duty-free.

European-made crystal and china—Wedgwood, Royal Crown Derby, Villeroy & Boch, Waterford, and Orrefors, to name a few—are available at prices at least 25% lower than those in the United States. Figurines from Lladro, Royal Doulton, and Hummel are also sold at significantly discounted prices. European fragrances and cosmetics are priced about 25%–30% less than in the United States, as are Rolex, Tissot, Patek Philippe, and other watches.

Bermuda has a thriving population of artists and artisans, whose work ranges from sculpture and paintings to miniature furniture, hand-blown glass, and dolls. Other Bermuda-made specialties include delicious local honey, which you can find in most grocery stores. Outerbridge's Sherry Peppers condiments add zip to soups, stews, drinks, and chowders. The original line has been expanded to include Bloody Mary mix, pepper jellies, and barbecue sauce.

Bermuda rum is another popular item, and a variety of rum-based liqueurs is available, including Bermuda Banana, Banana Coconut Rum, and Bermuda Gold. Gosling's Black Seal Rum is excellent mixed with ginger beer to make a Dark 'n' Stormy, a famous Bermuda drink that should be treated with respect and caution. Rum is also found in quantity in Fourways Dark 'n' Stormy cakes, which are made in Bermuda and can be mailed home.

U.S. citizens age 21 and older who have been out of the country for 48 hours are allowed to bring home 1 liter of duty-free liquor each (☞ Customs & Duties *in* the Gold Guide). In an odd catch-22, however, Bermuda requires a minimum purchase of 2 liters or five 75-centiliter bottles to qualify for in-bond (duty-free) prices. The airport has no duty-free shop of its own, but you can order duty-free liquor at any store; it will make arrangements to deliver your purchase to the airport departure lounge or your cruise ship. It is best to buy duty-free liquor at least 24 hours before your departure, or by 9:30 AM on the day of an afternoon departure, either of which will allow for delivery to your point of departure. With liquor, it pays to shop around, because prices vary: Grocery stores usually charge more than liquor stores. Some stores allow customers to create their own mixed packs of various liquors at in-bond prices, while others offer a selection of prepackaged sets (the five-pack is most common). Below are some sample prices at press time for 1 liter of liquor: Tia Maria, $16.35; Grand Marnier, $27.50; Chivas Regal (12-year-old), $29.05; J&B Rare, $14.20; Johnnie Walker Black, $27.50; Stolichnaya vodka, $9.50; Beefeater gin, $13.25; and Gosling's Black Seal rum, $8.30.

For products other than liquor, comparison shopping within Bermuda is usually a waste of time, because the merchants' association keeps prices almost identical island-wide. Again, it is worth checking the price of items at home—especially crystal and china—before you embark on a shopping spree in Bermuda. Ask your local department store if any sales are scheduled and check the prices of designer and name-brand products at local factory outlets.

Although the numbering of houses is becoming more common—houses have traditionally been known only by their picturesque names rather than numbers—buildings in Hamilton are still numbered rather whimsically. If you check the phone directory for a store address, you may find a listing on Front Street or Water Street, for example, but no street number. In fact, some Front Street buildings have two numbers, one of them an old historic address that has nothing to do with the building's present location. Fortunately, almost all Bermudians can give you precise directions.

In general, shops are open Monday–Saturday 9–5 or 9–5:30, closed on Sunday (although some supermarkets remain open) and public holidays. Some Hamilton shops stay open late on Wednesday for Harbour Night festivities from April through October. From late November through Christmas Eve, stores often stay open until 9 on Friday; in the two weeks before Christmas, many stores stay open until 9 most nights. When cruise ships call (from April through October), some Front Street shops open Sunday. The shops in the newly extended area at the Royal Naval Dockyard are usually open Monday–Saturday 10–5 from April through October (11–5 in winter) and Sunday 11–5; some extend their hours around Christmas. Almost all stores close for public holidays.

In most cases in this chapter, if a store has several branches or outlets, only the main branch phone number has been listed.

Shopping Districts

Hamilton has the greatest concentration of shops in Bermuda, and **Front Street** is its pièce de résistance. Lined with small, pastel-color buildings, this most fashionable of Bermuda's streets houses sedate department stores and snazzy boutiques, with several small arcades and shopping alleys leading off it. A smart canopy shades the entrance to the **55 Front Street Group,** which houses several upmarket boutiques. **The Emporium** on Front Street, a renovated old building that encloses an open atrium, is home to an eclectic collection of antiques, jewelry, souvenir, and low-quality art shops. The statue on top of the atrium fountain is of Bermudian Gina Swainson, who ruled as Miss World in 1979–80. **Windsor Place** is a modern mall on Queen Street where you can get anything from running shoes, sunblock, and greeting cards to haircuts, handblown glass, and cash (there are ATM machines on the lower and upper levels).

In St. George's, **Water Street, Duke of York Street,** and **Somers Wharf** are the sites of numerous renovated buildings that house branches of Front Street stores. Historic **King's Square** offers little more than a couple of T-shirt and souvenir shops. In the West End, **Somerset Village** has a few shops, but they hardly merit a special shopping trip. However, the historic **Clocktower Mall** and the newer **Victorian Mall at Royal Naval Dockyard** have a plethora of shops, including branches of Front Street shops and specialty boutiques. The Dockyard is also home to the **Craft Market,** the **Bermuda Arts Centre,** and **Island Pottery,** where local artisans display their wares and visitors can sometimes watch them at work. Several other small plazas are sprinkled around the island. They typically contain a few shops, and often a grocery store.

Department Stores

Bermuda's three leading department stores are A. S. Cooper & Son, Trimingham's, and H. A. & E. Smith's, the main branches of which are on Front Street in Hamilton. The third or fourth generations of the families that founded them now run these elegant, venerable institutions, and customers stand a good chance of being waited on by a Cooper, a Trimingham, or a Smith. In addition, many of the salespeople have worked at the stores for two or three decades; they tend to be unobtrusive, but polite and helpful when you need them.

A. S. Cooper & Son (⊠ 59 Front St., Hamilton, ☎ 441/295–3961; other branches in all major hotels, the Clocktower Building at Dockyard, and in St. George's at 22 Water St.). This store is best known for its extensive inventory of Waterford and Swarovski crystal; china, including Wedgwood, Royal Doulton, Belleek, Villeroy & Boch, and Royal Copenhagen; and Lladro figurines. A five-piece place setting of the Wedgwood Countryware pattern costs $63 ($79 including shipping to the United States, with duty, freight, and insurance). Prices on the stock of china and crystal are similarly attractive. A free home-delivery service with up to 40% savings (without affecting the $400 duty-free allowance) is available to United States customers who order Waterford chandeliers, tableware by Royal Doulton, Royal Crown Derby, Minton, Wedgwood, Villeroy & Boch, Royal Copenhagen, French Quimper, and stemware by Orrefors, Kosta Boda, and Atlantis Crystal. A. S. Cooper & Son's private-label collection of clothing can be found in the well-stocked men's, women's, and children's departments. The gift department on the Front Street level carries a large selection of tasteful Bermudian gifts and souvenirs.

H. A. & E. Smith's (⊠ 35 Front St., Hamilton, ☎ 441/295–2288; branches in the Belmont and Southampton Princess hotels and at 18 York Street in St. George's). Founded in 1889 by Henry Archibald and Edith Smith, this is arguably the best men's store in Bermuda—and exclusive agents for Burberry, William Lockie cashmeres, and Church shoes. Burberry raincoats are priced from $395 to $550, and William Lockie cashmeres sell from $245 to $375. You can buy English tweed jackets for $240, men's 100% cashmere topcoats for $395, and Italian silk ties for $26 and up. There is a large selection of Shetland and cotton sweaters, which go for about $30 each. Smith's is also a good place to buy kilts.

Women can find Fendi handbags here (the only place in Bermuda), for about $175 for a medium size, as well as cashmere-lined leather gloves for $58 and $65 (unlined $42). The women's department also has an extensive selection of formal and casual wear: Cashmere turtleneck sweaters are priced from $198; Burberry raincoats start at $395. The women's shoe department offers a broad choice of fine Italian styles, both classic and contemporary.

The Front Street–level china department carries a large selection of patterns from Royal Doulton, Royal Crown Derby, Royal Worcester, and Rosenthal, and crystal of all types is sold. French perfume sells for 20% to 30% less than in the States. As with many of the island's older buildings, the store has a confusing layout that makes it easy to get lost. The staff here is especially genteel, however, and they will help orient you.

Marks & Spencer (✉ 18 Reid St., Hamilton, ☎ 441/295–0031). A franchise of the large British chain, it's called Marks and Sparks by everyone in Bermuda and England. This large store is usually filled with thrift-minded locals attracted by its moderate prices for men's, women's, and children's clothing. Summer wear, including swimsuits, cotton jerseys, and polo shirts, is a good buy. High-quality men's and women's cashmere and woolen sweaters are also sold at substantial discounts.

Trimingham's (✉ 37 Front St., Hamilton, ☎ 441/295–1183). A Hamilton fixture since 1842, this is Bermuda's largest department store— home of Daks Bermuda shorts and tailored-for-Trimingham's sportswear. Famous women's designers, such as Dana Buchman, Nicole Farhi, and Calvin Klein, have complete lines here, and fine tableware by Lenox, Mikasa, Noritake, Aynsley, Portmeirion, Waterford, Royal Worcester, and Spode is sold for up to 30% less than in the United States. The store has an impressive display of perfumes and cosmetics, and it is Bermuda's exclusive distributor of Christian Dior, Estée Lauder, and Yves Saint Laurent. Shoppers will also find a potpourri of fine leather, jewelry, children's fashions, and gift items. Trimingham branches—10 in all—can be found all over the island, including at Somers Wharf in St. George's, South Shore Road in Paget, and in Somerset Village.

Grocery Stores

Many of the accommodations on Bermuda, usually guest houses and housekeeping apartments, allow you to do your own cooking. Self-catering vacations are cheaper than those where you pay full board or dine out at every meal; considering how expensive Bermuda is, this option has widespread appeal for both families and budget travelers. Still, foodstuffs in Bermuda are quite expensive. For example, a dozen imported large eggs costs about $1.75 (locally raised eggs are even dearer: about $3 a dozen), a loaf of Bermuda-made bread is $3, a six-pack of Coke is about $4.75, and a 13-ounce can of coffee is $5. Listed below are some of the major supermarkets in Bermuda. Unless stated otherwise below, grocery stores carry liquor.

A-One Paget (✉ Middle Rd., Paget, ☎ 441/236–0351). This grocery is near Barnsdale Guest Apartments and the Sky Top Cottages. Be warned, however, that the route between Sky Top and the store takes in a significant hill, which could make for a difficult hike if you buy a large amount of groceries.

A-One Smith's (✉ Middle Rd., Smith's Parish, ☎ 441/236–8763). Although part of the Marketplace chain, this mart doesn't have as large a supply of goods because it is a smaller shop. It's near Angel's Grotto and Brightside Apartments, but not quite within walking distance.

Giant Foods (✉ Middle Rd., Warwick, ☎ 441/236–1344). A medium-size store, Giant is within walking distance of the Pretty Penny guest house—except when you're heavily laden with groceries.

Harrington Hundreds Grocery & Liquor Store (✉ South Rd., Smith's Parish, ☎ 441/293–1635). Near Spittal Pond and not far from Angel's Grotto apartments, it is still a long go to walk with bags.

Heron Bay Marketplace (✉ Middle Rd., Southampton, ☎ 441/238–1993). One of the island-wide Marketplace chain of stores, this one has a large selection of fresh vegetables. It's convenient to Longtail Cliffs and Marley Beach, but again, not on foot.

The Hitching Post (✉ Somerset Rd., near Somerset Bridge, Sandys, ☎ 441/234–0951). Finally, a convenience store that does not overcharge.

And, the big bonus is that it's open Sunday 11 AM–7 PM, when other grocery shops are closed. No liquor is sold.

The Marketplace (✉ Reid St., near Parliament St., Hamilton, ☎ 441/292–3163). The headquarters for a moderately priced chain with stores around the island, this is the island's largest grocery store. You can take out hot soups, stir-fried meats and vegetables, dinners, salads, and desserts for $4.99 a pound. This branch also opens Sundays, 1–5.

Maximart (✉ Hog Bay Level, Sandys, ☎ 441/234–1940). Near Whale Bay Inn, this is a good place to stock up on snacks if you are staying at Lantana Colony Club. Surprisingly, there's a good selection of meats here, too.

Miles Market (✉ Pitts Bay Rd., near the Princess, Hamilton, ☎ 441/295–1234). Here you'll find a large selection of Häagen-Dazs ice cream, an excellent choice of high-quality imported and local meats and fish, and specialty foods found nowhere else on the island. Many items are on the expensive side, but the quality here is unsurpassed in Bermuda. The market delivers goods anywhere on the island.

Modern Mart (✉ South Shore Rd., Paget, ☎ 441/236–6161). Part of the Marketplace chain, it is smaller than its flagship Hamilton store but has all the essentials. It is easily accessible from Sky Top Cottages, Loughlands, and other south-shore accommodations.

Shelly Bay Marketplace (✉ North Shore Rd., Hamilton Parish, ☎ 441/293–0966). Another store in the Marketplace chain, this one has a good selection. It is the only large grocery store on North Shore Road.

Somerset Marketplace (✉ Somerset Rd., Sandys, ☎ 441/234–0626). The largest grocery store on the island's western end, it is convenient to Whale Bay Inn, but take a moped or taxi.

Somers Supermarket (✉ York St., St. George's, ☎ 441/297–1177). There's a large selection here despite its small size. Hot items, salads, and sandwiches are available and are made fresh daily. It is within walking distance of the St. George's Club and Hillcrest Guest House.

The Supermart (✉ Front St., near King St., Hamilton, ☎ 441/292–2064). In addition to the normal goods, there's a well-stocked salad bar, prepackaged sandwiches, and hot coffee. This store and Miles Market are a long hike—particularly with heavy bags—from the Ferry Terminal in Hamilton, but once aboard the boat it's an easy ride across the harbor to Greenbank Cottages and Salt Kettle House. Island-wide deliveries are available.

Specialty Stores

Antiques

Heritage House (✉ 2 W. Front St., Hamilton, ☎ 441/295–2615). Browsers will find it difficult to tear themselves away from the antiques section in this small shop. Owner John Bluck regularly scours Great Britain and Europe for treasures, such as a 19th-century mahogany corner washstand, handmade chess sets, a wind-up gramophone, and more. He also stocks mahogany reproductions of English furnishings. Do not expect to find any bargains in this store, particularly on imported goods. The original works of esteemed local artists, including Sheilagh Head, Diana Amos, and Otto Trott, are also on display, and internationally known marine artists Stephen Card and Mark Boden are represented exclusively by Heritage House. The shop has its own framing department with a computerized system that allows for less expensive production. Harmony Kingdom animal boxes are among the many gift items. You can find tasteful Bermudian souvenirs here, too.

Pegasus (⌧ 63 Pitts Bay Rd., Hamilton, ☎ 441/295–2900). This Dickensian place in an old house with creaky wood floors is a few minutes' walk from downtown Hamilton on Front Street West, near the Princess. The store has bins and bins of antique prints and a small selection of antique maps. In particular, look for the original Leslie Ward (Spy) *Vanity Fair* caricatures that were published between 1869 and 1914 (from $70) and the Curtis botanicals ($50). Topographical engravings of America, Canada, Ireland, and Scotland by Bartlett are $40–$100. French fashion scenes and early lithographs of fruit, butterflies, and shells are priced from $50. There is a huge selection of greeting cards and wrapping paper from England, and you can order beautifully crafted ceramic house signs from England here. The shop provides certificates of antiquity for buyers to show to U.S. Customs (antiques are duty-free and do not affect the $400 allowance). You can browse here to your heart's content 10–5, but never on Sunday.

Arts and Crafts

ARTISTS

Buying artwork by someone you know is always more satisfying than buying it blind, and a number of Bermuda's resident artists—some of whose works are in the collections of famous collectors worldwide—encourage visits to their studios. Call ahead first, however, to find out if it's convenient to stop by. Be sure to check about payment before going: Although commercial shops that sell original art usually accept credit cards, most artists on the island do not. Remember that there are no duties levied on Bermudian arts and crafts.

Diana Amos (⌧ "Corncrake," Warwick, ☎ 441/236–9056). An art teacher at Bermuda College, Ms. Amos has a discerning eye that is revealed in her Bermudian scenes. She uses pastel watercolor tones to render the beauty of the island's unique architecture, landscapes, and seascapes. Her work is in galleries throughout the island and costs between $500 and about $2,000.

Alfred Birdsey Studio (⌧ "Rosecote," 5 Stowe Hill, Paget, ☎ 441/236–6658). In January 1996, Alfred Birdsey died, and the island mourned his loss. His studio, operated by family members, remains open. Renowned on the island, Mr. Birdsey received the Queen's Certificate of Honour and Medal in recognition of "valuable services given to Her Majesty for more than 40 years as an artist of Bermuda." His watercolors of Bermuda hang in myriad places on the island, including Cambridge Beaches cottage colony, as well as in select U.S. galleries. At the studio, watercolors (all originals) cost from $40 to $100, and lithographs cost as little as $10. The studio is usually open weekdays 9–1, Saturday 9–noon, and by appointment; call before going because hours vary.

Stephen Card (⌧ Scaur Hill, Somerset, ☎ 441/234–2353). A native Bermudian, this fine marine artist was for many years a captain in the British merchant marine. He relinquished full-time life at sea some years ago to devote himself to painting. Many of his ships from yesteryear are painted only after much careful research. Mr. Card's work hangs in private collections in the United States and can be seen aboard major cruise passenger ships. He often travels, but you can also find his work at Heritage House (☞ *above*). His prices are based on detail and size and range from $2,000 to $20,000.

Will Collieson (⌧ 18 York St., St. George's, ☎ 441/297–0171). One of the island's most talented and versatile artists, Mr. Collieson works in many media, and his sense of humor shines in many of his zany three-dimensional contemporary collages, made with materials found around the island. His creations can be seen daily in the window displays at H. A. & E. Smith's department store. Prices vary, depending on the medium used, but a collage costs between $200 and $800.

Joan Forbes (✉ Art House, 80 South Shore Rd., Paget, ☎ 441/236–6746). Ms. Forbes's watercolors and lithographs of local architecture, horticulture, and seascapes are made for visitors as inexpensive mementos. Her lithographs sell for $10–$45. She also produces cards, notepaper, and envelopes.

Desmond Fountain (☎ 441/238–8840). This award-winning sculptor's works are on display all over the island, whether it's a life-size bronze statue perched beside a lagoon or a lolling figure seated in a garden chair. Fountain created the Land Ho! statue of Sir George Somers on Ordnance Island in St. George's, and other works of his can be seen in the Sculpture Gallery on the mezzanine of the Southampton Princess. Prices start at about $4,500 for a small bronze and soar to dizzying heights.

Sheilagh Head (☎ 441/238–0173). One of the island's finest painters, Mrs. Head, schooled in Italy and England, works with colors better than any other local painter. Her oils stand apart because she explores light and shadow, illuminating the soft hues of the surroundings. Whether it is an abstract, an old Bermudian chimney, a cluster of buildings, or the sky rising above a swathe of foliage or the ocean, this artist's sensitivity shines forth in every canvas. Mrs. Head's work hangs in private collections in the United States, Europe, and Britain. Her paintings are sold through the Bermuda Society of Arts (✉ West Wing, City Hall, Church St., Hamilton); prices range from about $500 to $2,500.

Carole Holding Print & Craft Shops (✉ King's Square, St. George's, ☎ 441/297–1373; ✉ Clocktower Mall, Dockyard, ☎ 441/297–1373; ✉ 81 Front St., Hamilton, ☎ 441/297–1373 or 800/880–8570, ℻ 441/297–8374). Commercial artist Ms. Holding mass-produces watercolors of Bermuda's scenes and flowers; many of the same works are sold as signed prints and limited editions. Crafts, both imported and by local artists, are also available. Prices range from $12 (small prints) to $200 (framed watercolors).

John Kaufmann (✉ 16 Tranquillity Hill, Sandys, ☎ 441/234–4095 or 441/235–2232). Mr. Kaufmann works solely with oils to execute his well-known seascapes and landscapes. He has had successful one-man shows at the Windjammer Gallery, which is the only gallery to carry his work. Prices range from $1,500 for an 810 to about $2,500 for a 1020.

Elmer Midgett (✉ Scaur Hill, Somerset, ☎ 441/234–1936). Using an uncompromising style in oils that employs bold strokes reminiscent of those of van Gogh, Mr. Midgett focuses on the island's unusual buildings and angles. He is also a master at stained glass. His paintings—priced from $600 to about $1,200—are often on display at the Bermuda Society of Arts Gallery (☞ City Hall *in* Chapter 3).

Ann Proctor (✉ Harbour Rd., Paget, ☎ 441/292–8339). This artist's delicate, beautifully executed, and much sought-after watercolors of Bermuda plants and flowers have the quality of botanical drawings. Prices start at about $550.

Bruce Stuart (✉ Windjammer Gallery, Reid and King Sts., Hamilton, ☎ 441/292–7861). The island's unique architecture appears in his paintings, which have a near-photographic quality. Original work ranges in price from $1,100 to $5,000.

Otto Trott (✉ Clearview Gallery, Crawl Hill, Hamilton Parish, ☎ 441/293–4057). A Bermudian who is known for his sensitive use of light and shade, Mr. Trott renders beautiful oil paintings of landscapes and local characters. His work can be found at other island galleries, but he owns the Garden Gallery, and often his best pictures are found there. Works are priced from about $600 to about $2,000. Mr. Trott will give lessons to Bermuda visitors.

Sharon Wilson (✉ Turtle Pl., Southampton, ☎ 441/238–2583 or 441/238–0823). Ms. Wilson occupies a special place in the local art scene because she is one of the few artists who depict Bermuda's people. This talented woman has had many successful shows, and her work—priced between $5,500 and $7,000—sells well to visitors and locals alike. She employs a radiant range of pastels and often captures people absorbed in their own private world.

Dr. Charles Zuill (☎ 441/236–9000). One of the island's most innovative artists, Dr. Zuill is also the head of the art department at Bermuda College. His most recent exhibit at the Bermuda Society of Arts, consisting of "Earth Paintings" on square and rectangular canvases, employed a new medium that combined paint and sand from beaches in several parts of the world. His prices begin around $500.

Mary Zuill (✉ 10 Southlyn La., off South Shore Rd., Paget, ☎ 441/236–2439). In a tiny studio attached to her house, Ms. Zuill, a cousin of author Willam Zuill, paints delightful watercolors of Bermuda's flowers, architecture, and seascapes. She accepts commissions and will either design a painting or work from a photograph you've taken in Bermuda. Watercolors cost between $85 and $450. She welcomes visitors Tuesday–Friday, 10–noon and 2:30–5, from about mid-March to November only.

CRAFTSPEOPLE

Celia and Jack Arnell (☎ 441/236–4646). The miniature cedar furniture crafted by this husband-and-wife team is displayed in a dollhouse at the Craft Market (☞ *below*). The fine details on the breakfronts and chests of drawers include tiny metal drawer knobs, and the wonderful four-poster bed comes complete with a canopy. A four-poster bed sells for $125, chairs for about $35, depending on the model.

Kathleen Kemsley Bell (✉ 7 Seabright La., ☎ 441/236–3366). A director of the Bermuda Arts Centre at Dockyard, Ms. Bell creates exquisite dolls of persons from different periods of Bermuda's history. Each doll is unique, and each is researched for historical accuracy. The bodies are sculpted of papier-mâché, then hand-painted with marvelously expressive faces. Costumes are all hand-stitched. The base of each doll is signed and carries a description of the historical period on which the doll's fashions are based. Call to make an appointment at the studio, or visit the Bermuda Arts Centre at Dockyard, where her work is on display. Ms. Bell works on commission and will visit your hotel with samples of her work. Prices start at $250.

Ronnie Chameau. Ms. Chameau creates Christmas angels and dolls from dried palm, banana, and grapefruit leaves gathered from her yard and byways around the island. The 9-inch dolls ($55), with palmetto-leaf baskets and hats, palm-tree matting for the hair, and pecan heads with painted faces, are intended as table ornaments, while the dainty 4-inch angels ($15) are designed to hang on the Christmas tree. Colorful hand-painted Bermuda cottage doorstops ($65) are Ms. Chameau's other specialty. Trimingham's (☎ 441/295–1183) is the exclusive purveyor of her works.

FINE-ART PHOTOGRAPHERS

Mark Emmerson (⊠ Belvedere Bldg., Hamilton, ☎ 441/292–6283). This photographer produces rich black-and-white prints on platinum and other specialized photographic papers. His portfolio is extensive, and he occasionally shows his work at the Arts Centre at Dockyard as well as his studio in the Belvedere Building. Prices vary according to size and paper used.

Ian MacDonald-Smith (⊠ 175 Clarendon La., Flatts, ☎ 441/292–3295). Bold, bright, and large Cibachrome prints—many images are 2024 priced at about $450—are this photographer's passion. Unusual angles and portions of the island's unique architecture are the subjects of many pictures. He has produced several books, which are available throughout the island and make a good substitute if his originals are more than your budget allows.

Graeme Outerbridge (⊠ Heritage House, 2 W. Front St., Hamilton, ☎ 441/295–2615; ⊠ Windjammer Gallery, corner of Reid and King Sts., ☎ 441/292–7861). A photographer who contributed to the acclaimed *Day in the Life* book series, Mr. Outerbridge captures Bermuda in original photographic prints, silk screens, and posters.

DeForest Trimingham (⊠ South Shore Rd., Paget, ☎ 441/236–2727). After he retired from working in the family's Front Street department store, Mr. Trimingham resumed working with his camera. He has traveled the world and produced numerous fine Cibachromes of remote places, but most visitors seem to prefer his sensitive Bermuda compositions, which are priced from about $650 for an 1114.

Judith Wadson (⊠ Box 223, Hamilton HMAX, ☎ 441/236–3522). This photographer's specialty consists of hand-colored black-and-white prints as well as photographic prints of Bermuda's architecture and landscapes on archival watercolor paper and high-quality photographic papers. Ms. Wadson, who formerly was a staff photographer for *Yachting* magazine, focuses on the old-world side of Bermuda. Prices for her work range from about $200 to $400, depending on the size, and whether the image is framed.

GALLERIES AND CRAFTS SHOPS

Bermuda Arts Centre at Dockyard (⊠ Museum Row, Dockyard, ☎ 441/234–2809). Sleek and modern, with well-designed displays of local art, this gallery is housed in one of the stone buildings of the former British naval dockyard. The walls are adorned with paintings and photographs, and glass display cases contain exquisitely crafted quilts as well as costume dolls, jewelry, and wood sculpture. Exhibits change frequently. Several artists' studios inside the gallery are open to the public.

Bermuda Glassblowing Studio & Show Room (⊠ 16 Blue Hole Hill, Hamilton Parish, ☎ 441/293–2234). A restored village hall in the Bailey's Bay area houses this glassblowing studio, where eight artists have created more than 200 examples of handblown glass in vibrant, swirling colors. You can watch glassblowers at work daily in the studio, and sometimes at the Dockyard outlet (⊠ Bermuda Craft Market, Dockyard, ☎ 441/234–3208). The works are sold for retail at the studio and the outlet as well as at a retail store in Hamilton (⊠ 18 Windsor Place Mall, Queen St., ☎ 441/295–6970). Prices range from $10 to $1,600.

Bermuda Society of Arts (⊠ West Wing, City Hall, Hamilton, ☎ 441/292–3824). Many highly creative Society members sell their work at the perennial members' shows and during a revolving series of special group exhibits. You will find watercolor, oil, and acrylic paintings and pastel and charcoal drawings, as well as occasional photographs, collages, and pieces of sculpture. The Society's second gallery, Harbour Gallery, is on Front Street West.

Bridge House Gallery (✉ 1 Bridge St., St. George's, ☎ 441/297–8211). Housed in part of a Bermuda home that dates to 1700, this gallery is of historical and architectural interest in its own right. In the 18th century, the two-story white building was the home of Bermuda's governors; today it is maintained by the Bermuda National Trust. Original works by local artists, inexpensive prints, and souvenirs are for sale.

Craft Market (✉ The Cooperage, Dockyard, Ireland Island, ☎ 441/234–3208). Occupying part of what was once the cooperage, this large stone building dates from 1831. This is one of the few places that has island-made handicrafts. Anna and Glenn Correia's wooden creations are beautifully executed and reasonably priced. Outstanding is Judith Faram's exquisite—but expensive—handmade jewelry, which is of world-class standard.

Island Pottery (✉ Dockyard, Ireland Island, ☎ 441/234–3361). Potters throw their wares on wheels here in a large stone building at Dockyard, and the results are sold on the premises.

Masterworks Foundation Gallery (✉ 97 Front St., Hamilton, ☎ 441/295–5580). Formed in 1987, the foundation exhibits well-known Canadian, British, French, and American artists, including Georgia O'Keeffe and Winslow Homer, whose works were inspired by Bermuda. The Bermudiana Collection contains more than 400 works in watercolor, oil, pencil, charcoal, and other media. The Bermuda National Gallery at City Hall, Camden House, and Waterloo House all display selected pieces from this collection.

Windjammer Gallery (✉ King and Reid Sts., Hamilton, ☎ 441/292–7861; ✉ 95 Front St., ☎ 441/292–5878). The island's largest selection of local and imported art is in a charming four-room cottage whose colorful garden has life-size bronze sculptures. Individual and group shows are held regularly, and work is exported to collectors worldwide. The knowledgeable staff can help with your selection and shipping arrangements. Prints and lithographs are also available. Prints Plus, at 95 Front Street, is Windjammer's print shop, where there is an extensive collection of local prints, cards, books, photographs, and art-related gifts as well as wearable art. All purchases may be shipped, and a catalog is available.

Bookstores

Bermuda Book Store (✉ Queen St., Hamilton, ☎ 441/295–3698). Book lovers, beware! Once you set foot inside this musty old place, you'll have a hard time tearing yourself away. Stacked on a long table is a host of books about Bermuda. The proprietor can probably answer any questions you have about the island.

The Book Cellar (✉ Water St., St. George's, ☎ 441/297–0448). This small shop below the National Trust's Tucker House crams in a large selection of Bermudian books and an interesting assortment of novels by English and American authors that make for more meaningful reading than any current best-sellers. Coffee-table books cover a range of subjects, and there is a variety of British children's books that are hard to find in the United States. Owner Jill White and her well-read staff will be happy to help you search for an obscure title or let you browse at your leisure.

The Bookmart (✉ The Phoenix Centre, 3 Reid St., Hamilton, ☎ 441/295–3838). The island's largest bookstore specializes in best-sellers and paperbacks. There is a complete selection of Bermuda titles, as well as a large children's book section.

The Children's Bookshop (⊠ International Centre, 26 Bermudiana Rd., Hamilton, ☎ 441/292–9078). A wonderful selection of hard-to-find British titles is geared to all ages.

Ship's Inn Book Gallery (⊠ Clocktower Building, Dockyard, Ireland Island, ☎ 441/234–2807). Sherlyn Swan carries an ever-changing assortment of used books as well as some rare and antique titles. The only new books are about Bermuda.

Washington Mall Magazine (⊠ Washington Mall, Reid St., Hamilton, ☎ 441/292–7420). Come here for Bermuda's best selection of magazines, including hard-to-find periodicals. This is also the place to find a best-seller for the beach or the journey home, children's books, and coffee-table publications about the island.

Boutiques

Archie Brown & Son (⊠ 51 Front St., Hamilton, ☎ 441/295–2928; ⊠ Clocktower Building, Dockyard, ☎ 441/234–1017; ⊠ York St., St. George, ☎ 441/297–0036). Top-quality woolens, Pringle of Scotland cashmeres, Shetland and lamb's wool sweaters, and 100% wool tartan kilts are among the specialties here.

Aston & Gunn (⊠ 2 Reid St., Hamilton, ☎ 441/295–4866). An up-market member of the English Sports Shops that dot the island, this handsome store carries men's and women's clothing and accessories. Men's European clothing, including Hugo Boss and Van Gils, costs up to 30% less than in the United States. Aston & Gunn cotton dress shirts sell for $40–$50. Women's wear, including designs by Calvin Klein and Anne Klein, is mainly from the United States, but because there's no sales tax it's less expensive. Good-quality soft leather carry-on bags are priced from $185.

Bananas (⊠ 93 W. Front St., Hamilton, ☎ 441/295–1106; ⊠ 7 E. Front St., Hamilton, ☎ 441/292–7264; ⊠ Princess, Hamilton, ☎ 441/295–3000; ⊠ 3 King's Sq., St. George's, ☎ 441/297–0351; ⊠ Sonesta Beach Hotel & Spa, Southampton, ☎ 441/238–3409). Sportswear and T-shirts make this a teenager's dream. Brightly colored Bermuda umbrellas cost less than $20.

Bermuda Railway Co. (⊠ Reid and Burnaby Sts., Hamilton, ☎ 441/296–1577; ⊠ Clocktower Mall, Dockyard, ☎ 441/296–1290; ⊠ 29 Mangrove Bay, Somerset, ☎ 441/292–3682; ⊠ 30 Water St., St. George's, ☎ 441/297–0546; ⊠ 90 South Shore Rd., Paget, ☎ 441/292–3518; ⊠ Crystal Cave, Wilkinson Ave., Hamilton Parish., ☎ 441/293–0942). The main Hamilton location of the Railway Co. is called "Grand Central Station," and the various branches are known as "stations." All carry accessories and casual, color-coordinated cotton separates for men (sized up to XXL), women, and children. In addition to skirts, shirts, shorts, and the like, belt buckles and even beach towels are sold. A best-selling item is the Bermuda Railway cap, branded with the company logo.

Calypso (⊠ 45 Front St., Hamilton, ☎ 441/295–2112; other branches at Princess Hotel, Hamilton; Coral Beach & Tennis Club; Sonesta Beach Hotel & Spa, Southampton; Southampton Princess, Southampton; Victorian Mall, Clocktower Building, Dockyard). This expensive women's clothing shop carries an array of sophisticated leisure wear. It has the island's largest selection of swimwear and is Bermuda's only purveyor of Jantzen merchandise. Expect to shell out $265 for a small French purse and $845 for a soft briefcase. Accessories, including Italian leather shoes and straw hats, are plentiful. Eclectic novelty items from Europe make great gifts.

Cecile (⊠ 15 Front St., Hamilton, ☎ 441/295–1311; ⊠ Marriott's Castle Harbour Resort, Hamilton Parish, ☎ 441/293–2841; ⊠ Southampton Princess Hotel, South Shore Rd., Southampton, ☎ 441/238–1434). Specializing in upscale off-the-rack ladies' fashions, Cecile carries designer labels such as Mondi, Basler, and Louis Feraud of Paris. There's a good selection of swimwear, including swimsuits by Gottex, and of European lingerie, especially La Perla. An expanded accessories department carries shoes as well as scarves, jewelry, handbags, and belts.

Constable's Woolen Fashions (⊠ Duke of York St., St. George's, ☎ 441/297–1995). Icelandic woolen clothing is the specialty of this store, and prices are generally 30%–50% lower than those in the United States. This is the place to come for heavy woolen coats, ski sweaters, ponchos, and jackets in smoky colors. Travel blankets are also a hot item.

Cow Polly (⊠ Somers Wharf, St. George's, ☎ 441/297–1514). Phoebe Wharton's store brings together expensive hand-painted clothing and attractive accessories from the far corners of the globe. Beautifully crafted straw bags and hats are worth the trip from Hamilton. And you won't find the store's unusual pottery, jewelry, or men's ties sold anywhere else on the island.

Crown Colony Shop (⊠ 1 Front St., Hamilton, ☎ 441/295–3935). This branch of the English Sports Shop features quality formal and business wear for women. The shop's signature item is a line of Parisian-designed Mayeelok silk dresses and two-piece skirt and pant sets in polyester and silk, which sell for $235 and $295.

Davison's of Bermuda (⊠ 27 and 73 Front St., Hamilton, ☎ 441/292–7137; ⊠ Water St., St. George's, ☎ 441/297–8363; ⊠ Princess Hotel, Hamilton, ☎ 441/292–1980; ⊠ Marriott's Castle Harbour Resort, Hamilton Parish, ☎ 441/293–8044; ⊠ Southampton Princess Hotel, South Shore Rd., Southampton, ☎ 441/238–1036; ⊠ Clocktower Building, Dockyard, ☎ 441/234–0959). High-quality cotton sportswear items include sweaters and slacks, tennis and sailing clothing, golf and tennis hats, and children's sportswear. They also carry gift packages of Bermuda fish chowder, clam chowder and sherry peppers ($18 for a six-pack), and a collection of deliciously vicious-looking stuffed trolls—a huge one guards the doorway and claims to "bite" if touched. Back in the States, you'll find branches of this store in Miami, San Diego, New Orleans, Baltimore, Newport (RI), and Myrtle Beach.

English Sports Shop (⊠ 95 Front St., Hamilton, ☎ 441/295–2672; ⊠ Water St., St. George's, ☎ 441/295–2672). This shop specializes in British woolens: Harris Tweed jackets for men cost $225, and Shetland woolen sweaters are priced at $26.95. You can buy two cashmere sweaters at $52, with more expensive cashmere sweaters going for $195–$210.

Frangipani (⊠ Water St., St. George's, ☎ 441/297–1357). This little store is filled with colorful women's fashions that have an island resort look. Cotton, silk, and rayon leisure wear are the backbone of the stock, but vibrant Caribbean art is also sold. Frangipani also sells a collection of unusual accessories to offset various styles.

London Shop (⊠ 22 Church St., Hamilton, ☎ 441/295–1279). Next to a Häagen-Dazs ice cream parlor, this small men's shop has shelves piled high with Pierre Cardin dress shirts for about $45. European designer suits are priced from $395; Dutch and British trousers start at $59. A good selection of European silk ties is priced from $35. This is a good place to find polyester and cotton safari suits ($135–$150) and Bermuda shorts at $55.

Stefanel (✉ 12 Reid St., Hamilton, ☎ 441/295–5698). This very smart, very expensive boutique stocks the snazzy cotton knits of Italian designer Carlo Stefanel. Look for men's cotton and linen suits and cotton dress shirts, and women's patterned wool skirts, trousers, and leggings with hand-knit, contrasting jackets.

Triangle's (✉ 55 Front St., Hamilton, ☎ 441/292–1990). The star attractions of this boutique are Diane Freis's original, colorful, and crushable mosaic dresses, priced between $300 and $420—almost half what they cost in the United States.

Upstairs Golf & Tennis Shop (✉ 26 Church St., Hamilton, ☎ 441/295–5161). As befits Bermuda's role as a golfing paradise, this store stocks clubs and accessories from some of the best brands available, including Ping, Callaway, and Titleist. Tennis players can choose a racquet by Yonex or Dunlop. Men's and women's sportswear is also sold.

Cigars
Chatham House (✉ 65 Front St., Hamilton, ☎ 441/292–8455). The politically correct be warned: Not only is the air here thick with the aroma of cigar and cigarette smoke, but there is a lifesize wooden Indian princess to greet customers. In business since 1895, this shop has the ambience of an old-time country store. It stocks not only top-quality cigars from Cuba (Romeo y Julietta, Bolivar, Partagas, and Punch), but Briar and Meerschaum pipes, Swiss Army knives, Dunhill lighters, shades, gum, and postcards. A sign advises that it is illegal to bring Cuban cigars into the United States.

Tienda de Tabacs (✉ Emporium Building, 69 Front St., Hamilton ☎ 441/295–8475). As sleek as the Chatham House is rustic, this store (which also displays the cigar advisory) focuses almost exclusively on cigars, Cuban and otherwise. The hardwood floors are polished to a high sheen, and shelves and glass cases are lined with boxes of stogies. At the rear of the long room there are three huge soft leather armchairs grouped around a coffee-table appropriately set with ashtrays. So even if you can't take the Cubans into the States, you're surely invited to smoke 'em right here in the store, along with the sales staff.

Crystal, China, and Porcelain
Bluck's (✉ 4 W. Front St., Hamilton, ☎ 441/295–5367; ✉ Reid and Queen Sts., Hamilton, ☎ 441/292–3894; ✉ Water St., St. George's, ☎ 441/297–0476; ✉ Southampton Princess Hotel, South Shore, Southampton, ☎ 441/238–0992). A dignified establishment that has been in business for more than 150 years, this is the only store on the island devoted exclusively to the sale of crystal and china. Royal Doulton, Royal Copenhagen, Villeroy & Boch, Herend, Lalique, Minton, Waterford, Baccarat, and others are displayed on two floors in the main Front Street location. Herend Rothschild Bird is $235.50 for one five-piece place setting; a five-piece place setting of Hermès Toucans is $357. There is a substantial stock of the popular Kosta Boda Swedish crystal, and a large gift section includes an abundant selection of Limoges boxes. The courteous staff will provide you with price lists upon request.

Vera P. Card (✉ 11 Front St., Hamilton, ☎ 441/295–1729; ✉ 9 Water St., St. George's, ☎ 441/297–1718; ✉ Marriott Castle Harbour Resort, Hamilton Parish, ☎ 441/293–8463; ✉ Sonesta Beach Hotel & Spa, South Shore Rd., Southampton, ☎ 441/238–8122). Lladro and Swardovski "Silver Crystal" figurines are widely available all over the island at almost identical prices, but this store has the most extensive selection, including open-edition and limited-edition gallery pieces. The Lladro Bermuda Moongate and several other works are carried here exclusively. The shop's collection of more than 250 Hummel figurines is one of the world's largest. The impressive selection of beautifully crafted Swiss and German watches and clocks includes the Bermuda Time collection; and the stock of fine and costume jewelry includes 14-carat gold earrings, charms, and pendants.

Jewelry

Astwood Dickinson (✉ 83–85 Front St., Hamilton, ☎ 441/292–5805; ✉ Walker Arcade, Hamilton, ☎ 441/292–4247). Established in 1904, this store has an exquisite collection of European jewelry, unmounted stones, and a wide range of Swiss watches. Elegant timepieces by Patek Philippe, Omega, Cartier, Baume & Mercier, Tiffany, and Tag Heuer are sold for as much as 20% less than in the United States. Jewelry from Tiffany and Mikimoto·is also available. The shop's exclusively designed 18-karat gold mementos in the Bermuda Collection sell for $50–$1,000. The collection includes the Bermuda dinghy pendant priced from $75 (earrings are $230), a tall-ship pin or pendant for $690, a Bermuda Island pendant from $50, and a Gibbs Hill Lighthouse tie-pin for $150.

Crisson's (✉ 55 and 71 Front St., 16 Queen St., and 20 Reid St., Hamilton, ☎ 441/295–2351; ✉ Marriott Castle Harbour Resort, Hamilton Parish, ☎ 441/293–2852; ✉ Elbow Beach Hotel, South Shore Rd., Paget, ☎ 441/236–9928; ✉ Sonesta Beach Hotel & Spa, South Shore Rd., Southampton, ☎ 441/238–0072; ✉ York and Kent Sts., St. George's, ☎ 441/297–0672; ✉ Water St., St. George's, ☎ 441/297–0107). The exclusive Bermuda agent for Rolex, Ebel, and Raymond Weil, this upscale establishment offers discounts of 20%–25% on expensive merchandise, but don't expect to find cheap Timex or Swatch watches. The gift department carries English flatware, Saint Louis crystal, and imported baubles, bangles, and beads.

Solomon's (✉ 17 Front St., Hamilton, ☎ 441/292–4742 or 441/295–1003). This is the sole store on the island to carry only genuine stones and minerals in its collection of modern and classic designs. Prices for artisan-crafted one-of-a-kind pieces range from $70 to more than $100,000. Though hardly inexpensive, the designs are often whimsical and charming. Manager Allan Porter and his friendly staff will guide you in making your choice.

Vera P. Card (☞ *above*).

Linens

Irish Linen Shop (✉ 31 Front St., Hamilton, ☎ 441/295–4089; ✉ Cambridge Rd., Somerset, ☎ 441/234–0127). In a cottage that looks as though it belongs in Dublin, the Hamilton branch is the place for Irish linen tablecloths. Prices range from $10 to more than $3,000. Antique tablecloths can cost as much as $1,600. The best buys in this shop are the exclusively designed Irish linen tea towels for $7. From Madeira come exquisite hand-embroidered handkerchiefs from $8.50, linen sheets and pillowcases, and cotton organdy christening robes with slip and bonnet, hand-embroidered with garlands and tiers of Valenciennes lace (from $220 to more than $800). Pure linen hand-rolled handkerchiefs from Belgium with Belgian lace are priced under $20, while Le Jacquard Français cotton kitchen towels cost about $13. The shop's Bermuda Cottage Collection includes quilted tea cozies ($28), with matching place mats and pot holders (less than $15). The store has an exclusive arrangement with Souleiado, maker of the vivid prints from

Provence that are available in tablecloths, place mats, and bags, as well as by the yard—the last at a huge savings over U.S. prices.

Liquors and Liqueurs

The following liquor stores sell at identical prices; each has branches sprinkled around the island from St. George's to Somerset; and each will allow you to put together your own package of Bermuda liquors at in-bond (duty-free) prices: **Burrows Lightbourn** (⊠ Front St., Hamilton, ☎ 441/295–0176; ⊠ Queen St., Hamilton, ☎ 441/295–0176; ⊠ Harbour Rd., Paget, ☎ 441/236–0355; ⊠ Water St., St. George's, ☎ 441/297–0552; ⊠ Main Rd., Somerset, ☎ 441/234–0963); **Frith's Liquors Ltd.** (⊠ Front St., Hamilton, ☎ 441/295–3544; ⊠ York St., St. George's, ☎ 441/297–0684; ⊠ Mangrove Bay, Somerset, ☎ 441/234–1740; ⊠ Sonesta Beach Hotel, Southampton, ☎ 441/238–8122); **Gosling's** (⊠ Front St., Hamilton, ☎ 441/295–1123; ⊠ York and Queen Sts., St. George's, ☎ 441/297–1364; ⊠ Main and Cambridge Rds., ☎ 441/234–1544).

Perfume

Bermuda Perfumery (⊠ 212 North Shore Rd., Bailey's Bay, ☎ 441/293–0627 or 800/527–8213). This highly promoted perfumery is on all taxi-tour itineraries. Regularly scheduled guided tours of the facilities include a walk through the ornamental gardens and an exhibit on the distillation of flowers into perfume. At the Calabash gift shop you can purchase the factory's Lili line of fragrances as well as imported soaps and an assortment of fragrances.

Peniston-Brown's Perfume Shop (⊠ 23 W. Front St., Hamilton, ☎ 441/295–0570; ⊠ 6 Water St., St. George's, ☎ 441/297–1525) and the **Guerlain Shop** (⊠ 19 Queen St., Hamilton, ☎ 441/295–5535), which is the exclusive agent for Guerlain products, stock more than 127 lines of French and Italian fragrances, as well as soaps, bath salts, and bubble bath. The Guerlain Boutique (⊠ 53 Front St., Hamilton, ☎ 441/295–8843) carries only Guerlain products, including its quality line of cosmetics.

Perfume & Gift Boutique (⊠ 55 Front St., Hamilton, ☎ 441/295–1183), Trimingham's fragrance salon, carries Chanel No. 5, Laura Ashley No. 1, Elizabeth Taylor's Passion and White Diamonds, and Calvin Klein's Obsession, among others.

Miscellaneous

Flying Colours at Riihuolma's (⊠ 5 Queen St., Hamilton, ☎ 441/295–0890). This family-owned and -operated shop, established in 1937, has the island's largest selection of T-shirts with creatively designed island logos in hundreds of styles. The selection of quality souvenirs and gifts is plentiful, and educational toys are a specialty. This shop also carries everything for the beach—hats, beach towels, toys, and more.

Hall of Names (⊠ Bank of Butterfield Mall, Hamilton, ☎ 441/234–3410). This is a fun place to learn the origins of your family name, or of any nickname. Friendly owner John Doherty punches the pertinent information into a computer and for $15 per surname ($10 for derivatives and nicknames) gives you a nicely presented document with facts compiled from an extensive bibliography, with your family coat of arms at the top. The store is a franchise of a Canadian-based company, whose team of researchers and historians compiles the information into a database.

Hodge Podge (⊠ 3 Point Pleasant Rd., Hamilton, ☎ 441/295–0647). Just around the corner from the Ferry Terminal and Visitors Center Service Bureau in Hamilton, this cluttered little shop offers pretty much what its name implies: postcards, sunblock, sunglasses, film, and T-shirts.

Rising Sun Shop (✉ Middle Rd., Southampton, ☎ 441/238–2154). This country store, the only one on the island, is easy to spot—a flag, a horse's head, and other eye-catching inventory usually hang outside the entrance. Owner Anne Powell's warmth and humor infuse her novelty gift items, which may include toilet plungers priced from $27, a ship's decanter for $45, Portuguese wine coolers for $24, or picnic hampers priced from about $45—though inventory changes frequently. There are usually skads of wicker baskets in stock, as well as more expensive items such as antique hobby horses starting at $2,000. A large selection of quality tack (stable gear) is always on hand.

Sail On (✉ Old Cellar La., off Front St., Hamilton, ☎ 441/295–0808, FAX 441/295–2712). Owned and run by Hubert Watlington, a former Olympic windsurfer and top local sailor, this must-visit shop is tucked up a quaint alleyway, opposite Number One Shed and a cruise ship dock. It's the best place on the island for casual clothing and swimwear for adults and children, as well as gifts that appeal to those with a wacky sense of humor. Road Toad and Famous Onions clothing are sold here exclusively. T-shirts, designed by Bermudians, earn ongoing kudos for their originality in the Best of Bermuda merchant awards. Shades of Bermuda, a part of the shop, carries the island's largest selection of sunglasses. Mail order is available.

Treats (✉ Washington Mall, Reid St., Hamilton, ☎ 441/296–1123). This candy store is filled with bulk candy in just about every flavor. Buy sweets by the piece or the pound. The Candygramme gift box is filled with candy of your choice and decorated with a balloon—prices start at $15. You will find whimsical gifts here, too.

9 Portraits of Bermuda

Bermuda's Hidden Landscapes

America's Rebel Colonies and Bermuda: Getting a Bang for Their Buckwheat

Off Bermuda's Beaten Track

Bermuda at a Glance: A Chronology

BERMUDA'S HIDDEN LANDSCAPES

AT THE PUB on the square in St. George's, Bermuda, there is a sign on the second-floor veranda that everyone ignores. "Do not feed the birds," it says, but the clientele keeps handing out crumbs to the sparrows that dart through the open railings.

I sat on that veranda on a sultry October afternoon, finishing a pint of Watney's and looking out over King's Square. I had just enjoyed my first cup of Bermuda fish chowder, which the Pub, like most local restaurants, lets you fine-tune with cruets of dark rum and a fiery concoction called sherry peppers.

At the next table an English toddler was singing a song about a little duck. The 18th-century square below was quiet, partly because it had just rained and partly because at the moment there was no cruise ship anchored at St. George's. I crumbled a few morsels from the bun of my fish sandwich, tossed them to the sparrows, and made up my mind on another Watney's. After all, I wasn't playing golf that afternoon.

Not playing golf? The Bermuda Islands, conventional wisdom has it, are a place where you live on the links. But I was after a different place—a traveler's Bermuda, if I could find it.

On an archipelago roughly 21 mi long and seldom more than a mile wide, traveling can be a difficult order—unless you severely limit your pace. Fortunately, automobiles are out of the question. Visitors can't rent them (even residents weren't allowed to own cars until 1946), and the only option for exploring Bermuda on four wheels is to engage a taxi driven by an accredited guide. But why risk seeing the whole place in a day? If you move at a speed faster than a walk, you miss details like the sign I saw on a small, shuttered yellow building: "Dot & Andy's Restaurant. Operated by Barbara and Donna."

Until recently, walking in Bermuda has meant edging gingerly along the nearly nonexistent shoulders of narrow lanes, ready to press yourself into the hibiscus

hedges when a car comes by. A few years ago, though, some enterprising Bermudians got the idea of turning the right-of-way of the abandoned Bermuda Railway into an island-length hiking trail. (The entire railway, down to the spikes, was sold to British Guiana, now Guyana, in 1948.)

My first choice, as a rail enthusiast, would have been to have the narrow-gauge locomotive and cars still rattling along the tracks. But being able to walk the route, or part of it, is clearly the next best thing. My problem was that I chose a section that skirted a residential district along Bailey's Bay, near the northeastern end of the main island. Here the old roadbed was frequently severed by sharp inlets of the sea, and the trestles that had once bridged them had long since gone to South America. I'd walk a hundred yards or so and have to go back to the road, often finding no signs to tell me when I could pick up the trail again. (Farther west on the islands, the old route is less frequently broken.) On one side was the ocean, on the other a series of relentlessly suburban backyards—there are no raffish little shacks here like the ones you find on other islands. Finally, after I had inadvertently wandered into my fourth backyard, it began to rain. It was the kind of rain that makes you so wet in the first couple of minutes that there's no sense in hurrying out of it. I walked to a bus shelter and admitted defeat . . . and some success, having got into a situation in which I could hardly be mistaken for a tourist, even in Bermuda.

It was in the bus shelter that I met a young American who was waiting out the storm with his two toddlers. He was a civilian worker at the U.S. naval air station, a submarine-watching facility now largely dedicated to operating the islands' commercial airport. His most telling comment had to do with his younger child, who had been born in Hamilton: "She's a real Bermuda Onion."

He knew, of course, that genuine Bermudian citizenship requires at least one native parent, or jumping through more bureaucratic hoops than most people would care to deal with, but the fact that he liked thinking of his little girl as a Bermudian meant that he wasn't just serving a remunerative sentence in a faraway place. To a wet traveler like me, the message was that there was a community here, and foreigners could become part of it.

The rain that ended my railway trail walk was part of the tail end of Hurricane Nana, which had threatened to strike the island in full force before being pushed off track by a continental cold front. "We don't have hurricanes in Bermuda," a hotel bartender had told me with a wink, obviously remembering 1987's Emily, with her 116-mph winds, 50 injuries, and $35 million damage.

"No," I replied. "I live in Vermont, and we don't have snow."

Nana was a hurricane that missed, although she faded and veered away with great theatrical effect. By 9 that evening the rain returned, sheeting sideways against the windows of the hotel restaurant while tall palms thrashed in wild abandon. From the hotel bar the storm was a terrific backdrop—the room was all Key Largo atmosphere heightened by the adrenal tingle that comes with a sudden pressure drop. It didn't last long. Within an hour, all that remained of Nana in Bermuda was a random gusting among the palm tops, and it was fine outside for a walk down to the bay.

The next day I reverted to the vehicle of choice for covering ground in Bermuda. Motorized or "auxiliary" cycles, and the more modern motor scooters—none for rent with engines larger than 50cc, but powerful enough for islands with a 20-mph speed limit—have become a virtual postcard cliché in Bermuda, and to strap on your de rigueur white helmet is to feel as if you've somehow become part of the landscape.

A lot of visitors are afraid the scooters can too easily help them accomplish just that, but the bikes aren't all that dangerous, once you learn the controls and remember to stay on the left, British style. There is, however, a common motorbike injury the locals call "road rash," a nasty abrasion of whatever appendage happens to meet with the road, or with one of Bermuda's limestone walls, during a badly executed turn.

What I most wanted the bike for was exploring the Bermuda hinterlands. I had already visited St. George's, the islands' oldest settlement and former capital, with its narrow meandering streets, lovely State House (built in 1620), and cedar-beam, 18th-century church of St. Peter. I had been particularly intrigued with a local attraction called the Confederate Museum, headquarters of blockade-running operations during the U.S. Civil War. (What really caught my interest there was the attitude of the black docent, "proud," as she put it, of a building that housed the branch office of a desperate effort to keep her ancestors in chains. In Bermudian race relations, bygones are bygones to a remarkable degree.)

TOWNS are best explored on foot, even though it did get to be great fun to breeze into the capital for dinner after dark and have maître d's take my helmet. The bike, though, would let me discover the countryside, with its quiet lanes and tended meadows and fragments of old estates. One of those estates—Verdmont, in Smith's Parish, now a Bermuda National Trust property—lay at the end of a delightfully convoluted route I had devised, one that was designed to take me buzzing along as many back roads as possible.

It was on St. Mark's Road, rounding Collector's Hill, that the essence of this miniature landscape suddenly came clear: I was looking, I realized, at a near-perfect combination of Martha's Vineyard and the Cotswolds. On the Vineyard account was the gently rolling countryside with the sea not far away, as on a New England seacoast farm; the Cotswolds element was provided by a little jewel of a limestone Gothic church, by narrow byways with names like Pigeon Berry Lane, and by the faultless juxtaposition of every stand of trees, half-acre of greensward, and carefully clipped hedgerow.

As it turned out, I wasn't the first to get this feeling about the place: I saw later that two of the local streets were named Nantucket Lane (close enough) and Cotswold Lane. And why not? The Cotswold Hills, Bermuda, and the Massachusetts islands are all essentially English places, the latter two offering their settlers an Englishness of landscape even before any art was applied to it. And that art, in all three locales, was the particular English genius for conjuring tremendous diversity within the most compact of areas. Consummately ordered yet always romantically picturesque, the English landscape aesthetic depends on constant variety and small surprises, and never upon great vistas.

THE RESULT is a sense of much in little, of no space wasted; the effect in Bermuda is to shrink the visitor into the islands' scale, rather than to leave him feeling like a scooter-mounted giant in a hibiscus garden.

There was another aspect of Bermuda to consider, one that counters the islands' persona as a serene, ocean-borne fragment of English countryside. This is its past history as fortress Bermuda, a 21-square-mi dreadnought permanently anchored in the Atlantic. Fort St. Catherine, at the colony's extreme northeastern tip, is now decommissioned and restored to reveal its vast warren of tunnels, built to feed shells to guns commanding the northern and eastern approaches to the islands. St. David's Island, too, has its battery, a rusting line of World War II–era shore artillery where feral house cats pad about the empty magazines.

From the 17th to the 20th centuries dozens of promontories and harbor entrances throughout Bermuda bristled with guns, reflecting Britain's confrontations with forces that ranged from imperial Spain to the newly independent United States to the U-boats of the Third Reich. And no single installation loomed so mightily as the Royal Navy Dockyard, at the barb of Bermuda's fishhook-shape western end.

From 1810 to 1950 the dockyard was the "Gibraltar of the West," providing a heavily fortified anchorage for British warships and a citadel of massive limestone support structures. Approaching by ferry from Hamilton, I immediately was struck by the orderliness and permanence of it all, by the twin towers of the main building with clock faces showing the time and the hour of the next high tide, and by the ubiquitous initials VR—"Victoria Regina," shorthand for one of history's most remarkable imperial achievements. The dockyard looks as if it were built to last

a thousand years, and it may, though now it houses a cluster of museums, crafts galleries, restaurants, and boutiques. Like the rest of Bermuda's defenses, the dockyard was never tested by a serious attack; its bristles were too formidable a challenge.

Time and again in Bermuda, one encounters the opposing tidal pull of British and American influences. This, after all, is a place where they still refer to the panorama of harbor islands as seen from the top of Gibbs Hill as the "Queen's View," because Elizabeth II admired it in 1953. But this British colony also conducts its financial affairs in dollars, not sterling, and nearly 90% of its visitors are American.

There is a continuing Bermudian tradition that many residents link with the long British military presence, and that is a certain formality of dress. I was reminded of it one day in downtown Hamilton, when I saw a white-haired gentleman wearing a blue blazer, a white shirt, and a rep silk tie, along with pink Bermuda shorts, white kneesocks, and pink tassels on his garters. The shorts themselves are a throwback to the military and got their start as a local trademark when Bermuda tailors began refining officers' baggy khaki shorts for civilian wear. They are now ubiquitous as Bermudian business attire, but the most striking thing about them is not the fact that they expose gentlemen's knees but that they are integrated into a very correct, very formal men's civilian uniform. I never once saw a businessman's collar and tie loosened on a hot day in Bermuda—a sure sign that the stiff upper lip can outlast even the presence of the Royal Navy.

I thought about where I might find the quintessence of Bermudian formality and local tradition, and concluded that the place to look was probably afternoon tea at the venerable Hamilton Princess Hotel. I was staying elsewhere and thought it might be appropriate to call the Princess first to see if outsiders were welcome. "Are you serving tea at four?" I asked the English-accented woman who answered the telephone.

"Yes."

"Is it all right to come if you're not registered at the hotel?"

"Are you registered at the hotel?"

"No. That's why I'm asking."

"I'll switch you to dining services."

"Hello?" (Another Englishwoman's voice.)

"Hello, I'm wondering if I can come to tea if I'm not registered at the hotel. "

"What is your name, sir?" I gave her the name and spelling. At this point, I was tempted to add "Viscount."

"I don't have you listed as a guest."

"I know that. I'm calling to ask if it's all right to come to tea if I'm not a guest."

"No, sir."

Now we were deep in Monty Python territory, and I had the John Cleese part. Clearly, there was nothing to do but get dressed, scoot into Hamilton, and crash tea at the Princess. But when I sauntered into the hotel with my best ersatz viscount air, all I found was a small antechamber to an empty function room where a dozen people in tennis clothes stood around a samovar and a tray of marble pound cake slices. I poured a cup, drank it, and was gone in five minutes. Crashing tea at the Princess had been about as difficult, and as exciting, as crashing lunch at my late grandfather's diner in New Jersey.

Hamilton is a tidy, cheerful little city, but as the days drew down I returned more and more to the countryside, particularly to the back roads where small farms survive. Bermuda was once a mid-ocean market garden, in the days before the United States restricted imports, and property values skyrocketed beyond the reach of farmers; now, an occasional neat patch of red earth still produces root crops, broccoli, cabbage, and squash. I even saw a truck loaded with onions go by—a reminder of a Bermuda before golf.

— William G. Scheller

William G. Scheller is a contributing editor to *National Geographic Traveler*. His articles have also appeared in the *Washington Post Magazine, Islands,* and numerous other periodicals.

AMERICA'S REBEL COLONIES AND BERMUDA: GETTING A BANG FOR THEIR BUCKWHEAT

WHEN THE WAR of American Independence began, Bermudians at first felt little personal concern. There was some sympathy for the colonists; quarrels between arbitrary executive power and people, which in America had now led to real trouble, had also been part of Bermuda's history, and besides this there were ties of blood and friendship to make for a common understanding. But for all that, Bermudians, while expressing discreet sympathy, were chiefly concerned for their ships and carrying trade, and realizing their helpless position, they believed their wisest course lay in continued loyalty to the Crown. The wisdom of this policy was suddenly brought into question when the Continental Congress placed an embargo on all trade with Britain and the loyal colonies, for as nearly all essential food supplies came from the Continent, the island faced starvation unless the decree was relaxed. Thus there was a swift realization that Bermuda's fate was deeply involved in the war.

The drama now began to unfold and soon developed into a struggle between the governor, George Bruere, and the dominant Bermuda clique led by the Tuckers of the West End. Bruere's chief characteristic was unswerving, unquestioning loyalty, and the fact that two of his sons were fighting with the royalist forces in America—one of them was killed at Bunker Hill—made the ambiguous behavior of Bermudians intolerable to him, both as a father and as an Englishman.

Of the Tuckers, the most prominent member of the family at this time was Colonel Henry, of the Grove, Southampton. His eldest son, Henry, colonial treasure and councillor, had married the governor's daughter, Frances Bruere, and lived at St. George's. There were also two sons in America, Thomas Tudor, a doctor settled in Charleston, and St. George, the youngest, a lawyer in Virginia. The two boys in America, caught up in the events around them and far removed from the delicacies of the Bermuda situation, openly took the side of the colonists.

Up to the time of the outbreak of the war there had been warm friendship between the Tuckers and the Brueres, a relationship made closer by the marriage of Henry Tucker to Frances Bruere. But when it became known in Bermuda that the Tuckers abroad were backing the Americans, Bruere publicly denounced them as rebels and broke off relations with every member of the family except his son-in-law. But Colonel Henry was more concerned with the situation in Bermuda than he was with the rights and wrongs of the conflict itself, and he believed that unless someone acted, the island was facing serious disaster. So, privately, through his sons in America, he began to sound out some of the delegates to the Continental Congress as to whether the embargo would be relaxed in exchange for salt. This move, never in any way official, had the backing of a powerful group, and before long it was decided to send the colonel with two or three others to Philadelphia to see what could be arranged. Meanwhile another less powerful faction took form and likewise held meetings, the object of which was to oppose in every way these potential rebellions.

Colonel Henry and his colleagues reached Philadelphia in July 1775 and on the 11th delivered their appeal to Congress. Though larded with unctuous flattery, the address met a stony reception, but a hint was thrown out that although salt was not wanted, any vessel bringing arms or powder would find herself free from the embargo. The fact that there was a useful store of powder at St. George's was by now common knowledge in America, for the Tucker boys had told their friends about it and the information had reached General Washington. Thus, before long, the question of seizing this powder for the Americans was in the forefront of the discussions.

Colonel Henry was in a tight corner. Never for an instant feeling that his own loyalty was in question, he had believed himself fully justified in coming to Philadelphia to offer salt in exchange for food. But these new suggestions that were now being put to him went far beyond anything he had contemplated, and he was dismayed at the ugly situation that confronted him. It is evident that the forces at work were too strong for him. The desperate situation in Bermuda, verging on starvation, could only be relieved by supplies from America, and an adamant Congress held the whip hand. After some agonizing heart-searching, he gave in and agreed with Benjamin Franklin to trade the powder at St. George's for an exemption of Bermuda ships from the embargo.

Colonel Henry returned home at once, arriving on July 25. His son St. George, coming from Virginia, arrived about the same time, while two other ships from America, sent especially to fetch the powder, were already on their way.

ON AUGUST 14, 1775, there was secret but feverish activity among the conspirators as whaleboats from various parts of the island assembled at Somerset. As soon as it was dark, the party, under the command, it is believed, of son-in-law Henry and a Captain Morgan, set off for St. George's. St. George, lately from Virginia and sure to be suspect, spent the night at St. George's, possibly at the home of his brother Henry, and at midnight was seen ostentatiously walking up and down the Parade with Chief Justice Burch, thus establishing a watertight alibi. Meanwhile the landing party, leaving the boats at Tobacco Bay on the north side of St. George's, reached the unguarded magazine. The door was quickly forced, and before long, kegs of powder were rolling over the grass of the Governor's Park toward the bay, where they were speedily stowed in the boats. The work went on steadily until the first streaks of dawn drove the party from the scene. By that time 100 barrels of powder were on the way to guns that would discharge the powder against the king's men.

When Bruere heard the news he was frantic. A vessel that he rightly believed had the stolen powder on board was still in sight from Retreat Hill, and he determined to give chase. Rushing into town, the distraught man issued a hysterical proclamation:

POWDER STEAL
Advt
Save your Country from Ruin, which may hereafter happen. The Powder stole out of the Magazine late last night cannot be carried far as the wind is so light.

A GREAT REWARD
will be given to any person that can make a proper discovery before the Magistrates.

News of the outrage and copies of the proclamation were hurried through the colony as fast as riders could travel. The legislature was summoned to meet the following day. Many members of the Assembly doubtless knew a good deal, but officially all was dark and the legislature did its duty by voting a reward and sending a wordy message expressing its abhorrence of the crime.

But no practical help was forthcoming, and after several days of helpless frustration Bruere determined to send a vessel to Boston to inform Admiral Howe what had happened. At first no vessels were to be had anywhere in the island; then, when one was found, the owner was threatened with sabotage, so he withdrew his offer. Another vessel was found, but there was no crew, and for three whole weeks, in an island teeming with mariners, no one could be found to go to sea. At last, on September 3, the governor's ship put to sea, but not without a final incident, for she was boarded offshore by a group of men who searched the captain and crew for letters. These had been prudently hidden away in the ballast with the governor's slave, who remained undiscovered. The captain hotly denied having any confidential papers, so the disappointed boarders beat him up and then left.

In due course the ship reached Boston, and Admiral Howe at once sent the *Scorpion* to Bermuda to help Bruere keep order. Thereafter for several years His Majesty's ships kept a watchful eye on the activities of Bermudians, and in 1778 these were replaced by a garrison. It has always seemed extraordinary that no rumor of this bargain with the Americans reached Bruere before the actual robbery took place. It is even more amazing that within a stone's throw of Government House such a desperate undertaking could have continued steadily throughout the night without discovery.

The loss of the powder coincided with the disappearance of a French officer, a prisoner on parole. At the time it was thought that he had been in league with the Americans and had made his escape with them. But 100 years later when the foundation for the Unfinished Church was being excavated, the skeleton of a man dressed in French uniform was disclosed. It is now believed that he must have come on the scene while the robbery was in progress and, in the dark, been mistaken for a British officer. Before he could utter a sound he must have been killed outright by these desperate men and quickly buried on the governor's doorstep.

— William Zuill

A native Bermudian who was a member of the Bermuda House of Assembly, William Zuill wrote several historical works about the island. This excerpt about the role of Bermuda in the American War of Independence is taken from his book *Bermuda Journey*. William Zuill died in July 1989.

OFF BERMUDA'S BEATEN TRACK

BERMUDA IS LOVELY, but a walk along its narrow roads can involve close encounters with countless madcap moped drivers and a stream of cars. A more serene way to sample Bermuda's lush terrain, stunning seascapes, and colorful colonies of island homes is to follow the route of the railroad that once crossed this isolated archipelago. The Bermuda Railway Trail goes along the old train right-of-way for 18 mi, winding through three of the several interconnected islands that make up Bermuda.

Opened in 1931, the railway provided smooth-running transportation between the quiet village of Somerset at the west end and the former colonial capital of St. George's to the east. But by 1948 it had fallen victim to excessive military use during World War II, soaring maintenance costs, and the automobile. The railroad was closed, and all its rolling stock was sold to Guyana (then called British Guiana). In 1984, Bermuda's 375th anniversary, the government dedicated the lands of the old railway for public use and began to clear, pave, and add signs to sections of its route.

The trail's most enchanting aspect is that it reveals a parade of island views hidden from the public for nearly 30 years, scenes similar to what the first colonists must have found here in the early 1600s. In a few places the trail joins the main roads, but mostly it follows a tranquil, car-free route from parish to parish, past quiet bays, limestone cliffs, small farms, and groves of cedar, allspice, mangrove, and fiddlewood trees. Short jaunts on side trails and intersecting tribe roads (paths that were built in the early 1600s as boundaries between the parishes, or "tribes") bring you to historic forts and a lofty lighthouse, coral-tinted beaches, parks, and preserves.

I explored the Railway Trail on foot, moped, and horseback, using an 18-page guide available free at the Visitors Service Bureau in Hamilton. (You can also find the guide at some of the big hotels.) The booklet contains historical photos, a brief history of the railroad, maps, and descriptions of seven sections of trail, which range from 1¾ to 3¾ mi.

Sporting a pair of proper Bermuda shorts, I revved up my rented moped and headed out to the Somerset Bus Terminal, one of eight former railroad stations and the westernmost end of the trail. From there I followed the paved path to Springfield—an 18th-century plantation house used by the Springfield Library. A leisurely stroll in the adjoining 5-acre Springfield & Gilbert Nature Reserve took me through thick forests of fiddlewood. I also saw stands of Bermuda cedars that once blanketed the island but were nearly wiped out by blight in the 1940s.

Back on the trail I spotted oleander, hibiscus, bougainvillea, and poinsettia bursting through the greenery at every turn. In backyards I could see bananas, grapefruit, oranges, lemons, and limes growing in profusion, thanks to Bermuda's consistent year-round subtropical climate.

I parked the moped at the trailhead to Fort Scaur—a 19th-century fortress built by the Duke of Wellington, conqueror of Napoleon at Waterloo—and strolled up to its mighty walls and deep moat. Through a dark passage I reached the grassy grounds with their massive gun mounts and bunkers. A telescope atop the fort's walls provided close-up views of the Great Sound and Ely's Harbour, once a smuggler's haven. A caretaker showed me around the fort, one of the three largest in Bermuda.

On my moped again, I motored past Skroggins Bay to the Lantana Colony Club, a group of beachside cottages. I stopped to sip a Dark and Stormy—a classic Bermudian rum drink—and to enjoy the view of the sail-filled Great Sound. My post-swizzle destination: Somerset Bridge. Only 32 inches wide, this tiny bridge was built in 1620 and looks more like a plank in the road than the world's smallest drawbridge—its opening is just wide enough for a sailboat's mast to pass through.

I ended my first Railway Trail ride at the ferry terminal near the bridge, where I boarded the next ferry back to Hamilton. Had I continued, the trail would have taken me through what was once the agricultural heartland of Bermuda. The colony's 20 square mi of gently rolling landscape, graced by rich volcanic soil and a mild climate, once yielded crops of sweet, succulent Bermuda onions, potatoes, and other produce. But tourism has become bigger business here, and today only some 500 acres are devoted to vegetable crops.

Just west of Sandys Parish the trail runs for some 3¾ mi through Warwick Parish. The path, now dirt, overlooks Little Sound and Southampton, where fishing boats are moored. Here the Railway Trail begins to intersect many of Bermuda's tribe roads, which make interesting diversions. Tribe Road 2 brings you to the Gibb's Hill Lighthouse, built around 1846. This 133-ft structure is one of the few lighthouses in the world made of cast iron. You pay $2 for the dubious privilege of climbing 185 steps to the lens house, where you're rewarded with far-reaching views of the island and Great Sound. The 1,500-watt electric lamp can be seen as far away as 40 mi.

Spicelands, a riding center in Warwick, schedules early-morning rides along sections of the Railway Trail and South Shore beaches. I joined a ride to follow part of the trail where it cuts deep into the rolling limestone terrain—so deep that at one point we passed through the 450-ft Paget Tunnel, whose walls are lined with roots of rubber trees.

We rode through woodlands and fields, past stands of Surinam cherry trees and houses equipped with domed water tanks and stepped, pyramid-shaped roofs designed to catch rainwater. As we trotted through the cool darkness beneath a dense canopy of trees it was hard to imagine a time when noisy rolling stock rattled along the same route, carrying some of the 14 million passengers who rode the railway while it was in operation. Finally, a tribe road led us through tropical vegetation to the clean, coral-pink beaches of Bermuda's beautiful South Shore.

EAST OF HAMILTON, the Railway Trail follows the North Shore, beginning in Palmetto Park in the lush, hilly parish of Devonshire. It hugs the coastline past Palmetto House (a cross-shaped, 18th-century mansion belonging to the Bermuda National Trust) and thick stands of Bermuda cedar to Penhurst Park, where there are walking trails, agricultural plots, and good swimming beaches.

Farther east the trail hits a wilder stretch of coast. The Shelley Bay Park and Nature Reserve along here has native mangroves and one of the few beaches on the North Shore. After a short walk on North Shore Road, the trail picks up again at Bailey's Bay and follows the coast to Coney Island. The park here has an old lime kiln and a former horse-ferry landing.

The remaining sections of the trail are in St. George's. Start at the old Terminal Building (now called Tiger Bay Gardens) and stroll through this historic town. The trail passes by Mullet Bay and Rocky Hill Parks, then heads to Lover's Lake Nature Reserve, where nesting long tails can be seen amid the mangroves. The end of the trail is at Ferry Point Park, directly across from Coney Island. In the park there's a historic fort and a cemetery.

Evenings are perhaps the most enchanting time to walk along the Railway Trail. As the light grows dim, the moist air fills with songs from tiny tree frogs hidden in hedges of oleander and hibiscus. The sound sets a tranquil, tropical mood that, for nearly a half century, has been undisturbed by the piercing whistle and clickety-clack of Bermuda's bygone railroad.

— Ben Davidson

BERMUDA AT A GLANCE: A CHRONOLOGY

1503   Juan de Bermudez discovers the islands while searching for the New World. The islands are eventually named after him.

1603   Diego Ramirez, a Spanish captain, spends several weeks on Bermuda making ship repairs.

1609   An English fleet of nine ships, under the command of Admiral Sir George Somers, sets sail for Jamestown, Virginia, with supplies for the starving colony. Struck by a hurricane, the fleet is scattered, and the admiral's ship, the *Sea Venture,* runs aground on the reefs of Bermuda. The colonization of Bermuda begins.

1610   After building two ships, *Deliverance* and *Patience,* from the island's cedar trees, the survivors depart for Jamestown, leaving behind a small party of men. Admiral Sir George Somers returns to Bermuda a few weeks later but dies soon afterward. He requests that his heart be buried on the island.

1612   Asserting ownership of the islands, the Virginia Company sends 60 settlers to Bermuda under the command of Richard Moore, the colony's first governor. The Virginia Company sells its rights to the islands to the newly formed Bermuda Company for £2,000.

1616   The islands are surveyed and divided into shares (25 acres) and tribes (50 shares per tribe). The tribes, or parishes, are named after investors in the Bermuda Company. The first slaves are brought to Bermuda to dive for pearls and to harvest tobacco and sugarcane.

1620   The Bermuda Parliament meets for the first time, in St. Peter's Church in St. George's, making it the third-oldest parliament in the world after those of Iceland and Great Britain.

1684   The Crown takes control of the colony from the Bermuda Company. Sir Robert Robinson is appointed the Crown's first governor.

1775   The American Continental Congress announces a trade embargo against all colonies remaining loyal to the Crown. Dependent on America for food, Bermuda negotiates to give the rebellious colonies salt if they will lift the embargo. The colonies refuse but state that they will end sanctions in exchange for gunpowder. Without the knowledge of Governor George Bruere, a group of Bermudians breaks into the magazine at St. George's and steals the island's supply of gunpowder. The gunpowder is delivered to the Americans, who lift the embargo.

1780   The "Great Hurricane" hits Bermuda, driving ships ashore and leveling houses and trees.

1784   Bermuda's first newspaper, the *Bermuda Gazette & Weekly Advertiser,* is started by Joseph Stockdale in St. George's.

1804   Irish poet Thomas Moore arrives in Bermuda for a four-month stint as registrar of the admiralty court. His affair with the married Hester Tucker was the inspiration for his steamy love poems to her (the "Nea" in his odes), which have attained legendary status in Bermuda.

1810   The Royal Navy begins work on Dockyard, a new naval base on Ireland Island.

1812 In response to American raids on York (now Toronto) during the War of 1812, the British fleet attacks Washington, D.C., from its base in Bermuda.

1815 Hamilton becomes the new capital of Bermuda, superseding St. George's.

1834 Slavery is abolished.

1846 The first lighthouse in the colony, the 117-ft-high Gibbs Hill Lighthouse, is built at the western end of the island in an effort to reduce the number of shipwrecks in the area.

1861 Bermuda enters a period of enormous prosperity with the outbreak of the American Civil War. Sympathetic to the South, Bermudians take up the lucrative and dangerous task of running the Union blockade of southern ports. Sailing in small, fast ships, Bermudians ferry munitions and supplies to the Confederates and return with bales of cotton bound for London.

1883 Princess Louise, daughter of Queen Victoria, visits Bermuda. In honor of her visit, the new Pembroke Hotel changes its name to the Princess.

1901 Afrikaner prisoners from the Boer War are incarcerated in Bermuda. By the end of the war, approximately 5,000 prisoners are housed on the islands.

1915 A 120-man contingent of the Bermuda Volunteer Rifle Corps (B.V.R.C.) departs for service in France during World War I. In action at the battles of the Somme, Arras, and the Third Battle of Ypres, the unit loses more than 30% of its men. In 1916, the Bermuda Militia Artillery also heads for France.

1931 Constructed at a cost of £1 million ($4.5 million), the Bermuda Railway opens years behind schedule. Maintenance problems during World War II cripple train service, and the whole system is sold to British Guiana (now Guyana) in 1948.

1937 Imperial Airways begins the first scheduled air service to Bermuda from Port Washington in the United States.

1940 During World War II, mail bound for Europe from the Americas is off-loaded in Bermuda and taken to the basement of the Princess Hotel, where it is opened by British civil servants trying to locate German spies. Several spies in the United States are unmasked. As part of the Lend-Lease Act between Prime Minister Churchill and President Roosevelt, the United States is awarded a 99-year lease for a military base on St. David's Island. Construction of the base begins in 1941.

1944 Women landowners are given the vote.

1946 For the first time, automobiles are permitted by law on Bermuda.

1951 The Royal Navy withdraws from Dockyard and closes the base.

1953 Winston Churchill, Dwight D. Eisenhower, and Prime Minister Joseph Laniel of France meet on Bermuda for the "Big Three Conference."

1959 NASA opens a space tracking station on Coopers Island, which is part of the American base.

1971 Edward Richards becomes Bermuda's first black government leader (a title later changed to premier).

1973 Governor Sir Richard Sharples and his aide, Captain Hugh Sayers, are shot dead. In 1976, Erskine "Buck" Burrows is convicted of the murder, as well as several other murders and armed robberies. He is hanged in 1977.

1979 Gina Swainson, Miss Bermuda, wins the Miss World Contest. An official half holiday is announced and Gina Swainson postage stamps are released in 1980.

1987 Hurricane Emily hits Bermuda, injuring more than 70 people and causing millions of dollars in damage.

1990 President Bush and Prime Minister Thatcher meet on Bermuda.

1994 Her Royal Highness Queen Elizabeth II and Prince Philip make an official visit to Bermuda.

1995 The Royal Navy closes its Bermuda headquarters after having maintained a presence on the island for 200 years. The U.S. Naval Air Station base closes; it had operated since September 1940.

BOOKS AND VIDEOS

THE WELL-RESPECTED historian William Zuill wrote extensively about the island. Published in 1945 and now somewhat outdated, Zuill's 426-page *Bermuda Journey: A Leisurely Guide Book* provides a fascinating look at the island and its people, with historical notes and anecdotes. The book is out of print; check with the Bermuda Book Store in Hamilton (☎ 441/295–3698) to see if used copies are available. Zuill's other books include *The Wreck of the Sea Venture,* which details the 1609 wreck of Admiral Sir George Somers's flagship and the subsequent settlement of the island, and *Tom Moore's Bermuda Poems,* a collection of odes by the Irish poet who spent four months on Bermuda in 1804.

For a charming account of growing up in Bermuda during the 1930s and 1940s, refer to *The Back Yard,* by William Zuill's daughter Ann Zuill Williams. And W. S. Zuill, son of the historian, wrote *The Story of Bermuda and Her People,* a recently updated volume tracing the history of the island from the *Sea Venture* wreck to the present.

Bermuda, by John J. Jackson, contains an abundance of facts on Bermudian business, economics, law, ecology, and history, as well as tourist information. John Weatherill's *Faces of Bermuda* is a marvelous collection of photographs, and those curious about the legendary Bermuda Triangle can read about its history in *The Bermuda Triangle Mystery Solved,* by Larry David Kusche.

For lovers of railroad history, *"Rattle and Shake": The Story of the Bermuda Railway,* by David F. Raine, and *The Bermuda Railway: Gone But Not Forgotten,* by Colin Pomeroy, tell the tale of the fabled narrow-gauge railroad in photos and prose. You'll find both in the Railway Museum and in other shops on island.

Bermuda's traditions and the unique culinary lineup that accompanies special holidays are the highlight of *The Seasons of Bermuda* by Judith Wadson. The island is showcased in several coffee-table books of color photographs, such as *Bermuda,* by Scott Stallard, *Bermuda Abstracts,* by Graeme Outerbridge, and *Bermudian Images,* by Bruce Stuart. Among the books for younger audiences are Willoughby Patton's *Sea Venture,* about the adventures of a young boy on the crew of the ill-fated ship; E. M. Rice's *A Child's History of Bermuda,* which tells the story of the island in terms children can readily understand; Dana Cooper's illustrated book, *My Bermuda ABC's* and *My Bermuda 1,2,3;* and Bermudian artist Elizabeth Mulderig's three *Tiny the Tree Frog* books.

Panatel VDS has produced several half-hour videos, including "Bermuda Highlights," "Dive Bermuda," and "Bermuda Bound, Paradise Found." Priced at $29.95 and available for both North American and European systems, the videos are sold at several stores and shops around the island.

INDEX

NOTES

NOTES

NOTES

NOTES

NOTES

NOTES

NOTES

Fodor's Travel Publications

Available at bookstores everywhere, or call 1–800–533–6478, 24 hours a day.

Gold Guides

U.S.

Alaska

Arizona

Boston

California

Cape Cod, Martha's Vineyard, Nantucket

The Carolinas & Georgia

Chicago

Colorado

Florida

Hawai'i

Las Vegas, Reno, Tahoe

Los Angeles

Maine, Vermont, New Hampshire

Maui & Lāna'i

Miami & the Keys

New England

New Orleans

New York City

Pacific North Coast

Philadelphia & the Pennsylvania Dutch Country

The Rockies

San Diego

San Francisco

Santa Fe, Taos, Albuquerque

Seattle & Vancouver

The South

U.S. & British Virgin Islands

USA

Virginia & Maryland

Walt Disney World, Universal Studios and Orlando

Washington, D.C.

Foreign

Australia

Austria

The Bahamas

Belize & Guatemala

Bermuda

Canada

Cancún, Cozumel, Yucatán Peninsula

Caribbean

China

Costa Rica

Cuba

The Czech Republic & Slovakia

Eastern & Central Europe

Europe

Florence, Tuscany & Umbria

France

Germany

Great Britain

Greece

Hong Kong

India

Ireland

Israel

Italy

Japan

London

Madrid & Barcelona

Mexico

Montréal & Québec City

Moscow, St. Petersburg, Kiev

The Netherlands, Belgium & Luxembourg

New Zealand

Norway

Nova Scotia, New Brunswick, Prince Edward Island

Paris

Portugal

Provence & the Riviera

Scandinavia

Scotland

Singapore

South Africa

South America

Southeast Asia

Spain

Sweden

Switzerland

Thailand

Toronto

Turkey

Vienna & the Danube Valley

Special-Interest Guides

Adventures to Imagine

Alaska Ports of Call

Ballpark Vacations

Caribbean Ports of Call

The Complete Guide to America's National Parks

Disney Like a Pro

Europe Ports of Call

Family Adventures

Fodor's Gay Guide to the USA

Fodor's How to Pack

Great American Learning Vacations

Great American Sports & Adventure Vacations

Great American Vacations

Great American Vacations for Travelers with Disabilities

Halliday's New Orleans Food Explorer

Healthy Escapes

Kodak Guide to Shooting Great Travel Pictures

National Parks and Seashores of the East

National Parks of the West

Nights to Imagine

Rock & Roll Traveler Great Britain and Ireland

Rock & Roll Traveler USA

Sunday in San Francisco

Walt Disney World for Adults

Weekends in New York

Wendy Perrin's Secrets Every Smart Traveler Should Know

Worldwide Cruises and Ports of Call

Fodor's Special Series

Fodor's Best Bed & Breakfasts

America

California

The Mid-Atlantic

New England

The Pacific Northwest

The South

The Southwest

The Upper Great Lakes

Compass American Guides

Alaska

Arizona

Boston

Chicago

Colorado

Hawaii

Idaho

Hollywood

Las Vegas

Maine

Manhattan

Minnesota

Montana

New Mexico

New Orleans

Oregon

Pacific Northwest

San Francisco

Santa Fe

South Carolina

South Dakota

Southwest

Texas

Utah

Virginia

Washington

Wine Country

Wisconsin

Wyoming

Citypacks

Amsterdam

Atlanta

Berlin

Chicago

Florence

Hong Kong

London

Los Angeles

Montréal

New York City

Paris

Prague

Rome

San Francisco

Tokyo

Venice

Washington, D.C.

Exploring Guides

Australia

Boston & New England

Britain

California

Canada

Caribbean

China

Costa Rica

Egypt

Florence & Tuscany

Florida

France

Germany

Greek Islands

Hawaii

Ireland

Israel

Italy

Japan

London

Mexico

Moscow & St. Petersburg

New York City

Paris

Prague

Provence

Rome

San Francisco

Scotland

Singapore & Malaysia

South Africa

Spain

Thailand

Turkey

Venice

Flashmaps

Boston

New York

San Francisco

Washington, D.C.

Fodor's Gay Guides

Los Angeles & Southern California

New York City

Pacific Northwest

San Francisco and the Bay Area

South Florida

USA

Pocket Guides

Acapulco

Aruba

Atlanta

Barbados

Budapest

Jamaica

London

New York City

Paris

Prague

Puerto Rico

Rome

San Francisco

Washington, D.C.

Languages for Travelers (Cassette & Phrasebook)

French

German

Italian

Spanish

Mobil Travel Guides

America's Best Hotels & Restaurants

California and the West

Major Cities

Great Lakes

Mid-Atlantic

Northeast

Northwest and Great Plains

Southeast

Southwest and South Central

Rivages Guides

Bed and Breakfasts of Character and Charm in France

Hotels and Country Inns of Character and Charm in France

Hotels and Country Inns of Character and Charm in Italy

Hotels and Country Inns of Character and Charm in Paris

Hotels and Country Inns of Character and Charm in Portugal

Hotels and Country Inns of Character and Charm in Spain

Short Escapes

Britain

France

New England

Near New York City

Fodor's Sports

Golf Digest's Places to Play

Skiing USA

USA Today The Complete Four Sport Stadium Guide

WHEREVER YOU TRAVEL, *H*ELP IS NEVER FAR AWAY.

From planning your trip to providing travel assistance along the way, American Express® Travel Service Offices are always there to help you do more.

Bermuda

Meyer Agencies Ltd. (R)
35 Church Street
Hamilton
441/295-4176